COBOL/370 for
Power Programmers

COBOL/370 for
Power Programmers

David Shelby Kirk

A Wiley–QED Publication

John Wiley & Sons, Inc.

New York • Chichester • Brisbane • Toronto • Singapore

Printed in the United States of America

10 9 8 7 6 5 4 3 2

To Linda Jane, my wife and my best friend.

Contents

List of Figures

Preface

So, Why a Second Edition?

When I wrote the first edition of this book, little did I know that a superset of COBOL II was in the works at IBM. I should have known better. IBM has been consistent in their efforts to periodically upgrade the programming environment, and a superset of COBOL II should have been predictable. Fortunately for those of us who write the code, IBM's newest version of COBOL, SAA AD/Cycle COBOL/370 (referenced as COBOL/370 in this book), builds on the foundation of COBOL II. While COBOL II is certainly a major enhancement to the COBOL language and changed the perception that COBOL is a dead language, COBOL/370 ties many loose ends together from an environmental perspective. We'll see more on that later. As you read this book, you will find that COBOL/370 is actually several products, not just the compiler. I'll cover that shortly.

When I wrote the first edition, I felt strongly that COBOL programmers finally had a compiler worthy of professionals. In the two years since that book, I have had this consistently proved to me. Now, COBOL/370 carries forward what was begun with COBOL II, the flexibility to carry an application beyond the mainframe to other platforms. Programmers developing applications at programmable workstations (PWS) now have a compiler that is accessible either from the mainframe or from the PWS.

If you're wondering why I didn't write a separate book for COBOL/370, the answer is that the two languages have more similarities than differences. IBM announced COBOL/370 as a superset of COBOL II and I can't improve on those words. In case you read the first edition, you will find that all of the programming features introduced for COBOL II are also in COBOL/370. Additionally, if your shop is using COBOL II, you would probably like to be able to keep the same text when your shop eventually migrates to COBOL/370. By having both languages in one text, you can ensure that your COBOL II applications will continue to function properly in that new world.

Authors look forward to the opportunity to write a second edition. First, it speaks to the success of the first edition. Second, it gives the author the opportunity to update and expand on the original material. Throughout my first book I encouraged reader feedback—and I got it. Thanks to all of you who took the time to write. Your praise, your questions, and your criticism all helped direct me to where the book could be expanded and improved. While this new edition now includes information on COBOL/370, there are many enhancements and changes for COBOL II, as well. You will find more information on tables, on CICS, and on several COBOL statements that weren't in the first edition (such as STRING) that I've added as a result of your feedback.

Like the first edition, this book focuses on the programming and design aspects of building applications. I preserved the nontypical structure of the first edition, keeping the major focus on techniques that work, not on just the syntax differences. This remains a book of power techniques, not a reference for COBOL syntax. That reflects the reader responses, since many of them related to the non-COBOL topics (such as compile options, JCL, and performance issues) that aren't routinely available. You didn't buy this book to learn COBOL concepts. You bought it (I hope) because you want to be a better MVS programmer.

What This Book Is

Writing quality, high-performance code is what this book is about. This book was written for the professional COBOL programmer who wants to always write the best, most efficient, and cleanest code possible and who needs a ready reference for day-to-day use of COBOL II or COBOL/370 in an MVS environment. With that focus, the book is not organized in the way in which COBOL books for the novice are. This book, knowing the demands for maintenance and compatibility that the professional programmer faces, devotes a majority of its pages to explaining differences and demonstrating techniques. While new COBOL techniques are the foundation of the book, other techniques are also given. The book will also be useful to managers and others planning to convert to COBOL II or COBOL/370 who want to understand more about the features. Many topics appear in several places because I felt you might look for the topic in several places.

While the major portion of the book focuses on COBOL II and COBOL/370, it attempts also to assist you in other challenges you face in the programming process, such as interfacing with programs written in OS/VS COBOL and using the Linkage Editor and DFSORT. There are reference aids on other topics, too, ranging from hexadecimal tables to the EBCDIC collating sequence and even to a summary of JCL. These references are not complete, but they include the information most likely to be needed by a COBOL programmer working with MVS.

In addition to providing reference material, this book includes suggested design and coding guidelines for programs. While your shop may already have guidelines, those in this book focus on simplicity, compatibility with prior versions of COBOL, and on avoiding terms that may be unfamiliar. Emphasis is on clarity, structure, and style, using the minimum syntax required.

What This Book Is Not

This is a desk reference, not an encyclopedia. This book does not contain every facet of information available about COBOL II, COBOL/370, or MVS, nor does it attempt to tutor you in programming fundamentals or elementary COBOL syntax (e.g., you won't find the definition of a COBOL paragraph or the purpose of a SELECT statement in this book). This book also does not attempt to explain the ANSI standards and their many levels, because those topics typically do not interest the professional programmer who has little or no say in such issues, anyway. There are references to specific environments, such as CICS and IMS but, again, there is no tutorial information on basics of programming for their environments.

How This Book Is Organized

Chapter 1: Introduction. Read this chapter thoroughly for an overview of new features. If your shop hasn't yet converted to COBOL II or COBOL/370, this chapter will highlight some of its benefits.

Chapter 2: Coding Differences. This chapter is designed to help you get over the hurdle of learning a new version of COBOL by answering the question, "What's different?" This is the chapter of instruction. You will want to read this chapter more than once.

Chapter 3: Programming with COBOL II and COBOL/370. This chapter is designed not to be read sequentially but to be used to address specific COBOL design and coding issues. The chapter is organized by topic, not by feature, so some COBOL features may appear more than once or be cross-referenced. Included in the chapter is information on JCL, the Linkage Editor, and DFSORT. If it is a topic related to coding, compiling, linking, or executing COBOL programs, you will find it here. Where Chapter 2 explained the new features of COBOL II and COBOL/370, this chapter demonstrates how to use the new features (and some old features) effectively.

Chapter 4: Debugging Techniques. No, this chapter does not teach dump reading, although it does have a brief tutorial on debugging concepts for the less experienced reader. Instead, this chapter gives some tips and information on debugging facilities that are new and that are most likely to be used. This includes several tips and techniques for your "testing toolkit."

Debugging is an area where COBOL/370 and COBOL II differ widely. As with the first edition, the focus will remain on prevention, not on correction. Also, while basic COBOL II debug facilities and techniques are specific and detailed, the information presented on the COBOL/370 debug facilities is more conceptual. This is because I have had limited exposure to the COBOL/370 debug facility (known as CODE/370 and explained further on).

I mention this because, for COBOL/370, most debug facilities are provided on a programmable workstation (PWS) via IBM's AD/Cycle CODE Debug Tool. Since many/most programmers still do COBOL debugging on the mainframe (and because debugging is not a focus of this book), in-depth information on the AD/Cycle CODE Debug Tool is not in this book. (Yes, I'm aware that there are several software products available that allow programmers to write, compile, and debug COBOL programs on a PC. When I refer to debugging, however, I am referring to the process of debugging a COBOL program running under control of the mainframe run-time environment, not under control of a PC in a simulated environment. CODE/370 provides that cooperative capability.) Again, to paraphrase my earlier comment, this book focuses on building power applications and building them well—not on fixing bugs.

Chapter 5: Design Guidelines. This chapter is designed to assist those professionals who do not have well-defined standards for program design at their shop or who have difficulty developing GO TO-less programs. Techniques to design SORT applications are also included.

Chapter 6: Coding Guidelines. Several topics in this chapter are also in Chapter 3. The difference is that, where Chapter 3 focuses on using COBOL II and COBOL/370 effectively, this chapter focuses on the mechanics of coding, with a suggested coding format for each COBOL division. Even if your shop already has a set of COBOL coding standards, you may find that this chapter provides different ideas to consider.

Chapter 7: Summaries, Tables, and References. If it isn't here, either I overlooked it or you don't need it. This summary includes charts and information on much besides COBOL. Information on JCL, acronyms, comparisons to OS/VS COBOL, and common ABEND codes are among the topics available here for instant reference.

Chapter 8: Sample Programs. These sample programs demonstrate some new COBOL features, plus examples of OS/VS COBOL compatibility. All examples demonstrate the design and coding guidelines from Chapters 5 and 6.

Chapter 9: Related Publications. Earlier in this preface, I mentioned that this book doesn't contain everything there is to know about COBOL II, COBOL/370, or MVS. No book could. This chapter serves to help you quickly locate related texts from QED and IBM. As a professional programmer, I know one of your personal goals is to build and maintain a library of useful reference materials. This chapter can help you make those choices.

Who This Book Is For

If you have difficulty with some topics in this book, the reasons may be that the topics add depth to subjects you thought you already knew or they uncover areas of MVS of which you were unaware. As the saying goes, "Just do it." As you explore the various topics, you may find yourself learning about more than the topic at issue.

Programmers who see their jobs as just a way of earning a paycheck will benefit little, if at all, from this book. They know all the COBOL they need to make a program function. The readers who will benefit from this book are those who continually seek a better way. Making a program function correctly is part of the job; making the program work better and more efficiently is a higher goal. They know, as I do, that being a professional programmer is one of the most interesting and challenging of the technology professions. By having this book in your hands, I assume you are one of us. Welcome. I hope you find the book useful.

To any grammarians among you, I confess that I knowingly used "programmerese" when discussing many topics. I used this approach because that is how most programmers discuss programming. For example, you will find that the word ABEND has been used as a noun, as an intransitive verb, as a transitive verb, and as an adjective. While that may not be proper use of the language, I doubt that any programmer misunderstands such expressions as "the program ABENDed," or "locate the ABENDing instruction."

To paraphrase a sentence in this preface, this book was written for you, the professional programmer. If I've omitted some useful topic, made a technical error, or included information you haven't found to be useful, please let me know. I would enjoy hearing from you.

David Shelby Kirk
Cicero, New York

Acknowledgments

No book that attempts to move COBOL to a higher level can do so without acknowledging that much has been done by others through the years to bring COBOL to its current level. It was not only improvements in COBOL, but improvements in many other technologies that have made it possible to write this book. I have attempted to list here specific acknowledgment of those efforts.

Extract from Government Printing Office Form Number 1965-0795689:

Any organization interested in reproducing the COBOL report and specifications in whole or in part, using ideas taken from this report as the basis for an instruction manual or for any other purpose is free to do so. However, all such organizations are requested to reproduce this section as part of the introduction to the document. Those using a short passage, as in a book review, are requested to mention COBOL in acknowledgment of the source, but need not quote this entire section.

COBOL is an industry language and is not the property of any company or group of companies, or of any organization or group of organizations.

No warranty, expressed or implied, is made by any contributor or by the COBOL Committee as to the accuracy and functioning of the programming system and language. Moreover, no responsibility is assumed by any contributor, or by the committee, in connection therewith.

Procedures have been established for the maintenance of COBOL. Inquiries concerning the procedures for proposing changes should be directed to the Executive Committee of the Conference on Data Systems Languages.

The authors and copyright holders of copyrighted material:

FLOW-MATIC (Trademark of Sperry Rand Corporation),
Programming for the UNIVAC (R), I and II, Data Automation Systems copyrighted 1958, 1959, by Sperry Rand Corporation; IBM Commercial Translator, Form No. F28-8013, copyrighted 1959 by IBM; FACT, DSI 27A5260-2760, copyrighted 1960 by Minneapolis-Honeywell,

have specifically authorized the use of this material in whole or in part, in the COBOL specifications. Such authorization extends to the reproduction and use of COBOL specifications in programming manuals or similar publications.

References in this book to the ANSI Standard or to ANSI 85, are to the American National Standard Programming Language COBOL, X.3.23-1985, and to ANSI Programming Language—Intrinsic Function Module for COBOL, X3.23a—1989.

Use of the following terms in this book are references to these specific IBM products:

Term used	IBM product and program number
MVS	MVS/SP, MVS/XA, and MVS/ESA, unless noted
IMS	IMS/VS or IMS/ESA, unless noted
CICS	CICS/MVS or CICS/ESA, unless noted
COBOL/370	SAA AD/Cycle COBOL/370 (5688-197)
LE/370	SAA AD/Cycle Language Environment/370 (5688-198)
CODE/370	SAA AD/Cycle CoOperative Development Environment/ 370 (5688-194)
COBOL II	VS COBOL II Compiler & Library & Debug (5668-958)
OS/VS COBOL	OS/VS COBOL Compiler & Library (5740-CB1)
DFSORT	DFSORT (5740-SM1)
Assembler H	Assembler H Version 2 (5668-962)

The following terms used in this book are trademarks of International Business Machines Corporation:

MVS/SP, MVS/XA, MVS/ESA, CICS/MVS, DB2, IBM, SAA, DATABASE 2, Systems Application Architecture, AD/Cycle, CICS/ESA, IMS/ESA, System/360, System/370, Operating System/2, OS/2

Introduction to COBOL II and COBOL/370

This first chapter of the book is different from those that follow. Instead of dealing with the day-to-day issues you face as a programmer, it addresses concepts and features of COBOL II and COBOL/370 that are appropriate for a wider audience than programmers (maybe your boss would enjoy reading it on a cold winter's night). Oh, reading the other chapters will also help your boss, but those other chapters are designed explicitly for you. They are intended for desktop reference, to be used for specific questions, or for design and coding issues.

This chapter addresses the programmer who is new to COBOL II or COBOL/370 and wants to know the differences between these and earlier versions and who also wants to know what some of the benefits are. As a professional programmer, you take pride in your skills, and the need to learn a new version of COBOL may seem threatening. It won't be. While there are many differences, you will find that much of what you've always done in COBOL programs will still work. In many ways, COBOL II and COBOL/370 free you to do tasks more simply, more efficiently, and with better structure.

1.1. WHAT ARE COBOL II AND COBOL/370?

As a reader of this book, you already know the fundamentals of COBOL, so you may be wondering, "Why are COBOL II and COBOL/370 considered different?" Let's hold that question for a moment and cover some COBOL history.

1.1.1. Overview of COBOL History

Until the early 1970s, COBOL was bundled with the equipment (i.e., if you bought/rented IBM's hardware, COBOL was available at no extra charge). For reasons beyond this book, IBM began pricing hardware and software separately, and while customers considered it a disadvantage at the time, it proved to benefit everyone. With a fee being charged for software, IBM and other vendors began to develop a software industry, providing superior software designed to run on IBM or compatible hardware.

IBM's first proprietary version of COBOL was COBOL Version 3, which provided some enhancements such as debugging assistance. This was followed a couple of years later by COBOL Version 4, which also included an optimization facility. Then, around 1976, IBM released OS/VS COBOL, embodying all features of earlier compilers, plus many more. Until the announcement of COBOL II, OS/VS COBOL was the major version used. Throughout this book, key differences will be identified.

Compiler	Approximate year	Standard level
COBOL F	1968	DOD (Department of Defense)
ANS COBOL Ver 2	1970	ANS 1968
ANS COBOL Ver 3	1972	ANS 1968
ANS COBOL Ver 4	1974	ANS 1968 and extensions
OS/VS COBOL	1976	ANS 1968 and ANS 1974
COBOL II	1984	ANS 1985
COBOL/370	1991	ANS 1985 and ANS 1989

Figure 1.1. COBOL releases for OS/MVS.

Now, back to your question, "Why are COBOL II and COBOL/370 considered different?" There are two primary reasons, and I'll try to give you some information as well as background on each.

One, COBOL II and COBOL/370 support the American National Standards Institute (ANSI) 1985 standards, which are the first major upgrade to the COBOL language since its inception, embodying structured programming components and removing obsolete features. Since IBM introduced COBOL II prior to approval of the 1985 standards, the earlier versions of COBOL II (versions 1 and 2) did *not* meet ANSI 1985 standards and are not covered in this book. My assumption is, since version 3 has been available since 1988, your shop is using version 3.0 or a later version.

Two, IBM developed COBOL II and COBOL/370 to be a part of the operational environment. What does that mean? It means that they are not just compilers, but are active parts of the resident software environment on your mainframe and the compiler-generated code expects to run within control of the COBOL run-time facilities. It also means that COBOL can now take advantage of new operating software, such as MVS/XA and MVS/ESA. It means that CO-BOL is an environment in itself, not just a compiler, and recognizes other environments such as CICS and IMS.

The importance of those two reasons isn't obvious until you assess the history of COBOL. When COBOL first became available in the early 1960s, many people felt it would eliminate the need for programmers, allowing business analysts to write application logic in English. COBOL's terminology supported that belief, using terms such as verb, sentence, statement, and paragraph. While the dream of eliminating programmers proved untrue, COBOL remained a language that had no proper structure, as did other procedural languages. COBOL was shackled by its attempt to appear as English prose.

PL/1, for example, has DO and END structural components to contain procedural substructures, allowing procedural control of any grouping of statements. For COBOL, the only structural components available in earlier versions of COBOL were paragraphs, sections, statements, and sentences. For structured programs, sections are too big to control effectively (and open to misuse of GO TOs), sentences are uncontrollable, and statements are controllable only within the confines of a sentence. That left only the paragraph as an element that could be controlled, normally with the PERFORM statement. The restrictions imposed by the other structures, combined with the limited conditional logic of IF, ELSE, and NEXT SENTENCE, left the professional programmer with few structural tools. With ANSI 85, COBOL now qualifies as a professional's language, since true structured code is now possible. The opportunities for structured code will be addressed in other parts of the book, including Chapter 3 (Programming with COBOL II and COBOL/370), Chapter 5 (Program Design Guidelines), and Chapter 6 (COBOL Coding Guidelines).

Also true in earlier versions of COBOL was a total dependence on a shop's technical staff and trial and error to determine what compile and link-edit options should be used with COBOL. COBOL object code was insensitive or unaware of the presence of CICS or IMS and reference manuals for the earlier versions of COBOL rarely, if ever, acknowledged the existence or programming considerations necessary for MVS, CICS, or IMS. Today's IBM manuals are a far cry from those earlier versions, with extensive information and guidance on using COBOL with other environments.

COBOL, then, is no longer just a language. As such, it is more complex, more flexible, and more sensitive to an environment. Therefore, the need exists for this book. As you read through it, the importance of these issues will become apparent.

Before proceeding into a review of the features, let's briefly look at each of the two languages. Although most programming features are shared between COBOL II and COBOL/370 (see Figure 1.2), each arrived on the scene with different objectives, primarily because they each arrived at different times (as shown in Figure 1.1). By the way, none of the features in Figure 1.2 are available with OS/VS COBOL.

	COBOL/370	COBOL II
1. Run-time environments		
a) LE/370[1]	X	X
b) COBOL II run-time library		X
2. Debug environments		
a) AD/Cycle CODE/370[2]	X	
b) COBTEST[3]		X
c) Formatted dump	X	X
d) Subscript checking	X	X
3. Dictionary Services/MVS[4]	X	
4. SAA support		
a) SAA Level 2	X	
b) SAA Level 1	X	X
c) SAA flagging	X	X
5. Programming features		
a) Reference modification-DBCS	X	
b) Reference modification	X	X
c) De-edit feature	X	X
d) Procedure-pointer	X	
e) GLOBAL linkage section	X	
f) GLOBAL & EXTERNAL data items	X	X
g) Improved CICS interface	X	X
h) Enhanced VSAM file-status codes	X	X
i) Nested COPY statements	X	X
j) INITIALIZE statement	X	X
k) CONTINUE statement	X	X
6. Structured programming features		
a) Nested programs	X	X
b) Scope terminators	X	X
c) In-line PERFORM statement	X	X
d) EVALUATE statement	X	X
7. COBOL features		
a) Enhanced compiler listing options	X	X
b) Standards support/enforcement	X	X
c) FASTSRT feature	X	X
d) Reentrant code option	X	X
e) 31-bit addressing	X	X

Note 1: LE/370 is required for COBOL/370.
       2: CODE/370 is an optional IBM product for COBOL/370.
       3: COBTEST is an optional IBM product for COBOL II.
       4: Dictionary Services/MVS is an optional IBM product for
          COBOL/370.

Figure 1.2. Summary of new features of COBOL/370 and COBOL II.

1.1.2. Overview of COBOL II

COBOL II is the most popular of these two compilers, primarily because it has been around since 1984 and many shops may not have COBOL/370 for many more years. Actually, I still find large MIS departments that use ANSI 1968 programming standards with OS/VS COBOL with no plans yet for COBOL II. (Yes, with IBM's formal withdrawal of support for OS/VS COBOL, these companies are now beginning to use COBOL II, but they still lack any plan.)

The announcement of COBOL II was a surprise to many IBM customers and watchers, primarily because most of us thought IBM would just add new features to OS/VS COBOL, not announce a new product instead. MVS/XA had been announced, and many customers wanted to take advantage of its features with their application programs, something that OS/VS COBOL could not do. Also, the ANSI 1985 standard had been in committee for so long that many referred to it as the ANSI 198x standard. The new ANSI level reached far beyond earlier ANSI levels, and there was, not unexpectedly, much discussion about it.

This was a time when companies were becoming interested in being able to move COBOL applications from one operating platform to another, something that wasn't possible at the time without major rework. IBM decided (wisely, I think) that addressing these (and more) issues would be better served by writing a new compiler instead of refurbishing OS/VS COBOL. A particular decision that I applauded was that IBM kept COBOL II focused on performance and environmental compatibility, not on upward compatibility for all the archaic COBOL standards from the 1960s. (In shop after shop, it is almost always the continued use of out-of-date features that causes companies to face costly conversions to be able to use COBOL II (or COBOL/370).

IBM had also announced a long-range strategy called System Application Architecture (SAA) that would integrate computer applications across many operating platforms and standardize many features (more on this later). A version of COBOL was clearly needed to form a foundation for customers to develop SAA-compatible applications. COBOL II was that vehicle. As shown in Figure 1.3, COBOL II works on all major MVS platforms, allowing MVS customers to implement COBOL II at their shop to take advantage of available opportunities. *NOTE:* For the record, COBOL II, under other product names, is available on a wide variety of IBM platforms. That is beyond the scope of this book, but applications developed with COBOL II or COBOL/370 can be ported across many IBM platforms. For more information on this, see the IBM manual *SAA Common Programming Interface, COBOL Reference* (Chapter 9, Related Publications).

(*NOTE:* Figure 1.3 only identifies the environment in which a particular compiler-generated application can operate. You should not infer that similar features are exploited in each. Additionally, Figure 1.3 only shows the minimum level of IBM products for a given feature. For example, since IMS/ESA is a later release than IMS/VS Version 2.2, it isn't shown, although it is supported.)

Environment	CICS				IMS			DB2		
Release & Level No.	ESA 3.2.1	ESA 3.1.1	MVS 2.1	VS 1.7	VS 2.2	VS 2.2	VS 1.3	Ver 2	Ver 2	Ver 1
MVS/ESA 3.0	X	X	X	X	X	X	X	X	X	X
MVS/XA			X	X		X	X		X	X
MVS/SP			X	X		X	X		X	X
LE/370	X				X			X		
COBOL/370	X				X			X		
COBOL II	X	X	X	X	X	X	X	X	X	X
OS/VS COBOL	X	X	X	X	X	X	X	X	X	X

Figure 1.3. Comparison of COBOL and IBM environmental software.

What makes COBOL II so powerful from an IBM customer perspective is that, since it is sensitive to the operating platform, it generates object code that takes advantage of what is available. This allowed companies to start using COBOL II even when they hadn't yet upgraded other aspects of their system, clearly a plus. In fact, COBOL II also works in the VSE environment, so VSE shops can develop COBOL II applications in anticipation of migrating those applications to MVS. (COBOL II for the VSE environment is covered in my book *VSE COBOL II Power Programmer's Desk Reference*, available from QED.)

As this book goes to press, the most recent release of COBOL II is Version 4.0, announced in November 1992. This new release, instead of extending features available in Version 3.2, added full 31-bit addressability and object code compatibility to VSE. So , don't look for new features in Version 4.0 in your MVS environment. This was just another step toward achieving COBOL portability for IBM platforms.

1.1.3. Overview of COBOL/370

All of the power of COBOL II—indeed, every positive aspect of COBOL II—is carried forward in COBOL/370. Other than a different set of debug tools, productional applications developed with COBOL II will work fine in COBOL/370 (assuming the programs had been compiled with the NOCMPR2 compile option with COBOL II). As you can see in Figure 1.2, there are a few topics where COBOL/370 stands alone, but for the most part those are environmental topics. In the area of the COBOL language, COBOL/370 offers only a few (but significant) enhancements, which will be clarified later. So, what's the big deal? Simple. COBOL/370 sets the pace for extended environmental expansion. Rather than have you wondering what *environmental expansion* is (that's *my* term, not IBM's), let me review it briefly here.

By environmental expansion I am referring to the need for companies to be protected in the future from the requirement to continually recompile, relink, and otherwise modify application programs just to be able to use the current software facilities. In other words, as the environment expands, whether to new operating systems or different hardware platforms, companies will expect their applications to continue to perform. If you have ever participated in a migration from one compiler to another (such as from VS/COBOL to COBOL II), you know that, after all the effort, the only value you had added to the programs was that they were now using a current version of the compiler. In today's economy, that's hardly the place where any company wants to invest resources. Today's clients are demanding new applications, new features, and portable platforms for applications.

COBOL II set the initial step here by being supported by other IBM products, such as CICS. Now, with COBOL/370, the language itself is being separated from the operating platform, and the debug facilities are being offloaded to a programmer workstation. This is largely transparent to the COBOL programmer (other than the debug facilities), but it is still important to know.

So, what's special about COBOL/370 to a programmer? Well, for one thing, you will see that there is no longer a COBOL-specific subroutine library. That eliminates the concern about using RES or NORES as a compile option, since it is impossible to link run-time modules within the load module. This is an example of the portability of COBOL/370. You will also find that the functions performed by a subroutine library are now handled by a new IBM product, SAA AD/Cycle Language Environment/370 (referred to in this book as LE/370). While COBOL/370 introduces some of its own new features, many (most?) of the benefits come from its implicit association with LE/370. In fact, LE/370 is an environmental prerequisite to COBOL/370 (i.e., if LE/370 isn't installed at your shop, COBOL/370 will not function, nor will the other AD/Cycle products, such as CODE/370, function.) Earlier, I mentioned that COBOL/370 was more than "just a compiler." This is probably a good place to pause and explain that.

LE/370 and AD/Cycle products.

With COBOL II, the compiler, the subroutine library, and the debug tool, were all tightly connected. The products would only operate with each other. COBOL/ 370 separates all that. The products (loosely described) are

- LE/370—Not really part of COBOL/370, but certainly a prerequisite for COBOL/370 and the provider of several of the new features available via COBOL/370. When installed, COBOL II programs can also benefit from some of its features, as we will see later.
- COBOL/370—This is the compiler—nothing more, nothing less.
- CODE/370—This separate product is available on both the mainframe

and also on the PWS (although it is on the PWS that maximum function- ality is found). CODE/370 is an optional product, as some debug features are provided by LE/370.

While there have been PC-based compilers and debuggers available for several years, this integration of mainframe and workstation products is, to me, significant. Instead of debugging the application in stand-alone mode on the workstation and then uploading the program to the mainframe, the structure of LE/370, COBOL/370, and CODE/370 provides a true cooperative processing en- vironment where the location of the source code, the location of the test files, and the source of the debug features are all transparent (well, as transparent as these things get). In this text, focus for COBOL/370 features will be on using LE/ 370 and COBOL/370 to build applications, not on the features of CODE/370. The following chart depicts symbolically the interrelationship between LE/370, CODE/370, and both COBOL/370 and COBOL II.

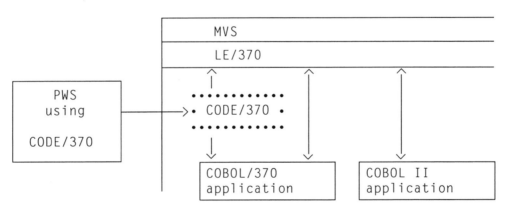

LE/370 is the language building block that will, as new compilers are devel- oped, provide coexistence from one language to another. While initial support was for only COBOL and C (as implemented in IBM's C/370), it has been ex- panded to support FORTRAN and PL/I. If you've ever needed to get programs in different languages to speak to each other, you can visualize what a blessing this is. Also, by having a common set of routines, programmers using different lan- guages can use the same services.

With COBOL/370, you will have access to a series of intrinsic functions of LE/370, as well. Those of you who have worked with mathematical languages such as FORTRAN are familiar with functions, those implicit subroutine CALLs that can be imbedded within another statement. For example, with COBOL/370 your program can directly request such services as MAX, MEAN, MEDIAN, and many others. We'll see examples of intrinsic functions later.

An additional benefit of LE/370 is that it can also support COBOL II, allow- ing a shop to mix COBOL II and COBOL/370 applications. LE/370 has many CALLable services and both COBOL II and COBOL/370 can access those since they are invoked by the normal CALL statement. Again, we'll see more of that later. If your shop has LE/370 installed, your COBOL II load modules that were compiled with the RES attribute will automatically be under its control (but for limited features).

1.2. MAJOR FEATURES OF COBOL II AND COBOL/370

Converting your applications to COBOL II or COBOL/370 has many benefits, some for the application (user) and some for you, the professional programmer. Since conversion is a one-time process, it isn't a special topic within this book. Also, your technical support area may have installed some conversion assistance software, either from IBM or other vendors. If such conversion software is available, your efforts to change your programs from OS/VS COBOL to COBOL II or COBOL/370 will be less: not eliminated, but less. For more information that may assist you in such a conversion from OS/VS COBOL to COBOL II, see Chapter 2 (Coding Differences) and Chapter 3, Section 2 (Module Structures).

1.2.1. Newer IBM Features Supported

One of IBM's major points when COBOL II was announced was that this language would be kept current with IBM's plans. IBM has kept its word on this, as COBOL II has had major upgrades and enhancements since its announcement. This will undoubtedly also be true for COBOL/370. As new announcements continue, OS/VS COBOL will be left further and further behind. Keeping your applications (and you) current on technology is important. You will stay aware of new technology and continue to grow in your profession and your application takes advantage of new operating opportunities. What follows is an overview of some of the enhanced capabilities of COBOL II and COBOL/370. Where a technique requires a conscious effort on your part, it will be covered in detail in later chapters. **PLEASE NOTE:** Since COBOL/370 supports all COBOL II features, I will use the term COBOL II when referring to features shared by both compilers.

31-bit addressability.
With COBOL II, your application can use features, either consciously or automatically, of your shop's operating environment. For example, if your shop is running MVS/XA or MVS/ESA, there is memory available beyond 16 megabytes, yet OS/VS COBOL programs are unable to be loaded there. COBOL II can generate object code with 31-bit address capability, allowing COBOL II programs to be loaded into any memory space. The address space above the 16 megabyte level can be compared to the sunshine above the clouds during a storm. Down below, most programs and systems software are thrashing and competing for the same memory space. Up above, the memory is virtually (pardon the pun) empty. This is a significant part of COBOL II's ability to improve application performance.

You may be wondering why current programs can't run in that upper ad-

There's not much up here . . .
16-megabyte line
Large components of systems software (e.g., MVS, VTAM)
On-line applications (e.g., CICS, IMS) in VS/COBOL
Batch applications in VS/COBOL

Figure 1.4. Symbolic representation of 31-bit opportunity.

dress space. The reason is that application programs written for the IBM System/360, System/370, 4300, and 30xx series, prior to the availability of MVS/XA, used a 24-bit addressing scheme, allowing a maximum address of 16 million. Not too many years ago, that sounded like an infinite number. No longer.

Reentrant code.

Your applications can also be reentrant, making the applications available to multiple users without being reloaded into memory. This applies especially to a CICS environment, where an application may be used concurrently by many terminal users. Before COBOL II, reentrant code was available only from skilled assembler programmers. The RENT option will be covered more thoroughly in Chapter 3.

Faster sorting.

Although there are restrictions, most SORTs will run more efficiently in COBOL II. In addition to this enhancement, you will find much about using SORT within COBOL programs throughout this book.

VSAM enhancements.

If you use VSAM files, COBOL II now provides the opportunity for your application to get detailed feedback from any VSAM I/O request. This is not a replacement to the FILE-STATUS clause, but an enhancement to it.

Higher compiler limits.

If you're like I am, you never think about compiler limits. The size of an 01-level, the number of data items possible, and other such limits seldom interfere with designing an application. By increasing the limits significantly (due largely to availability of MVS/XA and successors), COBOL II provides the opportunity to rethink how WORKING STORAGE should be used in a program. Imagine what you could do if you could define an 01-level to be 16 million bytes. That is larger than many databases. What if you loaded that data file into a table in memory to improve response time for that critical application of yours? Hmm . . .

CALLable services (LE/370 only).

If your shop installs LE/370—normally done along with COBOL/370, but not necessarily—there are many prewritten CALLable subroutines that let your program dynamically tune its performance and also use many other services, such as mathematical services (e.g., sine, cosine, log, square root). This eliminates the need to write all these routines yourself and can add previously unavailable functionality to your applications. Since these services are available with CALL statements, both COBOL II and COBOL/370 can use them. (*NOTE:* For COBOL II programs to use LE/370, they must be relinked with the LE/370 subroutine library to get the LE/370 version of IGZEBST. The specifics of relinking will be covered later.)

In this book I will explain only a few of these CALLable services. My intent in this text is to make you aware of them and to provide documentation on common ones of general interest. The ones that relate to mathematics are also provided with intrinsic functions (see next topic), and the others are for complex application interaction with LE/370. That topic is beyond the scope of this book.

Intrinsic functions (COBOL/370 only).

COBOL/370 provides many functions that are invoked by appearing within a source statement. For example, computing the present value or annuity of a set of numeric variables no longer requires that the programmer know the mathematics of doing it. You will find all intrinsic functions documented in Chapter 7 and there are several examples of their use in Chapter 3.

1.2.2. ANSI 85 Support

Being at the latest ANSI level may not seem important to you, but this issue has a wide ripple effect in the industry. New features implemented from the latest ANSI level represent the evolving sophistication of COBOL. As COBOL continues to evolve, the language gets more power and becomes more consistent across multiple platforms. When COBOL was new (early 1960s), people envisioned that a COBOL program would be able to operate properly on any computer with no need for a conversion. In hindsight, those early dreams had little chance of success. Every vendor implemented COBOL a little differently, and there was little consistency even within the products of one vendor. The industry now has an opportunity to achieve a level of standardization not possible back then. With your application compatible with the ANSI 1985 standard, you will stand a better chance than ever that much of it will be compatible in a future environment.

Although books could, and have been, written about the many modules and levels of ANSI, you won't find that information in this book. Programmers rarely want to know what modules and subsets of ANSI are available. Instead, they want to know what works and what doesn't. This isn't to criticize those other books. Some people need to know that information (I did, to write this book), but the scope of this book is what you probably need on a regular basis. *The major benefit you will see with ANSI 85 features is the ability to do true structured programming.*

1.2.3. Standards Control Opportunities

You'll need to check with your shop to find if this feature is implemented. COBOL II can restrict what statements are used (yes, some programmers still use the ALTER statement), provide customized messages for designated statements, and even restrict what compile options are allowed. For an individual programmer, this isn't a benefit, but for a large MIS shop, knowing what options are specified and what statements are or aren't used is important for departmental planning. Good standards can also protect you, the programmer, from inheriting maintenance responsibility for programs that only work correctly with a non-standard use of compile options or with unfamiliar statements.

Actually, COBOL II provides the opportunity to do much more, such as providing shorthand for certain statements or even support for languages other than English. Since that pertains to customizing COBOL II for an entire installation, it isn't part of this book. For more information on how to do this, see Chapter 9 (Related Publications).

1.2.4. SAA Opportunity

IBM's strategic plan to integrate a variety of operating platforms is called Systems Application Architecture (SAA). This is a major step for the industry and provides impetus for companies to start standardizing how they use computers. One of the SAA building blocks is COBOL II. If your company has decided to move toward an SAA environment, COBOL II provides a monitoring facility to warn you if incompatible features are used.

SAA is an exciting concept, especially if your company wants to share applications across mainframes, midframes, and PCs. With COBOL II, programs you develop for a mainframe environment can be more easily transported to other environments, freeing you from the requirement to program for different platforms. For more information on how COBOL II fits in with SAA, see Chapter 9 (Related Publications).

1.2.5. Improved Tuning and Cost Control

Although much of this is done by your systems programmers, COBOL II can be configured for specific environments. There are new compile options that cause different code to be generated, depending on how data are defined and used within your application. These options are explained in Chapter 3 (Programming with COBOL II and COBOL/370).

Optimization.

Have you ever placed an "*" in column 7 to comment out procedural code that was not to be executed? Most of us have, at one time or another. Now, COBOL II locates code that is out of the logic flow and flags it and doesn't generate code for it. So, if you have code that is not to be deleted but is not to be executed, just move it out of the logic path and you're done. Providing that service is part of the enhanced OPTIMIZE facility, but it does much more. COBOL II will restructure the object code if that is more efficient, and, in some situations, it will even eliminate redundant computations within the application.

Batched compiles.

Another cost control feature is the ability to batch several programs together and invoke the compiler once to generate several object programs. This concept was available in OS/VS COBOL, but required special control statements to activate. COBOL II further builds on this facility by providing the option to generate appropriate Linkage Editor statements to cause separate load modules to be generated in one invocation of the Linkage Editor.

Environment management.

COBOL II. COBOL II now provides specific opportunities for your systems programmers to preload IMS/DC applications and improve their performance. Systems programmers may also package specific COBOL runtime modules to improve performance of specific environments, such as CICS. Since those tasks are specialized and do not affect the development and coding of COBOL programs, no additional information on preloading is provided in this book.

COBOL/370 (via LE/370). Throughout this text, you will often see references to LE/370 instead of to COBOL/370. This is because, if COBOL/370 is installed, LE/370 is a prerequisite and assumed to be present. For example, the improvements in tuning that are provided for COBOL/370 are, in fact, delivered via LE/370, not COBOL/370. This is because IBM has (finally) separated the compiler from the run-time environment. Whereas the COBOL II run-time environment focused on specific performance concerns (such as preloads for IMS), LE/370 provides more extensive opportunities for performance tuning. Since environmental performance tuning is beyond the scope of this book, I won't dwell on it.

1.3. BENEFITS TO AN APPLICATION

Applications benefit from many of the above features, primarily because they reduce resource usage and allow programs to be created that are less costly to maintain. Some of the features, however, provide the opportunity for applications to expand and to incorporate new services. Until MVS/XA broke the 16-megabyte barrier, many shops had been facing a continual problem: finding virtual storage constraint relief (VSCR) for their mission-critical applications. This means that there wasn't enough memory for the application to run efficiently. This occurred for two reasons. One, the application probably continued to grow in size as new functions were added. Two, IBM and other vendors kept adding new functions to the operating software to meet customer needs. A shop running CICS, TSO, IMS, VTAM, MVS, JES, and other software, in addition to your application, eventually finds that memory is full.

IBM's introduction of 31-bit addressability provided the opportunity for programs to operate above the old environment of 16 megabytes, thereby freeing the programs from the constraints of competing for memory with other applications in a finite space. This ability to free a program from memory constraints is one of the major benefits an application can realize with COBOL II.

Another benefit the application realizes is the opportunity to develop programs that are cleaner and easier (cheaper) to maintain. By consciously applying the new structured components of COBOL II, you create applications that are easier to read, easier to debug, and less costly to maintain.

1.4. BENEFITS TO A PROGRAMMER

Much of what COBOL II means to you has already been mentioned, and after you finish this book, you will probably feel this list is too short. COBOL II provides such a large menu of features that it is difficult to sample them all. These are what I believe are the features most impressive to programmers.

Structured programming.
Yes, for the first time, COBOL has the ability to implement a true DO-UNTIL or CASE statement and can contain nested conditional statements within a paragraph. With prior levels of COBOL, a programmer could always justify a situation where the GO TO statement was necessary. Not so with COBOL II. This gives you the opportunity to create cleaner code than you could with OS/VS COBOL.

Documentation.

Okay, so documentation isn't the programmer's favorite word. All the more reason to use COBOL II. With COBOL II, you can control what error messages you get and where they appear. The cross-reference facility even tells you where data fields are modified, not just referenced. There are summaries of statements used, programs CALLed, and you can even control what portions of the source program are listed. The operative word is CONTROL. These features weren't in OS/VS COBOL. You will find more information on these techniques in Chapter 3 (Programming with COBOL II and COBOL/370) and in Chapter 4 (Debugging Techniques with COBOL II and COBOL/370).

Another documentation improvement is more subtle. Finally, you can mix upper- and lower-case text, making the program more readable. No longer must you code

```
IF DS1-INCOME IS NUMERIC
   MOVE WS1-TAX-ID TO PR1-TAX-ID.
```

Instead, you may now code

```
If Ds1-income is numeric
   Move Ws1-tax-id to Pr1-tax-id.
```

Many people feel that mixed upper- and lower-case text is easier to read than all upper case. Whether you prefer that isn't the issue, however. The point here is that you are in *control*. An extension of this concept is that you may now specify whether you want the COBOL II messages and other information on the source listing to appear in upper case or in both upper and lower case. Again, your choice. In this book, for purposes of contrast against the text, all COBOL statements will be upper case.

Debugging.

What I haven't mentioned yet is that COBOL II includes improved debugging facilities that have their own chapter (see Chapter 4, Debugging Techniques). There, you will find that COBOL II provides even more debugging aids than were available in OS/VS COBOL, including a new COBTEST debug tool that has three modes: full-screen mode, line mode, and batch mode. The on-line facility receives little mention in this book because, being on-line with instant help available, using it is largely a matter of practice, probably much the same as learning ISPF.

There are two other debugging aids you will find useful and easier to use than COBTEST. One is the new subscript range intercept feature (SSRANGE), which intercepts subscripts that go beyond the range of a table. If you've ever had the 2:00 A.M. phone call for an 0C4 ABEND of a critical productional program, you will appreciate the benefits of this new feature.

The other debugging aid is the new formatted dump (FDUMP). Whereas OS/VS COBOL's equivalent facility required additional JCL and was somewhat clumsy (few programmers I've met ever used it), the new compile option for formatted dumps embeds the debug code directly within the object code, eliminating the need for additional compile-time JCL. This new dump presents your DATA DIVISION areas in readable format and can save valuable time when you need to determine the content of a number of data fields.

Earlier, I mentioned that this book did not include detailed information on IBM's AD/Cycle CODE/370 Debug Tool. That is because this is an optional product and normally used from a PWS. Still, there are several debug facilities that are explicit whenever a program is operating with LE/370. The dump produced by LE/370 is application-oriented and there are CALLable services to obtain diagnostic information not previously available from a high-level language such as COBOL. In fact, the debug facilities of COBOL/370 are so extensive that they would justify their own book. (As a matter of fact, IBM has developed several such books that are specific to this topic. See Chapter 9, Related Publications.)

CICS enhancements.

Do you use CICS? If so, the coding becomes simpler with some coding requirements removed. For example, no longer do you need to maintain base locator pointers (BLLs) for your LINKAGE SECTION. More details for CICS are in Chapter 3 (Programming with COBOL II and COBOL/370). Yes, you will need to convert CICS COBOL programs that make heavy use of LINKAGE SECTION, but there are software aids for that. See your technical support staff for availability of any in-house conversion aids.

1.5. DEVELOPING AN APPROACH TO LEARNING COBOL II OR COBOL/370

When you first learned COBOL, you probably studied many parts of the language before you were able to code a simple application. My recommendation to learning this new version of COBOL is quite different. Rather than read this entire book before attempting any of the new facilities, just jump in and swim. Here is my recommended approach to get you up and running in COBOL II quickly:

1. **Compile a known OS/VS COBOL program.** Assuming that you know the name of the COBOL II JCL PROC to use for your shop (I'll cover JCL in Chapter 3), compile a program with which you're familiar using the COBOL II compiler. This will give you some immediate feedback on some of the errors that might occur. If you've been using the LANGLVL(2) and MIGR options in your OS/VS COBOL compiler, you might find no errors at all. If so, you are positioned to move quickly toward mastering COBOL II. If there were errors, don't worry. Most are

not difficult to correct. Don't attempt to correct the errors yet, as I'll get to that shortly.

2. **Read Chapter 2.** In Chapter 2 (Coding Differences), you will discover the more visible differences between the compilers. Although COBOL II can't be so easily dissected, I have attempted to organize the chapter by three categories: what was dropped, what was changed, and what is new. In your first reading, focus on what was dropped and what has changed, not on what is new. Your immediate goal is to learn which, if any, of your current programming techniques must be changed. Since changing old techniques is much harder than learning new ones, address this first. Also, Chapter 2 does not cover every nuance of COBOL II. Instead, it covers the most likely features you'll encounter or use.

3. **Compare compile options.** There is a summary of compile options in Chapter 7 (Summaries, Tables, and References). Don't worry about new ones, just concentrate on the differences (e.g., the equivalent of PMAP in OS/VS COBOL is LIST in COBOL II). With this information, you can use COBOL II as you used OS/VS COBOL.

4. **Remove syntax errors from a known program.** Now, go back to that listing you compiled and start removing syntax errors. If you've used some coding techniques that aren't in this book, you may need additional assistance. With new compiler releases, there are usually several little known or undocumented features that are changed. Your goal is reaching the level of proficiency where you can use COBOL II to compile programs without using new features. (*NOTE:* If you are going to be working in an environment where you must continue to maintain applications in OS/VS COBOL and also write applications in COBOL II, you will find specific help in Chapter 3, Section 2 (Module Structures) and Chapter 8 (Sample Programs).

5. **Try EVALUATE and remove all occurrences of FILLER.** By now, you're familiar with COBOL II and have successfully compiled a program with the COBOL II compiler. Now is the time to experiment with some new features, preferably those that are visible and that will let you feel comfortable with new features. I recommend some experimental use of the EVALUATE statement, since it can replace a variety of nested IF statements, or even replace some table searches. If you are using an on-line text editor, such as ISPF, also try replacing all FILLER by spaces. Although a small item, this makes a DATA DIVISION noticeably more readable.

6. **Reread Chapter 2 and remove unnecessary items.** On the second reading of Chapter 2, focus on removing all paragraphs and clauses that aren't needed. You might remove some that are still in your shop standards, but your standards may need to be reviewed and updated if they still reflect OS/VS COBOL (Chapter 6 in this book might be a good place to start). For example, the LABEL RECORDS ARE STANDARD clause

and the DATA RECORDS clause are required in FDs at many shops, yet both are obsolete statements in ANSI 85, and COBOL II treats them as comments—so why bother coding them? You will also discover that the ENVIRONMENT DIVISION isn't needed at all in several circumstances (e.g., an on-line IMS/DC or CICS application with no FD statements).

By removing every item that doesn't cause the compile to fail, you will start to discover changes you may want to make in how you develop applications. Clinging to old techniques and continuing to code obsolete statements prevents you from improving your coding productivity—and may cause you to spend extra time at some future date removing those statements because a future release of the compiler might no longer recognize them.

7. **Set a goal to use three new features in your next program.** This is the hard part. Now that you feel confident with COBOL II, there is a normal tendency to get on with it and to stop learning new features. As an example, over the years I've encountered many OS/VS COBOL programmers who did not know how to get a Symbolic Dump (SYMDMP) or to use a binary search (SEARCH ALL). It happens. Learning all the primary features of a compiler takes work. Otherwise, the pressure of the project causes all of us to keep doing things the same old way.

SUMMARY

This chapter has touched on the differences you will experience in using COBOL II or COBOL/370. The following chapters will provide information that clearly demonstrates that COBOL II and COBOL/370 are, indeed, different animals. In teaching COBOL II and COBOL/370, I am continually enthused by the excitement of programmers who suddenly see COBOL as a true programming language. I'm sure you will too. COBOL/370 especially excites me for the vision it offers.

2

Coding Differences between COBOL II, COBOL/370, and OS/VS COBOL

To learn COBOL II or COBOL/370, your first priority is to understand what you must unlearn. This is normal, as new versions of COBOL have traditionally dropped some features and modified others. This chapter is intended to serve as a periodic reference on these features for you, and to serve as a first-time tutorial on the differences between COBOL II and COBOL/370 and their predecessor, OS/VS COBOL.

For purposes of readability, the terms *components* or *elements* are used throughout this book when referring to a collection of terms that form the syntax of COBOL programs. This includes, but is not limited to, paragraphs, clauses, statements, sections, divisions, and data description entries. The term, *feature*, will normally be used to describe a capability of COBOL, which would also include any components that implement that feature. For example, Report Writer is a feature, but GENERATE is a component of Report Writer.

To assist you, this chapter is organized in decreasing order of importance from a maintenance or conversion perspective, covering first the elements that are no longer available, followed by the elements that have been modified, followed by elements that are new to the language. Determining whether a feature was dropped, modified, or new wasn't always obvious and was subject to my interpretation. You may feel, after reading the chapter, that some features I listed as modified were, indeed, sufficiently changed to be classified as new.

Overall, most changes reflected here are because COBOL is evolving into a cleaner, simpler language. The trend is to

- Remove elements that belong elsewhere within the software inventory (such as the Communications feature).
- Remove features that were hardware or vendor dependent (such as ISAM or CLOSE WITH DISP).

- Eliminate overlapping elements (e.g., EXAMINE and TRANSFORM).
- Remove requirements that have outlived their intent (such as SEGMENT-LIMIT and LABEL RECORDS ARE STANDARD).
- Remove requirements for elements where a general default is sufficient (such as SOURCE-COMPUTER).
- Provide a debugging language that is separate from the source language (e.g., READY TRACE is removed).
- Provide new facilities to improve program-to-program communications and to use memory more effectively.
- Provide new facilities to give the programmer more control of processes and more opportunities to use structured techniques.

With practice, you will soon find that your programs use fewer lines of code and are easier to read.

How to read the syntax charts.

Throughout this book, and in IBM books as well, you will encounter a new format to represent COBOL syntax. The format is simpler than earlier versions, but let me explain briefly. Below is the syntax for minimum items for the IDENTIFICATION DIVISION. The basic rules are

- Entries appearing on a top line are mandatory.
- Items appearing beneath a line are optional for the above line.
- Entries appearing beneath another entry are alternatives.
- New elements will be shown in **BOLD**.
- The symbol to continue to the next line is shown by "—>".
- The end of a statement is shown by "—><".

In the example on the first line the format is indicating that IDENTIFICATION DIVISION is mandatory, but since there is an element beneath it, that element may be used instead.

On the second line, PROGRAM-ID and program-name are mandatory and may be followed, optionally, by either COMMON or INITIAL or both.

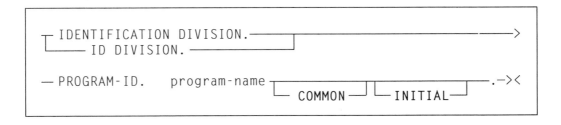

Figure 2.1. Example of COBOL syntax chart.

If you compare the charts in this book with those in IBM reference manuals, you will find that IBM's are more complete and identify all options. The ones used in this book are subsets intended to highlight new features. Options rarely used and those that haven't changed may not appear. These charts are usually all you will need if you are already comfortable with the basics of COBOL syntax.

REMINDER: Earlier, I mentioned that I would use the term COBOL II whenever referring to a topic that applied to both COBOL II and to COBOL/370. I mention that because you will find the term COBOL/370 does not appear frequently in this chapter, since most new features are available in both COBOL II and COBOL/370. This seemed preferable to continually stating "COBOL II and COBOL/370." Where there is a difference, or where it may be confusing, I will state that the topic at hand applies to both.

2.1.   OS/VS COBOL FEATURES THAT WERE DROPPED

This section lists the most visible (most commonly used) elements of OS/VS COBOL that are not in COBOL II. The dropped elements were either ANSI 1968 components or were early IBM extensions of COBOL. If your shop used ANSI 74 COBOL, you should have few problems in a move to COBOL II. If you are unfamiliar with any particular element, so much the better, because that means you won't need to unlearn that element. Most, if not all, of the elements in this section may be converted to their COBOL II equivalent (if one exists) by using conversion software on the market. Your technical support staff can assist you.

2.1.1.   Report Writer

Many shops didn't discover Report Writer until the 1980s, although it has been in use at some shops since the 1960s. Report Writer is still a module in the full ANSI 1985 standard (although an optional module), and IBM chose not to incorporate it into COBOL II.

When COBOL II was introduced, there was no choice: you had to abandon use of Report Writer. Since then, IBM has developed a Report Writer preprocessor that converts Report Writer code into equivalent COBOL II code, allowing a shop to use the preprocessor either 1) on a one-time basis to convert existing applications, or 2) on a routine basis, converting programs with Report Writer prior to each compile. The choice here is not easy or simple. Consider:

1. If a shop does a one-time conversion, the shop is free from the Report Writer issue, but loses the productivity feature that caused the shop to use it initially.
2. If a shop continues using Report Writer, the preprocessor increases the cost of each compile, the generated COBOL code does not match what the programmer wrote and may be more difficult to debug, and when

report output is incorrect, the problem may be in one of three places: the compiler, the preprocessor, or the program logic.

Whether Report Writer should be used at your shop, then, is something I can't tell you. It is not part of COBOL II, but you can continue to code Report Writer if your shop uses the preprocessor. Neither choice is perfect.

Report Writer (supported by a preprocessor)

Communications

ISAM & BDAM

Segmentation

Macro-level CICS

EXAMINE & TRANSFORM

READY/RESET TRACE, EXHIBIT, USE FOR DEBUGGING

CURRENT-DATE & TIME-OF-DAY

NOTE & REMARKS

ON (the statement, not the clause within statements)

WRITE AFTER POSITIONING

STATE & FLOW Compile options

OPEN & CLOSE obsolete options

Figure 2.2. Major OS/VS COBOL components absent in COBOL II and COBOL/370.

2.1.2. ISAM and BDAM

If you use ISAM or BDAM, you need to convert such files to an equivalent VSAM format before using COBOL II. While conversion software may address all, or most, of the COBOL changes, the files must be separately converted.

2.1.3. Communications Feature

This feature, which required a CD entry and used SEND, RECEIVE, ENABLE, and DISABLE statements, has been removed, and no equivalent feature exists. This was a feature that allowed COBOL programs to interact with a user-written TCAM program. Most likely, your shop uses other software for sending and receiving messages, such as CICS or IMS/DC, anyway.

2.1.4   Segmentation Feature

While this is no longer supported, any such references are treated as comments. With virtual storage, the need for segmenting COBOL programs is considered obsolete.

2.1.5.   Macro-Level CICS

If you have CICS programs at the macro level, they need to be converted to CICS command level before using COBOL II. There are some conversion programs on the market that address this conversion issue.

2.1.6.   EXAMINE and TRANSFORM

EXAMINE and TRANSFORM have been eliminated in favor of INSPECT. OS/VS COBOL supported all three verbs.

2.1.7.   READY/RESET TRACE, EXHIBIT, and USE FOR DEBUGGING

COBOL II is evolving to a point where no debugging facilities will exist in the code proper. At this writing, READY TRACE and RESET TRACE are obsolete. USE FOR DEBUGGING is still supported, but it will be removed from the next revision of the ANSI standard, so I don't encourage its use. For debugging assistance, IBM provides the COBOL debugging facility (see Chapter 4, Debugging Techniques). If READY TRACE or RESET TRACE appear within a COBOL II program, they are ignored. The EXHIBIT statement will cause a compile error.

2.1.8.   CURRENT-DATE and TIME-OF-DAY

Removing CURRENT-DATE and TIME-OF-DAY is part of COBOL's evolution toward using procedural elements to accomplish objectives, rather than relying on special registers. OS/VS COBOL supported both ANSI 68 and ANSI 74 facilities to access date and time. These ANSI 68 statements are not allowed:

```
MOVE CURRENT-DATE TO data-name
MOVE TIME-OF-DAY TO data-name
```

Whereas these ANSI 74 statements work in OS/VS COBOL and in COBOL II:

```
ACCEPT data-name FROM DATE      (implicit PIC is 9(6))
ACCEPT data-name FROM TIME      (implicit PIC is 9(8))
```

The PIC definitions are *changed* from ANSI 68. In ANSI 68, CURRENT-DATE was X(8), for MM/DD/YY (slashes were included) and TIME-OF-DAY was X(6), for HHMMSS. In COBOL II, DATE is 9(6) for YYMMDD (different order and no slashes), and TIME is 9(8) for HHMMSShh (for hours, minutes, seconds, and hundredths of seconds).

For more information on additional options of ACCEPT, see the next section of this chapter.

2.1.9. NOTE and REMARKS

Neither of these is listed in the IBM OS/VS COBOL Reference Manual, but both were acceptable. Use the * in column 7, instead.

2.1.10. ON Statement

This is part of the debugging extensions IBM provided with OS/VS COBOL. You possibly have never used it. This is *not* a reference to ON clauses, such as ON SIZE ERROR, which continue to be valid.

2.1.11. WRITE AFTER POSITIONING Statement

This statement was a carryover from pre-OS/VS COBOL compilers. It is replaced by WRITE AFTER ADVANCING.

2.1.12. STATE and FLOW Compile Options

While not COBOL elements, these two debug options were popular in some shops and unknown in others. Their functions are available in the new COBTEST debug facility for COBOL II and CODE/370 for COBOL/370.

2.1.13. OPEN and CLOSE Obsolete Options

Those optional clauses that were hardware dependent, the LEAVE, REREAD, and DISP options for the OPEN statement, and CLOSE WITH DISP and CLOSE WITH POSITIONING are no longer valid. In both cases, other options have been available for several years, so I don't anticipate these changes will cause application problems. Also, these OPEN and CLOSE options, as were many of the changes listed in this section, were *not* specified as being part of OS/VS COBOL proper, but they were documented in the appendix as IBM extensions.

As I mentioned earlier, the best way to evaluate the implication of the dropped features is to compile one or more of your programs. Also, specifying the LANGLVL(2) and MIGR options when compiling with OS/VS COBOL will help sensitize you to incompatible elements.

2.2. MODIFIED COBOL COMPONENTS

This section requires a careful reading because the fundamental syntax of these components existed in OS/VS COBOL. Features identified in the prior section (e.g., Report Writer) will not be repeated here.

Only those options and syntax that are sufficiently different to warrant your interest will be presented. The examples shown in this section may be incomplete, not displaying all options of a particular clause. The purpose for this approach is to focus on what has changed without requiring you to cope with the full syntax of COBOL. (Note: A listing of COBOL statements and their syntax is in Chapter 7, Summaries, Tables, and References). I have classified entries in this section as "modified COBOL components," rather than as "new COBOL components" because the features are made available using clauses or statements with which you are probably already familiar.

2.2.1. IDENTIFICATION DIVISION

The major change in the IDENTIFICATION DIVISION is that it now allows you to specify how the program will participate within a run unit. This is accomplished by the PROGRAM-ID clause. No other entries are required, nor should they be used.

Required entries (those that must always be present): IDENTIFICATION DIVISION or ID DIVISION, PROGRAM-ID.

Obsolete, treated as comments: All other entries, including AUTHOR, INSTALLATION, DATE-WRITTEN, DATE-COMPILED, and SECURITY.

Obsolete and not allowed: REMARKS.

Enhanced elements (descriptions follow this list): PROGRAM-ID.

```
 ┌─ IDENTIFICATION DIVISION.──────┬──────────────────────────>
 └───── ID DIVISION. ─────────────┘

 ─ PROGRAM-ID.    program-name ┬──────────────────┬──.─><
                               └─ COMMON ──┘└─ INITIAL ─┘
```

Figure 2.3. IDENTIFICATION DIVISION requirements.

PROGRAM-ID modifications.

The new features of PROGRAM-ID are intended to provide additional features for multi-module structures, where one program is CALLed by another. The optional clause, COMMON, specifies that the program may be accessed from any other programs sharing a nested run unit (see Chapter 3, Programming with COBOL II and COBOL/370, for more information on module structures). Unless your shop starts using nested programs, you won't have use for this feature.

The clause, INITIAL, specifies that the program is to be in its initial state every time it is CALLed. Even without INITIAL coded, a program is in its initial state the first time it is CALLed and on the first CALL following a CANCEL statement. Use of INITIAL should be reserved for those structures where a sub-program does not reinitialize variables, does not maintain any information from one CALL to the next, and the program logic always assumes that it will be CALLED only once. Your use of INITIAL will be dependent on how your shop writes and mixes subprograms.

Recommendation for using IDENTIFICATION DIVISION features.

Instead of using the obsolete elements, use the COBOL comment facility (an * in column 7) to provide any needed documentation. The date the program was compiled appears on source listings and is imbedded within the object program. Be careful not to misinterpret COBOL syntax messages (this applies to all divisions, not just the IDENTIFICATION DIVISION entries). For example, consider this error from a compile listing (notice how COBOL embeds the error message in the source listing—a nice improvement):

```
        PROGRAM-ID.
            DKA101BN.
        AUTHOR.
==> IGYDS1128-W "AUTHOR" PARAGRAPH COMMENTARY WAS FOUND IN AREA "A".
            PROCESSED AS IF FOUND IN AREA "B".
            DAVID S. KIRK.
        REMARKS.
            THIS SUBPROGRAM CALCULATES VACATION DAYS.
```

It appears that AUTHOR is incorrect, yet no error appears for using RE-MARKS. This appears to contradict my previous statements. In fact, because COBOL II ignores obsolete elements, the compiler saw REMARKS in column 8 and assumed it was part of the AUTHOR paragraph. Errors such as this can be confusing.

2.2.2. ENVIRONMENT DIVISION

The major change of the ENVIRONMENT DIVISION is that you may now get full VSAM status code feedback for your VSAM files. This is provided by the

FILE STATUS clause. Other notable changes are a continuing reduction of required and optional clauses. In fact, there are now many situations where this division serves no purpose and need not be coded.

Required entries (those that must always be present): None. (This would be true if all defaults were acceptable and there were no files to SELECT.)

Obsolete, treated as comments: MEMORY SIZE, SEGMENT LIMIT, and MULTIPLE FILE TAPE.

Obsolete and not allowed: ACTUAL KEY, NOMINAL KEY, TRACK-AREA, TRACK-LIMIT, PROCESSING MODE.

Optional entries (ignored): ORGANIZATION IS in SELECT statement.

Enhanced elements (descriptions follow this list): FILE STATUS.

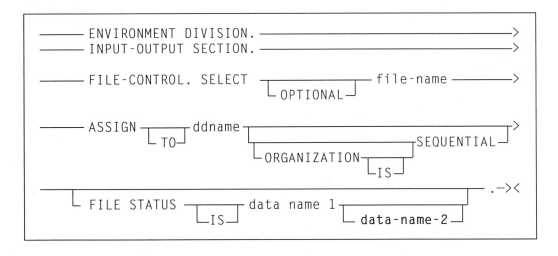

Figure 2.4. Example of FILE STATUS for sequential file (all SELECT options not shown).

Use of expanded FILE STATUS codes for VSAM.

From the example in Figure 2.4, the "data-name-1" entry is the normal FILE STATUS field from OS/VS COBOL. The new entry is "data-name-2," which must be defined in the WORKING-STORAGE SECTION (or the LINKAGE SECTION, if appropriate) as a six-byte group item. The group item must contain three subordinate entries, each a half-word binary entry. An example:

```
01 VSAM-STATUS-CODE.
    05  VSAM-RETURN-CODE         PIC S99  BINARY.
    05  VSAM-FUNCTION-CODE       PIC S99  BINARY.
    05  VSAM-FEEDBACK-CODE       PIC S99  BINARY.
```

This new feature allows a COBOL program to access the status for a variety of VSAM processes. The returned codes are from Access Method Services. For more information on the content and use of these fields, see the appropriate VSAM Macro Instruction Reference manual (Chapter 9, Related Publications). (Note: Notice the use of the word *BINARY* in the example. COBOL II allows programs to use BINARY in place of COMP, and PACKED-DECIMAL in place of COMP-3 if desired. COMP and COMP-3 still work fine.)

Recommendation for using ENVIRONMENT DIVISION features.

The ENVIRONMENT DIVISION contains many optional entries that are rarely used. If you use VSAM files, you already know what options are necessary and where the new VSAM status codes will help your applications. From programs I've seen or worked on, the example in figure 2.4 exhibits the complete syntax that is adequate for more than 90% of programs. If your application uses the default collating sequence (most do) and has no special names to define (few do), then you need to define the ENVIRONMENT DIVISION *only* when there are files to process.

2.2.3.   DATA DIVISION

Most of the big changes in the DATA DIVISION were identified earlier in Section 2.1 (COBOL Features Dropped). Other changes reflect an on-going process of cleaning up the COBOL language, removing the requirement for clauses that are either irrelevant or self-evident. For example, labels for a file are handled via MVS and JCL, so the LABEL RECORDS clause is irrelevant. The 01-level that follows an FD is always identified with the FD, so the DATA RECORD clause is also irrelevant. Since FILLER always means a data description with no name, the word FILLER only documented what would be self-evident if FILLER were omitted. Now it can be.

These changes don't require that you modify existing programs, but they do allow you to code less and achieve the same results.

Required entries (those that must always be present): None. (Having no entries would be rare.)

Obsolete, treated as comments: LABEL RECORDS clause in FD (illegal in SD), DATA RECORD clause, and VALUE OF clause (in FD).

Obsolete and not allowed (see Section 2.1): Report Writer statements, Communications statements, ISAM & BDAM statements.

Optional entries (Described below): FILLER.

The FILLER entry.

This is an easy and optional change that improves readability of a program. The word *FILLER*, used to define data descriptions with no name, may be replaced by spaces. For years, it was a meaningless entry in COBOL. Now, it is no longer needed. Consider the example in Figure 2.5. The second entry for the record is easier to read.

Enhanced elements (descriptions follow this list): USAGE clause, VALUE clause, OCCURS DEPENDING ON, and COPY statement.

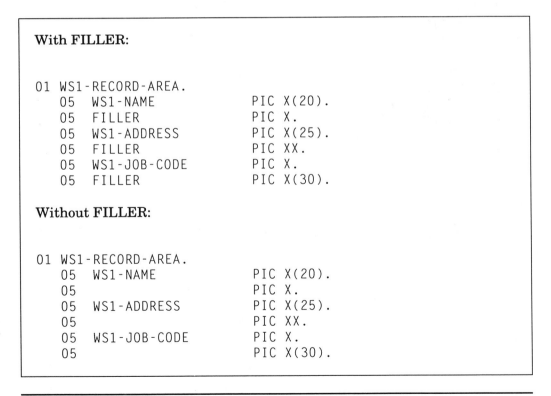

```
With FILLER:


01 WS1-RECORD-AREA.
    05   WS1-NAME            PIC X(20).
    05   FILLER              PIC X.
    05   WS1-ADDRESS         PIC X(25).
    05   FILLER              PIC XX.
    05   WS1-JOB-CODE        PIC X.
    05   FILLER              PIC X(30).

Without FILLER:


01 WS1-RECORD-AREA.
    05   WS1-NAME            PIC X(20).
    05                       PIC X.
    05   WS1-ADDRESS         PIC X(25).
    05                       PIC XX.
    05   WS1-JOB-CODE        PIC X.
    05                       PIC X(30).
```

Figure 2.5. Example with and without FILLER.

Modifications to the USAGE clause.

One of the changes to USAGE was mentioned earlier: the ability to use BINARY instead of COMP, and PACKED-DECIMAL instead of COMP-3. This is nice, but old habits die hard. In developing example programs for this book, I continued to use COMP and COMP-3, and I plan to continue using them since they require fewer keystrokes.

The addition of POINTER, however, opens up new doors that will be explored more in the next chapter. POINTER provides to COBOL programs the facility to treat addresses of data as data, a technique that was previously available only to assembler programmers.

The USAGE IS PROCEDURE-POINTER clause applies only to COBOL/370. This is to provide the facility of passing the address of one program to another program. This could be desirable if program A wants to specify to program B which of several programs to CALL. This would normally be done when a COBOL/370 program wants LE/370 to invoke a specific user-written routine for a specific condition or where a user application needs such dynamic controls. There is no PIC clause with this elementary item, defaulting to an 8-byte, system-controlled field. Data items that are PROCEDURE-POINTERs are modified with a new format of the SET command (covered later).

Modifications to the VALUE clause.

The extension to VALUE that will be most appreciated is that it may now be used in OCCURS statements. In OS/VS COBOL, a table could not be defined and initialized in the DATA DIVISION, requiring either a REDEFINES entry or a PERFORM VARYING statement in the PROCEDURE DIVISION. Consider

In OS/VS COBOL

```
01  JOB-CODE-TABLE.
    05  JOB-CODE-ENTRIES OCCURS 8 TIMES INDEXED BY JOB-CODE.
        10  JOB-TITLE      PIC X(8).
        10  JOB-MAX-SAL    PIC S9(5)V99.
        10 JOB-MIN-SAL     PIC S9(5)V99.
         .
         .

    PERFORM 0100-INIT-TABLE VARYING JOB-CODE FROM 1 BY 1 UNTIL
        JOB-CODE > 8.
         .

         .
0100-INIT-TABLE.
    MOVE SPACES TO JOB-TITLE (JOB-CODE)
    MOVE ZEROS TO JOB-MAX-SAL (JOB-CODE)
                  JOB-MIN-SAL (JOB-CODE).
```

In COBOL II

```
01  JOB-CODE-TABLE.
    05  JOB-CODE-ENTRIES OCCURS 8 TIMES INDEXED BY JOB-CODE.
        10 JOB-TITLE       PIC X(8) VALUE SPACES.
        10 JOB-MAX-SAL      PIC S9(5)V99 VALUE ZERO.
        10 JOB-MIN-SAL      PIC S9(5)V99 VALUE ZERO.
          .
          .
```

Techniques such as this can save procedural complexity and reduce programming efforts. Later on, you will see a new statement, INITIALIZE, that can replace the above PERFORM logic when needed in a program.

Another option in the VALUE clause is that you may now code in hexadecimal, just as assembler programmers do (Note: The hexadecimal literal may now be used where other alphanumeric literals are valid, not just in the VALUE clause). The literal must be preceded by *X* and the data must follow hexadecimal conventions (a multiple of 2 bytes, with values of 0 through 9 and A through F). Nice trick, but should you use this feature? One of the strengths of COBOL is its avoidance of machine dependencies. There are several situations, primarily between COBOL and non-COBOL modules, where hex literals may be effective, but I encourage you to be c-a-r-e-f-u-l. Here is an example of possible use:

```
05  WS5-PROCESS-SWITCH  PIC  X  VALUE X'01'.
    88  BIT-0-SET             VALUE X'80'.
    88  BIT-0-1-SET           VALUE X'C0'.
    88  BIT-0-2-SET           VALUE X'A0'.
    88  BIT-0-3-SET           VALUE X'90'.
    88  BIT-0-4-SET           VALUE X'88'.
    88  BIT-0-5-SET           VALUE X'84'.
      .
      .
```

This initializes the field to a binary value of 1 and provides 88-level entries to allow setting or testing of various bit combinations. This technique might be helpful if your system interacts with assembler programs that use one byte for multiple switches. This does *not* mean you can change individual bits. The down side of hex values is that it is easy to make mistakes with them and difficult to figure them out. For more information on bits and hexadecimal, see Chapter 7.

The new NULL option can't be explained without first laying some groundwork. NULL is related to POINTER and PROCEDURE-POINTER. I'll show you later.

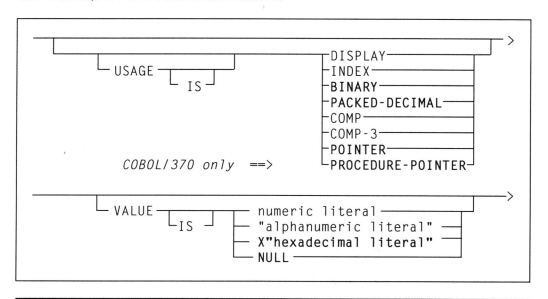

Figure 2.6. Example of USAGE and VALUE clauses (all options not shown).

Modifications to OCCURS DEPENDING ON.

With COBOL II, you may now have variable length data subordinate to variable length data, as demonstrated in Figure 2.7. Notice that the control fields (named here VALUE-A and VALUE-B) are in the fixed portion of the record and are not allowed to be in the variable portion. While this facility is now available, do you want to define files this way? The strong move towards data normalization has significantly reduced the number of variable length records and I applaud the change.

The COPY statement.

OS/VS COBOL supported both the ANSI 1974 standard and the IBM extension to the ANSI 1968 standard. COBOL II supports the ANSI 1974 and the ANSI 1985 standard. The format of the COPY statement that met the ANSI 1968 standard is no longer allowed. That format was

```
01 data-name COPY membername.
```

whereby data-name replaced the associated data-name from the copy member. See the example in Figure 2.8. COPY statements in OS/VS COBOL that follow the ANSI 1974 standard should work satisfactorily.

```
01   RECORD-NAME.
     05  1ST-GROUP-NAME.
         10  VALUE-A          PIC S9    COMP.
         10  VALUE-B          PIC S9    COMP.
     05  2ND-GROUP-NAME OCCURS 1 TO 10 TIMES
         DEPENDING ON VALUE-A.
         10  FIELD-C          PIC XX.
         10  FIELD-D  OCCURS 1 TO 30 TIMES
             DEPENDING ON VALUE-B.
             15 FIELD-E        PIC S9(5) COMP-3.
             15 FIELD-F        PIC XXX.
```

Figure 2.7. Example of nested OCCURS DEPENDING ON.

COPYbook member EMPREC:

```
01   EMP-REC.
     05   EMP-NAME        PIC X(30).
     05   EMP-JOB-CODE PIC X.
```

COPY statement extension in OS/VS COBOL:

```
01   WORK-REC   COPY   EMPREC.
```

Generated source code with OS/VS COBOL:

```
01   WORK-REC.
     05   EMP-NAME        PIC X(30).
     05   EMP-JOB-CODE PIC X.
```

Generated source code with COBOL II (causes syntax error):

```
01   WORK-REC
01   EMP-REC.
     05   EMP-NAME        PIC X(30).
     05   EMP-JOB-CODE PIC X.
```

Example of allowable format:

```
COPY EMPREC.
```

Figure 2.8. COPY format that is no longer allowed.

An additional change in COBOL II is that you may have COPY statements imbedded within other COPY statements. This nesting was not allowed in OS/VS COBOL. In writing this, my first feeling was "Why would anyone want to do this? Programming is hard enough without adding this complexity." I encourage you to not use it unless you have a very specific need for it.

Recommendation for using DATA DIVISION features.

Assuming you aren't using Report Writer or other no-no's, these changes in the DATA DIVISION do not require that you change the way you code COBOL programs (Exception: The COPY statement example I mentioned). Also, making any of these changes prevents your program from compiling with OS/VS COBOL again.

I recommend you take advantage of the opportunity to omit FILLER and the opportunity to leave obsolete statements out of your FDs and SDs. Anytime you can stop coding obsolete statements, the program becomes cleaner. Also, if you continue coding LABEL RECORDS ARE STANDARD and DATA RECORD IS, all COBOL II will do with the statements is check if you spelled them correctly. If you did, it ignores them. If you didn't, you will get a syntax error. Is that any way to play the odds? So stop it, already.

2.2.4. PROCEDURE DIVISION

Changes to existing statements in the PROCEDURE DIVISION add several new options to your tool kit. Many of the changes qualify as all new. They are included here because they are extensions to existing statements. The issues that will require you to change any entries in this division were highlighted earlier in Section 2.1 of this chapter (OS/VS Features That Were Dropped).

Required entries (those that must always be present): None. (This would be true for a program within a run unit that consisted of no procedural code. I'll show you an example in Chapter 3.)

Obsolete, treated as comments: Not applicable in PROCEDURE DIVISION.

Obsolete and not allowed (see section A, above): References to CURRENT-DATE and TIME-OF-DAY, EXAMINE, EXHIBIT, READY/RESET TRACE, TRANSFORM, Report Writer statements, Communications statements, ISAM and BDAM statements, NOTE (use * in column 7, instead), ON statement (was used primarily for debugging), and OPEN and CLOSE obsolete options.

Changed elements: This is a bit unusual, having a feature remain yet be different. That's what happened to the WHEN-COMPILED special register. In OS/VS COBOL, this special register returned the time, followed by the date. With COBOL II, that sequence has been reversed and now has a different format, as well. For example, a program compiled on November 14, 1994, at 10:05 A.M. would cause these results in this special register:

```
OS/VS COBOL:    10.05.00NOV 14, 1994    <== total of 20 bytes
COBOL II:       11/14/9410.05.00        <== total of 16 bytes
```

COBOL/370 also offers an intrinsic function for this feature, which has yet another data format. Since intrinsic functions are covered together, I'll discuss it then.

Enhanced elements: Scope Terminators, CALL, INSPECT, PERFORM, READ and RETURN, SET, SORT, and NOT ON SIZE ERROR and NOT IN-VALID KEY.

Scope terminators.

Scope terminators are the easiest of COBOL II's new PROCEDURE DIVISION enhancements to start using. Until now, the scope of a conditional statement extended for the duration of a sentence (i.e., the scope was terminated by a period). That sometimes caused clumsy coding practices. Consider the following from OS/VS COBOL:

```
2100-PRODUCE-REPORT.
    PERFORM 2300-READ-RECORD
    IF NOT END-OF-FILE
        IF VALID-CONTROL-BREAK
            PERFORM 2400-WRITE-SUBTOTALS.
    IF NOT END-OF-FILE
        PERFORM 2500-ASSEMBLE-DETAIL-LINE
        PERFORM 2600-WRITE-DETAIL.
```

While you may have done that code differently, this technique is not unusual and is an example where a period was necessary to end the scope of the nested IF statement. Because there were additional processes dependent on the first IF statement, that statement had to be repeated. A *scope terminator* is a new COBOL II element that allows you to define the end of a conditional statement's scope without the need for a period. The syntax is straightforward: the letters *END-*, followed by the name of the affected verb. For example:

> END-IF is the scope terminator for the IF statement
> END-COMPUTE is the scope terminator for the COMPUTE statement (remember, with an ON SIZE ERROR clause, any arithmetic statement can be conditional)
> END-READ is the scope terminator for a READ statement.

Any statement that has conditional elements may use a scope terminator where a period is not needed (and my philosophy is *never* to code anything that is not needed—more on this in the chapter on program design, Chapter 5). There is an exception to the first sentence in this paragraph, as a new format for PER-FORM has a mandatory scope terminator, yet it is NOT conditional. More on that a bit further on when new PERFORM features are addressed. For now, let's redo that prior example:

```
2100-PRODUCE-REPORT.
    PERFORM 2300-READ-RECORD
    IF NOT END-OF-FILE
        IF VALID-CONTROL-BREAK
            PERFORM 2400-WRITE-SUBTOTALS
        END-IF
        PERFORM 2500-ASSEMBLE-DETAIL-LINE
        PERFORM 2600-WRITE-DETAIL.
```

Notice how the logic is clearer. I finished the example with a period as it is the end of the paragraph, although an END-IF could have been coded if the logic flow were to continue. My preference is to code scope terminators every time I code a conditional statement and to avoid using periods except at the end of paragraphs. Scope terminators make the structure clear and, as I never use unnecessary periods, I never have to worry about an improperly placed one.

Changes to the CALL statement.

The opportunities that come with the new features in the CALL statement are not immediately apparent. The new features are extensions of, and do not conflict with, CALL statements from OS/VS COBOL (Exception: In OS/VS COBOL, you were allowed to have a paragraph-name as an identifier following USING. COBOL II does *not* allow that). There are several changes, each of which needs clarification. Let's look at each option, keeping in mind that they can be combined within the same CALL statement.

Use of BY REFERENCE or BY CONTENT in CALL statement. This new option lets you control whether your program will let a subprogram have access to the data in your program or only the value of the data in your program. Confusing? Remember, in OS/VS COBOL, a subprogram that accessed a passed parameter list (CALL USING . . .) was accessing the data directly within the CALLing program. That meant the subprogram could modify the data, even if you didn't want it modified. Now, by specifying BY CONTENT when you CALL a subprogram, the subprogram receives what appears to be your data area, but it is actually a separate area. If the subprogram changes it, your program's data area is not affected. If you code neither of these options, BY REFERENCE is assumed, as that is compatible with OS/VS COBOL coding conventions.

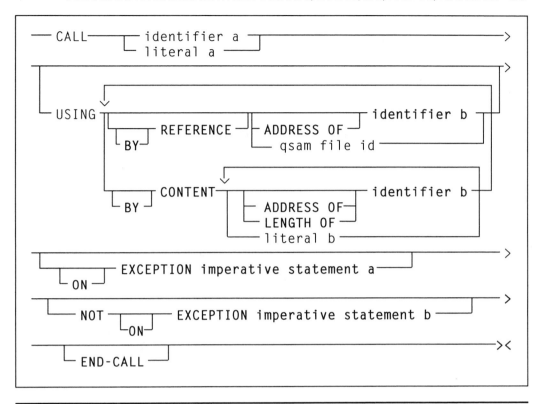

Figure 2.9. CALL syntax in COBOL II.

Use of LENGTH OF clause in CALL statement. Did you ever want to pass data to a subprogram, but the length of the passed data varied? Now you can also pass the length of the data, so the subprogram can respond according to your intent. This is useful whenever variable data must be exchanged between programs. Errors can still occur, of course, if the program logic is incorrect, but now the information is available so such a program can be cleanly constructed. The LENGTH OF clause is not restricted to the CALL statement, as it is a new special register provided by COBOL II. The receiving program must have an identifier defined in the LINKAGE SECTION with PIC S9(9) COMP. Here is an example of that technique:

```
CALL 'SUB1'    USING WS3-WORK-REC
               BY CONTENT LENGTH OF WS3-WORK-REC
```

The subprogram, SUB1, would need the following:

```
LINKAGE SECTION.
01  LS1-WORK-REC.
    .
    .
01  LS2-LENGTH     PIC S9(9)  COMP.
PROCEDURE DIVISION USING LS1-WORK-REC LS2-LENGTH.
```

Use of ADDRESS OF clause in CALL statement. This will be covered later, along with POINTER data elements. The ADDRESS OF clause is not restricted to the CALL statement, as it is a new special register provided by COBOL II.

Use of ON EXCEPTION and NOT ON EXCEPTION in CALL statement. These are conditional expressions that receive control depending on whether the subprogram was accessed by your CALL statement. They apply only to dynamic CALLs. For example, your program periodically CALLs a large subprogram dynamically, but the REGION may be of insufficient size. You might code

```
CALL LARGE-PROG USING data-name
    ON EXCEPTION
        DISPLAY 'Program not loaded, increase REGION'
        MOVE 16 TO RETURN-CODE
        STOP RUN
END-CALL
```

(OS/VS COBOL had an option, ON OVERFLOW, that was equivalent to ON EXCEPTION. COBOL II supports that syntax, also.)

Changes to the INSPECT statement.

With EXAMINE and TRANSFORM no longer available, the INSPECT statement gets new respect. A major enhancement has been the ability to duplicate the capabilities of the TRANSFORM statement. Previously, the INSPECT statement could only address 1-byte entries, whereas TRANSFORM could address groups of data. Now, with the new format, INSPECT can do a one-for-one replacement of TRANSFORM statements. The new format allows statements such as the following:

```
01  DATA-FIELD    PIC X(300).

01  CHARS-A       PIC X(26)
    VALUE 'abcdefghijklmnopqrstuvwxyz'.

01  CHARS-B       PIC X(26)
    VALUE 'ABCDEFGHIJKLMNOPQRSTUVWXYZ'.

    INSPECT DATA-FIELD CONVERTING CHARS-A TO CHARS-B
```

This ability to change character sets across a complete data area was not previously possible with a single INSPECT statement. This simplifies the manual coding required to convert OS/VS COBOL programs to either COBOL II or COBOL/370.

Changes to the PERFORM statement.

The PERFORM statement has always been one of my favorites and now it has even more flexibility, although the new features are a mixed blessing. First, I want to tell you about the new features, and then I'll get back to that point about a mixed blessing.

PERFORM now has two major new syntax structures that can be useful if you do structured programming. The first is full implementation of the DO-UNTIL format. (Refresher: a DO-UNTIL statement executes the code before testing the condition; a DO-WHILE tests the condition prior to executing the code.) Until now, the PERFORM UNTIL (a DO-WHILE statement) had to serve both needs. Now you can specify the PERFORM UNTIL statement adding WITH TEST AFTER to it and it becomes a DO-UNTIL format. (Note: If not coded on a PERFORM UNTIL statement, WITH TEST BEFORE is assumed for compatibility with existing code.)

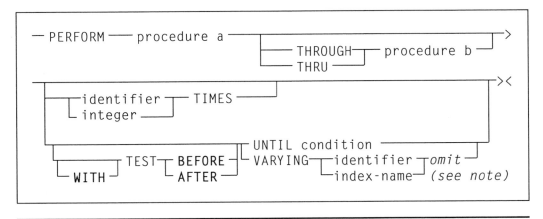

Figure 2.10. Basic PERFORM syntax. (Note: For clarity of new features, the syntax following VARYING is omitted from the diagram where omit appears, including FROM, BY, UNTIL, and AFTER.)

For me, the big question was "When would I ever need the WITH TEST AFTER clause?" I never found a satisfactory answer, but I can offer an example. WITH TEST AFTER has a potential advantage when you are using the VARYING clause to load a table and want the index-data-item to reflect the number of entries in the table, not one greater than the number in the table. Consider these two options:

```
PERFORM 3300-LOAD-PREMIUM-TABLE VARYING PREM-INDEX FROM 1 BY
    1 UNTIL END-OF-FILE

PERFORM 3300-LOAD-PREMIUM-TABLE WITH TEST AFTER VARYING
    PREM-INDEX FROM 1 BY 1 UNTIL END-OF-FILE
```

Assuming there were 1,000 premium entries to be loaded to the table, the contents of PREM-INDEX after the first statement would refer to a 1,001st entry, whereas the contents of PREM-INDEX in the second example would reflect that the table had 1,000 entries, not 1,001. Assuming the END-OF-FILE condition-name is not already set at the time either statement is executed, the choice becomes one of style.

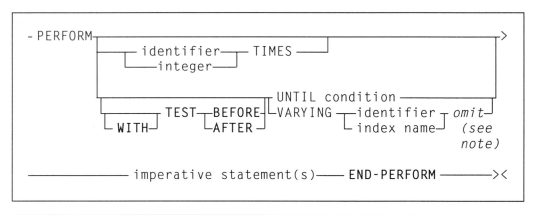

Figure 2.11. Inline PERFORM syntax. (Note: For clarity of new features, the syntax following VARYING is omitted from the diagram, including FROM, BY, UNTIL, and AFTER. This is where omit appears.)

The second option is the inline PERFORM, with all PERFORMed code following the PERFORM statement. From the syntax in Figure 2.11, a sample inline PERFORM might be

```
PERFORM VARYING STATE-INDEX FROM 1 BY ONE UNTIL END-OF-FILE
    PERFORM 2100-READ-RECORD
    IF NOT END-OF-FILE
        MOVE STATE-DATA TO STATE-TABLE (STATE-INDEX)
    END-IF
END-PERFORM
```

Earlier, I mentioned that the PERFORM verb was an exception to my statement about using scope terminators on conditional statements. The END-PERFORM statement is the *only* scope terminator that applies to a nonconditional statement. Also, it must be coded at the end of all inline PERFORMs.

In my first paragraph on these PERFORM enhancements, I mentioned a mixed blessing. Although I admit it is a matter of style, I prefer not to use either statement. Why? While teaching programmers I learned that most programmers do best when they have a few simple tools. The PERFORM WITH TEST AFTER is so subtle in its difference that many novice programmers may not recognize what you are doing with the code. The inline PERFORM is nice in concept, but it can increase the density of paragraphs and reduce readability, especially when the code is to be maintained later by less experienced programmers.

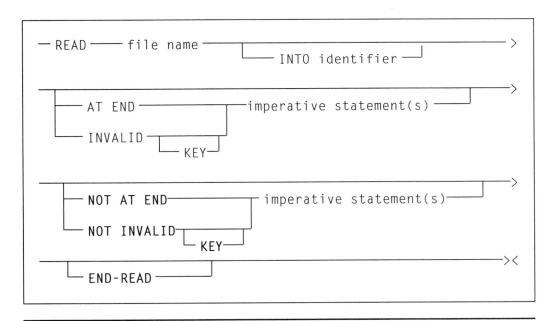

Figure 2.12. Basic READ syntax. For clarity, I omitted little used options, such as NEXT RECORD. (Note: AT END/NOT AT END *cannot* be intermixed with INVALID KEY/NOT INVALID KEY.)

Changes to READ and RETURN statements.

The changes to these two statements are so obvious and easy that one might wonder why these enhancements weren't done years ago. Anyway, they provide some interesting program structure opportunities. (Example 8.2, in Chapter 8, Sample Programs, is one.) By adding a NOT AT END clause, much of the clumsiness of READs and RETURNs is eliminated.

In OS/VS COBOL, I typically had a paragraph similar to this:

```
2300-READ-PAYROLL.
    READ FD3-PAYROLL-FILE
      AT END
        MOVE 'Y' TO FD3-EOF-SWITCH.
      IF FD3-EOF-SWITCH = 'N'
        ADD 1 TO FD3-RECORD-COUNT.
```

Now I can use the following replacement:

```
2300-READ-PAYROLL.
    READ FD3-PAYROLL-FILE
      AT END
        MOVE 'Y' TO FD3-EOF-SWITCH
      NOT AT END
        ADD 1 TO FD3-RECORD-COUNT
    END-READ.
```

I think you will agree that the COBOL II approach is much cleaner. (Being the end of the paragraph, the END-READ wasn't required. I use it for clarity.) This feature also provides the opportunity to change a typical programming style that is common in structured programming.

Typical PERFORMed READ, followed by test for end of file:

```
PERFORM 2300-READ-PAYROLL
IF FD3-EOF-SWITCH = 'N'
    imperative statements to process data
    .
    .
```

Opportunity for a different approach with COBOL II:

```
READ FD3-PAYROLL-FILE
  AT END
    MOVE 'Y' TO FD3-EOF-SWITCH
  NOT AT END
    imperative statements to process data
    .
    .
```

It works, but I suggest you use the approach carefully. I prefer decomposition of a program to keep I/O statements in separate paragraphs. While the READ statement fits well in the above example, it will tempt a maintenance programmer to add another READ statement in the future. Your shop may have standards on that, too.

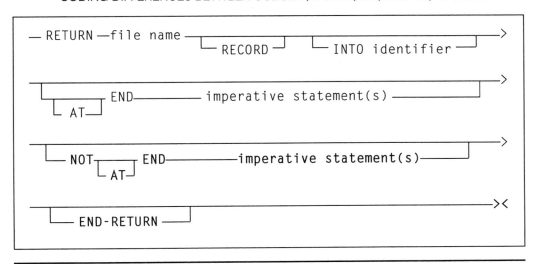

Figure 2.13. RETURN syntax.

SET enhancements.

Many programmers have never used this statement. Lack of use is indicative of a lack of experience with managing indexes in programs (more on that in Chapter 3, Programming with COBOL II). For now, let's look at a new capability. The SET statement may now reference 88-level condition names. Demonstrating is easier than explaining.

```
01  WS3-EMPL-DATA.
    05  EMPL-NAME            PIC X(30).
    05  EMPL-JOB-CODE        PIC X.
        88  PROGRAMMER       VALUE '1'.
        88  ANALYST          VALUE '2'.
        88  MANAGER          VALUE '3'.

01  FD2-PRINT-REC.
    05  FD2-EMPL-NAME        PIC X(30).
    05  JOB-TITLE            PIC X(10).
        88  PROGRAMMER-TITLE  VALUE 'PROGRAMMER'.
        88  ANALYST-TITLE     VALUE 'ANALYST'.
        88  MANAGER-TITLE     VALUE 'MANAGER'.
        88  UNKNOWN-TITLE     VALUE '**********'.
```

Where the application is to interrogate EMPL-JOB-CODE and move the appropriate value to JOB-TITLE, in OS/VS COBOL, you might code:

```
IF PROGRAMMER
    MOVE 'PROGRAMMER' TO JOB-TITLE
```

```
ELSE
    IF ANALYST
        MOVE 'ANALYST' TO JOB-TITLE
    ELSE
        IF MANAGER
            MOVE 'MANAGER' TO JOB-TITLE
        ELSE
            MOVE '**********' TO JOB-TITLE
```

In COBOL II, you can code this:

```
IF PROGRAMMER
    SET PROGRAMMER-TITLE TO TRUE
ELSE
    IF ANALYST
        SET ANALYST-TITLE TO TRUE
    ELSE
        IF MANAGER
            SET MANAGER-TITLE TO TRUE
        ELSE
            SET UNKNOWN-TITLE TO TRUE
```

As you can see, this use of SET removes literals from the PROCEDURE DIVISION and moves them where they belong, to the DATA DIVISION. Readability is improved too, as all options appear beneath the data name. When you get to the EVALUATE statement in the next section, you will discover an even cleaner way to write the above logic by using both the EVALUATE statement and the SET statement.

I haven't yet covered all the new features of the SET statement. I have more on SET in the next section, where I include it with a definition of POINTER data elements and PROCEDURE-POINTER elements.

SORT enhancements.

People have debated with me on whether what I'm about to describe is an enhancement or not. To me, anything that makes a program cleaner is an enhancement. SORT hasn't changed, so what's the big deal? Well, SORT no longer requires that procedural logic be organized by SECTION names. That's it. Why is that important? Anytime an unnecessary coding element is removed, you have the opportunity for a cleaner structure. This is what I call a style issue. If you consider that most programmers never use SECTIONs except when they do SORT programs, there is a tendency to use both paragraphs *and* SECTIONS. This practice creates programs that are unstructured and rife with GO TOs. It is not unusual to find SORT programs where an INPUT PROCEDURE is something like this:

```
1000-INPUT SECTION.
1010-INITIALIZE.
    initialization logic
    .
    .
    .
1030-PROCESS-DATA.
    PERFORM 1040-READ-RECORD
    IF EOF-SWITCH = 'Y'
        GO TO 1050-EXIT.
    process record...
    .
    .
    .
    GO TO 1030-PROCESS-DATA
1040-READ-RECORD.
    input statements
    .
1050-EXIT.
    EXIT.
```

Have you seen programs such as this? Often, they occur because the requirement for a SECTION caused the programmer to think that all paragraphs had to be within the SECTION, mandating a GO TO statement. It wasn't true, but it happened a lot and I've even seen corporate standards manuals that *dictated* this technique. Removing the requirement for SECTIONs lets programmers write simpler SORTS. (See Chapter 8, Sample Programs, for an example.) (Note: later versions of OS/VS COBOL did not require SECTION names, but many programmers used older manuals and the compiler continued to issue warning messages.)

NOT ON SIZE ERROR and NOT INVALID KEY clauses.

These are straightforward. Wherever you may currently place an ON SIZE ERROR clause (e.g., ADD, SUBTRACT), you may now also, or instead of, place the NOT ON SIZE ERROR clause. Likewise, wherever you could place an INVALID KEY clause (e.g., READ, WRITE), you may now also, or instead of, place the NOT INVALID KEY clause.

Recommendation for using PROCEDURE DIVISION features.

My first recommendation is that you rethink how you do nested IF statements and start restructuring with END-IF and other scope terminators. This quickly improves your program structure. Next, I suggest using EVALUATE and the expanded features of READ and RETURN, as they also improve structure and readability. Familiarity with the new option of SET comes quickly if you already use 88-levels. To help you change your approach to SORT programs, I included an example in Chapter 8 (Sample Programs).

The extensions to CALL and PERFORM should be approached more cautiously. The CALL enhancements offer some opportunities for new systems you are developing, but make sure you're comfortable with the features before committing to a large project. As I indicated earlier, the PERFORM enhancements are powerful, but you may want to postpone using them until you have more experience with scope terminators.

2.3. NEW COBOL COMPONENTS

By now, you may feel that you've already read about the new features of COBOL II. New, yes, but the components described in the prior section were enhancements to existing COBOL elements. This section introduces some new features that have their own syntax. Making the decision to separate COBOL features this way was not easy. As I mentioned at the beginning of this chapter, my guiding light was to address the learning requirements of the maintenance or conversion programmer. By first learning what was dropped, followed by learning what is different, and ending by learning new features, you will be more productive more quickly than if I had glossed over differences and jumped here immediately.

While these elements are new, many benefit from using them in combination with each other or with the expanded capabilities described for current components.

2.3.1. Nested Programs/END PROGRAM Statement

I've picked nested programs first because it is an interesting concept that may take time to absorb and your shop may decide never to use this approach to application development. From previous material in this book, you have probably surmised that program structure is more flexible with COBOL II (e.g., INITIAL in PROGRAM-ID and extensions to CALL and PERFORM statements). If so, you're right on target. This feature, and those that follow, support and expand on flexibility in program structure.

First, let's get our terms straight. A *nested program* is one that is contained WITHIN another program, a concept that did not previously exist in COBOL, although PL/1 and FORTRAN have always had such capabilities. Placing a program within another program requires that a means be defined to identify the end of a program. That new COBOL element is the END PROGRAM statement. See Figure 2.14 for an example.

In the example, MAIN1 calls SUB1. Notice how the END PROGRAM statements make clear to the compiler that SUB1 is within MAIN1. The program name in END PROGRAM must match that in the PROGRAM-ID statement or a syntax error occurs. Because SUB1 exists only within MAIN1, it has no identifier within the object module from a compile and is invisible to the Linkage Editor (i.e., SUB1 cannot be CALLed from separately compiled programs).

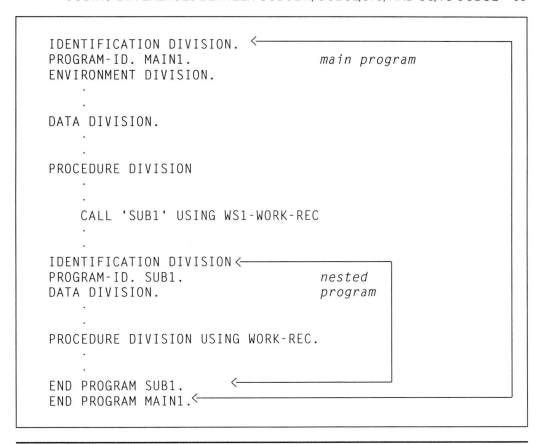

```
    IDENTIFICATION DIVISION.  <
    PROGRAM-ID. MAIN1.                    main program
    ENVIRONMENT DIVISION.
         .
         .
    DATA DIVISION.
         .
         .
    PROCEDURE DIVISION
         .
         .
       CALL 'SUB1' USING WS1-WORK-REC
         .
         .
    IDENTIFICATION DIVISION <
    PROGRAM-ID. SUB1.                     nested
    DATA DIVISION.                        program
         .
         .
    PROCEDURE DIVISION USING WORK-REC.
         .
         .
    END PROGRAM SUB1.        <
    END PROGRAM MAIN1.<
```

Figure 2.14.   Sample of nested program. SUB1 is CALLed by MAIN1,
                   yet exists within MAIN1.

When used, END PROGRAM must be the last statement for a program. The statement may be used, if desired, for any program, even one that is not nested, as a means to let the compiler validate the last statement. Other terms that have meaning to nested programs are COMMON (in PROGRAM-ID) and GLOBAL (in FD and data descriptions).

You are probably wondering "Why would I ever use such a structure?" When I first learned about nested programs, that was my question too. At first, it appears to be an unwieldy structure with nothing positive about it. Actually, it is more a change in the way you build structure than in the way you write code. This is an exciting feature, one that will receive special treatment in Chapter 3 in a section titled Module Structures. For now, it is sufficient that you are aware of the concept and how the basic structure is formed. There is an example of a nested program in Chapter 8.

2.3.2. EVALUATE.

The EVALUATE statement is an extension of the IF statement and provides the CASE concept for structured programming. Many programmers attempted to implement a form of CASE in earlier versions of COBOL by using the GO TO DEPENDING ON statement. That worked with limited success, but it required many GO TO statements to support it and had other restrictions in its structure.

The EVALUATE can take one or more data elements or conditions and specify the action to take. The entries following the word EVALUATE specify *what* will be evaluated and *how many* evaluations will be made. For example:

```
EVALUATE WS1-SEX-CODE ALSO WS3-MARITAL-STATUS
```

The above statement specifies that there will be two evaluations, each against a data-name. Entries following WHEN could then specify values that might be in those fields. The number of comparisons following WHEN must match the number of entries following EVALUATE. For example:

```
EVALUATE WS1-SEX-CODE   ALSO   WS3-MARITAL-STATUS
WHEN          'F'       ALSO          'S'
```

would be a possible entry. The imperative statement(s) following that entry would be executed if BOTH conditions were true. For example:

```
EVALUATE WS1-SEX-CODE   ALSO   WS3-MARITAL-STATUS
WHEN          'F'       ALSO          'S'
                    PERFORM 3100-SINGLE-FEMALE-EMP
```

The appearance of the next WHEN entry or END-EVALUATE terminates the scope of the WHEN clause. It is easier to understand the statement by looking at one, so I refer you to the following examples. Keep your use of EVALUATE simple at first as you build on experience. You will find EVALUATE can make what would have been long IF statements much more readable and much easier to maintain.

Generally, the TRUE options provide more flexibility because a condition may be any valid COBOL condition (e.g., 88-levels, data-name followed by relational operator followed by literal or data-name, conditions separated by AND or OR). Although the syntax in Figure 2.15 may imply that you can mix and match, you cannot. The combination of possible entries must provide three components:

1. A value (e.g., data-name, expression, or literal)
2. A value to compare to the first value
3. A condition (e.g., true or false)

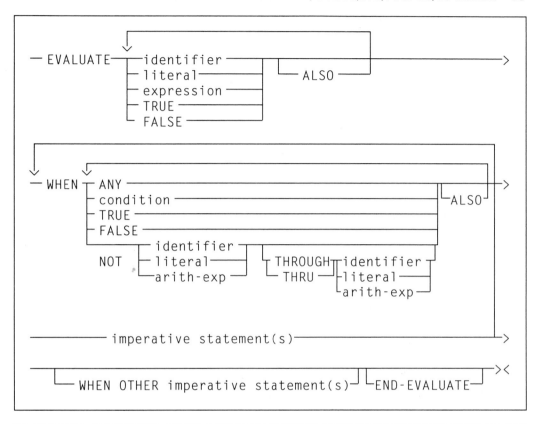

Figure 2.15. EVALUATE syntax.

For example, an 88-level-name defines a data-name and a value and could be used with TRUE or FALSE, but it could not be combined with literal or identifier as those are already defined by the 88-level-name. Likewise, condition entries and 88-levels may *not* be used where a data-name follows the EVALU-ATE verb because that provides more than the three required components. The following examples do not include all options of the EVALUATE statement and are intended to show examples of concept, features, and format. There is an IF statement following each one for comparison purposes.

Testing value of a single field:

```
EVALUATE WS1-SEX-CODE
    WHEN 'M' PERFORM 2100-MALE-APP
    WHEN 'F' PERFORM 2200-FEMALE-APP
    WHEN OTHER PERFORM 2300-ERROR-RTN
END-EVALUATE
```

IF equivalent:

```
IF WS1-SEX-CODE = 'M'
    PERFORM 2100-MALE-APP
ELSE
    IF WS1-SEX-CODE = 'F'
        PERFORM 2200-FEMALE-APP
    ELSE
        PERFORM 2300-ERROR-RTN
    END-IF
END-IF
```

Testing truth of a single 88-level or condition:

```
EVALUATE TRUE
    WHEN 88-level-name    PERFORM 2100-RTNA
                          PERFORM 2300-RTNB
                          MOVE 'Y' TO WS1-SWITCH
    WHEN 88-level-name2 OR condition-a
                          PERFORM 2500-RTNC
    WHEN OTHER            MOVE 'N' TO WS1-SWITCH
END-EVALUATE
```

IF equivalent:

```
IF 88-level-name
    PERFORM 2100-RTNA
    PERFORM 2300-RTNB
    MOVE 'Y' TO WS1-SWITCH
ELSE
    IF 88-level-name OR condition-a
        PERFORM 2500-RTNC
    ELSE
        MOVE 'N' TO WS1-SWITCH
    END-IF
END-IF
```

Testing more than one 88-level or condition:

```
EVALUATE
            TRUE        ALSO        TRUE
    WHEN 88-level-a  ALSO condition-b
                     PERFORM 2100-RTNA
    WHEN condition-c ALSO 88-level-d
                     PERFORM 2200-RTNB
```

```
        WHEN 88-level-e    ALSO ANY
                           PERFORM 2300-RTNC
        WHEN OTHER         MOVE 'N' TO WS2-SWITCH
END-EVALUATE
```

IF equivalent:

```
IF 88-level-a AND condition-b
    PERFORM 2100-RTNA
ELSE
    IF condition-c AND 88-level-d
        PERFORM 2200-RTNB
    ELSE
        IF 88-level-e
            PERFORM 2300-RTNC
        ELSE
            MOVE 'N' TO WS2-SWITCH
        END-IF
    END-IF
END-IF
```

Testing more than one data field:

```
EVALUATE
    WS1-SEX-CODE   ALSO WS2-MAR-STATUS
    WHEN 'M'       ALSO    'S'   PERFORM 3100-SGL-MALE
    WHEN 'M'       ALSO    'M'   PERFORM 3200-MAR-MALE
    WHEN 'F'       ALSO    'S'   PERFORM 3300-SGL-FEM
    WHEN 'F'       ALSO    'M'   PERFORM 3400-MAR-FEM
    WHEN OTHER                   PERFORM 3500-ERROR
END-EVALUATE
```

IF equivalent:

```
IF WS1-SEX-CODE = 'M' AND WS2-MAR-STATUS = 'S'
    PERFORM 3100-SGL-MALE
ELSE
    IF WS1-SEX-CODE = 'M' AND WS2-MAR-STATUS = 'M'
        PERFORM 3200-MAR-MALE
    ELSE
        IF WS1-SEX-CODE = 'F' AND WS2-MAR-STATUS = 'S'
            PERFORM 3300-SGL-FEM
        ELSE
            IF WS1-SEX-CODE = 'F' AND WS2-MAR-STATUS = 'M'
                PERFORM 3400-MAR-FEM
```

```
                    ELSE
                        PERFORM 3500-ERROR
                    END-IF
              END-IF
         END-IF
    END-IF
```

Testing expressions and literals:

This short example demonstrates that you may use EVALUATE for situations other than comparing data names to values. All other above combinations may also be used here.

```
EVALUATE LOAN-BAL + NEW-LOAN-AMT
    WHEN 0 THRU LOAN-LIMIT  PERFORM 3100-ISSUE-NEW-LOAN
    WHEN LOAN-LIMIT + 1 THRU LOAN-LIMIT * 1.10
                               PERFORM 3200-WRITE-CHECK-DATA
    WHEN OTHER                 PERFORM 3300-REJECT-LOAN
END-EVALUATE
```

Finally, you needn't always code an action for each WHEN statement. For example, you might have a situation where several values are true, such as:

```
EVALUATE GRADE-LEVEL
    WHEN  7
    WHEN  8
    WHEN  9  PERFORM 2300-JUNIOR-HIGH
    WHEN 10
    WHEN 11
    WHEN 12  PERFORM 2400-SENIOR-HIGH
END-EVALUATE
```

The easiest way to learn the EVALUATE statement is to start using it. I have found novice programmers pick this statement up quickly because it is easier (and quicker) to code than nested IF statements and the logic is easier to see in the code.

2.3.3. CONTINUE

CONTINUE is a new statement that does *nothing* except meet the requirement of having a procedural statement where required. You might be thinking, "Wasn't that what NEXT SENTENCE did?" No. NEXT SENTENCE is really a GO TO statement that transfers control to an unnamed sentence following the current sentence. By now, you can probably guess that I don't like the NEXT SENTENCE clause for that reason. A GO TO is a GO TO, even when it is a NEXT

SENTENCE clause. In COBOL II, there is never a need for NEXT SENTENCE if you use the new features of COBOL II and use periods sparingly.

In the previous paragraph, I stated that the CONTINUE statement did nothing. Well, that's not exactly true. What it does is allow the procedural logic to continue to the next procedural statement within the program. Unlike NEXT SENTENCE, it does not determine what that statement is. Let's look at some examples where CONTINUE fills a gap.

Example 1

```
EVALUATE  FD3-SEX-CODE
WHEN  'M'  PERFORM 3200-PROCESS-MALE-APP
WHEN  'F'  CONTINUE
WHEN OTHER MOVE 'Y' TO FD3-INVALID-TRANS-CODE
END-EVALUATE
```

Here is a situation where CONTINUE allows the EVALUATE syntax to contain a WHEN condition for code "F" when no processing is to be done on that condition, preventing the WHEN OTHER from being executed for what is a valid code.

Example 2

```
IF APPL-AGE > 17 OR APPL-PARENT-CONSENT = 'Y'
    CONTINUE
ELSE
    PERFORM 3100-ISSUE-REJECTION-NOTICE
```

This is a less obvious example. Often it is much clearer to code positive logic than to code negative logic, even when the processing is for the negative condition. If example 2 had been coded for the negative condition, it would have read:

```
IF APPL-AGE NOT > 17 AND APPL-PARENT-CONSENT NOT = 'Y'
    PERFORM 3100-ISSUE-REJECTION-NOTICE
```

The need for the two NOT conditions and the use of AND are sometimes lost on novice (and a few senior) programmers. Turning the statement around is cleaner and the CONTINUE fills the requirement that a procedural statement be present.

Here is a more typical case, where a nested IF has a condition that is not to be processed. Coding CONTINUE makes the logic clearer, as it denotes (in this example) that if SEX-CODE is 'M" and MARITAL-STATUS is other than "M', nothing is to process.

Example 3

```
IF SEX-CODE = 'M'
    IF MARITAL-STATUS = 'M'
        PERFORM 3100-MALE-MARRIED-APP
    ELSE
        CONTINUE
ELSE
    PERFORM 3200-TEST-FEMALE-APPS
END-IF
```

Without CONTINUE, the following is also valid (just in case you were wondering if END-IF could work also.)

```
IF SEX-CODE = 'M'
    IF MARITAL-STATUS = 'M'
        PERFORM 3100-MALE-MARRIED-APP
    END-IF
ELSE
    PERFORM 3200-TEST-FEMALE-APPS
END-IF
```

2.3.4. INITIALIZE

Have you ever had some initialization (or reinitialization) code in a program where you had to reset a myriad of program switches or storage areas? It is usually tedious to code and you always wonder if you remembered all of them. That's where INITIALIZE can help.

First, you need to organize your data areas so one statement can reset all of them. I recommend placing all accumulators or switches that affect a particular logic path into a single 01-level entry. This is important because the INITIALIZE statement acts on data fields based on their data type, not their data name.

The function performed by INITIALIZE is to reset numeric fields to zero and alphanumeric fields to spaces, although there is an optional clause that does a REPLACING BY. The most common use of INITIALIZE is:

```
INITIALIZE data-name.
```

Here are some examples. If you have the following data areas,

```
01   WS2-COMMON-ITEMS.
     05   WS2-TRANS-SWITCH    PIC   X.
     05   WS2-HEADER-SWITCH   PIC   X.
     05   WS2-LINE-COUNT      PIC   S999    COMP-3.
     05   WS2-TOTAL-DEP       PIC   S9.
     05   WS2-JOB-CODE        PIC   X.
```

```
01  WS3-PREMIUM-TABLE.
    05  WS3-PREM-ENTRY        PIC   S9(5)V99    COMP-3 OCCURS 100
                              TIMES   INDEXED BY PREM-INDEX.
```

you can set all of them to appropriate spaces or zeros by:

```
INITIALIZE WS2-COMMON-ITEMS WS3-PREMIUM-TABLE
```

Compare the simplicity of this with the extra coding you would need if using OS/VS COBOL. Your programs may never need to do this type of processing, but if your programs do need the logic, this is the way to go.

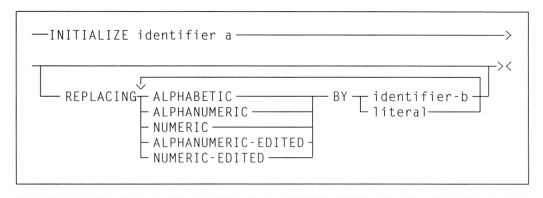

Figure 2.16.   INITIALIZE syntax.

While I find INITIALIZE a powerful statement, you should be sensitive to a couple of aspects that could cause you grief. One is that INITIALIZE only initializes valid data elements. That means FILLER elementary items are NOT initialized. (In case you thought maybe they were initialized to spaces, they aren't.) Also, if there is a REDEFINEd element within the area being initialized, it will be bypassed. (After all, there is no way of determining which PIC clauses to honor.) Finally, the INITIALIZE statement also bypasses any POINTER items, index data items, and (for COBOL/370) any PROCEDURE-POINTER items.

I have been criticized by a few technicians for recommending INITIALIZE, since it generates a few more machine instructions than the proper number of MOVE statements. I mention it here because these technicians may also work at your shop. If machine cycles become more expensive than your time, I'll change my views, but I think the industry passed that mark two decades ago.

2.3.5.   TITLE

I like the ability to place comments in a document where they will be seen more than once. TITLE generates no code and is active only during the compile process. It serves to place a custom title line on your source listing on every page until another TITLE statement is encountered. Here is an example:

```
TITLE  'PREMIUM CALCULATION PROGRAM'
IDENTIFICATION DIVISION.
    .
    .
    .
PROCEDURE DIVISION.
TITLE  ' TERM POLICY CALCULATIONS'
    .
    .
    .
TITLE  ' WHOLE LIFE POLICY CALCULATIONS'
    .
    .
```

In addition to printing a title on your source listing, TITLE also causes a page eject to occur. If you're thinking, "Doesn't the "/" in column 7 do that, too?", you're right. The difference is that the "/" causes the comment to appear only one time, not on all following pages. This simple line of text improves a program's documentation. As a matter of style, I like to use it just prior to the IDENTIFI-CATION DIVISION statement.

2.3.6. Data Manipulation Enhancements/Changes

I've saved these enhancements until the end because they add subtle opportunities for rethinking program structure and data manipulation techniques. Because they are different, your shop may not allow their use, so you may want to get the corporate scoop before using these particular features. Topics here relate to the many new ways data may be defined both for system management and for data manipulation. Most of the entries here are new features, although some changes may require that you change how you write some pre-COBOL II statements.

LENGTH OF and ADDRESS OF special registers.

You saw these two elements previously as part of the CALL statement. They are new special registers (some other special registers you may be familiar with are TALLY, RETURN-CODE, and several relating to SORT, such as SORT-CORE-SIZE). Special registers are facilities provided by the compiler and are not de-fined within the source program.

The LENGTH OF special register is a value kept by the generated code for each 01-level item. You may never have need for it in your programs, but it makes a significant improvement to CICS programs by eliminating the need to manipu-late or specify LENGTH in EXEC CICS statements (covered in Chapter 3).

The ADDRESS OF special register is a value kept by the generated code for the address of each 01-level item in the LINKAGE SECTION. (Use of ADDRESS

OF with POINTER is explained further in this chapter.) In addition to being used in the CALL statement, it also simplifies CICS programs by eliminating the need for CICS programmers to use BLL cells (covered in Chapter 3).

GLOBAL and EXTERNAL data elements.

This is a major enhancement, providing extensive new options for program design. In OS/VS COBOL, data elements were part of the source program in which they were defined. Access to the data elements from other programs could only be done via a CALL USING statement. No more. COBOL II can define data areas separately from the program in which they are used or where their definitions appear (more on this in Chapter 3). Let's examine each term separately.

Global. When appended to a data or file definition (01-level or FD), that data element or FD may be referenced by any nested program within the run unit. I reviewed the concept of nested programs earlier, but I didn't explain why it might have advantages. Here is one possibility: being able to define an FD or 01-level that is directly accessible from within other programs. See Figure 2.17 for an example. The module, SUB1, has no DATA DIVISION, yet can reference all defined GLOBAL entries in the program in which it is nested.

That prior sentence is important. A GLOBAL item is global ONLY to those programs that are contained *within* it. Programs that do not share the same parentage do not have access to the data. Examine Figure 2.18. While most COBOL code is missing from the example, the structure is based on the module relationships that follow: Outermost module: MAIN1. MAIN1 may access data or FDs only from within itself. (MAIN1 isn't contained within any other module.)

Directly contained modules: SUB1 and SUB2. SUB1 and SUB2 may access any data area or FD within their own programs or that are GLOBAL in their parent, MAIN1 (i.e., SUB1 may NOT access any data area or FD defined in SUB2).

Indirectly contained module: SUB2A. SUB2A is directly contained within SUB2 and indirectly contained within MAIN1. It has no relationship to SUB1. Therefore, SUB2A may access data areas within itself, that are GLOBAL within its parent, SUB1, or within SUB1's parent, MAIN1.

Use of GLOBAL is an excellent technique to maintain control of data accessibility and eliminate the need to code definitions of the FDs or data areas within each module.

External. The external clause may be used on FDs and 01-level entries also. Where GLOBAL applied to nested programs, EXTERNAL applies to traditional, external structures where each program in the run unit is separate, often being separately compiled (and link-edited, if DYNAM is used). This can be advantageous if it is desirable for several programs to share the same files or data areas. Whereas GLOBAL elements were accessible only from programs that were contained within a program, EXTERNAL elements may be accessed from ANY program in the run unit that has the same definitions.

```
IDENTIFICATION DIVISION. ←─────────────────┐
PROGRAM-ID.  MAIN1                 main     │
ENVIRONMENT DIVISION               program  │
  .                                          │
DATA DIVISION.                               │
FD FD1-INPUT GLOBAL                          │
  .                                          │
WORKING-STORAGE SECTION.                     │
01 WS1-WORK-REC GLOBAL.                       │
  .                                          │
  .                                          │
PROCEDURE DIVISION.                          │
  .                                          │
  CALL 'SUB1'                                │
  .                                          │
IDENTIFICATION DIVISION        ←──────┐      │
PROGRAM-ID.  SUB1                nested│      │
                                program│      │
  .                                    │      │
                                       │      │
PROCEDURE DIVISION.                    │      │
  READ FD1-INPUT INTO WS1-WORK-REC     │      │
  .                                    │      │
END PROGRAM SUB1.          ←───────────┘      │
END PROGRAM MAIN1.←───────────────────────────┘
```

Figure 2.17. Sample of GLOBAL file and record definition.

From a coding perspective, the difference between GLOBAL and EXTERNAL is that the EXTERNAL items must be coded in all programs *exactly* the same. If the element is spelled differently, for example, it compiles with no errors, and executes, but the defined EXTERNAL element is unique and processing errors (or ABENDs) will depend on the process attempted. Elements that will be EXTERNAL should be defined as COPYbooks to eliminate this possible error. Also, EXTERNAL 01-level items may NOT have a VALUE clause.

For an example of EXTERNAL, assume the following COPYbooks:

PAYSEL

```
SELECT FD1-PAYROLL-FILE
   ASSIGN TO PAYMAST  FILE STATUS IS FD1-STAT.
```

PAYFD

```
FD FD1-PAYROLL-FILE EXTERNAL
    RECORD CONTAINS 100 CHARACTERS
    RECORDING MODE IS F.
01 FD1-PAYROLL-REC.
   05  FD1-EMP-NUMBER PIC X(5).
    .
    .
```

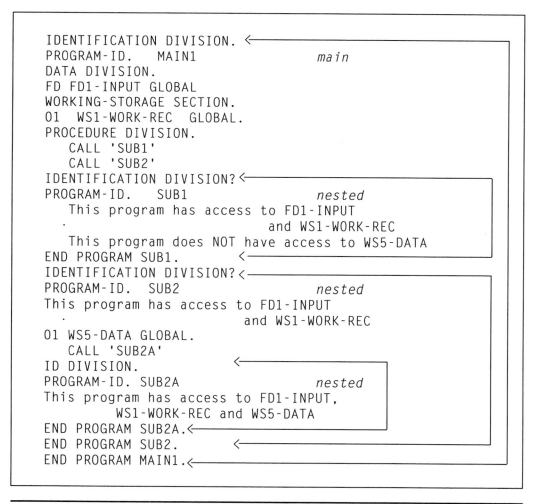

```
IDENTIFICATION DIVISION.  ←
PROGRAM-ID.   MAIN1                   main
DATA DIVISION.
FD FD1-INPUT GLOBAL
WORKING-STORAGE SECTION.
01  WS1-WORK-REC  GLOBAL.
PROCEDURE DIVISION.
   CALL 'SUB1'
   CALL 'SUB2'
IDENTIFICATION DIVISION? ←
PROGRAM-ID.   SUB1                 nested
   This program has access to FD1-INPUT
    .                          and WS1-WORK-REC
   This program does NOT have access to WS5-DATA
END PROGRAM SUB1.          ←
IDENTIFICATION DIVISION? ←
PROGRAM-ID.  SUB2                 nested
This program has access to FD1-INPUT
    .                        and WS1-WORK-REC
01 WS5-DATA GLOBAL.
   CALL 'SUB2A'
ID DIVISION.                ←
PROGRAM-ID. SUB2A                 nested
This program has access to FD1-INPUT,
       WS1-WORK-REC and WS5-DATA
END PROGRAM SUB2A.←
END PROGRAM SUB2.        ←
END PROGRAM MAIN1.←
```

Figure 2.18.   Sample of GLOBAL access by subprogram.

PAYWORK

```
01  WS1-PAYROLL-WORK EXTERNAL.
    05 FD1-STAT     PIC XX.
    .
    .
    .
```

Using these three COPYbooks, you could develop the program structure in figure 2.19. It helps to visualize the structure by considering that all EXTERNAL elements are separate from all programs. The true in-memory structure for the example in Figure 2.19 is:

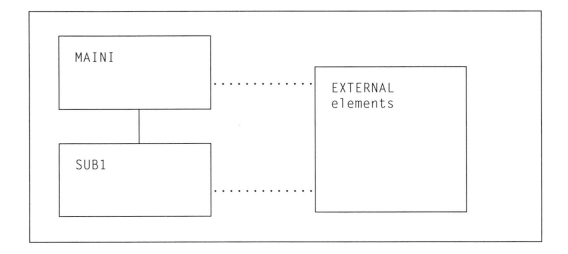

Note: EXTERNAL elements are treated as 24-bit addressable items that will be placed BELOW the 16-megabyte line with COBOL II, regardless of whether DATA(31) or DATA(24) is specified. This restriction does not appear in COBOL/370.

As you saw, EXTERNAL and GLOBAL bring new structure opportunities to COBOL programs. Both offer their own advantages that may change the way you design programs. Also, you can use EXTERNAL and GLOBAL definitions together. Suggestions on when to use these features in program design are in Chapter 3 (Programming with COBOL II).

NULL value, POINTER data items, SET, and ADDRESS OF.

Earlier in the book, while describing changes to the USAGE and VALUE clause, I mentioned that NULL and POINTER were new terms and would be explained later. I also postponed an addition to the SET statement and use of ADDRESS

```
ID DIVISION.
PROGRAM-ID.  MAIN1.                          Unlike GLOBAL,
ENVIRONMENT DIVISION.                         there is
INPUT-OUTPUT SECTION.                         nothing unique
FILE-CONTROL.                                 about the
    COPY PAYSEL.                              main program
DATA DIVISION.                                regarding use
FILE SECTION.                                 of EXTERNAL.
    COPY PAYFD.
WORKING-STORAGE SECTION.
    COPY PAYWORK.
PROCEDURE DIVISION.
1.   OPEN INPUT FD1-PAYROLL-FILE
     CALL 'SUB1'
      .

END PROGRAM MAIN1.
ID DIVISION.                                  This subprogram
PROGRAM-ID.  SUB1.                            could be
ENVIRONMENT DIVISION.                         CALLed either
INPUT-OUTPUT SECTION.                         statically or
FILE-CONTROL.                                 dynamically.
    COPY PAYSEL.
DATA DIVISION.                                The linkage
FILE SECTION.                                 is established
    COPY PAYFD.                               at run-time,
WORKING-STORAGE SECTION.                      not during
    COPY PAYWORK.                             compile or
PROCEDURE DIVISION.                           link-edit.
1.   READ FD1-PAYROLL-FILE
      .

END PROGRAM SUB1.
```

Figure 2.19. Example of EXTERNAL use.

OF with the CALL statement. This is as good a place as any to discuss those features. The features here are needed to replace BLL manipulation in CICS programs and allow use of dynamic SQL (SQLDA) in DB2 programs (see Chapter 3). Some programmers will probably never need to code any of these entries, but they create interesting opportunities for new structures (also in Chapter 3).

All of these elements relate, since they support manipulating addresses within an application. I don't foresee these options being used much (other than for CICS and DB2), but they do offer unique opportunities. While they don't have to be used together, it will be simpler to grasp them that way. Let's start with ADDRESS OF. The term, ADDRESS OF, represents an internal register for each 01-level item in the LINKAGE SECTION. One of the new CALL formats uses it this way:

```
CALL 'SUB1' USING ADDRESS OF  WS3-DATA-AREA
```

This CALL statement passes the address of the data element *as data*. The CALLed subprogram must move it to where it can use the address to access the data the address points to. Here is an example of a CALLed subprogram, demonstrating the concept.

```
LINKAGE SECTION.
01  LS1-ADDRESS           .      POINTER.

01  LS2-DATA-AREA.
    .
    .

PROCEDURE DIVISION USING LS1-ADDRESS.
1.  SET ADDRESS OF LS2-DATA-AREA TO LS1-ADDRESS
    .
    .
```

Before the program can work with the data elements in LS2-DATA-AREA, it first establishes addressability to it. That is accomplished by the SET statement. The SET statement takes the passed address in LS1-ADDRESS and establishes it for addressability to LS2-DATA-AREA. LS1-ADDRESS is defined as a POINTER item. This is because it contains an address of data, not data. Notice there is no PIC clause.

If this were the typical way of using POINTER items, it would be easier to code in the traditional way, since COBOL has always provided addressability to data areas in CALLing programs. For example:

Calling program

```
CALL 'SUB1' USING WS3-DATA-AREA
```

Called program

```
LINKAGE SECTION.
01  LS2-DATA-AREA.
    .
    .

PROCEDURE DIVISION USING LS2-DATA-AREA.
```

This typical structure passes the address of the data-name, but it does so as an address for the internal code to manage, not as data for the application logic to manage. Obviously, POINTERs are not intended for use in traditional CO-BOL-to-COBOL structures.

While this technique isn't needed in typical COBOL applications, there is a use for it if your application must interact with assembler programs that pass addresses of addresses between programs instead of addresses of data. With CICS, for example, the list of BLL cells is an address of addresses that requires attention prior to using the data areas.

The example showed one form of the SET. Here are the two basic forms it takes when ADDRESS OF is used.

```
SET pointer-item TO ADDRESS OF data-name <— This stores the
                                             address of the
                                             data-name in the
                                             pointer-item.


SET ADDRESS OF data-item TO pointer-item <— This establishes
                                             addressability of
                                             the data-item
                                             within the COBOL
                                             program.
```

To summarize the elements described here:

- NULL may appear in a VALUE clause for a POINTER item or within a SET (SET pointer-item TO NULL).
- POINTER items are valid only for use as one of the operands in the form of the SET statement using ADDRESS OF.
- ADDRESS OF exists only for elements in the LINKAGE SECTION.

Examples of these techniques are explored in Chapter 3 under the sections Module Structures and CICS/IMS/DB2 Issues.

If you're very, very careful, there is another feature you can exploit with POINTER data items. Since they contain the absolute memory address of a data field, you can manipulate them similar to a subscript without all the overhead. So, how to do it? Watch me.

```
05  DATAREA-POINTER          POINTER.
05  DATAREA-INCR  REDEFINES DATAREA-POINTER  PIC S9(9) COMP.

LINKAGE SECTION.
01  MY-DATA-AREA.
    05  A-DATA-ELEMENT        PIC X(25)  OCCURS 10.
```

```
SET DATAREA-POINTER TO ADDRESS OF MY-DATA-AREA
COMPUTE DATAREA-INCR = DATAREA-INCR + 50
CALL 'PROGA' USING DATAREA-POINTER
```

In this example, we pass the address of the third appearance of the field called A-DATA-ELEMENT. Do we need to do this? Should we do this? I don't know. As a power programmer, you call the shots. My goal is to demonstrate some of the possibilities because you may see where a specific capability fits a need in your application. *WARNING:* TRUNC(BIN) is mandatory when you're fooling around with memory addresses.

PROCEDURE-POINTER data items (COBOL/370 only).

As I mentioned previously, this allows a COBOL/370 application to pass the address of one program to another. To fully grasp this, you also need to have a good knowledge of how the CALL statement works with DYNAM and NODYNAM. If you aren't familiar with that subject, you might want to first read Section 3.2.10, Static versus Dynamic CALL Structures. This knowledge is necessary because use of a PROCEDURE-POINTER item with a SET statement causes implicit execution of a partial CALL. First let's review the syntax of this form of the SET statement. See Chapter 7, Summaries, Tables, and References, for the full syntax.

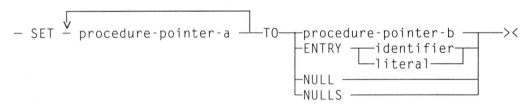

Before reviewing some examples of this SET format, let's go over what actually happens:

- The normal sequence of statements would be a SET statement, followed by a CALL statement.
- The SET statement must reference the name of an external run unit name (e.g., load module name or ENTRY name).
- When a SET statement referencing a PROCEDURE-POINTER is executed, LE/370 receives control.
- If the reference from the SET statement was a literal, LE/370 determines what action to take, based on whether the program executing the SET statement was compiled with DYNAM or NODYNAM. If NODYNAM was specified, LE/370 attempts to locate the program name from within the same load module as the program that issued the SET statement and to store the entry address in the PROCEDURE-POINTER data item. If

DYNAM was specified, LE/370 assumes this to be the name of a separate load module. LE/370 then loads that module into memory and stores the address of the load module's entry point in the PROCEDURE-POINTER data item.

- If the reference was a dataname that contained the name of the module whose address is required, LE/370 follows the logic flow specified above for DYNAM, regardless of the use of DYNAM or NODYNAM for the application.

This will be clearer if we show some examples. Let's assume we have two load modules, one that consists of two programs and one that does not (or, for our purposes, doesn't need to). The first we'll call MODA (I know, I'm not too original). Load module MODA was formed by linkediting two programs, PROGA and PROGB (PROGA and PROGB would have been the PROGRAM-ID statements if they were COBOL). The other load module is called (what else?) MODB.

```
MODA                        MODB

┌──────────────────┐        ┌──────────────────┐
│ PROGA            │        │                  │
│                  │        │                  │
├──────────────────┤        │                  │
│ PROGB            │        │                  │
│                  │        │                  │
└──────────────────┘        └──────────────────┘
```

Within WORKING STORAGE for the program named PROGA, we have these entries. (*NOTE:* If used with a PROCEDURE-POINTER, the VALUE clause can only specify NULL or NULLS.)

```
        .
        .
        .
05   MODULE-POINTER      PROCEDURE-POINTER.
05   MODULE-NAME         PIC X(8)   VALUE  'MODB'.
```

Since PROGA and PROGB are in one load module, we can assume (at least in this situation) that PROGA was compiled with NODYNAM. If this statement is coded

```
SET MODULE-POINTER TO ENTRY 'PROGB'
```

LE/370, by seeing that a literal was used, looks within MODA to find the desired entry address. If the statement had been

```
SET MODULE-POINTER TO ENTRY MODULE-NAME
```

LE/370 ignores DYNAM and NODYNAM and searches for a load module with the name MODB, loading it into memory also. These two examples work fine, but you're probably wondering, "Gee, what would happen if the first example had referenced a literal of MODB or the second example had used the value PROGB in MODULE-NAME?" If you have had experience with ABENDs in the past by coding similar errors with the CALL statement, then you can understand how misuse of the SET statement can cause similar results. Using PROCEDURE-POINTERs is a powerful feature of COBOL/370, but you need to be careful.

Class tests—alphabetic and numeric.

This is a good news/bad news situation. The good news is that you may now test for ALPHABETIC-UPPER and ALPHABETIC-LOWER when you are validating an alphanumeric field for all upper-case or all lower-case text. The bad news is that ALPHABETIC now allows both upper- and lower-case text. In OS/VS CO-BOL, the statement

```
IF data-name ALPHABETIC
```

would only be true if the field contained characters *A* through *Z* and the space. Now, it will be true if the field contains *A* through *Z*, *a* through *z* and the space. If you will be converting programs from OS/VS COBOL to COBOL II, I suggest you change all occurrences of ALPHABETIC to ALPHABETIC-UPPER.

The NUMERIC situation is not as clear. The NUMERIC class test operates differently, depending on a compile-time option, NUMPROC. Your shop has set a default value for this option and your technical staff can probably answer your questions about this. The NUMPROC option is explained in chapter 3, along with all other compile options. The good news about the NUMPROC option is that it provides some performance improvements if your numeric data elements are always properly signed.

Reference modification.

Reference modification is another addressing technique that has been lifted from other languages. This is a technique whereby you may access part of a data area without using the REDEFINES clause in the DATA DIVISION. For example, assume you have a data area defined that contains a phone number, including parentheses, [e.g., (555) 555-1212]. Counting parentheses, spaces, and the hyphen, that comes to 14 positions. With the data area defined as

```
05 FD3-EMPL-PHONE-NUMBER    PIC X(14).
```

you could access the area code (you know it is the second, third, and fourth characters in the field) by coding

```
MOVE FD3-EMPL-PHONE-NUMBER (2:3) TO WS1-AREA-CODE
```

In case you didn't figure out the example, the first digit specifies the starting byte within the field. In this case 2 for the second byte. The digit following the colon represents the length of the field (in bytes) for this statement, in this case 3 because the area code is 3 bytes long.

Since reference modification applies to bytes, this technique should be used for alphanumeric fields. (It could be used for other data types, but it would become a maintenance nightmare.) The complete syntax is

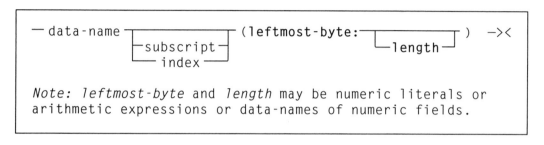

Figure 2.20. Reference modification syntax.

From Figure 2.20, you see that if subscripts or indexes are used, they are placed first, following the data name. The length operand is optional. When length is omitted, the compiler assumes a length that represents the remaining bytes in the field. Therefore, to use the previous example of a phone number, the code to move the seven-digit phone number and the hyphen would be

```
MOVE FD3-EMPL-PHONE-NUMBER (7:8)  TO WS3-LOCAL-PHONE
```

or

```
MOVE FD3-EMPL-PHONE-NUMBER (7:)  TO WS3-LOCAL-PHONE
```

As you can see, this can be non productive. Counting the bytes in the field to code this statement takes time and can be difficult to read. When not needed, I don't encourage this approach because it adds one more element to possibly debug. Finally, if you use an arithmetic expression to compute the starting position and length at run-time, results may be unpredictable if your computations do not fall within the defined data field length (e.g., a starting position of -5 or a length of 0). A new compile option, SSRANGE, can assist in debugging. (SSRANGE also supports debugging OCCURS clauses and is covered in Chapter 3 and in Chapter 4, Debugging.)

An example of a potentially powerful (and dangerous) use of reference modification is the following two-statement CALLed subprogram that I developed to assist a group migrating from OS/VS COBOL.

```
ID DIVISION.
PROGRAM-ID. MOVEDATA.
DATA DIVISION.
LINKAGE SECTION.
01  FROM-FIELD        PIC X(1000).
01  TO-FIELD          PIC X(1000).
01  FROM-START        PIC S9(4)   COMP.
01  TO-START          PIC S9(4)   COMP.
01  FROM-LENGTH       PIC S9(4)   COMP.
PROCEDURE DIVISION USING FROM-FIELD TO-FIELD FROM-START
                         FROM-LENGTH TO-START.
1.  MOVE   FROM-FIELD (FROM-START:FROM-LENGTH) TO
           TO-FIELD   (TO-START:FROM-LENGTH)
    GOBACK.
```

The two-statement COBOL program replaced a complicated assembler program that had been previously used to move data by specifying the byte location of a field within a record and its length, the byte location within a receiving field to place the data, plus the location of sending and receiving records. Although this works and demonstrates the power of reference modification, this example can do serious damage.

The reason serious damage can occur is because the compiler can't generate code to check to ensure that the MOVE stays within bounds of the records since a record of any length could be passed to the subprogram. (In case you're wondering, the FROM-FIELD and TO-FIELD could have been specified with any PIC length. The program has successfully moved data in records of 30,000 bytes and more.) Also, since the movement of data is to a record of unknown length, the SSRANGE compile option can't provide meaningful test results. As mentioned previously, the only reason I wrote this was to replace an existing assembler module to simplify migration to COBOL II. Otherwise, I would frown on such an unprotected coding practice.

Finally, although it's probably obvious, reference modification should only be used with DISPLAY fields, since it is byte-oriented. Use with COMP or COMP-3 data would yield unpredictable results.

De-editing numeric data.

The term *de-edit* means to be able to MOVE from a data element that is edited (i.e., has PIC characters such as $, Z, and decimal points, as in PIC $,$$$.99) to a numeric data element that is not edited [i.e., has PIC characters that depict a numeric value for computation, such as PIC S9(5)V99]. This was never possible before. This can be handy if you are pulling numeric entries from a data entry screen (e.g., CICS) and want the screen to be edited for the terminal operator but also want it in numeric format for processing. This ability requires no special coding on your part. It is just a capability for the MOVE statement that was not allowed in earlier releases of COBOL.

DAY-OF-WEEK.

Earlier, I explained that CURRENT-DATE and TIME-OF-DAY were replaced by a form of the ACCEPT statement. That capability existed in OS/VS COBOL, since the ACCEPT statement is an ANSI 74 statement. Here is an additional extension to the ACCEPT statement you can use with COBOL II:

```
ACCEPT data-name FROM DAY-OF-WEEK
```

where the implicit PIC for DAY-OF-WEEK is PIC 9(1). The values range from 1 for Monday through 7 for Sunday. For example, the value 5 represents Friday.

Extended compiler limits.

Normally, you probably never think about how large a data item can be. In fact, you probably never knew the limit when working with OS/VS COBOL programs. I didn't. Since data elements were used to store copies of data records in memory, the limit didn't usually matter because the limiting factor was usually the data record size. That has changed with COBOL II. Consider the following comparison:

	Maximum data size	
	OS/VS COBOL	**COBOL II**
Working-Storage	1 megabyte	128 megabytes
01-level size	1 megabyte	16 megabytes
Linkage Section	1 megabyte	128 megabytes

Note: A megabyte is not one million bytes. It is 1,048,576 bytes. That means that 128 megabytes is really 134,217,727 bytes and 16 megabytes is really 16,777,215 bytes.

This extension offers possibilities of using an 01-level for an in-memory database, something you couldn't consider in OS/VS COBOL. While there are always other considerations when designing a high-performance application, one option might be to load a database into a table in memory and then access it by using an index. MVS/XA offers programmers the opportunity to reevaluate their use of memory, once considered more precious than other resources.

2.3.7. Intrinsic Functions for COBOL/370

Intrinsic functions have long been available for most high-level languages (HLL), and they are a welcome addition to COBOL/370. The advantage of intrinsic functions is that they produce a given value from within a statement, as opposed to using a CALL for the same result. Let's jump quickly to a simple comparison.

As an example, you might have a CALLable subroutine at your shop that converts alpha data from lower or mixed case to upper case. If so, to move data from DATA-FIELD to RECEIVING-FIELD and convert it to upper case, you might do it with something like

```
CALL 'UPCASE' USING DATA-FIELD RECEIVING-FIELD.
```

That works, but it's clumsy. Intrinsic functions that produce the same value can be imbedded within another statement, such as:

```
MOVE FUNCTION UPPERCASE (DATA-FIELD) TO RECEIVING-FIELD
```

From that example, you may have already figured out the syntax for using intrinsic functions. In the MOVE example, the FUNCTION replaced an elementary data value within a COBOL statement on a one-for-one basis. Another trait of FUNCTIONs is that they can never be a receiving field. This makes sense, since they produce a value. That is true for all FUNCTIONs. You may use a FUNCTION in place of any elementary data item in any COBOL statement where it is not a receiving field. (Exception: FUNCTIONS cannot be passed with a CALL ... USING statement, since that passes a data area or address.) In addition to being elementary items, data elements must be DISPLAY if alphanumeric and signed numeric if for a numeric value.

The syntax for specifying a FUNCTION is pretty simple. Just precede the function name with the word FUNCTION, followed by the arguments for the function. Here is the complete syntax:

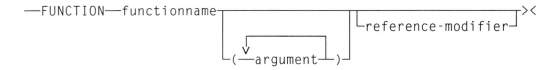

Although this diagram of the syntax is correct, it is somewhat misleading, implying that arguments are always optional. Of 42 supplied functions, only 3 (CURRENT-DATE, RANDOM, and WHEN-COMPILED) allow arguments to be omitted. (*NOTE:* As shown in the previous sentence, some FUNCTIONs have the same name as existing special registers. Don't let that confuse you, since the values returned are different.)

The only reason that the syntax includes reference modification is to remind you that reference modification is only for use with FUNCTIONs that yield alphanumeric results, for example

```
MOVE FUNCTION UPPERCASE ('Computer') (3:4) TO FIELD-A
```

would cause FIELD-A to contain "MPUT" after the MOVE. (*NOTE:* Reference modification was covered in Section 2.3.6.)

FUNCTION results fall into three categories: alphanumeric, numeric, and integer. (Numeric returns a value that may include a decimal place, whereas integer returns only digits.) In most cases, this is self-evident in the FUNCTION itself. Also, a FUNCTION that produces a numeric or integer result may only be used in a COBOL statement where an arithmetic expression is allowed.

Earlier, I mentioned that there are 42 FUNCTIONs. If your work environment is similar to mine, you will probably find that some apply to your needs, while others are never used. That is because the intrinsic functions fall loosely into several categories (my categories, not IBM's): text and character manipulation, date and time management, statistics, finance, and mathematics. That means that you will not need to learn all 42, just the ones you need.

A special feature of using an OCCURS entry with FUNCTIONs is that you may substitute ALL for any or all subscripts for the table. This technique can be used for any of the FUNCTIONs that allow an unrestricted number of arguments. For example, if we have a table of salaries, here is how we might add them up *without* intrinsic functions:

```
05 SALARY-ENTRY  PIC S9(5)V99  OCCURS 100 INDEXED BY SAL-CT.

    MOVE 0 TO SALARY-TOTAL
    PERFORM VARYING SAL-CT FROM 1 BY 1 UNTIL SAL-CT > 100
        ADD SALARY-ENTRY (SAL-CT) TO SALARY-TOTAL
    END-PERFORM
```

That works, of course, but it took several lines to code. If we hadn't used the inline PERFORM, it would have even required a separate paragraph. Here is how we would do that using ALL for a subscript with a FUNCTION:

```
COMPUTE SALARY-TOTAL = FUNCTION SUM (SALARY-ENTRY (ALL))
```

I included this example to demonstrate the power of using intrinsic functions. If you find that this power doesn't fit your style of programming, it may be that your programs rarely use arrays (OCCURS entries) to store data. We "data processing types" have long been used to processing one element at a time, sorting the data, and then summarizing. You may want to revisit the use of arrays for your next project to see if these FUNCTIONs can help you.

Earlier, I mentioned that some FUNCTIONs can have an unrestricted number of arguments. Since most of the examples in this text use the ALL example demonstrated above, you also should know that, when using such a FUNCTION, you can explicitly state each argument or combine with the ALL feature. Here is an example:

```
COMPUTE TOT-AMT = FUNCTION SUM (FLD-A TABLE-B (ALL) FLD-C FLD-D)
```

In this book, you will not find examples of all 42 FUNCTIONs. In fact, there are only a few, primarily to demonstrate their use. This was a conscious gesture on my part. My attempts to give you realistic examples of the scientific FUNCTIONs would annoy those of you who understand and can readily use them, and the rest of us would just skip over them. Likewise, I didn't attempt to demonstrate all of the FUNCTIONs for working with alphanumeric and numeric arrays. Those of you who understand and can use MEAN, MEDIAN, and VARIANCE only need to know that they are available and the syntax. A complete listing of the FUNCTIONs is in Chapter 7. If you are using COBOL/370, you should take some time to review them as they can noticeably improve your productivity. Examples using some of them are in the next chapter.

2.3.8. LE/370 CALLable Services

Unlike intrinsic functions, which can only be used within COBOL/370 programs, the LE/370 CALLable services are also available to COBOL II programs running under LE/370. This is because these services are accessed with a CALL statement.

The LE/370 CALLable services may be CALLed either statically or dynamically from your program. All parameters must be defined, either explicitly or implicitly, as BY REFERENCE, for example,

```
CALL 'CEEGPID' USING WS-VER, WS-PLAT, WS-FUNC
```

All services provide a feedback code (i.e., status code) as the last parameter, allowing the CALLing program to interrogate the value to determine the results of the request.

LE/370 CALLable services fall into several categories: dynamic storage management, condition handling, message handling, national language support, date and time services, math routines, and general services. Since LE/370 was developed to support several languages, some of the services duplicate what is already provided in COBOL/370's intrinsic functions.

In Section 3.13 you will find a few of these services documented with examples. There is a summary listing of all of the services in Chapter 7, but without the details necessary to use them. This is because many require in-depth knowledge of LE/370 and its memory and resource management techniques. If you need such in-depth LE/370 information, you should reference the IBM *LE/370 Programming Guide*, referenced in Chapter 9. That is a 490+ page manual with extensive details on these services and other considerations for LE/370. Those are topics clearly beyond the scope of this book. Instead, I have included information on those LE/370 CALLable services that you might readily use. The examples in the next chapter should demonstrate adequately how the services are invoked.

SUMMARY

This has been a hefty chapter of the book. I encourage you to read it more than once, highlighting and underlining those elements that affect your programming techniques. COBOL II and COBOL/370 are a major step forward for COBOL. You don't need to read the next chapter (and probably shouldn't) until you have experimented with several of these different features and developed a feeling of comfort with and enthusiasm for COBOL II and COBOL/370. The language structure should feel natural before you start looking for new techniques.

3

Programming with COBOL II and COBOL/370

This chapter is designed to provide some tips and techniques for day-to-day programming assignments and for maximizing a program's design and performance. I assume you have read the previous chapter and also that you have experimented some with COBOL II or COBOL/370. This chapter does not, however, focus solely on new components. Instead, it focuses on whatever technique is appropriate to the topic. This will often include a new feature, but not always.

This chapter is not written to be read from beginning to end as was the previous chapter. Instead, use this chapter as a ready reference for COBOL techniques. You will find many topics are duplicated to some degree elsewhere in the book and you may be wondering why some topics appear twice. I did this because, as a desk reference, you should find topics where you look for them, not where I think they should go. So, this means many topics appear in several places. I hope they appear in a sufficient number of locations to ease your use of the chapter.

3.1. USING STRUCTURED PROGRAMMING COMPONENTS

First, if you're not familiar with structured programming, see Chapter 5 (Program Design Guidelines). For the rest of you, you know whether or not you use structured programming practices. Structured programming means

- no GO TOs (that's right, *none*)
- no EXIT statements

- no PERFORM THRU statements
- one entry and one exit for all statements/paragraphs/modules

If you coded those statements only in pre-1980 OS/VS COBOL SORT programs or early (pre-Version 1.6) CICS programs (when only **EXEC CICS HANDLE** was available to check PFkeys and errors), that's okay, as there was often little choice. If you still violate any of those pointers, you're creating problems for yourself. **EXIT** and **PERFORM THRU** don't explicitly violate structured programming concepts, but they do violate top-down design techniques since they do not decompose logic.

Furthermore, such statements not only present the opportunity for maintenance programmers to insert additional paragraphs within the logic flow, but they also tempt the best of us to use a GO TO to get to the **EXIT** statement. To help you, I've assembled here a brief review of COBOL statements that provide structured programming components (SEQUENCE, SELECTION, DO-WHILE, DO-UNTIL, and CASE).

3.1.1. SEQUENCE Component

SEQUENCE means that a statement's scope places it in sequence with the preceding statement. A set of sequence statements are, therefore, all sharing in the same scope. When you execute the first statement in a sequence, the structure takes you through all of them. So, what does that mean? It means that you must *not* contain the scope by inserting any periods that aren't required.

```
MOVE A TO B
MOVE C TO D
```

are two statements that meet the definition of SEQUENCE. The first is executed and then the second. If we were to precede those two statements by an **IF** statement,

```
IF condition
    MOVE A TO B
    MOVE C TO D
```

we know that both MOVE statements would be executed. However, some programmers are in the habit of placing periods after *every* statement. Preceding such statements with an IF statement would give us this:

```
IF condition
    MOVE A TO B.
    MOVE C TO D.
```

Obviously, that would be an error. It has been this practice over the years that has sensitized many people to "always check for missing periods." In truth, the reverse is the proper approach. Instead of checking for missing periods, you should avoid placing unnecessary periods and spot check for them. They are only appropriate at the end of a paragraph. Throughout this book, the approach is "if you don't need it, don't code it."

3.1.2. SELECTION Component

If you're thinking that this is accomplished by the IF and ELSE statement, you're correct—but there are many more selection statements. For example, other statements that provide selection options are

```
Statement     Selection clause

ADD           ON SIZE ERROR, NOT ON SIZE ERROR
CALL          ON EXCEPTION, NOT ON EXCEPTION
COMPUTE       ON SIZE ERROR, NOT ON SIZE ERROR
DELETE        INVALID KEY, NOT INVALID KEY
DIVIDE        ON SIZE ERROR, NOT ON SIZE ERROR
EVALUATE      WHEN
MULTIPLY      ON SIZE ERROR, NOT ON SIZE ERROR
READ          AT END, NOT AT END, INVALID KEY, NOT INVALID KEY
RETURN        AT END, NOT AT END
REWRITE       INVALID KEY, NOT INVALID KEY
SEARCH        WHEN
START         INVALID KEY, NOT INVALID KEY
STRING        ON OVERFLOW, NOT ON OVERFLOW
SUBTRACT      ON SIZE ERROR, NOT ON SIZE ERROR
UNSTRING      ON OVERFLOW, NOT ON OVERFLOW
WRITE         INVALID KEY, NOT INVALID KEY
```

Because all of these provide the SELECTION component, all of them also have scope terminators associated with them to avoid prematurely terminating the scope of the statement (for example, END-MULTIPLY, END-WRITE). It is the extensive use of scope terminators for SELECTION statements that maintains the integrity of your structured program, since scope terminators ensure the SELECTION components are also eligible to be SEQUENCE components as well.

3.1.3. The DO-WHILE Component

Nothing new here. The PERFORM UNTIL statement accomplishes this. You have a choice of using the traditional approach, where the executed code is in a separate paragraph, or using the new inline format where the executed code immediately follows the PERFORM statement. Remember; a DO-WHILE component tests a condition BEFORE executing the code, whereas a DO-UNTIL component tests the condition AFTER executing the code.

Traditional

```
PERFORM 2300-PROCESS-RECORDS UNTIL EOF-SWITCH = 'Y'
```

Inline

```
PERFORM VARYING TAB-INDEX FROM 1 BY 1 UNTIL END-OF-FILE
    PERFORM 2400-READ
    IF NOT END-OF-FILE
        MOVE FD1-REC TO WS3-TABLE (TAB-INDEX)
    END-IF
END-PERFORM
```

Remember, the inline PERFORM requires the scope terminator END-PER-FORM.

3.1.4. The DO-UNTIL Component

This was never before available in COBOL and many analysts who develop programming specifications for COBOL applications avoid using DO-UNTIL. Anyway, you now have it with the WITH TEST AFTER clause appended to a PERFORM statement. You have a choice similar to that offered above for the DO-WHILE component, either using the traditional PERFORM where the executed code is in a separate paragraph, or using the new inline format where the executed code immediately follows the PERFORM statement.

Traditional

```
PERFORM 2300-PROCESS-RECORDS UNTIL EOF-SWITCH = 'Y' WITH
  TEST AFTER
```

Inline

```
PERFORM WITH TEST AFTER VARYING TAB-INDEX FROM 1 BY 1 UNTIL
  END-OF-FILE
    PERFORM 2400-READ
    IF NOT END-OF-FILE
        MOVE FD1-REC TO WS3-TABLE (TAB-INDEX)
    END-IF
END-PERFORM
```

This example appears identical to the earlier example for DO-WHILE. The difference is in the status AFTER execution. Remember, the inline PERFORM requires the scope terminator END-PERFORM.

3.1.5. The CASE Component

This component is provided by the new EVALUATE statement, of which there were many examples in the previous chapter. Do NOT use the GO TO DEPEND-ING ON statement to attempt this.

3.1.6. How to Avoid the GO TO Statement

There is additional material in Chapter 5 (Program Design Guidelines) that addresses this topic. I include the topic here because it is a common concern of programmers who have trouble with the concept. My approach is to concentrate on decomposing the program design and not to concentrate on GO TOs. The need for GO TO statements disappears in an application where each paragraph decomposes downward and outward to accomplish the scope of the paragraph.

When dealing with structure, I create analogies with an office environment where the main module/paragraph is the "manager" and the other modules/paragraphs are "subordinates" or "junior managers." For example, a manager wanting to review records for employees eligible for a pay raise in the current month would not say to a subordinate, "Please get me all the employee records." Instead, the manager would say, "Please get me the records of the employees eligible for a pay raise this month."

Sound simple? Compare that simple logic to a program that needs to read a file but wants to process only certain records. Often, we see something like this:

```
2100-PROCESS.
    PERFORM 2300-READ-RECORD
    IF NOT END-OF-FILE
        IF ELIGIBLE-FOR-PAY-RAISE
            process, etc
              .
              .
        ELSE
            GO TO 2100-PROCESS.

2300-GET-READ-RECORD.
      READ FD1-PAYROLL-FILE
        AT END
            SET END-OF-FILE TO TRUE
      END-READ.
```

This is poor code, primarily because the process of getting input has not been decomposed. Why not try the office analogy approach and do this:

```
2100-PROCESS.
    PERFORM 2300-GET-VALID-RECORD
    IF NOT END-OF-FILE
        process, etc
        .
        .
        .

2300-GET-VALID-RECORD.
    PERFORM UNTIL END-OF-FILE OR ELIGIBLE-FOR-PAY-RAISE
        READ FD1-PAYROLL-FILE
          AT END
              SET END-OF-FILE TO TRUE
        END-READ
    END-PERFORM.
```

This "delegates" the process of simple validation to a subordinate module, freeing the "manager" module to make processing decisions instead of doing simple edits as well. You will probably find your programs have more paragraphs, and smaller ones at that. You will probably also find that junior programmers can maintain them too. The use of the GO TO statement will continue to be used by a portion of programmers, but it will always be indicative of either an inadequate or incomplete program design.

3.2. MODULE STRUCTURES

This section contains suggestions and tips if you are building a new application, adding a subprogram to an existing structure, or contemplating different ways to link your logic subsets together. If you're unfamiliar with combining programs, read the first two topics for an overview.

3.2.1. Main Modules and Submodules

This section introduces the term *run unit*, which appears throughout the book. (NOTE: In LE/370 you will see run units referred to as *enclaves*.) A run unit is the logical collection of programs executed under control of a main program. This may be one or more programs in one or more languages formed into one or more load modules. For example, in a batch environment a run unit begins at the JCL EXEC statement. Also, a run unit is normally one load module.

A main program/module is one that is invoked from MVS (for example,

PGM= on JCL EXEC statement). A main program is to a great degree coded the same way as a subprogram. Differences lie in the way they are terminated (see next topic) and how they share data with other programs in the run unit (see topics on Sharing Data and on Sharing Files). For example, a main program using the PROCEDURE DIVISION USING statement is receiving data from MVS (via the JCL PARM parameter) in a format different from the same statement being used in a subprogram. Where a LINKAGE SECTION is used in a main program, it is typically to store the above-mentioned PARM data from a JCL statement. The main program is the highest element in a run unit. As in other components of a run unit, a main program should have one entry point and one exit. (Note: If the first COBOL program is CALLed from an assembler program, there are some differences. See that topic later in this section.)

Subprograms/submodules are invoked from another program (CALLed from another application or from a software environment, for example, IMS or CICS). Subprograms use PROCEDURE DIVISION USING to accept data from a calling program in a format determined by the CALLing program. Subprograms can in turn also CALL other subprograms. As in other components of a run unit, a subprogram should have one entry point and one exit.

Example of a batch main program and subprogram

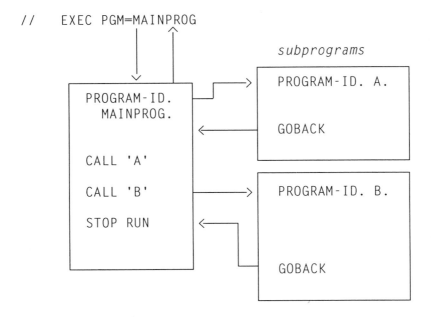

From the JCL, MVS gives control to MAINPROG. MAINPROG in turn transfers control first to program A and then to program B. The subprograms use

GOBACK to return control and the main program uses STOP RUN to return control to MVS.

3.2.2. Terminating a Program/Module

COBOL provides five ways to terminate an application.

1. **STOP RUN.** The STOP RUN statement, used by main programs, returns control back to the system environment. The system environment is normally established by MVS at the time the first program (the main program) is initiated. Therefore, a subprogram should NOT use STOP RUN. Another function of the STOP RUN statement closes any files in the run unit that are still open. One STOP RUN, at most, should be within a run unit. While COBOL II has removed many of the restrictions on using STOP RUN for CICS and IMS applications, I recommend you not use it. (Note: For other considerations on the environment, see the topic on assembler language.)

2. **GOBACK.** The GOBACK statement returns control to the CALLing program and should be used by subprograms. GOBACK is the preferred statement for CICS and IMS applications. (Note: GOBACK may also be used by main programs, but the resource cleanup that would have been done by STOP RUN is dependent on various installation defaults, primarily the RTEREUS run-time option. Check with your technical staff before standardizing on this approach.)

3. **EXIT PROGRAM.** The third option is the EXIT PROGRAM statement, which performs differently depending on whether it is executed from within a main program or from within a subprogram. If executed in a CALLed subprogram, it functions as GOBACK. If executed in a main program, it is ignored. Note: An EXIT PROGRAM statement is implicitly defined at the end of every COBOL program, (that is, if the last statement in a program falls through to the next available statement, an EXIT PROGRAM statement will be executed). This is avoided by PERFORMing paragraphs and not allowing fall-through logic (for example, PERFORM THRU or GO TO). Most shops do not use EXIT PROGRAM; they use GOBACK instead. Because CICS and IMS applications treat this statement differently depending on whether EXIT PROGRAM is in the highest level module or not, I recommend that you do not use it. Anytime a statement acts differently in different settings, it is only a matter of time before you forget which setting you are in. This is a statement to avoid.

4. **EXEC CICS RETURN.** The fourth option applies to CICS programs.

CICS provides a specific statement, EXEC CICS RETURN, to terminate run units in the CICS environment. CICS programs should use EXEC CICS RETURN when the run unit is finished and control is to be returned to CICS. Note: Under COBOL II, STOP RUN no longer crashes the CICS environment as it did in OS/VS COBOL, but it lacks environmental cleanup functions of EXEC CICS RETURN.

5. **ABEND.** The final option is to force an ABEND. While this isn't a clean technique, there may be times when you do not want the application to appear to have terminated with no errors. Any ABEND code you use should not be in the range of 1000 to 1999, as those are used by the COBOL II run-time routines. Your shop may have some home-grown subprograms that do this, or for CICS you can probably use the EXEC CICS ABEND command. If so, use them. Otherwise, here are some techniques to consider:

Use IBM's ABEND routine, ILBOABN0. This subroutine is supplied by IBM with other COBOL run-time modules and requires a parameter passed to it that is PIC S9(4) COMP, containing a value between 0 & 4095 (this will be the ABEND code). Here is an example:

```
05  WS1-ABEND-CODE   PIC  S9(4)  COMP  VALUE +5.
  .
  .
    CALL 'ILBOABNO'  USING WS1-ABEND-CODE
```

This example produces a printed dump if there is a SYSUDUMP or SYSABEND DD statement in the step. In this example, the User ABEND code is 0005.

Even though ILBOABN0 still functions, I recommend that you pick one of the other options. This is because any module whose name begins with ILBO is a carry-over from OS/VS COBOL and will eventually be incompatible. Also, an ABEND with ILBOABN0 shows the save area two levels back from where the ABEND actually occurred.

Use your own ABEND routine. You can control whether the dump is printed. This can be advantageous when you need the ABEND termination code but do not want the added expense and waste of printing a dump. While I don't guarantee this assembler program for all environments, it does work and it is simple. (Note: As with all other assembler examples in this book, this module is not reentrant, although it does execute in 31-bit or 24-bit mode.) It uses the same parameter list as IBM's, but there is no dump produced.

Sample assembler program to ABEND with no dump

```
ABEND      CSECT
ABEND      AMODE 31
ABEND      RMODE ANY
R1         EQU   1
R2         EQU   2
R12        EQU   12
R13        EQU   13
R14        EQU   14
R15        EQU   15
           USING ABEND,R12
           SAVE  (14,12),,*
           LR    R12,R15
           LA    R14,SAVEAREA
           ST    R14,8(,R13)
           ST    R13,4(,R14)
           LR    R13,R14
           L     R1,0(,R1)
           LH    R2,0(,R1)
           ABEND (2)
SAVEAREA   DC    18F'0'
           END   ABEND
```

Using the above example, this would be executed as

```
CALL 'ABEND' USING WS1-ABEND-CODE
```

One benefit (drawback?) of this module is that, if it ABENDs, it does not activate any debugging function. Be sure to assemble it with IBM's Assembler H product. (Note: Changing ABEND (2) in the above listing to ABEND (2),DUMP causes it to force a system dump, if that is preferred.)

If you are using LE/370, the drawback of using the assembler ABEND is that LE/370 condition handling gains control **AFTER** the ABEND occurs. The following option is preferable.

Use LE/370 CALLable services. LE/370 provides a CALLable service, CEE3ABD, to terminate an enclave. The basics of these services are covered later in Section 3.13.2, Using LE/370 CALLable Services.

STOP RUN versus GOBACK.

Some people are confused by differences between STOP RUN and GOBACK. If a subprogram uses STOP RUN, it exits back *past* the program that CALLed it, defeating the concept of structured programming (Note: also affected by RTEREUS run-time option). Consider this example:

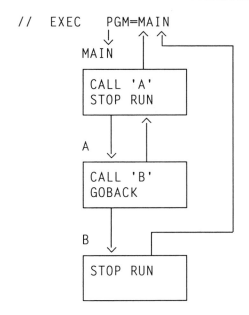

```
//  EXEC  PGM=MAIN
```

MAIN

```
CALL 'A'
STOP RUN
```

A

```
CALL 'B'
GOBACK
```

B

```
STOP RUN
```

Module MAIN does a STOP RUN back to the system. That's proper. Module A executes a GOBACK to return control to the CALLing program. That's proper too. Module B executes a STOP RUN, bypassing all prior modules, creating a GO TO environment. That can cause structural problems in an application.

Some programmers writing in IMS or CICS code STOP RUN (in error) because they visualize their program as receiving control from MVS. Actually, the program that receives control from MVS is the IMS or CICS control program, which in turn invokes the application program. An IMS or CICS application then is *always* a subprogram. IMS applications should use GOBACK to terminate processing. If you're ever in doubt, GOBACK is safer than STOP RUN since GOBACK works with both main programs and with subprograms. CICS programs have a specific CICS statement, called EXEC RETURN, which should be used for the highest level module. (Note: COBOL II now allows CICS and IMS programs to use STOP RUN, primarily (my opinion) because so many programmers kept using it. My suggestion is to follow the above guidelines, using GOBACK and EXEC RETURN, because they are compatible across all supported environments for IMS and CICS.)

3.2.3. COBOL to COBOL

This is the simplest approach to a multimodule application. When all COBOL programs in a run unit are COBOL II or COBOL/370, you may use all functions available from the environment. This includes the ability to use reentrant code, to reside above the 16-megabyte line, or to share data and files as documented later in this section. There are no special techniques to use here, but I mention it to encourage you to develop (or convert) all modules that constitute a run unit to COBOL II or COBOL/370 to minimize any incompatibilities and to ensure you full access to COBOL facilities.

You will also receive maximum benefit (and ensure compatibility) by always specifying the same or compatible compile options. For example, COBOL II programs with RENT and RES are most compatible with COBOL/370 programs that are RENT. This is because these options establish the same RMODE and AMODE attributes.

OS/VS COBOL programs can be shared with COBOL II and COBOL/370 programs, but there are difficulties, due mostly to OS/VS COBOL's limitation to 24-bit addressing. This is covered more fully in Section 3.2.6, Using OS/VS CO-BOL Programs, and in Figure 3.1. If you will be dynamically accessing OS/VS COBOL programs with COBOL/370 (i.e., via LE/370 at run-time), you will also need to read information further in the text regarding the ALL31 option.

3.2.4. Nested Programs in COBOL

Nested programs, with examples, were introduced in the previous chapter. The primary advantage to this approach is the extra features that are available to you when sharing data or files with other programs (explained later in this section). A secondary benefit is that the compiler sees the programs as one program, not several. This means the documentation from the compile process (for example, cross-reference listings, program assembler code, or offset listings) is more thorough and you never encounter a situation in which one of the modules has several different object copies and the Linkage Editor used the wrong copy. You also receive a listing from the compiler showing the hierarchy of your structure, which can be helpful to a maintenance programmer unfamiliar with the application.

From a structured programming point of view, the benefit of nested programs is that you can insert new subprograms quickly. One technique I encourage is putting subprograms in COPYbooks, making it simpler to share them across an application.

The debugging advantage is that there is only one true program. The added complexity of doing hex arithmetic to determine in which module the ABEND occurred is history.

From this material, you probably feel I think it is a good approach. I do. Having all the code together, getting one cross-reference listing, not having to pass data back and forth to subprograms, not having to remember to insert COPY statements for all the common items are big benefits to a maintenance staff. Let's look at an example: If we have a new application that has been designed to use several subprograms and share a common file and table data, the traditional approach would be to develop several COPYbooks, develop the various applications using the COPY statements, compile and link them and then test to see if they communicate together. Whew! Here is a nested way: Develop all common data and files and place them in one master COPYbook, something like this:

COPYbook   Name: PAYMAST

```
IDENTIFICATION DIVISION.
PROGRAM-ID.  PAYMAST.
ENVIRONMENT DIVISION.
INPUT-OUTPUT SECTION.
FILE-CONTROL.
    SELECT FD1-PAY-FILE ASSIGN TO PAYDD
        FILE STATUS IS PAY-STAT.
DATA DIVISION.
FILE SECTION.
FD FD1-PAY-FILE GLOBAL
    .
    .

WORKING-STORAGE SECTION.
01 WS1-PAY-WORK GLOBAL.
    .
    .

PROCEDURE DIVISION.
1.  CALL 'PAYRUN01'
    STOP RUN.
```

Now, all you need to do to use this program is to code

```
COPY PAYMAST
ID DIVISION.
PROGRAM-ID.  PAYRUN01.
PROCEDURE DIVISION.
    .
    .
END PROGRAM PAYRUN01.
```

This is much simpler than coding all the normal entries for a program and remembering which COPY statements to code.

The down side of nested programs is that you must recompile all of them even when you changed only one of them. Whether that issue is more important than the benefits is something for your shop to decide. (Note to CICS users: A nested program, including all nested CALLed modules, must be processed as one unit by the CICS translator.)

3.2.5. Assembler Language to COBOL

Assembler language has special considerations because it is outside the COBOL environment. By COBOL environment, I am referring to the run-time modules that are invoked to provide integrity from one COBOL module to another. There are specific differences depending on whether the assembler program is the CALLing or the CALLed module.

Assembler programs as subprograms.

There is no problem for COBOL programs to CALL assembler programs provided that the assembler programs follow standard IBM linkage conventions (see the following sample programs for an example) and are able to function in the appropriate addressing mode (31-bit or 24-bit). If you are migrating an OS/VS COBOL application to COBOL II and the application CALLs some assembler modules, those modules may need to be reassembled using IBM's Assembler H product (and may need some coding changes) to operate properly in 31-bit mode. Your shop probably has a technical staff already familiar with the coding adjustments, and actual coding of assembler is beyond the scope of this book.

Assembler programs as main programs.

First, let's identify the concerns. The first issue to fix is the possibility that the assembler main program has only 24-bit addressability. If so, you have two approaches:

1. Reassemble the main program with IBM's Assembler H product (and possibly change some code) to get the program to have 31-bit addressability. If full reentrant access is desired, the effort increases considerably.
2. Compile the COBOL subprograms with compile options NORENT. This option prevents the run unit from taking advantage of MVS/XA and MVS/ESA performance enhancements in virtual memory, so while it is the easier of the two approaches, you will be better off to reassemble the assembler mainprogram.

The second concern is that COBOL II programs operate in a COBOL environment that is normally established when the COBOL main program is initiated. This environment stays active throughout the run unit without needing to be reinitialized for entry/exit of each COBOL module. If an assembler program is the *main program*, the possibility exists that, while the programs will function properly, the run-time environment will be reinitialized frequently and affect performance. Using assembler language, therefore, can create a performance issue if it is the highest level module in the run unit. (Note: In a CICS environment, assembler programs may not CALL a COBOL program.)

There are four ways of initializing the environment to prevent the performance degradation:

1. Use the RTEREUS run-time COBOL II or LE/370 option (documented later in this chapter). This is probably your shop's default setting for non-CICS applications (RTEREUS is ignored by CICS). The section on compiler options shows a way to determine what this setting is. This is the easiest approach because it requires nothing on your part. If RTEREUS is not your shop's default and does not conflict with your shop's standards, your systems programmers can establish the option for your particular program (more information on this facility, IGZEOPT, is in the section on compile options). Doing so requires a modification to your link-edit control statements (documented later in this chapter).

2. Use a COBOL program as the main program. Where RTEREUS is not the default and there are reasons not to establish it, this is the next simplest approach for you. By creating a small stub driver program, you cause the environment to be initialized for the run unit. For example:

```
ID DIVISION.
PROGRAM-ID. DRIVER.
PROCEDURE DIVISION.
1.   CALL 'assembler-program-name'
     STOP RUN.
```

The following chart depicts the possible structure:

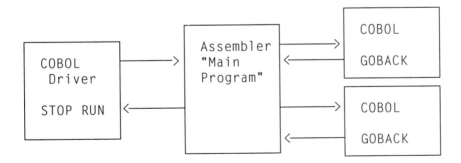

3. Modify the assembler program to initialize the run-time environment prior to the first CALL. IBM provides a module called IGZERRE that does this. (Note: This technique is not recommended for CICS or IMS/DC applications.) The main assembler program would need to include these statements:

Prior to first CALL

```
LA    1,1
CALL  IGZERRE
```

After last CALL

```
LA    1,2
CALL  IGZERRE
```

Simple assembler program to CALL a COBOL module

This is a simple program (it works) that initializes the COBOL environment and CALLs a program called MAINPROG.

```
              TITLE  'CALL COBOL subprogram and Initialize '
CALLCOB  CSECT
CALLCOB  AMODE 31
CALLCOB  RMODE ANY
         SAVE  (14,12),,*
         USING CALLCOB,12
         LR    11,13
         LR    12,15
         LA    13,SAVEAREA
         ST    13,8(0,11)
         ST    11,4(0,13)
         LR    4,1
         LA    1,1              A '1' in register 1 will
         CALL  IGZERRE          initialize environment
         LTR   15,15
         BZ    OKAY
         WTO   'IGZERRE Error',ROUTCDE=(11)
OKAY     LR    1,4
         CALL  COBPROG          Call PROGRAM-ID of 'COBPROG'
         LA    1,2              A '2' in register 1 will
         CALL  IGZERRE          terminate environment
         LTR   15,15
         BZ    QUIT
         WTO   'IGZERRE Error',ROUTCDE=(11)
QUIT     L     13,SAVEAREA+4
         LM    14,12,12(13)
         XR    15,15
         BR    14               RETURN TO MVS
```

```
SAVEAREA DC        18F'0'
        END        CALLCOB
```

For more information on parameter lists for IGZERRE, see the *IBM COBOL II Application Programming Guide* (Chapter 9, Related Publications).

4. Use the OS/VS COBOL assembler interface, ILBOSTP0, instead of IGZERRE. I include it here because you may encounter CALLs to that module in your current assembler programs. If so, that module is still supported by IBM, so there is no need to change it. (REMINDER: This is a 24-bit module.)

   If your application will use LE/370 (the default for COBOL/370 applications and for COBOL II RES applications where LE/370 is available), you will need to be aware of a couple of LE/370 run-time options, ALL31 and STACK (both are covered more fully later in the text). If ILBOSTP0 initializes the environment and no LE/370 options (via CEEUOPT, covered later) are defined, then LE/370 sets ALL31(OFF) and STACK(,,BELOW). If, for whatever reason, your application also uses CEEUOPT, then your application must force those options from within the CEEUOPT module.

5. Finally, with LE/370, there are additional tuning options that you might want to pursue with your shop's technical staff. LE/370 has significantly more tuning options that were not available prior to the availability of COBOL/370.

STOP RUN considerations when CALLed by an assembler program.

As stated elsewhere, subprograms should use GOBACK to return control to the CALLing program. That applies here, too, even if the CALLing program is written in assembler. However, there may be a reason you want to use STOP RUN at the highest level COBOL program and still treat it as a subprogram. The problem you face is that the STOP RUN statement normally returns control to either the program that CALLed the program that initiated the environment or to MVS, if MVS initiated the environment. To get around this, you need an *additional* assembler program between the high-level assembler program and your program. This will make it appear that the CALLing assembler and the CALLed COBOL program are communicating directly. (You also face *severe performance problems* if the COBOL program is CALLed frequently, because it must be reinitialized each time STOP RUN does resource cleanup.)

Anyway, assuming you're determined, here is a sample program that can be tucked between the assembler main program and your COBOL "main program." This example assumes the RTEREUS option is invoked. If not, use the previous example that included CALLs to IGZERRE. This works, but I don't recommend it. Here is the flow, showing both STOP RUN processing and GOBACK processing:

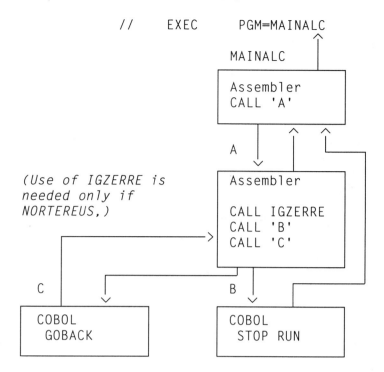

Sample program to CALL COBOL program without initialization

```
          TITLE 'CALL COBOL Main Program '
CALLMAIN  CSECT
CALLMAIN  AMODE 31
CALLMAIN  RMODE ANY
          SAVE  (14,12),,*
          USING CALLMAIN,12
          LR    11,13
          LR    12,15
          LA    13,SAVEAREA
          ST    13,8(0,11)
          ST    11,4(0,13)
          CALL  MAINPROG          Call PROGRAM-ID of MAINPROG
          L     13,SAVEAREA+4
          LM    14,12,12(13)
          XR    15,15
          BR    14
SAVEAREA  DC    18F'0'
                END  CALLMAIN
```

   The COBOL program in the diagram, module B, returns control at STOP
RUN, not to module A that CALLed it but to MAINALC, the program that

CALLed the program that CALLed B. The complexity of this solution may cause you to rethink why you prefer STOP RUN. As I mentioned earlier, GOBACK eliminates the need for the intermediate program.

All the considerations for assembler language are not addressed here, the goal of such a technical topic being to make you aware of issues to address if you are developing or maintaining such an application. If you are developing COBOL applications with no non-COBOL modules, your shop's run-time environment considerations have already been addressed by your technical staff.

This treatment of the topic is elementary, at best. If your shop is heavily into assembler interfaces, the complexities could fill several books. Check with your technical support staff for more assistance and direction and prior to using these sample programs. The issue of using non-COBOL languages with COBOL, especially if IMS or CICS are involved, often requires involvement and tuning considerations that are beyond this book.

3.2.6. Using OS/VS COBOL Programs

If you are maintaining an application where some of the modules in a run unit have been migrated to COBOL II while others remain in OS/VS COBOL, you have some special considerations. You should view a mixed environment as a temporary approach, because there is performance degradation when both CO-BOL versions are used. First, if it is a CICS transaction, either keep all modules OS/VS COBOL or convert them all to COBOL II or COBOL/370. A mixed approach is not supported in CICS (other than by EXEC CICS LINK or XCTL, which introduce their own performance degradation). There are also some headaches for IMS (see the section CICS/IMS/DB2 Issues for more information).

My concerns about OS/VS COBOL programs as discussed in this text apply only to those programs that interact with COBOL II or COBOL/370 programs, either through static or dynamic CALLS. Otherwise, OS/VS COBOL applications, whether compiled with RES or NORES, will continue to execute as before. The following information pertains ONLY to those OS/VS programs that must interact with COBOL II or COBOL/370 programs (other than via the EXEC CICS LINK or XCTL commands). Also, the examples depicted in Figure 3.1 apply equally to COBOL/370 when interacting with OS/VS COBOL programs.

Since OS/VS COBOL modules must reside below the 16-megabyte line, you must use appropriate COBOL compile options for downward compatibility to the OS/VS COBOL module. The options are NORENT for a static CALL and DATA(24) for a dynamic CALL. (See the section Static and Dynamic CALLs for more information.) See Figure 3.1 for a depiction of the structures available.

In all examples in Figure 3.1, the data areas will be below the 16-megabyte line. The COBOL II module above the 16-megabyte line does this because one of the compile options is DATA(24). The other structures accomplish this by specifying NORENT, which causes data areas to be allocated within the object mod-

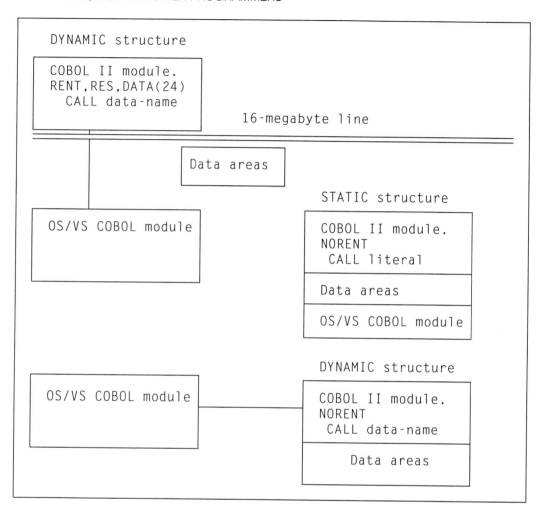

Figure 3.1. COBOL II & OS/VS COBOL structures.

ule. No changes are needed for an OS/VS COBOL module if it was compiled with RES and the appropriate (static or dynamic) CALL statement. Of the three structures, only the one with RENT (above the line) offers any COBOL II performance advantages, although all of the examples are less efficient than an all-COBOL II run unit. (REMINDER: All the above for COBOL II applies also to COBOL/370.)

For static CALLs where the OS/VS COBOL program was compiled with NORES, you would have one or more additional steps, since my assumption is that you will want to use RES for all COBOL II programs. (COBOL II and COBOL/370 require that all modules in a run unit share the same RES option. COBOL/370 is, by default, RES.) Your choices are

1. Convert the OS/VS COBOL program to COBOL II or COBOL/370 for a complete solution.
2. Recompile and link the OS/VS COBOL program with the OS/VS COBOL compiler, specifying RES, for a temporary solution.
3. Compile the COBOL II program with NORES for a temporary solution (You give up the performance opportunities provided by MVS/XA and MVS/ESA, as NORES requires NORENT.) (COBOL II only)

   If you are using COBOL/370, compile your COBOL/370 program with NORENT. (As with NORES for COBOL II, you give up many benefits of MVS/ESA. This forces the resulting load module to be in 24-bit mode for coexistence with the VS/COBOL module.)
4. If the OS/VS COBOL program is not to be converted or recompiled with RES, ensure that, during the link-edit process, all OS/VS COBOL versions of the ILBOxxxx modules are replaced by their equivalent modules from the COBOL II or LE/370 subroutine library. (See Creating a Load Module for more information on REPLACE.) This step can be combined with step 3 for a NORES environment, or with step 5 for a mixed environment.
5. If your choices from the above options cause you to have a mixed environment, use the run-time option MIXRES until the OS/VS COBOL modules have been converted. (COBOL II only)

If your choices included option 5 (MIXRES) you must ensure that MIXRES is specified as a run-time option. The section on compile options explains how to determine your shop default options. My guess is that it is not set to MIXRES. If it is not, you must ask your systems programming staff to assemble a special run-time module for you (IGZEOPT). You must explicitly include the IGZEOPT module in the link-edit process for any load modules in the run unit that contain the NORES option. (See the section in this chapter, Specifying COBOL II and COBOL/370 Options, for more information.) (This paragraph applies only to COBOL II.)

After reading this information, I hope you agree that converting the OS/VS COBOL applications is the preferred approach. The effort to create a coexisting environment with OS/VS COBOL modules will almost always be more costly than migrating the older programs and getting it finished.

3.2.7. Using RETURN-CODE

Every time a program returns control to a CALLing module, a return code is passed back to the CALLing module. At the highest level, this return code is made available to MVS. With the COND JCL parameter, this value can be tested. This technique may also be used within applications (even those with a mix of assembler and COBOL II, or COBOL II and OS/VS COBOL). This is because in every

COBOL program there is a special register called RETURN-CODE. It is initialized to zero at program initiation and the value is updated following each CALL statement. RETURN-CODE is implicitly defined as PIC S9(4) COMP VALUE ZERO. (Note: Prior to COBOL II, this was not allowed for CICS applications. Since EXEC CICS commands affect the RETURN-CODE, you need to test or change its value with that in mind.)

Using this special register requires no special coding on your part. What it does require is a disciplined set of values to be used within your application. The most widely known set of disciplined values are those developed by IBM for use by its language processors and utility programs. For example, we all know that

- A return code of 0 means no errors.
- A return code of 4 means minor warnings.
- A return code of 16 means serious error.

This is not magic. It just proves that when everyone on a project agrees to use certain values, communication improves. To send a value in RETURN-CODE to a CALLing module, all you need do is code:

In subprogram

```
MOVE numeric-literal  to RETURN-CODE
GOBACK
```

In CALLing program

```
CALL 'subprogram' ...
IF RETURN-CODE = numeric-literal...
    .
    .        insert appropriate processing here
    .
```

In the above example, the CALLing module must also include logic to set the value of RETURN-CODE prior to returning control via GOBACK or STOP RUN. Otherwise, it will contain the last value returned.

3.2.8. Sharing Files Among Modules

Sometimes, it is desirable to have several modules in an application have access to a file. I don't recommend it, preferring to keep tighter control on the read/write process. However, I recognize the need for it, as there are probably situations when good functional decomposition dictates it. There are different considerations for file sharing: one for assembler programs and two others for COBOL II programs.

Sharing files with assembler programs.

You have very little control here, and there is the (mostly theoretical) possibility that IBM will redo the format of the Data Control Block (the phrase "when pigs fly" comes to mind, but then I've been wrong before). Anyway, if the file is QSAM, you can share it with an assembler program by specifying the file name in the CALL statement. (*Don't* try this with COBOL subprograms.) The format is

```
CALL 'program-name" USING fd-name
```

This passes the address of the DCB to the assembler program. This can work if there is clear agreement on which program OPENs, CLOSEs, READs, and WRITEs to the file.

Sharing files with COBOL II programs.

There are two ways to share files with other COBOL II programs. One technique works with nested program structures and one with traditional, separately compiled structures. Since a program can have both nested modules and separately compiled modules, the two techniques can appear in a single run unit. (If any terms in this topic are unfamiliar to you, reread the sections on nested programs and on GLOBAL and EXTERNAL data elements in Chapter 2.) In both applicable cases, the logical processing of the file must not be violated. The options presented still require, for example, that the shared file be OPENed prior to issuing a READ to it, and so on.

For nested programs

In a nested program, use the GLOBAL clause on the FD, e.g.,

```
FD  FD2-PAYROLL-MASTER  GLOBAL
    RECORD CONTAINS 100 CHARACTERS.
01  FD2-PAYROLL-REC PIC X(100).
```

If this is specified in an outer program, all contained programs (both directly and indirectly) can access the file just as if the FD appeared in each contained program. Any program within the subset may issue any valid I/O statement for the file and has access to the 01-level entry for it, as well.

For separate programs

For separate programs, each participating program must have a common DATA DIVISION entry for the shared files and shared I/O areas. The FD entry must be similar to this:

```
FD  FD2-PAYROLL-MASTER  EXTERNAL
    RECORD CONTAINS 100 CHARACTERS.
01  FD2-PAYROLL-REC    PIC X(100).
```

The file description entries must be an *exact match*, even to the spelling. This is best done by COPYbook entries. There are examples of this in GLOBAL and EXTERNAL Data Elements in Chapter 2.

Note: External files are accessed below the 16-megabyte line with COBOL II. This should normally not be a major consideration, but you still need to be aware of it. EXTERNAL files may also be GLOBAL files. This is not a concern for COBOL/370, which can access EXTERNAL files anywhere.

3.2.9. Sharing Data Among COBOL II Modules

Sharing data other than files has many options, all of which can be combined with the file-sharing techniques if desired. Let's start with the simplest and proceed to the more complex:

Passing selected data via CALL BY REFERENCE statement.

This is the most common approach to sharing data, as a CALL statement uses, by default, the BY REFERENCE format. Until COBOL II, this was the only way to pass data to another program, so I encourage you to also consider the other options. In this approach, the original data exists within the CALLing module and it makes the data available to the CALLed module with something like:

```
CALL 'proga' USING data-name
```

Actually, this passes not the data, but addressability to the data, to the CALLed program. The CALLed program can not only reference the data, but it can change the data as well. This approach is well-documented, as the CALLed program must establish a LINKAGE SECTION to describe all data being passed from the CALLing program. The problem with this approach occurs when the two programs have different definitions of the data. Consider this:

CALLing module

```
01   WS1-REC        PIC X(24).
01   WS2-REC         PIC X(80).


     CALL 'suba' USING WS1-REC
```

CALLed module

```
LINKAGE SECTION.
01   WORK-REC    PIC X(50).
```

```
PROCEDURE DIVISION USING WORK-REC.
100-PROCESS.
    MOVE ZEROS TO WORK-REC
    GOBACK.
```

Examine what happens in this simple example. The CALLing program passes addressability of WS1-REC to suba. The CALLed subprogram uses this addressability to address not the intended 24-byte record, but the 24-byte record PLUS 26 bytes of WS2-REC in the CALLing program. This happens because the PIC clauses have different values. By moving zeros to WORK-REC, both WS1-REC and much of WS2-REC are set to zeros.

This is not untypical where the CALL statement is used, and it is a major cause for problems created by CALL statements. My recommendation is to use COPYbooks for passed data items and to have walkthroughs of all CALL statements and associated ENTRY or PROCEDURE DIVISION USING statements. (Although I included reference to the ENTRY statement, I don't recommend it. It gives more than one entry point to a COBOL program, a violation of structured programming rules. If you're thinking it is required, such as for IMS programs, it is not.)

Passing selected data via CALL BY CONTENT statement.

Similar to the above example, this approach is desirable if your program must pass selected data to another program, but the other program has no need to update the data. This also ensures some added control. The downside is that there is additional overhead: the system makes a copy of the data for the CALLed program. The format is

```
CALL 'suba' USING BY CONTENT data-name
```

With this format, the subprogram can change the data, but doing so does not change the data in the CALLing program and the potential problem in the previous example is avoided. This format, BY CONTENT, may be mixed with the previous approach, BY REFERENCE (that is, passing some fields by reference and others by content).

Passing variable selected data by CALL statement.

This technique can be combined with either of the two previous examples. It is useful if the data being passed may have a varying length. The format requires the clause, BY CONTENT LENGTH OF data-name. A sample CALL might be

```
CALL 'suba' USING WS1-WORK
            BY CONTENT LENGTH OF WS1-WORK.
```

The subprogram must be prepared to receive two data items:

```
LINKAGE SECTION.
01  LS-WORK.
      .
      .

01  LS-LENGTH        PIC S9(9)  COMP.

PROCEDURE DIVISION USING LS-WORK  LS-LENGTH.
```

The procedural code of the subprogram must include logic to interrogate LS-LENGTH and act appropriately according to application specifications.

Sharing data within a nested program.

This technique uses the GLOBAL clause discussed earlier for files in Chapter 2. If you use my recommendation earlier to use GLOBAL file structures, this complements the approach, making a complete set of data accessible from one program or COPYbook. The format applies to 01-level entries in WORKING-STORAGE. The format is

```
01 data-name GLOBAL.
   05...
     .
     .
```

GLOBAL may be combined with EXTERNAL if desired.

Sharing data externally.

This technique uses the EXTERNAL clause we discussed earlier. There are examples of this in Chapter 2. The advantage is that there is no need to pass data with the CALL statement, which can be a plus if specifications change for an application. As with EXTERNAL files, the data is maintained as DATA(24), below the 16-megabyte address (except for COBOL/370). The clause may only be used at the 01-level in WORKING-STORAGE. The format is

```
01 data-name EXTERNAL.
   05...
     .
     .
```

A note of caution: With EXTERNAL, the generated run-time code allocates a new data area if the EXTERNAL element cannot be located. (Remember, even the spelling must match. That is why I recommend use of COPYbooks for all such elements.) If, for example, a data item were spelled differently in a subprogram, the CALLed subprogram would access a new, uninitialized data area (VALUE clause isn't allowed for EXTERNAL) instead of the intended EXTERNAL data area. This causes no warning message to occur, as COBOL II cannot detect what the spelling should have been. This may, or may not, cause an ABEND, depending on how the program accesses the data. Finally, any indexes specified in an INDEXED BY clause are treated as local, not as EXTERNAL.

Accessing data within a CALLed program.

I include this technique, not because I anticipate frequent use of it, but to demonstrate that it is possible. This technique is appropriate if (1) there are data areas in a CALLed subprogram that the CALLing program wishes to access, and (2) you have decided that the data should not be EXTERNAL. Prior to COBOL II, this was impossible.

The technique is to establish a POINTER element in the CALLing program and have the CALLed program return the proper address for it. We accomplish this by using a combination of the POINTER data element and the SET statement with the ADDRESS OF clause. In the following example, note that the two SET statements are slightly different.

In this example, there are three programs:

1. MAINPROG, which desires direct addressability to the table in SUBPROG called PREM-TABLE. It CALLs SUBPROG, passing it the POINTER item in which the address of the PREM-TABLE is to be stored.
2. SUBPROG, which is CALLed by MAINPROG and contains a premium table that needs to be shared. It CALLs SETADDR, passing it PREM-TABLE and a data element in which to receive the address.
3. SETADDR, a necessary subprogram to establish the address of PREM-TABLE in SUBPROG. This process must be done in a separate program because the ADDRESS OF value exists only for entries in the LINKAGE SECTION. Since PREM-TABLE is in WORKING-STORAGE for SUBPROG, a third subprogram is needed. This program, upon receiving control from SUBPROG, uses the SET statement to store the address of PREM-TABLE.

Here is the structure:

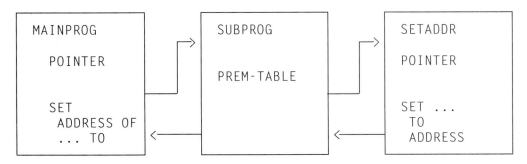

Here is the code:

```
TITLE 'Main Program'
IDENTIFICATION DIVISION.
PROGRAM-ID. MAINPROG.
DATA DIVISION.
WORKING-STORAGE SECTION.
01  WS1-WORK                    POINTER.
LINKAGE SECTION.
01  SUBPROG-AREA.
    05  SUBPROG-DATA-ITEM     PIC X(5) OCCURS 100.


PROCEDURE DIVISION.
1.
    CALL 'SUBPROG' USING WS1-WORK
    SET ADDRESS OF SUBPROG-AREA TO WS1-WORK
    ·   MAINPROG may now access the area, SUBPROG-AREA,
    ·   directly, without further CALLs to SUBPROG
    STOP RUN.
END PROGRAM MAINPROG.

TITLE 'Subprogram with sharable data area"
ID DIVISION.
PROGRAM-ID.  SUBPROG.
DATA DIVISION.
WORKING-STORAGE SECTION.
01  PREM-TABLE.
    05  PREM-TABLE-ITEM      PIC X(5) OCCURS 100.
01  MY-POINTER               PIC S9(9) COMP.
LINKAGE SECTION.
01  MAIN-POINTER             PIC S9(9) COMP.

PROCEDURE DIVISION USING MAIN-POINTER.
1.
    CALL 'SETADDR' USING PREM-TABLE MY-POINTER
    MOVE MY-POINTER TO MAIN-POINTER
    GOBACK.
    ·
    ·
END PROGRAM SUBPROG.

TITLE 'Subprogram that locates addresses'
ID DIVISION.
PROGRAM-ID. SETADDR.
```

```
DATA DIVISION.
WORKING-STORAGE SECTION.
LINKAGE SECTION.
01  LS-POINTER                POINTER.
01  LS-WORK.
    05                        PIC XXXXX.
PROCEDURE DIVISION USING LS-WORK LS-POINTER.
1. SET LS-POINTER TO ADDRESS OF LS-WORK
   GOBACK.
END PROGRAM SETADDR.
```

Note that SETADDR did not need to properly define the layout of PREM-TABLE, since it only needs to SET its address. SETADDR could be used to SET the address of any data area in any program, making this a reusable program.

While this technique has power, remember that MAINPROG's access to the premium table is dependent on SUBPROG. For example, if SUBPROG were dynamically CALLed and later CANCELed, MAINPROG would ABEND if it attempted to access the area.

Receiving data via a JCL PARM.

This technique is only valid for a main program, executed from the JCL EXEC statement. (Exception: An assembler main program could make this data available to subprograms.) Other than the previous example, this is the only occurrence where a main program has a LINKAGE SECTION.

First, we need an understanding of what a PARM is. Unlike other passed data, where we receive a pointer directly to the data, a PARM requires a different technique. The data from the PARM= parameter on the EXEC statement is preceded by a half-word binary field containing the number of bytes of data in the PARM. This data element is dynamically allocated and any attempt to access a larger PARM than that provided results in an ABEND (usually 0C4). For example, if we code

```
//    EXEC PGM=progid,PARM='07/24/93'
```

the data passed will be

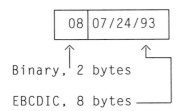

If we omitted the PARM, one is still allocated that looks like this:

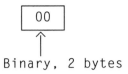

```
Binary, 2 bytes
```

The main program would need something like this:

```
LINKAGE SECTION.
01   PARM-DATA.
     05   PARM-LENGTH    PIC S9(4) COMP.
     05   PARM-CONTENT   PIC X(8).

PROCEDURE DIVISION USING PARM-DATA.
1.   IF PARM-LENGTH = 8
         MOVE PARM-CONTENT TO...
     ELSE

... Reminder: If PARM-LENGTH had a value less than 8, the
MOVE statement would cause an ABEND, since it moves 8 bytes.
```

3.2.10.   Static versus Dynamic CALL Structures

When deciding whether to use static CALLs to modules or dynamic CALLs, there are several considerations. First, let's clarify the terms.

Static CALL: A static CALL is where the CALLing and the CALLed modules are bound together in the same load module during link-edit processing. (See the section Creating a Load Module for more information on the process.)

Dynamic CALL: A dynamic CALL is one that is not resolved until the run unit needs to transfer control to the CALLed module. In this case, the CALLing and the CALLed modules are each processed separately by the Linkage Editor. (See the section CICS/IMS/DB2 Issues for applicability in CICS.)

You can combine the two, using both static and dynamic CALLs within a run unit.

Considerations of a static CALL.

Static CALLs are the format at most shops. When you do static CALLs, you can improve the performance of your application. This is because all programs, being in the same load module, are loaded into memory together. (Note: The jury is still out on this. Some systems performance experts believe that, while static CALLs improve a single application, dynamic CALLs are better for overall computer throughput.)

An additional benefit is that all modules are located and their references resolved during the link-edit process. Assuming you check your listings from the Linkage Editor, you are assured that all modules are in place. Finding that a module is not available is preferable now, rather than during run-time when you might ABEND. This can also be useful documentation, having a complete listing of all modules of the application.

If the Linkage Editor is not able to locate a requested module, it can still finish creating the load module (depending on options used), but it prints a warning message about the missing module and sets an error condition code. The load module will execute properly *unless* the logic causes it to CALL the missing module. If that occurs, you will normally get an 0C1 ABEND, with a PSW (Program Status Word) showing the address of the ABEND somewhere around 00000004. This is because the CALL transferred control to location zero and MVS attempts to locate the next sequential instruction from zero. Some programmers attempt to correct this situation by changing the STEPLIB or JOBLIB because "the program didn't find the needed module." Don't fall into this trap. Remember, a static CALL must be resolved at link-edit time, not at run-time. (The JOBLIB/STEPLIB technique is valid, however, for dynamic CALLs.)

Static CALLs may be done by coding (full syntax not shown):

```
CALL 'literal'
```

where 'literal' is the PROGRAM-ID of the desired program, and you have specified NODYNAM as a compile option.

Considerations of a dynamic CALL.

Dynamic CALLs are the most flexible because you control them at run-time, not at link-edit time. Their use also introduces more complexity into the application logic. Because each module is a separate load module, every application that uses it will get the same version, a definite plus if a program is used by several applications. With static CALLs, all affected modules would need to relink-edit when changes were made. In a dynamic CALL, no relinks are needed.

An additional benefit, depending on your shop's system environment, is that you can control memory requirements depending on which modules are needed. For example, if you have a large module that is rarely needed, it doesn't take up memory during the times it isn't used.

Since dynamic CALLs are resolved at the time the CALL is executed in the run unit, the Linkage Editor is unaware of the need for the module. That means the link-edit listing that is so useful for static CALLs has little use here (other than to validate RMODE and AMODE status). More important for dynamic

CALLs is to know in which load libraries the needed modules are. With this information, you can ensure the proper STEPLIB or JOBLIB statements are present. (Reminder: STEPLIB and JOBLIB DD's are mutually exclusive in a job step. MVS will search only one before searching through system libraries.)

If, at run-time, a needed module is not located, you will receive an 806 ABEND message, including a message with the name of the needed module (that is, you do not need to read the dump to solve this). If the module was too big to fit into memory, you will receive an 80A ABEND. The problem is corrected by locating the appropriate load library and making corrections to your STEPLIB or JOBLIB or by increasing the REGION. There is no need to recompile or to relink-edit. (Note: For dynamic CALLs, you can protect against these ABENDS by using the ON EXCEPTION and/or NOT ON EXCEPTION clauses of the CALL statement. For more information, see the previous chapter.)

Earlier, I mentioned that dynamic structures introduce complexity. That is because the application may now have both application logic in it and memory management logic. For example, while the CALL statement causes a dynamic module to be loaded into memory and given control, the CANCEL statement is used to release it from memory. A program CALLed again after being CANCELed will be in its initial state, with no saved values. Statements such as

```
CALL program-a USING data-namea
ON EXCEPTION
    CANCEL program-b
    CALL program-a USING data-namea
    END-CALL
END-CALL
```

can get you into trouble if CANCELing program-b did not free up sufficient memory or wasn't even in memory. These techniques can work well, but keep the added complexity of such techniques in mind.

An optional way to CANCEL a program is to define the program with the INITIAL clause on the PROGRAM-ID statement. For example:

```
PROGRAM-ID. program-name  INITIAL.
```

This specifies that the program must be CALLed in its initial state. If the program is also CALLed dynamically, it is CANCELed when the GOBACK is executed. Note: This can have severe performance degradation. If a module requires reloading each time it is called, it requires electro-mechanical processes (to the DASD load library) that are much slower than electronic processes. When a program must always be in its initial state, I recommend writing the procedural logic to initialize all work areas each time the program is entered.

Dynamic CALLs are done by coding

```
CALL 'literal'
```

where 'literal' is the PROGRAM-ID of the desired program and you have specified DYNAM as a compile option.

or

```
CALL data-name
```

where data-name is a data element of PIC X(8), containing the name of the desired program. The settings of DYNAM and NODYNAM have no bearing on this syntax. This is the only acceptable format for dynamic CALLs in CICS.

Converting a static CALL to a dynamic CALL (COBOL II only).

Creating a dynamic structure once required that the decision be made prior to compiling the affected programs. Now, with COBOL II, you can convert a run unit with static CALL statements into one with dynamic CALLs. While you should recompile and relink programs to create a dynamic CALL structure when possible, the conversion approach is still an option (normally desired where source code is not accessible). The conversion is done by supplying an intermediate module between the CALLing program and the dynamically CALLed programs.

To convert a structure, IBM provides a module called IGZBRDGE. This is an assembler language macro program that, when supplied with the proper parameters, generates an object module with ENTRY points for the names of the modules you want to be dynamically CALLed. The syntax for the macro is

```
name   IGZBRDGE  ENTNAMES=(prog1,prog2,...progn)
```

> where: name = the name you assign to the intermediate module (this can be any valid 8-character CSECT name)
> proga though progn = names of the load modules that you want to dynamically CALL (these names must already appear within the CALLing program as CALL 'literal')

Using the macro will require you to get assistance from your systems programmers (they usually control access to IBM-supplied software and use of assembler macros). The steps required are

1. Run IGZBRDGE to create the interface module
2. With the Linkage Editor, create load modules of all CALLed programs that are to be dynamically CALLed
3. With the Linkage Editor, create a load module consisting of the CALLing module and the IGZBRDGE-created module.

3.3. DEFINING, INITIALIZING, AND USING DATA AREAS

One of the main ways in which the professional programmer is distinguished from the novice programmer is the way in which data areas are defined and accessed. The approach used can affect memory allocation, the number of instructions generated, run-time efficiency, and program readability. Each of those topics is addressed in the following material.

3.3.1. Efficiencies in Data Definitions

This topic applies to two categories: memory efficiency and processing efficiency. Some of the guidelines have changed since OS/VS COBOL, especially for binary (COMP) data items. This section concentrates on the popular data formats: alphanumeric, packed-decimal, zoned decimal, and binary, plus implications for virtual storage allocation. While floating point data (COMP-2) does receive limited use, that format is not addressed in this book.

Memory efficiency.

With the amount of memory available in mainframes today, attaining memory efficiency may not seem to be an issue. While this is true for small, independent applications, it remains an issue for larger, corporate systems. The following topics might assist you.

Virtual storage constraint relief. The term "Virtual Storage Constraint Relief" (VSCR) refers to the process of reallocating memory from below the 16-megabyte address to above it. As mainframes increase memory, the increase will be in this address space and applications that don't take advantage of it will not benefit from the potential improvement. Realizing VSCR for an application includes allocation of both program memory and data memory. As this material is covered in more depth in specific topics, this is a summary list of that information.

Allocation of memory for programs. Whether a program is loaded above or below the 16-megabyte address is dependent on the RENT compile option. All program modules in a load module must have RENT for this to work. NORENT is primarily for compatibility with older programs. See Module Structures for more information.

Allocation of memory for data. Data areas are allocated above the 16-megabyte address if DATA(31) is specified and below if DATA(24) is specified. DATA(31) requires RENT. The compile option, NORES, also impacts on memory allocation as it restricts all memory allocations for addressability to be in 24-bit mode. With RENT, the DATA DIVISION is separate from the load module, but it is within the load module for NORENT.

  EXTERNAL data and file definitions are allocated in 24-bit mode (COBOL

II). See previous topics on sharing files and data for more information on when this technique is desired.

Alignment. First, remember that eight (8) bytes are the minimum allocated to 01-level entries (double-word alignment). Thus,

```
01  REC-A   PIC X.
01  REC-B   PIC X.
```

requires 16 bytes, not 2. That is why I recommend that switches and accumulators be combined into common 01-level items not only to improve readability, but also to reduce unnecessary memory use.

Packed-decimal field sizes. Another concern is the number of bytes allocated for COMP-3 items. If you recall that packed-decimal items contain 1 decimal digit in the rightmost byte and 2 decimal digits in all other bytes, you will know that the right technique is always to specify an odd number for COMP-3 items. Consider,

```
05  FLDA    PIC S9(4)   COMP-3   VALUE +5.
```

appears in memory as

00	00	5C

,

which is what would be assigned if the PIC had been S9(5). The difference is that additional instructions will be generated to truncate the high-order digit due to the even-numbered PIC clause.

Processing efficiency.

Although you may have been adept at determining processing efficiency for OS/VS COBOL programs, you will find some differences here. How you define data elements, plus what compile options you select, will make a noticeable impact on your processing efficiency.

Processing efficiency by sign definitions. With OS/VS COBOL, my recommendation was to put S in the PIC clause for every numeric item. Now, I have a different recommendation, but let me first share some background information. COBOL II has the facility to be forgiving with signs (the new NUMPROC compile option), which means that it can generate some inefficient code on demand. Many shops, fearing that some of their programs potentially misuse signed data, opted for the least efficient NUMPROC option, NUMPROC(NOPFD), which is explained later. If you want to use the most efficient option, NUMPROC(PFD), you must establish data in the following format:

- If the data will *never* be signed, omit the S in the PIC, for example, PIC 99. If such a field has a plus (C) or minus (D) sign, you will get incorrect results on IF NUMERIC.
- If the data is *always* signed with C or D (never *F*), place the *S* in the PIC clause. (Note: A MOVE from a PIC 9 to a PIC S9 field will set the sign to C.)

If all your data qualifies, you may specify NUMPROC(PFD) for your compiles. If you are unsure about C, D, and F, specify NUMPROC(MIG) and test the results. Here are some examples of the number of instructions generated, depending on selected options:

```
05   DISP-1        PIC 999.
05   DISP-2        PIC S999.
05   DISP-3        PIC 999.
05   PACKED-1      PIC S9(15)    COMP-3.
05   PACKED-2      PIC S9(15)    COMP-3.
```

This table lists the number of instructions generated for each compile option for these example statements.

MIG	NO PFD	PFD	
3	3	2	MOVE DISP-1 TO DISP-2
2	3	2	MOVE DISP-2 TO DISP-1
2	2	2	MOVE DISP-1 TO DISP-3
4	6*	4	ADD 1 TO DISP-1
5	7*	5	ADD DISP-1 TO DISP-2
3	4*	3	COMPUTE PACKED-1 = PACKED-1 * PACKED-2

*Included a CALL to a COBOL II run-time subroutine for additional validation and adjustment.

The above table may indicate that MIG and PFD are alike because they generate the same number of instructions for these few examples. Don't assume that, as these examples demonstrate only a few situations, and the choice of these options also affects how conditional statements are processed (e.g., IF NUMERIC, IF POSITIVE). For information on that subject, see Handling Conditional Statements in this chapter.

Processing efficiency considerations with binary data. This was an easy decision with OS/VS COBOL because you had a compile option choice of TRUNC or NOTRUNC. With COBOL II, you can choose TRUNC(BIN), TRUNC(STD), or

TRUNC(OPT). One IBM manual states that TRUNC(BIN) is the equivalent of NOTRUNC. Another IBM manual states that TRUNC(OPT) is the equivalent of NOTRUNC. Unfortunately, both are correct. In OS/VS COBOL, NOTRUNC caused the data to be stored as a full or half-word (not truncated) and *also* generated the least amount of code.

In COBOL II, the process of generating the most efficient code and the process of not truncating data have been separated into two different compile options. If you use binary arithmetic for efficiency and do not have a concern for truncation, use TRUNC(OPT). If you use binary arithmetic to store the maximum number of bits in the half or full-word, use TRUNC(BIN). Here are some examples of the instructions generated for different options:

```
05  BIN-F1      PIC S9(9)   COMP.
05  BIN-F2      PIC S9(9)   COMP.
05  BIN-H1      PIC S9(4)   COMP.
05  BIN-H2      PIC S9(4)   COMP.
05  BIN-F3      PIC S9(6)   COMP.
05  BIN-F4      PIC S9(6)   COMP.
```

This table lists the number of instructions generated for each compile option for these example statements.

BIN	STD	OPT	
17	1	1	MOVE BIN-F1 TO BIN-F2
4	1	1	MOVE BIN-H1 TO BIN-H2
19	4	3	COMPUTE BIN-F1 = BIN-F1 * BIN-F2
19	6	3	COMPUTE BIN-H1 = BIN-H1 * BIN-H2
20	11	10	ADD BIN-F1 TO BIN-F2
7	6	3	ADD BIN-H1 TO BIN-H2
11*	4	3	COMPUTE BIN-F3 = BIN-F3 * BIN-F4

* The BIN option generated 11 instructions, plus a CALL to a COBOL II runtime subprogram for further data validity.

From the data in the table, there are clearly performance differences. If you rarely use COMP data, the choice of compile options for your applications may not be critical, but if your applications require COMP data, you should be sensitive to the performance implications.

Processing efficiency considerations for field sizes. When considering data efficiencies, we often think only of the arithmetic statements. Too often overlooked is the importance of field sizes where the MOVE instruction is used. For example, where the data types, sizes, and signs match, you will get more efficient data moves than when they are different. A small point, but significant if your application does a lot of MOVE instructions.

3.3.2. Coding Literals

Literals may be numeric, nonnumeric, or hexadecimal. I encourage removing as many literals from the procedural code as possible, except for simple situations such as where a zero or one is obvious (e.g., ... VARYING FROM 1 BY 1 UNTIL ...). Here is a brief summary of common literal usage:

Numeric literals.

Length from 1 to 18 decimal digits, sign is optional, as is a decimal point. Number is assumed positive if sign is omitted.

Nonnumeric literals.

Length from 1 to 160 bytes, any EBCDIC character combination, enclosed in quotes or apostrophes, depending on choice of APOST compile option. If a quote or apostrophe must appear within the literal, it must occur twice, as in

```
'DON''T GET CONFUSED'
```

Hexadecimal literals.

Length from 2 to 320 hexadecimal digits (1 to 160 bytes), enclosed in quotes/apostrophes (depending on choice of compile options) and preceded by X, as in:

```
X'C8C5E7'
```

which occupies 3 bytes and, in EBCDIC, is 'HEX'.

3.3.3. Defining a Table

If tables are new to you, read this section for basic information on tables and their structure. This topic will explain how to define a table in WORKING-STORAGE. You may have heard terms such as *two-dimensional, three-dimensional*, or even *four-dimensional*. Let's get those terms simplified. The dimensions for a table are the number of search arguments that must be used to get a result. We'll take several examples to demonstrate this.

One-dimensional tables.

A one-dimensional table consisting of a single element type is merely a list. If unordered, I call it a laundry list because the only way to find anything is to read each item. This approach is useful if you have data that must be validated, where the validation itself affects the logic. For example, if you know one of your company's products is legal in ten states and not legal in the other 40, then a purchase order from the other 40 states should not be processed. To validate purchase orders, a table such as this might be defined using these sample two-character state codes:

```
01  LEGAL-TABLE-ENTRIES.
    05    PIC X(22)
       VALUE 'ALAZCOFLIDKSMAMONYOHZZ'.
01  LEGAL-TABLE REDEFINES LEGAL-TABLE-ENTRIES.
    05  VALID-STATE  PIC XX, OCCURS 11.
```

or this:

```
01  LEGAL-TABLE-ENTRIES.
    05    PIC XX      VALUE 'AL'.
    05    PIC XX      VALUE 'AZ'.
    05    PIC XX      VALUE 'CO'.
    05    PIC XX      VALUE 'FL'.
    .
    .
    .
    05    PIC XX      VALUE 'ZZ'.
01  LEGAL-TABLE REDEFINES LEGAL-TABLE-ENTRIES.
    05  VALID-STATE   PIC XX, OCCURS 11.
```

Notice the redefinition does not need to follow the PIC clause format as long as it is faithful to the number of bytes represented. There is an eleventh entry here, ZZ (although any unique code would do). The purpose of including an extra entry for tables is to allow better procedural control. For example, a control field, such as ZZ, is for tables where the last entry can't be otherwise predicted or where the size of the table is subject to change frequently (in this example, for instance, the number of states in which the product is legal will probably change).

Another type of one-dimensional table contains multiple data element types, usually a search element and a data component. For example, an insurance company might have a table containing premium amounts by age. That could be shown

```
01  PREM-TABLE.
    05  PREM-ENTRY    OCCURS 99   TIMES
                                ASCENDING KEY IS PREM-AGE
                                INDEXED BY AGE-INDX.
        10 PREM-AGE            PIC 99.
        10 PREM-MALE           PIC S9(5)V99 COMP-3.
        10 PREM-FEMALE         PIC S9(5)V99 COMP-3.
```

This table has more depth and structure than the previous one. Also, where the previous table needed only to be searched for a match to make processing decisions, this table isn't so simple. Searching the table presents different amounts to charge for the insurance policy. The ASCENDING KEY clause specifies that this table must be in ascending order by age *if* a SEARCH statement is used to process against it (covered in Improving Table Searches). The INDEXED BY clause specifies an index-name (covered in the topic on subscripting). Searching the above table requires knowledge of one variable, age.

Two-dimensional tables.

A two-dimensional table is a one-dimensional table with an added dimension. Let's take the table in the previous topic and add a new dimension, a smoking/ nonsmoking premium. Searching this table will require two variables: age and smoker/nonsmoker status. Here is one way of constructing the table:

```
01   PREM-TABLE.
     05   PREM-ENTRY    OCCURS 99   TIMES
                                    ASCENDING KEY IS PREM-AGE
                                    INDEXED BY AGE-INDX.
          10   PREM-AGE          PIC 99.
          10   PREM-SMOKE-OPTION  OCCURS 2.
               15   PREM-MALE        PIC S9(5)V99   COMP-3.
               15   PREM-FEMALE      PIC S9(5)V99   COMP-3.
```

This structure gives us four premium amounts for each age: two for smokers (male and female) and two for nonsmokers. Whether adding an INDEXED BY clause for the smoking option will improve performance will be a topic addressed in Subscripting versus Indexing. Tables of any complexity are usually initialized by reading a file of data and inserting data elements in the appropriate table entry. The PERFORM VARYING statement is effective here. (See Section 3.3.7 for an example of a four-dimensional table.)

3.3.4.   Initializing a Table

Initializing a table can be done in a variety of ways, usually dependent on how frequently the data changes and how complex it is. Here are some examples:

Redefine the table and store variable data

```
01   LEGAL-TABLE-ENTRIES.
     05      PIC X(22)
        VALUE  'ALAZCOFLIDKSMAMONYOHZZ'.
01   LEGAL-TABLE REDEFINES LEGAL-TABLE-ENTRIES.
     05   VALID-STATE PIC XX, OCCURS 11.
```

Initialize the table to spaces or zeroes with VALUE clause

```
01   LEGAL-TABLE.
     05  VALID-STATE   PIC XX   OCCURS 11   VALUE SPACES.
```

This feature did NOT exist in OS/VS COBOL.

Initialize the table to spaces or zeros at run-time

```
INITIALIZE LEGAL-TABLE
```

Note: INITIALIZE was reviewed in Chapter 2. With one statement, you can reset a table.

Some programmers accomplish this by using something like this, which *should be avoided*:

```
PERFORM 3400-RESET-TABLE VARYING STATE-CODE FROM 1 BY
  1 UNTIL STATE-CODE > 11
  .
  .
  .

3400-RESET-TABLE.
     MOVE SPACES TO VALID-STATE (STATE-CODE).
```

This works, but it is unnecessary with COBOL II, it is inefficient, and it is clumsy to code.

Initialize the table with variable data from a file

```
PERFORM VARYING AGE-INDX FROM 1 BY 1 UNTIL EOF OR
  PREM-AGE (AGE-INDX - 1) = 99
    READ FD3-PREM-FILE
      AT END
          SET EOF TO TRUE
      NOT AT END
          MOVE FD3-PREM-AGE TO PREM-AGE (AGE-INDX)
          MOVE FD3-ML-PREM-SM TO PREM-MALE (AGE-INDX, 1)
          MOVE FD3-FM-PREM-SM TO PREM-FEMALE (AGE-INDX, 1)
          MOVE FD3-ML-PREM-NOSM TO PREM-MALE (AGE-INDX, 2)
          MOVE FD3-FM-PREM-NOSM TO PREM-FEMALE (AGE-INDX, 2)
    END-READ
END-PERFORM
```

This example assumes that each record on the file contains the four premiums for an age group. This is an example where an inline PERFORM can be effective because the logic is contained within a few eye scans and does one function.

3.3.5. Improving Table Searches

One of the problems with tables is that, as we become familiar with them, we forget that a lot of computer time is spent calculating addresses and making comparisons that prove false. For example, if a table is unordered, the only way to locate a valid entry is to start at the beginning and test each variable until the end of the table is reached or a match is found. If this is done rarely, it may not be worth the effort to improve the process. However, many tables are used frequently. Any steps that improve the process will reduce costs and resource use. Here are some options that can improve table searches:

Use SEARCH statement. The SEARCH statement has several benefits over the PERFORM VARYING. One, the SEARCH statement is complete, able to increment the subscript value, make the comparison, test for the end of the table, and execute valid conditions, all with a few lines of code. Each dimension in a table requires a separate SEARCH statement. The SEARCH statement isn't new with COBOL II, although many programmers have never used it. Also, the SEARCH statement requires that the table be defined with an INDEXED BY clause. This is advantageous since it relieves you from needing to specify it as you would with a PERFORM VARYING statement. Here are examples using basic syntax

A sequential search

```
SET AGE-INDX TO 1
SEARCH PREM-ENTRY
   AT END    SET AGE-ERROR TO TRUE
   WHEN PREM-AGE (AGE-INDX) = APP-AGE
      PERFORM 3300-EXTRACT-PREMIUMS
END-SEARCH
```

Equivalent code with the PERFORM would require

```
SET AGE-ERROR TO TRUE
PERFORM VARYING AGE-INDX FROM 1 BY 1 UNTIL
 AGE-INDX > 99
   IF PREM-AGE (AGE-INDX) = APP-AGE
      PERFORM 3300-EXTRACT-PREMIUMS
      SET AGE-INDX TO 99
      SET AGE-OKAY TO TRUE
   END-IF
END-PERFORM
```

The above SEARCH statement searches the table from beginning to end until the AT END condition is met or the WHEN condition is met (there can be multiple WHEN conditions). The PERFORM accomplishes this also, but requires several extra statements that may not appear obvious, and if omitted cause errors in processing.

A binary search

```
SEARCH ALL PREM-ENTRY
   AT END     SET AGE-ERROR TO TRUE
   WHEN PREM-AGE (AGE-INDX) = APP-AGE
      PERFORM 3300-EXTRACT-PREMIUMS
END-SEARCH
```

This format of SEARCH appears similar to the sequential SEARCH statement, but it is quite different. For one, it requires that the table entry have the ASCENDING/DESCENDING KEY clause specified and that the variable following WHEN be that data-name.

The benefit is increased processing speed for large tables. This is accomplished by a technique called a "binary search." To gain an appreciation of this technique, assume you have a table with 10,000 entries. Sequentially searching the table for a match would, on average, require about 5,000 comparisons per attempt. For example, if your match value were the 5,061st entry, the SEARCH (or PERFORM VARYING) would execute the comparison 5,061 times before finding the match. This is both expensive and time consuming. A binary search divides the remaining elements in half and checks for high or low. For the example mentioned, it would start at the 5,000th entry and test for high or low. Since ours is the 5,061st, it would test higher than the 5,000th entry. (Remember, the ASCENDING KEY or DESCENDING KEY is required for this option.) The logic would then split the remaining items and test the 7,500th entry. The process would continue, splitting and testing high or low until the 5,061st entry were matched.

While computers may use slightly different numbers, the example is still valid. The concept is to narrow the remaining entries, based on discoveries already made. In my theoretical example, the 5,061st entry is located on the 12th compare, not the 5,061st.

Since the SEARCH statement is dependent on indexes, you will want to check a later section, Subscripting versus Indexes.

Arrange tables by probability of occurrence. Sometimes you know that of all the possible entries in a table, the majority of matches will match to a subset of the table entries. In that case, you may want to use a sequential search and initialize the table with the most frequently used data elements at the beginning. For example, if you have 100 job titles in a human resources table, but 95% of the employees have the title "Programmer," it wouldn't make sense to do a binary search to locate job title. Put the Programmer job title as the first entry in the table and do a sequential search.

There is a drawback to this easy approach. Over time the most probable job title may change. If, in our example, the department were restructured and programmers were reclassified as "Programmer/analysts," the performance of the application would suffer until changes were made to the table.

Arrange tables for direct access. This technique can rarely be used, but for that reason it is often overlooked when it is the best approach. Consider the case in which you want to print the name of the month but only have the number of the month. I've actually seen people do this inefficient technique:

```
01   MONTH-CONTENTS.
     05          PIC X(10)   VALUE '01JANUARY'.
     05          PIC X(10)   VALUE '02FEBRUARY'.
     05          PIC X(10)   VALUE '03MARCH'.
     .
     .

01   MONTH-TABLE REDEFINES MONTH-CONTENTS.
     05  MONTH-ENTRIES    OCCURS 12
             ASCENDING KEY IS MONTH-CODE
             INDEXED BY MONTH-INX.
         10   MONTH-CODE PIC 99.
         10   MONTH-NAME PIC X(8).
     .
     .

     SET MONTH-INX TO 1
     SEARCH MONTH-ENTRIES
       AT END
          DISPLAY ' INVALID MONTH'
       WHEN MONTH-CODE (MONTH-INX) = REP-MONTH
          MOVE MONTH-NAME (MONTH-INX) TO REP-TITLE
     END-SEARCH
```

The above example works, but with much unnecessary processing. A better and much simpler approach is to acknowledge that the appearance of entries within the table corresponds to the search argument (e.g., the seventh entry in the table happens to represent the seventh month), which gives us this simple approach:

```
01   MONTH-CONTENTS.
     05          PIC X(8)   VALUE 'JANUARY'.
     05          PIC X(8)   VALUE 'FEBRUARY'.
     05          PIC X(8)   VALUE 'MARCH'.
     .
     .
```

```
01   MONTH-TABLE REDEFINES MONTH-CONTENTS.
     05   MONTH-NAME        PIC X(8) OCCURS 12.
        .
        .

     IF REP-MONTH > 0 AND < 13
         MOVE MONTH-NAME (REP-MONTH) TO REP-TITLE
     ELSE
         DISPLAY ' INVALID MONTH'
     END-IF
```

This is a case where indexes are not beneficial, since the entry within the table is extracted in one statement. More on this concept in the next topic.

3.3.6.   Subscripting versus Indexes with Tables

If you work with tables, you've probably encountered discussions on using indexes to subscript through tables versus not using them (not using indexes is generally called subscripting). First let's identify the issue. Each time you request access to a table element, the run-time code must calculate the location of the data. Consider the following data description:

```
01   MONTH-TABLE.
     05   MONTH-NAME  PIC X(8)   OCCURS 12.
```

If this statement is encountered,

```
MOVE MONTH-NAME (REP-MONTH) TO REP-TITLE
```

the compiler will generate appropriate code to take the value of REP-MONTH and compute how many bytes the proper data element is beyond the starting point of the table. For example, if REP-MONTH contained the value 07, the generated code would need to do the following (approximately):

- Convert REP-MONTH to COMP format, if necessary.
- Subtract 1 from the value (7 - 1 = 6).
- Multiply the value by the length of MONTH-NAME (8 * 6) to get the offset in the table.
- Add the result to the memory location of MONTH-TABLE.
- Store the value temporarily as a base address and execute the MOVE statement.

Now, the resulting object code from compiling that statement may not generate the code quite that way, but my intent is to demonstrate that some work is needed every time a table element's address must be calculated. All of the above must be done each time the contents of the search argument REP-MONTH is changed, whether subscripting or indexing is used. The difference is that with indexes the result is saved for future use. With subscripting, the calculations are repeated for every access where there is the possibility that the value has changed. (Note: this is dependent, but only to a degree, on the OPTIMIZE compile option.)

So, what are your choices? If the table is accessed only once for each change of the search argument, it makes no difference which method you use. This rarely occurs, however. Usually you will access the table several times before changing the search argument, meaning that indexes will serve you better than subscripts. An example in which the table search does not change for several statements follows:

```
IF MONTH-CODE (REP-MONTH) > 3 AND MONTH-CODE (REP-MONTH) < 7
    MOVE MONTH-TITLE (REP-MONTH) TO REP-TITLE
    MOVE '2ND QUARTER' TO PAGE-TITLE
END-IF
```

The above calculations would be done three times (once for the first comparison, again for the second comparison, and once again for the move) if REP-MONTH is not defined as an index. If REP-MONTH were an index, no computations would be needed since the offset would have been previously calculated. That can mean a lot to an application. (The OPTIMIZE compile option minimizes this, but the need to do a computation of some degree still remains when indexes are not used.)

The main issue, then, is how many statements are executed after changing the value of an index. Indexes can be changed by three statements: the SET statement, the SEARCH statement, and the PERFORM VARYING statement.

Together with the ASCENDING KEY and INDEXED BY clauses of the DATA DIVISION, this gives good documentation and efficiency to an application. If you haven't used these statements before, I believe you will find that they complement each other.

Finally, if you're absolutely, positively committed to using subscripts and avoiding indexes—for whatever reason—then at least define your subscripts as PIC S9(4) COMP. You will miss out on the power techniques described here, but your code will be more efficient than it would be otherwise.

3.3.7. Using Large Table Space as a Database

This is a simple technique that was introduced in the previous chapter. There are no special coding requirements other than some form of table management technique. The big change is that you may define an 01-level item up to 16 million bytes. For example, if you are processing a keyed VSAM file, it may be much quicker to load the database into a table and use the SEARCH ALL statement instead of reading randomly from DASD. The limits of 01-levels changed considerably from OS/VS COBOL, giving this capability. Such a technique should not be used for EXTERNAL items, since they are allocated below the 16-megabyte address (only if using COBOL II). The following section shows a potential approach to using a large table.

Four-dimensional tables.

This example is included to demonstrate that adding more dimensions doesn't necessarily increase complexity by a significant factor. The previous table has been expanded here to include premiums for more than one policy type (e.g., term, whole life, variable life) and to include different premiums for each of the 50 states. A little arithmetic will show that the table, instead of containing 198 premiums in our two-dimensional example, now has 198,000 different premiums. At first glance, it might appear that the logic to search out the right premium for an applicant might be much more difficult. It isn't.

```
01   PREM-TABLE.
     05   STATE-PREMS            OCCURS 50  TIMES
                                   ASCENDING KEY IS STATE-CODE
                                   INDEXED BY STATE-INDX.
          10   STATE-CODE        PIC XX.
          10   POLICY-TYPES      OCCURS 20  TIMES
                                   ASCENDING KEY IS POL-CODE
                                   INDEXED BY POL-INDX.
               15   POL-CODE     PIC 99.
               15   PREM-ENTRY   OCCURS 99  TIMES
                                   ASCENDING KEY IS PREM-AGE
                                   INDEXED BY AGE-INDX.
                    20   PREM-AGE            PIC 99.
                    20   PREM-SMOKE-OPTION   OCCURS 2.
                         25   PREM-MALE      PIC S9(5)V99  COMP-3.
                         25   PREM-FEMALE    PIC S9(5)V99  COMP-3.
```

In most situations, the state code may have already been set and the policy type may have been on the policy application form. In that example (assuming a premium for all ages from 1 to 99), if the code for smoker was 1, we could access the female premium for a nonsmoker with

```
MOVE PREM-FEMALE (STATE-INDX, POL-INDX, AGE, 2) TO PREM-AMT
```

The examples I will demonstrate to search such a table build on the examples already shown. Since a sequential search would be prohibitive for such a large table, we would probably (as already mentioned) already know the state and policy codes. Knowing that would eliminate completely the need to search the table if age were a direct one-for-one key in itself (i.e., age 29 would be the

29th entry, age 47 would be the 47th entry). While that should happen—and often does—making such assumptions defeats the reason you're reading this book, doesn't it? So, let's see how a binary search might work.

When doing a binary search on a large table, you need to know that the SEARCH statement can only act on one dimension. Since we must identify the state before we can locate the policy type, that dictates this order:

```
SEARCH ALL STATE-PREMS
    AT END SET NO-PREM-FOUND TO TRUE
    WHEN STATE-CODE (STATE-INDX) = APP-STATE
        SEARCH ALL POLICY-TYPES
            AT END SET NO-PREM-FOUND TO TRUE
            WHEN POL-CODE (STATE-INDX POL-INDX) = APP-POL-CODE
                SEARCH ALL PREM-ENTRY
                    AT END SET NO-PREM-FOUND TO TRUE
                    WHEN PREM-AGE (STATE-INDX POL-INDX AGE-INDX)
                        = APP-AGE
                        MOVE PREM-FEMALE (STATE-INDX, POL-INDX,
                            AGE-INDX, SMOKE-CODE) TO PREM-AMT
                END-SEARCH
        END-SEARCH
END-SEARCH
```

While this is a nice "textbook example," I encourage you to consider other options that may eliminate the need for parts of it. One consideration is that the input file with policy applications might already be in sequence by state or by policy type. In that situation, you wouldn't need the SEARCH statement for those components for each policy application but could do a SEARCH for state or policy type only when it changed. You could then precede a smaller SEARCH statement by using the SET statement to set the appropriate values in the other indexes.

NOTE: In this example about insurance premiums, you will normally not see explicit fields for female and male as I have shown. I placed them there to make the table more readable to those of you who have not worked with insurance systems. Instead, you would normally want to add an additional OCCURS (making this a five-dimension table). This would require that we use a predefined code, such as 1 for female and 2 for male, eliminating the need to search that dimension. That entry would look something like this:

```
20  PREM-SMOKE-OPTION  OCCURS 2.
    25  PREM-AMOUNT     OCCURS 2 PIC S9(5)V99 COMP-3.
```

The reason for eliminating a female/male distinction is for coding efficiency. The above SEARCH example was for a female applicant. Unless we add the fifth dimension, a duplicate SEARCH statement would be needed for male applicants. Duplicate code we don't need.

Loading such a table would be a slight modification of the PERFORM VARY-ING covered previously. It might look like this, assuming the premium file is already in sequence by age within policy type within state:

```
MOVE ALL '9' TO PREM-TABLE
PERFORM 2400-VARY-POLICY VARYING STATE-INDX FROM 1 BY 1
    UNTIL STATE-INDX > 50
      AFTER POL-INDX FROM 1 BY 1 UNTIL POL-INDX > 20
      AFTER AGE-INDX FROM 1 BY 1 UNTIL AGE-INDX > 99
    .
    .
2400-VARY-POLICY.
    READ FD3-PREM-FILE
      AT END
          SET STATE-INDX TO 50
          SET POL-INDX TO 20
          SET AGE-INDX TO 99
      NOT AT END
          EVALUATE TRUE
              WHEN FD3-POL-CODE = 99
                  SET POL-INDX TO 20
                  SET AGE-INDX TO 99
              WHEN FD3-PREM-AGE = 99
                  SET AGE-INDX TO 99
              WHEN OTHER
                  MOVE FD3-STATE-CODE TO
                    STATE-CODE (STATE-INDX)
                  MOVE FD3-POL-CODE TO
                    POL-CODE (STATE-INDX POL-INDX)
                  MOVE FD3-PREM-AGE TO
                    PREM-AGE (STATE-INDX POL-INDX
                    AGE-INDX)
                  MOVE FD3-ML-PREM-SM TO
                    PREM-MALE (STATE-INDX POL-INDX
                    AGE-INDX, 1)
                  MOVE FD3-FM-PREM-SM TO
                    PREM-FEMALE (STATE-INDX POL-INDX
                    AGE-INDX, 1)
                  MOVE FD3-ML-PREM-NOSM TO
                    PREM-MALE (STATE-INDX POL-INDX
                    AGE-INDX, 2)
                  MOVE FD3-FM-PREM-NOSM TO
                    PREM-FEMALE (STATE-INDX POL-INDX
                    AGE-INDX, 2)
          END-EVALUATE
    END-READ.
```

This PERFORM VARYING is similar to the previous one and, for consistency, I kept the same assumptions, that one record from the premium file contained all premiums for one premium category (and in this case, state, policy type, age). The major difference is that, for this example, I assume that there may not be premiums for all states, all policy types, or all ages. In real situations, that is probably true.

For clarity, I also assume here that no policy is sold at age 99. Now, by first initializing the table to all 9s (the INITIALIZE statement could have done it, but a REDEFINES would have been necessary), the EVALUATE statement triggers the end of a policy type or age category when 99 is encountered. (The code 99 would have been programmatically set when the file was created.) In case it isn't obvious, the reason the table here is initialized to 9s is to support the binary search technique. Since my sample logic allows for less than a complete table, I can't afford to make assumptions about noninitialized areas.

If you read the code carefully, you will notice that I initialize the STATE-CODE table entry repeatedly, once for each premium age category. That is also true for POL-CODE. So, why am I doing this repeatedly? Because it's much simpler than writing the complex code required to only set STATE-CODE when the state value changes and to set POL-CODE when that value changes. Doing so would have required three (3) nested PERFORM VARYING statements, something I didn't want to do.

The table shown here is just under two million bytes, something not seen prior to COBOL II or COBOL/370. That's also why you rarely see such examples of the SEARCH or PERFORM statements. Furthermore, tables of this size, combined with use of GLOBAL or EXTERNAL or POINTER elements, would allow a wide number of programs to access this in-memory database concurrently without need of duplication.

3.3.8. Using STRING and UNSTRING

The STRING and UNSTRING statements have been available for almost 20 years, yet many programmers have never used them. Some of the reasons for that:

- They're taught in few training courses.
- They weren't allowed in previous versions of CICS and IMS.
- Being string-oriented, they require that a different perspective be used when programming.

My intent in including these here is not to cover all their possibilities, but to demonstrate some basic examples for those of you who have never used these statements. Earlier in the book, I indicated that I had no intention of explaining basic COBOL statements, preferring instead to explain techniques to write better programs. I decided to include this basic information on STRING and UN-STRING only after encountering many experienced programmers who are looking for help in using them. First, let's cover the concepts.

What makes the STRING and UNSTRING statements different from most other COBOL statements is that they operate on data one byte at a time, often based on content rather than a PIC clause, whereas other statements (such as MOVE) operate on a complete data field. To understand how a MOVE statement works only requires that you understand the PIC clauses of the data fields, plus be aware of the basic requirement of the MOVE instruction. With STRING and UNSTRING, you must also visualize the data itself. Now, let's review the statements. For the complete syntax for each, see Chapter 7.

STRING statement.

The STRING statement moves data from one or more fields to a single receiving field, one byte at a time. The move ends when the receiving field is full (setting the OVERFLOW condition) or there is no more data to move. Any remaining positions in the receiving field retain their previous value (i.e., the remainder of the field is not set to spaces). All data fields must be DISPLAY. Any literals used must be alphanumeric.

The DELIMITED BY clause specifies under what conditions the movement of data ceases. The DELIMITED BY SIZE causes an entire field to be moved. The DELIMITED BY literal/identifier causes each byte (or bytes) to be compared to the literal or contents of the identifier. If the two items do not match, the movement of bytes continues. If the two items do match, movement from that field ceases and the STRING command continues to the next sending field, if any. (*NOTE:* The delimiter value is never moved.) Here are some examples:

```
05  FIELD-1  PIC X(4)   VALUE 'A-BC'.
05  FIELD-2  PIC X(2)   VALUE 'DE'.
05  FIELD-3  PIC X(2)   VALUE 'HI'.
05  FIELD-4  PIC X(4)   VALUE 'JKLM'.
05  FIELD-5  PIC X(4)   VALUE 'NO*P'.
05  FIELD-6  PIC X(1)   VALUE '*'.
05  FIELD-7  PIC X(15)  VALUE '123456789012345'.
05  FIELD-8  PIC S9(4)  COMP.
05  FIELD-A  PIC S9(4)  COMP.
05  FIELD-B  PIC S9(4)  COMP.
05  FIELD-C  PIC S9(4)  COMP.

STRING FIELD-1 FIELD-2 DELIMITED BY '-'
       FIELD-3 FIELD-4 DELIMITED BY SIZE
       FIELD-5 DELIMITED BY FIELD-6
       INTO FIELD-7
```

In this example, the "A" in FIELD-1 will be moved, but the remainder of FIELD-1 will be bypassed because the second character matches the delimiter. All of FIELD-2 is moved because the delimiter was not found. All of FIELD-3 and FIELD-4 are moved because the delimiter is field SIZE. Finally, the first two characters of FIELD-5 are moved, as the third character matches the value specified in FIELD-6. That leaves FIELD-7 (the receiving field) with this value after the STRING is executed: "ADEHIJKLMNO2345".

The delimiter field, FIELD-6, was a single byte. That is typical, but is not a requirement, as the delimiter identifier (or literal) can be several bytes, if needed. For example, if we used DELIMITED BY '***' in a STRING command, there would need to be three consecutive asterisks in a field to delimit the string operation.

Throughout the STRING operation, a pointer field is maintained to keep track of the next available byte within the receiving field. In the prior example, the value would have been 12, since 11 bytes were moved. This internal pointer is maintained by the object code and is not available to your program. If, for some reason, you want to know the next available byte after the STRING operation (or you want to start the STRING operation at other than the first byte of the receiving field), you may specify your own pointer. Let's modify the previous example slightly to demonstrate this.

```
MOVE 2 TO FIELD-8
STRING FIELD-1 FIELD-2 DELIMITED BY '-'
       FIELD-3 FIELD-4 DELIMITED BY SIZE
       FIELD-5 DELIMITED BY FIELD-6
       INTO FIELD-7 POINTER FIELD-8
```

In this example, we are specifying that the STRING is to begin on the second byte. We caused this to happen by including a POINTER reference and setting it to the desired start byte (the value must not be set to less than 1 or greater than the size of the receiving field and that sets the OVERFLOW condition). This would have caused FIELD-7 to contain this value after the execution: "1A DEHIJKLMNO345". In this example, the POINTER field does not need to be COMP. I prefer it here because, if I specified COMP-3 or DISPLAY, the generated object code would convert it to COMP, anyway. This just makes it more efficient.

After the STRING operation, FIELD-8 contains 13, the location of the next available byte in the receiving field. This can be useful if you have additional STRING commands to execute against the same receiving field or if you want to use reference modification with that field. The STRING command, combined with the reference modification feature that was first introduced with COBOL II, gives you byte-manipulation capabilities that are yet to be fully explored. We are so field-oriented that the opportunities are just beginning to emerge.

Okay, so the examples may not have demonstrated typical uses of the STRING statement, my intent being to show its mechanics. Here is an example of setting a date field, where the receiving field is 8 bytes and each of the sending fields (for month, day, and year) are 2 bytes each:

```
STRING MONTH-FLD '/' DAY-FLD '/' YEAR-FLD DELIMITED BY SIZE
    INTO DATE-FIELD
```

Another possibility occurs when you have fields with an unknown number of spaces, yet you want the field contents to appear close together. An example of this would be printing a list of names so the first and last names are separated by a single space. Without the STRING command, such listings often look something like this:

```
Jane           Doe

William        Randolph
```

With this command:

```
STRING FIRST-NAME DELIMITED BY ' ',
        ' ' LAST-NAME DELIMITED BY SIZE
        INTO FULL-NAME
```

we generate data that looks like this:

```
Jane Doe
William Randolph
```

This topic only touched on the capabilities of the STRING statement, but it is probably sufficient for you to try it out. Go ahead. Just do it.

UNSTRING statement.

If you're thinking, "Well, the UNSTRING statement must be the reverse of the STRING statement," you are correct. Knowing one makes it easier to grasp the other, although they are generally used in different situations. I have known programmers who have used STRING for years, yet never had occasion to use UN-STRING. This happens because the STRING statement is generally used against data fields that have already been exposed to some degree of validation, such as the previous example of stringing month, day, and year. With UNSTRING, the program is often processing free-form data that has yet to be validated.

Also, thinking in reverse requires some practice. For example, the POINTER referred to the receiving field with STRING, but it refers to the sending field with UNSTRING. Likewise, while STRING was moving data, byte-by-byte, into a receiving field, leaving remaining bytes unmodified, the UNSTRING's purpose is to move data into valid data fields. Therefore, with UNSTRING, receiving fields are treated as receiving fields of an elementary MOVE statement.

The UNSTRING statement is normally used to parse data strings that are entered in a free-form format. An example might be a "user friendly" transaction that lets a terminal user enter a person's first name and last name in a single field. Transferring the first name to one data field and the last name to a separate data field is an ideal example of where UNSTRING can be helpful.

As with the STRING statement, UNSTRING moves data, one byte at a time, until either the receiving field is filled, the sending field is exhausted, or a delimiting value appears in the sending field. A special concern of using UNSTRING is determining how many occurrences of a delimiter are to be acknowledged. For example, let's assume, from our example above, that a person at a terminal enters this value (where b represents a space):

```
JANEbbDOEbbbbbbbbb
```

If we use the following command, it will cause a problem:

```
UNSTRING FULL-NAME DELIMITED BY 'b'
         INTO FIRST-NAME LAST-NAME
```

This happens because the first appearance of a space caused "Jane" to be stored properly in FIRST-NAME. That's when it gets sticky. The UNSTRING command continues with the next position after the delimiter and finds another space. Since it is now filling the LAST-NAME field, the UNSTRING assumes no data is to be stored there. This raises the ON OVERFLOW condition, since there are still remaining characters in the FULL-NAME field. We can correct the statement by adding ALL to the DELIMITED BY clause. This causes all contiguous appearances of a delimit character to be treated as a single delimiter. Let's go a step further in this example. If we, by experience, had found that the persons entering data into the terminals sometimes entered a period by habit, we would want the period to also be a delimiter. That modifies our example as follows:

```
UNSTRING FULL-NAME DELIMITED BY ALL 'b' OR ALL '.'
         INTO FIRST-NAME LAST-NAME
```

This is a definite improvement. Now, we will properly capture entries such as:

```
JANEbDOEb        JANEbbbbDOEb        JANEbDOE.b    JANE.DOEb
```

By now, you're possibly thinking, "What if a middle initial had been entered, messing up the logic?" Good question. We still have some work to do, don't we? UNSTRING provides a clause, COUNT IN. This is used to capture the number of bytes stored in a respective field. Now let's try it:

```
UNSTRING FULL-NAME DELIMITED BY '.b' OR ALL 'b' OR ALL '.'
          INTO FIRST-NAME COUNT IN FIELD-A
               MIDDLE-NME COUNT IN FIELD-B
               LAST-NAME COUNT IN FIELD-C
     ON OVERFLOW
          PERFORM routine for too many names entered
END-UNSTRING
EVALUATE TRUE
     WHEN FIELD-A = 0  PERFORM routine for no data entered
     WHEN FIELD-B = 0  PERFORM routine for only first name
                                found
     WHEN FIELD-C = 0
          MOVE MIDDLE-NME TO LAST-NAME
          MOVE ' ' TO MIDDLE-NME
END-EVALUATE
```

Depending on your processing requirements, here is an alternative approach that produces the same solution. In this example, I included the TALLYING IN clause, which references an elementary numeric item. The use of COUNT IN was omitted only because it isn't needed with this example, although you may use both COUNT IN and TALLYING IN, if desired. Notice that the TALLYING IN data item must be initialized prior to the UNSTRING operation.

```
MOVE 0 TO FIELD-8
UNSTRING FULL-NAME DELIMITED BY  '.b' OR ALL 'b' OR ALL '.'
          INTO FIRST-NAME
               MIDDLE-NME
               LAST-NAME
          TALLYING IN FIELD-8
     ON OVERFLOW
          PERFORM routine for too many names entered
END-UNSTRING
EVALUATE FIELD-1
     WHEN  0  PERFORM routine for no data entered
     WHEN  1  PERFORM routine for only first name found
     WHEN  2
          MOVE MIDDLE-NME TO LAST-NAME
          MOVE ' ' TO MIDDLE-NME
END-EVALUATE
```

Now we're cookin'. There are still more possibilities to address, such as titles, persons with four names, and so forth, but you get the idea. (The delimiter of '.b' was added because this is a common combination and we needed to ensure that it was treated as one delimiter, not as two.) I included the ON OVERFLOW only as an example. In this case, the overflow condition would be set if there were more than three names entered OR if the names were longer than anticipated. The above two examples let us capture more name formats, including the following:

```
JANEbDOEb  JANEbM.DOEb  JANEbM.bDOEb  JANE.M.DOEb  JANEbbDOEb
J.DOEb  J.M.DOEb  JANEbMARIEbDOEb  J.MARIEbDOEb  JbDOEb
```

This could still use improvement, but our users will applaud us for making the entry of a person's name this flexible. Neat, huh? There are more possibilities with UNSTRING, but I'm confident that, if you have never used it before, this is sufficient for you to add it to your inventory of COBOL statements. I'll call that a success.

3.4. HANDLING CONDITIONAL STATEMENTS

With COBOL II, you need to be sensitive to a few changes in conditional statements. While these differences appear elsewhere, they are summarized here for ease of access.

3.4.1. ALPHANUMERIC Tests

In OS/VS COBOL you could code IF ALPHABETIC and know you were testing for upper-case alphabetic characters. In COBOL II you must use IF ALPHABETIC-UPPER for the same results. IF ALPHABETIC still works, but it accepts both upper- and lower-case text as valid.

3.4.2. NUMERIC Tests

IF NUMERIC works the same for most situations. The difference depends on your choice of the compiler NUMPROC option. Here is an example of where the difference lies:

```
05 DATA-FLD PIC S999.
   IF DATA-FLD NUMERIC
```

will be true with all options if DATA-FLD contains a signed, positive or negative, number. That means the sign would be either "C" or "D". If DATA-FLD contains an unsigned value (sign of "F"), the test will be true for NUMPROC(MIG) and NUMPROC(NOPFD), but it will fail for NUMPROC(PFD). These same considerations should also be used when using the IF POSITIVE, ZERO, or NEGATIVE tests. (See Efficiencies in Data Definitions for more information.)

If you define data elements with the "S" (e.g., PIC S999), regardless of whether you anticipate a sign, you may want to use the NUMPROC(MIG) option to maintain compatibility with that coding technique.

3.5.   MAKING A PROGRAM MORE EFFICIENT

Making a program more efficient can be tough work, especially if major flaws exist in the design or if the program is already written. This section summarizes various techniques that can improve a program's performance, but none of these techniques go beyond COBOL (that is, if the file is poorly structured or if the logic flow is inefficient, you'll need more than some performance tuning to resolve the problem). Several of these topics will refer you to other topics for more information.

3.5.1.   File Blocking in QSAM

I'm still amazed at how this old-fashioned technique is ignored in many applications. Increasing the block size of a sequential file reduces the number of physical I/O requests that must occur, thereby reducing the elapsed time and cost of a program. Years ago many shops had standard guidelines such as "always block by 10." That may have been good advice in the early 1970s but no longer. A programmer doing small tests will not see the difference, but a full-scale productional run can be significantly affected. Since the maximum allowed in QSAM is 32,760 bytes, I recommend you use a block size as near to that as possible. If your DASD is larger than that (e.g., 3380s), use a block size that is slightly smaller than 1/2 the track size. Let's see an example:

Assuming you are using IBM 3380 DASD drives, the particulars are

```
Bytes per track:  47,476
Tracks per cylinder: 15
```

For this example, let's assume you have a record size of 376. Optimum blocking would be 32,712 (87 * 376), since this would give you 87 logical records processed for each READ or WRITE. Unfortunately, that leaves 14,764 bytes unused per track (47,476 - 32,712), or a wastage of 31 percent. That gives optimum I/O, but it compromises DASD usage. Let's try figuring nearer to half a track, 23,238 bytes [(47476 − 1000) ÷ 2]. By using slightly less than half the track, we can still get a good block size of 22,936 (61 * 376) and 61 logical records per block. Since 22,936 is less than half the size of the track, we get two blocks per track for a total track usage of 45,872 bytes (22,936 * 2). This is still an excellent block size and the DASD wastage is less than 4 percent, a significant improvement. (Note: Save your valuable time. IBM sells reference cards for their equipment so you don't need to do arithmetic. The card for the model 3380 is order number GX26-1678 and costs less than a dollar. The model 3390 reference is GX26-4577.

The FD needs the clause

```
BLOCK CONTAINS 0 RECORDS
```

The JCL DD statement (output ONLY) needs the clause

```
DCB=BLKSIZE=22936
```

You will further improve I/O for QSAM files on DASD by allocating in CYL-INDERS instead of TRACKS. While too deep for this book, this allocation causes fewer rotations of the DASD to transfer the file.

3.5.2. Data Formats

This subject is covered earlier in Efficiencies in Data Definitions. Here are my general guidelines:

- Always use packed-decimal for computational fields.
- Always specify an odd number of digits for the PIC clause.
- Always specify the sign in the PIC clause for computational fields.
- Always use indexes for tables. (If you refuse to accept my earlier arguments about indexes, then at least use COMP items for subscripts to minimize the inefficiencies.)
- Use COMP every time it is specified in an application or IBM documentation, since that normally means that either MVS or an application program expects it (but be careful of misuse of the SYNC clause, as that forces boundary alignment that may change desired record alignment).

If you're skeptical about guidelines beginning with the word Always, so am I. Even so, by following simple guidelines, I can concentrate on the programming assignment at hand instead of worrying about minor differences in performance. If you're convinced that binary arithmetic (COMP) is superior, review the earlier topic, Efficiencies in Data Definitions.

3.5.3. COMPUTE Statement

Years ago, I was advised to avoid the COMPUTE statement because it was inefficient. In hindsight, I was given poor advice. In test after test, the COMPUTE statement has been at least as efficient as other instructions, whether replacing a simple ADD with COMPUTE X = X + 1 or something more complex. The additional advantage of COBOL II is that, with OPTIMIZE specified, the compiler looks for sequences of arithmetic and saves those intermediate values for use later. The sequences can either begin the computation or be bound in parentheses to ensure they are identified. This can often create what appears to be amazing efficiency on a statement-by-statement basis. Consider this example:

```
COMPUTE A = A * (B / C)
    .

    .
COMPUTE Z = F * G + (B / C)
    .

    .
COMPUTE E = B / C
```

In all three statements, there is the sequence B / C. If the compiler determines the logic flow of the program cannot change the values of B and C between any two of the three statements, it saves the result of the division so it can be reused. In the last statement, for example, no division takes place. The generated machine code simply moves the result into field E.

While I encourage use of the COMPUTE statement, you need to be sensitive to the possibility of incurring large intermediate values that exceed machine capacity (see Chapter 7 for more information on machine capacities). As a general guideline, you can add the 9s in the PIC clauses to determine the largest intermediate value for multiplication or division. For example,

```
05  A   PIC  S9(15)   COMP-3.
05  B   PIC  S9(15)   COMP-3.
05  C   PIC  S9(15)   COMP-3.
05  D   PIC  S9(15)   COMP-3.
    .

    .
    COMPUTE A = A * B
```

will have an intermediate result of 30 digits (15 + 15), which is within the machine capacity for packed-decimal arithmetic. The generated machine code (using LIST compile option) would look something like this:

```
Assembler instructions          Compiler comments

ZAP    376(16,13),19(8,9)       TS2=0         B
MP     376(16,13),11(8,9)       TS2=0         A
ZAP    11(8,9),384(8,13)        A             TS2=8
```

You don't need to know assembler language to understand that this represents three instructions. The first one moves B to a temporary work area, the second multiplies the temporary work area by A, and the third moves the result to A. Very efficient. Now let's look at a different example:

```
    COMPUTE A = A * B * C * D
```

This will have an intermediate result of 60 digits (15 + 15 + 15 + 15). Since this number is too large for the machine, extra code must be generated to programmatically extend and validate the intermediate values. Explaining the generated assembler code is too complex for this book, but I show it here to highlight what pattern of assembly language indicates less efficient code (again, using the LIST compile option):

```
Assembler instructions              Compiler comments

        ZAP   360(16,13),11(8,9)    TS1=0          A
        MP    360(16,13),19(8,9)    TS1=0          B
        ZAP   376(16,13),19(8,9)    TS2=0          C
        L     2,92(0,13)            TGTFIXD+92
        L     15,188(0,2)           V(IGZCXMU)
        LA    1,782(0,10)           PGMLIT AT +766
        BALR  14,15
        CLC   401(8,13),0(12)       TS2=25         SYSLIT AT +0
        BC    2,484(0,11)           GN=13(0005E4)
        BC    15,494(0,11)          GN=14(0005EE)
GN=13   EQU   *
        L     15,460(0,2)           V(IGZEMSG)
        LA    1,754(0,10)           PGMLIT AT +738
        BALR  14,15
GN=14   EQU   *
        MVC   360(16,13),408(13)    TS1=0          TS2=32
        NI    360(13),X'0F'         TS1=0
        ZAP   376(16,13),27(8,9)    TS2=0          D
        L     15,188(0,2)           V(IGZCXMU)
        LA    1,782(0,10)           PGMLIT AT +766
        BALR  14,15
        ZAP   11(8,9),416(8,13)     A              TS2=40
```

First, instead of three instructions, you generate 20. However, that is just the visible portion. The highlighted instructions are the key to alert you to possible inefficiencies you may want to avoid. They represent the assembler language equivalent of CALL statements. The first is a CALL to module IGZCXMU, the second is a CALL to IGZEMSG, and the final CALL is to IGZCXMU again. While I have no idea how large those IBM-supplied programs are, I assure you they are each much larger than these 20 instructions. The guideline is not to look for these specific modules in arithmetic statements, but to watch for the pattern. (Note: You will see similar patterns in other, nonarithmetic instructions. In those instances, they are necessary for proper operation and may be ignored.) Whenever you have this pattern of instructions in COMPUTE statements and performance is important to you, consider using several COMPUTE statements, such as:

```
COMPUTE A = A * B
COMPUTE A = A * C
COMPUTE A = A * D
```

The preceding information is presented to sensitize you to possible inefficiencies. Yes, you can often avoid the appearance of these inefficiencies by coding many MULTIPLY and DIVIDE statements. They generate more code on average, however, since each MULTIPLY or DIVIDE statement edits and stores intermediate results, and they make the equation more difficult to read.

3.5.4. Compiler Options for Run-Time Efficiency

Some compile options have been discussed earlier in this section. This topic summarizes the impact on performance of various options and does not explain their functions in detail. A full discussion appears later in Specifying COBOL II Options.

Options that give maximum productional performance (some of them have implications on your data definitions):

Compile-time options

COBOL II and COBOL/370

OPTIMIZE
NUMPROC(PFD) or NUMPROC(MIG)
TRUNC(OPT)   (has potential implications for CICS,
                              IMS, & DB2)

NOSSRANGE
AWO
NODYNAM
FASTSRT
NOTEST

Run-time options

COBOL II		**COBOL/370**
NOAIXBLD	NOAIXBLD	DEBUG(OFF)
NOWSCLEAR	ALL31(ON)	RPTOPTS(OFF)
NOSSRANGE	CBLPSHPOP(OFF)	RPTSTG(OFF)
LIBKEEP	CHECK(OFF)	STORAGE(NONE, NONE,NONE)
		NOTEST

Compile options that generate maximum flexibility in the run-time environment, both for the application and for the computer:

COBOL II	**COBOL/370**
RESIDENT	RENT
RENT	DATA(31)
DATA(31)	

3.5.5. CALLs

A CALL statement generates a significant amount of executable code, often invisible. By invisible, I mean that the executed code is buried in the initialization code of the CALLed module, not in the CALLing module. Where a program is small (e.g., 50 statements or less), consider imbedding it in the parent program or using a nested structure, since either will minimize or eliminate some overhead code. If this isn't feasible, the most efficient CALL structure is the CALL BY REFERENCE format with the NODYNAM compile option. Don't worry about the GLOBAL and EXTERNAL options for data reference. Their use does not affect performance.

By including this information, I am not suggesting that you not use the CALL statement. I use it regularly. It has many benefits if a shop has reusable code or large applications. Just be aware that, of all statements, the CALL statement will normally execute the most overhead (nonproductive to the application logic) instructions.

3.5.6. SORTs

This chapter has a separate topic on SORT techniques and there is information on JCL for sorts further in this chapter. For a more thorough discussion, read those topics. What appears here is summary information.

First, assess your application data flow to see if the new sorted structure is needed in several places. If so, you will usually incur less cost by sorting the data once and saving to a permanent file, eliminating the need to resort the data later.

Second, consider using DFSORT to do the sort instead of COBOL. DFSORT is more efficient, and the control statements can be done in a matter of minutes, not hours or days. DFSORT is explained later in this chapter.

Third, never use the COBOL SORT statement format, SORT USING . . . GIVING . . . . Doing so accomplishes nothing that DFSORT could not do in less time with less coding and testing.

Fourth, consider using DFSORT control statements to replace an INPUT or OUTPUT PROCEDURE on those occasions where DFSORT cannot do all the necessary processing. This includes those situations in which an INPUT PROCEDURE is to do simple data selection and/or will reformat the data prior to sorting. This type of situation is much simpler to code with DFSORT control statements than by writing an INPUT PROCEDURE. (This technique has been available for years, yet many programmers are unaware of this possibility.) A program using this approach is in Chapter 8 (Sample Programs). See the section JCL Requirements for more information on the JCL for DFSORT and also see Chapters 5 and 6 for additional tips on sort applications.

Fifth, always use the FASTSRT compile option. If your SORT is anything other than SORT INPUT PROCEDURE . . . OUTPUT PROCEDURE . . ., you will receive improved performance.

3.5.7. SEARCH ALL

This is described previously in Improving Table Searches. If your application searches tables, see that topic. It explains and demonstrates the binary search process.

3.5.8. Indexes and Subscripts

This is described under Subscripting versus Indexes. If your application searches tables, see that topic. It explains and demonstrates the differences between use and nonuse of indexes to provide addressability to tables.

3.5.9. Data Structures and System Environments

There is no COBOL solution to this. I included the topic because you might be looking for a solution here. A poor data architecture can defeat the most well-written programs. Your data architecture should be designed prior to writing the programs that access them. If you believe your performance is being affected by poor data architecture or environmental considerations, see either your shop's data specialists about conducting a design review or your shop's technical staff to conduct performance monitoring of your application.

Some issues that may affect performance are mentioned below.

For VSAM files, check the control interval sizes, the free space allocations, alternate indexes, buffers, and keys. If you are using the defaults from Access Method Services, this should be investigated by a person familiar with VSAM. For more VSAM assistance, which is beyond the scope of this book, you might want another QED book, *VSAM: The Complete Guide to Optimization and Design* (See Chapter 9). That book addresses all issues that might affect VSAM performance.

For CICS applications, check your module structure, the number of EXEC LINK or EXEC XCTL commands that may occur within a transaction, and the number of I/O operations generated within a transaction. Converting LINKs to CALLs will improve performance significantly , as will minimizing the number of BROWSE operations. For more information on CICS that includes coding and tuning tips for COBOL II and COBOL/ 370, see another book of mine that is available from QED, *CICS: A How-to for COBOL Programmers*.

For IMS applications, review how often your logic makes a CALL to IMS (this is NOT the same as how many CALLs are in your program). By restructuring your SSAs (and your logic), you might be able to reduce the number of CALLs. Usually, simpler programs require more CALLs, while sophisticated programs require fewer CALLs. Thorough coverage is provided in a more appropriate QED book, *IMS Design and Implementation Techniques* (see Chapter 9). That text is appropriate not only for addressing performance issues, but also for its complete coverage of the IMS/VS environment.

For DB2 applications, I can only refer you to your shop's data specialists or to a couple of special interest QED publications in Chapter 9, *DB2 Design Review Guidelines*, and *DB2: Maximizing Performance of Online Production Systems*. As with the other books listed here, these focus on design and performance in mainframe applications, covering the full spectrum of the named system environments.

For information on developing a DB2 application with COBOL, see the QED book, *Embedded SQL for DB2: Application Design and Programming* (Chapter 9, Related Publications). While examples in that book use OS/VS COBOL, it complements this book by its coverage of building DB2/COBOL applications for MVS/XA or MVS/ESA environments.

Earlier in this book I mentioned that COBOL II is not just a language, but it is also an environment. By environment, I mean that it is involved not only with compilation, but also with execution. The other subjects mentioned in this topic are also full environments. While your COBOL II program is the heart of the application logic, how the program interacts within these other environments affects the quality, value, and performance of your applications.

3.6. MAKING A PROGRAM RESISTANT TO ERRORS

Is it really possible to make a program bullet proof? I don't think so, but I do know you can take steps to develop a program that will minimize ABENDs and other errors. In this topic, I have summarized various techniques that can help prevent an error.

3.6.1. FILE STATUS

If you use VSAM files, this technique is old hat to you, but what about those QSAM files? COBOL II provides special services to QSAM files that use the FILE

STATUS clause in the SELECT statement. For one, the program does not ABEND (honest!) even if the DD statement is absent. Of course, your program is expected to check the file status after each I/O to determine status and take appropriate action (e.g., after detecting that a file did not OPEN properly, your logic should ensure that no READ or WRITE went to that file). For file status codes, see Chapter 7. Here is a simple example showing the fundamentals (highlighted) to improve QSAM file integrity (some parts of the program are omitted). This example assumes that the absence of the file is acceptable (e.g., a file that is not always present). For that reason, the word OPTIONAL appears in the SELECT statement, although it is primarily to indicate that absence of the DD is anticipated. OPTIONAL also causes the status code to be different and supports CLOSE processing.

```
INPUT-OUTPUT SECTION.
FILE-CONTROL.
     SELECT OPTIONAL FD1-WEEKLY
        ASSIGN TO INPDD  FILE STATUS IS WS1-FD1-STAT.
DATA DIVISION.
FILE SECTION.
FD   FD1-WEEKLY
     BLOCK CONTAINS 0 RECORDS
     RECORDING MODE IS F
     RECORD CONTAINS 100 CHARACTERS.
     .
     .
WORKING-STORAGE SECTION.
01   WS1-FD1-STATUS.
     05   WS1-FD1-REC-CT    PIC S9(4)  COMP  VALUE 0.
     05   WS1-FD1-STAT      PIC XX.
     05   WS1-FD1-EOF-SW    PIC X              VALUE 'N'.
          88 FD1-EOF                           VALUE 'Y'.
     .
     .
PROCEDURE DIVISION.
1.   PERFORM 1000-INITIALIZE
     PERFORM 2000-PROCESS UNTIL FD1-EOF
     PERFORM 3000-WRAPUP
     IF RETURN-CODE > 15
         DISPLAY 'SERIOUS I/O ERROR ON FD1'
     END-IF
     STOP RUN.

 1000-INITIALIZE.
     OPEN INPUT FD1-WEEKLY
     IF WS1-FD1-STAT NE '00'
         SET FD1-EOF TO TRUE
```

```
        END-IF
        .

        .

2000-PROCESS.
    PERFORM 2100-READ
    IF WS1-FD1-EOF-SW  = 'N'
        .

        .              process the data record here
        .
2100-READ.
    READ FD1-WEEKLY
      AT END
          SET FD1-EOF TO TRUE
      NOT AT END
          IF WS1-FD1-STAT NE '00'
              SET FD1-EOF TO TRUE
              MOVE 16 TO RETURN-CODE
              DISPLAY 'FD1-WEEKLY I/O STAT ' WS1-FD1-STAT
          END-IF
END-READ.
```

In this example, notice that if an OPEN error occurs, the READ statement is not executed. This allows for different settings of the RETURN-CODE: 4 meaning that the weekly file was not present, and 16 meaning that it was present but an I/O error occurred.

3.6.2.   ON SIZE ERROR

There is nothing new here with COBOL II, just an old standby that is rarely used. If your applications could conceivably cause an overflow or divide by zero, this should be considered.

3.6.3.   PARM Processing

Validating PARM lengths was discussed earlier under the section on module structures. For more information, see that section.

3.6.4.   CALL Statement (LENGTH OF, ON EXCEPTION, and BY CONTENT)

These are all new features of COBOL II. The LENGTH OF clause lets a CALLed program validate the anticipated length of the passed data. The ON EXCEPTION clause is good for DYNAMically CALLed module structures, allowing you to prevent 806 or 80A ABENDs.

The BY CONTENT clause has some performance implications, but could be advantageous if your program CALLs other programs that need data from your program but are not to modify it. This not only protects your data, but it also prevents a CALLed program from inadvertently overwriting parts of your program through addressability to your DATA DIVISION.

All of these options of the CALL statement are explained in Chapter 2 and in this chapter under the section, Module Structures.

3.6.5. Data Validation

The 0C4, 0C7, 0C9, and 0CB ABENDs are probably the most familiar ABENDs in all shops, yet they can usually be prevented. Let's take them separately.

0C4 This ABEND is usually caused by a runaway subscript or index attempting to access unallocated memory. While it can occur for other reasons, the majority of programs ABENDing with 0C4 have an OCCURS clause. ABENDing can be prevented by testing the range of the subscript prior to use. Program testing can be supplemented by the SSRANGE compile option.

0C7 This ABEND is caused by using nonnumeric data in an arithmetic statement, which can be prevented by using the IF NUMERIC test. (See earlier topic, Data definitions, for implications of NUMPROC compile option.) Don't attempt to do your own range test for these two reasons:

1. If the field is PIC 99, you could get an 0C7 in your attempt to prevent one. This occurs because the generated code converts the data to numeric format and then compares it to other numeric values.
2. If the field is PIC XX, you could be accidentally "approving" nonnumeric data, getting an 0C7 anyway. Consider the following:

```
05   DATA-ITM PIC 999.
05   NEW-DATA-ITM REDEFINES DATA-ITM PIC XXX.

     IF NEW-DATA-ITM > '000' AND < '100'
        ADD DATA-ITM TO ...
```

In this innocent example, you need to be familiar with the EBCDIC collating sequence (Chapter 7). If you check it, you will find that "01 " (a zero, a one and a space) are between "000" and "100." In fact, quite a number of nonnumeric values are in that range (e.g., "03<") and several could cause the ADD statement to cause an 0C7 ABEND.

0C9 and 0CB These are, in fact, the same ABEND, a divide by zero. One is packed-decimal and the other is binary. It can be detected by an ON SIZE ERROR clause or by validating the divisor before the DIVIDE statement.

3.6.6. COPYbooks

The more data definitions, file definitions, common procedural statements, and program-to-program interfaces you put in COPYbooks, the less exposed you will be to programming errors. If you give the same programming specifications to 20 programmers, expect at least one of them to make a simple error that affects processing or ABENDs the program.

COPYbooks will not only reduce your exposure to misinterpretations, but they will also improve overall program documentation and communications among a project team.

Now that I've mentioned the positive aspects of COPYbooks, let me remind you of the downside impact as well. COPYbooks are at their best when defining data structures that are file-dependent, such as file record descriptions. However, when COPYbooks are used to establish generic work areas and 88-levels used across a broad band of programs, the problems outweigh the benefits. For example, a COPYbook established to contain valid codes for all corporate department codes creates havoc whenever any changes are needed.

Consider the maintenance programmer who, when asked to simply add a new department code, finds that 300+ programs use the COPYbook and all of them must be recompiled and retested. This is a gross misuse of COPYbooks, causing extensive testing and coordination efforts that are not justified. If your shop uses COPYbooks for documenting such generic codes, I recommend that you make an effort to persuade your management that your company would be better served by storing such data in files, *not* in COPYbooks.

3.6.7. RETURN-CODE Tests

While reviewed earlier in the section, Module Structures, RETURN-CODE is another technique to improve resistance to error. Anytime you CALL a program or PERFORM a paragraph that could have conditional outcome, ensure the program specifications include a status code to be returned. Doing so improves readability of the program, improves communication between the two modules, and provides incentive for the person writing the CALLed or PERFORMed code not to use a GO TO or issue an intentional ABEND. (The mechanics of issuing an intentional ABEND were covered in the topic Terminating a Program/Module, also in this chapter).

3.7. VSAM TECHNIQUES

This is *not* a treatment on VSAM programming techniques but a summary of new facilities available to you in COBOL II. COBOL II does not change the way VSAM files are handled, and all of these changes appear in various places in Chapter 2. They are here for a quick reference.

First, COBOL II provides a VSAM status code field to allow you to interrogate status codes from Access Method Services. Those codes are defined in the appropriate *VSAM Macro Instruction Reference* manual. (See Chapter 9 for the specific manual for your shop.) This is in addition to the standard file status field. (See chapter 7 for file status codes.) An example of a VSAM SELECT statement follows:

```
SELECT FD2-MASTER
    ASSIGN TO MASTDD
    ORGANIZATION IS INDEXED
    RECORD KEY IS FD2-KEY
    FILE STATUS IS WS1-FD2-STATUS
      WS1-FD2-VSAM-STAT.
    .
    .
    .
    05  WS1-FD2-VSAM-STAT          COMP.
        10   STAT-RETURN-CODE      PIC 99.
        10   STAT-FUNCTION-CODE    PIC 99.
        10   STAT-FEEDBACK-CODE    PIC 99.
```

These data elements may be checked in addition to the normal FILE STATUS field. Notice that the VSAM status field is the second named field in the FILE STATUS clause. The FD for a VSAM file need be only

```
FD   file-name
     RECORD CONTAINS nn CHARACTERS.
```

In the above FD, the RECORD CONTAINS clause is optional. I suggest using it, primarily for its documentation function.

Another new feature from COBOL II that could affect VSAM processing is the addition of NOT AT END and NOT INVALID KEY to the I/O statements. These are explained under the topic Scope Terminators in Chapter 2.

The final new technique available to the COBOL II programmer is that the START statement now has an additional option for the KEY clause that improves readability. That option is GREATER THAN OR EQUAL TO. For example, instead of coding this:

```
START file-name KEY NOT LESS THAN data-name...
```

you can code this:

```
START file-name KEY GREATER THAN OR EQUAL TO data-name...
```

It is a small item, but this option lets you think positively instead of negatively to state the same condition. Anytime you can avoid using NOT, you reduce the odds that a rookie programmer will make an error in the future when maintaining your program. For more specific VSAM considerations beyond those addressed within the scope of COBOL II, QED publishes *VSAM: The Complete Guide to Optimization and Design.* See Chapter 9, Related Publications, for information on this and related IBM VSAM publications.

3.8. SORT TECHNIQUES

A COBOL SORT requires several considerations, not only to have it work correctly, but also, to have it work efficiently. Additional sort information may be found in these sections: Making a Program More Efficient (in this chapter), JCL Requirements (in this chapter), plus sections in Chapter 5 and Chapter 6. First, let's review how the sort takes place. Let's use a simple SORT statement, such as

```
SORT SD-SORT-FILE ASCENDING KEY FIELD-A
    INPUT PROCEDURE 2100-PROCESS-INPUT
    OUTPUT PROCEDURE 3100-PROCESS-OUTPUT
```

3.8.1. SORT Logic Flow

A common perception of the logic flow from the above is an implied PERFORM UNTIL statement of 2100-PROCESS-INPUT, followed by the sort, followed by an implied PERFORM UNTIL of 3100-PROCESS-OUTPUT. If that were true, you could view the process as similar to any other PERFORM structures. Instead, here is what happens:

1. When the SORT statement is executed, it does NOT transfer control to an INPUT PROCEDURE. Instead, it *dynamically loads* the SORT utility program (DFSORT, the same one used for stand-alone sorts) into memory and transfers control to that application, passing the addresses of any INPUT or OUTPUT PROCEDURES, plus the address of some sort control statements. (For efficiency, you should allocate more memory to the run unit than the application itself requires.)

2. DFSORT is now in control. First, DFSORT checks for the existence of a control data set that might have stand-alone control statements (ddname would be either IGZSRTCD or SORTCNTL). If present, DFSORT includes these with those received from your SORT statement. Next, it does an implied PERFORM of your INPUT or OUTPUT procedure. This means your code is running subordinate to DFSORT, not subordinate to your parent paragraph with the SORT statement, and certain programming practices should not be done. These include using such statements as STOP RUN, GOBACK, or (horrors!) a GO TO to a different logic path in the application. For the application to terminate cleanly, you *must* return control back by the same path following normal structured practices. (If you're wondering how to stop a sort in progress, I'll get to that shortly.)

3. As each RELEASE statement is executed, DFSORT feeds the next record into the sorting process, which is occurring *concurrently* with your INPUT or OUTPUT processing. Likewise with the RETURN statement, each execution of it causes DFSORT to pass back the next record available from the sort. An important point, explained shortly, is that DFSORT also checks contents of a special register called SORT-RETURN *each time* it receives control from a RELEASE or RETURN.

4. As your code exits the INPUT or OUTPUT paragraph, DFSORT uses this as a signal to finish that sort phase or to return control back to the statement following the SORT statement. When control is returned to the statement following the SORT statement, DFSORT exits memory. If an error occurred at any time, DFSORT sets a nonzero value in the SORT-RETURN special register.

The following diagram is a symbolic representation of what is happening. The dotted lines represent the conceptual flow. The solid lines represent the actual flow.

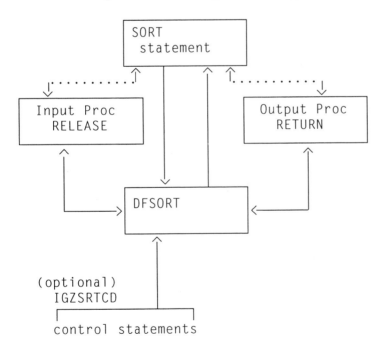

3.8.2.   SORT Components

A COBOL SORT requires several components: A SELECT statement, an SD definition, an INPUT PROCEDURE of procedural code if the data is to be modified or selected prior to the sort, and an OUTPUT PROCEDURE of procedural code if the data is to be modified or otherwise processed after the sort. The optional INPUT PROCEDURE requires a RELEASE statement to transfer a record to the sort process and the optional OUTPUT PROCEDURE requires a RETURN statement to read records back from the sort process. An example sort program is included in Chapter 8 (Sample Programs). Let's look at each of the SORT components:

The SELECT statement
Since DFSORT allocates its own work files, this is a comment. Use:

```
SELECT sort-file-id ASSIGN TO SORTWORK.
```

The SD statement
Because the actual sort files are allocated by DFSORT, your goal here is to use the minimum acceptable syntax to COBOL II. All data fields that will be keys for the sort process must be defined within the 01-level.

```
Specify:   SD   sort-file-name
                RECORD CONTAINS nn CHARACTERS.
           01   sort-record-name.
                05 sort-key-a      PIC ...
                05 sort-key-b      PIC ...
                  .
                  .
```

The PROCEDURE DIVISION
First, a SORT statement must be used. Usually, there will be one or both of the possible PROCEDURES. The INPUT PROCEDURE, if used, needs to have a RELEASE statement somewhere within the logic flow (i.e, the RELEASE statement does not have to be in the named paragraph). This also applies to the OUTPUT PROCEDURE, in that the RETURN statement need not be physically within the named paragraph.

3.8.3. SORT Performance Tips

Terminating a SORT.

Earlier I reviewed the logic flow of a sort. You may recall that I stated that DFSORT checked the status of SORT-RETURN after receiving control via a RELEASE or RETURN statement. This is the key. If you are in an INPUT or OUTPUT procedure and decide to terminate the sort or the application itself, follow these steps:

1. Set a flag so DFSORT knows to terminate. Do this by a statement such as:

```
MOVE 16 TO SORT-RETURN
```

2. Next, RETURN or RELEASE one more record. Since DFSORT checks SORT-RETURN first, the next record will not be processed. Instead, DFSORT will shut down and return control to your statement following the SORT statement.

3. Those two steps cause the sort process to terminate. Now you can terminate the application or whatever is appropriate. Use something such as this following your SORT statement:

```
IF SORT-RETURN > 0
    your error termination process goes here
ELSE
    your normal next process goes here
END-IF
```

Improving performance of a SORT.

Much of this was covered in an earlier section, Making a Program More Efficient. Here are some specifics.

1. Use an INPUT PROCEDURE (or the IGZSRTCD interface) to restructure your input records so that only the needed fields are sorted. Since much of the sort process occurs in memory, this increases the number of records that can be sorted this way. (How to use IGZSRTCD is explained in the next topic.)

2. Use selection logic to ensure no records are sorted that are not needed. For example, why sort 100,000 records when the OUTPUT PROCEDURE (or the following program) has logic that bypasses many of the records. This logic can be in either an INPUT PROCEDURE or the IGZSRTCD interface.

3. Specify the FASTSRT option. This improves I/O for any USING or GIVING clauses (i.e., ignored for programs with both an INPUT and an OUTPUT PROCEDURE).

4. Never use a SORT USING... GIVING... statement. A stand-alone sort is quicker and easier to code.

5. Specify more memory than you think you need. Because DFSORT is a "smart" program, it does the best it can with what it gets. This doesn't mean it is working efficiently, only that it is working functionally. Your technical staff may have guidelines for your shop.

6. Don't specify many SORT work files in your JCL. Modern sort techniques generally work best with fewer, not more, work files.

Using DFSORT control statements (IGZSRTCD).

Although seldom used, the SORT control statements may be used from within COBOL SORT programs. Their advantage is that they are easy to code and can eliminate the need for an INPUT or OUTPUT PROCEDURE, depending on the complexity of your requirements. They can also supplement processing if the program already has INPUT or OUTPUT PROCEDURES or both. For example, an INCLUDE or OMIT statement could determine what records are sorted or an OPTION statement could provide special performance information to SORT. When used within COBOL, the statements must have DDNAME of IGZSRTCD or SORTCNTL. This can be changed by the SORT-CONTROL register in a CO-BOL program if desired. The syntax is identical to that used in a stand-alone sort (remember, it is the same program).

Your choice of statements must coincide with processing steps of the application. For example, if you use an INREC statement to realign data fields, the data fields must appear in the SD record description as they will appear after the realignment. (Note: Don't show a smaller record size in the SD record description, however, as DFSORT opens the file before processing the INREC statement. That generates a run-time error.) Likewise, use of OUTREC would change, again, the record's description. For that reason, you cannot use both INREC and OUTREC in an application (nor can I think of a reason why you would need to). The format of each statement is in the section, JCL Requirements. Here are some suggested uses.

1. To select records for the sort: Use INCLUDE statement.
2. To omit records from the sort: Use OMIT statement.
3. To realign and shorten (lengthen) records prior to the sort process: Use INREC.
4. To realign and shorten (lengthen) records after the sort process: Use OUTREC.

A coding example is in the section JCL Requirements. For additional information on using DFSORT, see your appropriate reference manual (Chapter 9, Related Publications).

CONTROL STATEMENTS (in order of processing)

OPTION	provides temporary overrides to defaults
INCLUDE or OMIT	specifies what records to sort
INREC	reformats input records
SORT or MERGE	*<— provided by COBOL SORT statement*
SUM	creates summary records and totals
OUTREC	reformats output records

Complete syntax on the DFSORT control statements is in the section JCL Requirements in this chapter.

3.9. CICS/IMS/DB2 ISSUES

Some of the material presented here appears in various other topics. This material is presented under the assumption that you know how to program applications for CICS, DB2, or IMS. In all cases, refer to your technical staff for specifics for your shop. CICS and IMS are complex system environments and there may well be differences from what is written here. There is also a topic in the next chapter (Debugging) about debug considerations for CICS, IMS, and DB2. (For more information on CICS and its use with COBOL II, COBOL/370, and CICS/ESA, see my other book from QED, *CICS: A How-to for COBOL Programmers.*)

I should also mention here that some of the material in this section is oriented to conversion from prior versions of COBOL, primarily from OS/VS COBOL. However, even if you are not converting an application to COBOL II or COBOL/370, you may find some performance information here. This happens because, all too often, the programmer doing the conversion is under time pressure to get the application productional and doesn't have the time or inclination to worry about performance issues. Another consideration is that you may have learned CICS or IMS or DB2 while programming with OS/VS COBOL and need to "unlearn" some obsolete techniques.

3.9.1. CICS Considerations

CICS receives major performance improvements from COBOL II, and most OS/VS COBOL programs do not require specific program changes to benefit from them. COBOL II simplifies several CICS processes and provides some features that weren't previously allowed.

The first release of CICS to support COBOL II was CICS/VS Release 1.6, although support for major features did not arrive until CICS/MVS Release 2.1. In this book, my assumption is that you are using either CICS/MVS or CICS/ESA. To use COBOL/370, your shop must be running CICS/ESA Release 3.2.1 or a later version.

Module structure and compile options. These are items that reflect new features or capabilities offered by COBOL II and COBOL/370. These do not usually require any program changes for existing programs but may offer new opportunities for new programs. You may also find that some compile option changes are necessary for current programs.

1. Specify the option, COBOL2, when running the CICS translator.
2. If your shop is using CICS/MVS Release 2.1 or CICS/ESA, specify the option, ANSI85, to use these features:
   - Lower-case characters in COBOL statements
   - Batched compilations

- Nested programs
- GLOBAL variables
- Reference modification

3. A run unit of COBOL/370 and/or COBOL II programs also may not contain any OS/VS COBOL programs.

4. Programs must use NOCMPR2, RES, RENT, NODBCS, and NODYNAM compile options.

5. IBM recommends you use TRUNC(BIN), although you may want to test other TRUNC options if your application makes extensive use of binary arithmetic. NOTE: TRUNC(BIN) is always required when the length of a CICS data area exceeds the PIC clause for its length field. For example, DFHCOMMAREA may be up to 32K, but EIBCALEN is PIC S9(4). Therefore, if the length of DFHCOMMAREA exceeds 9,999, use TRUNC(BIN).

6. Programs may not be CALLed from assembler programs, although they may CALL assembler subprograms.

7. While the DYNAM option is not allowed, the use of CALL identifier is valid with NODYNAM for CALLs to COBOL II subprograms.

8. Dynamically and statically CALLed subprograms may contain EXEC CICS commands if running under CICS/MVS or CICS/ESA. CALLed programs must be COBOL II or COBOL/370.

9. If the FDUMP, TEST, or SSRANGE compile options are used, the formatted information will be written to the temporary storage queue, CEBRxxxx. (COBOL II only) Information for COBOL/370 is written to CESE transient data queue.

10. The ON EXCEPTION and NOT ON EXCEPTION clauses are not allowed with CICS for COBOL II, but are allowed when LE/370 is used.

11. Programs that use macro-level CICS code will not compile with COBOL II, nor will those using BLL cells.

12. If you CALL another COBOL II program that will execute EXEC CICS statements, pass the DFHEIBLK and DFHCOMMAREA as the first two parameters. The CICS translator will insert the appropriate data definitions and adjustments to the PROCEDURE DIVISION USING statement for the CALLed program. Exception: When the CALLed module is a nested program, the PROCEDURE DIVISION USING statement must be manually coded. (Note: CALLing another program that also executes EXEC CICS statements was not allowed prior to COBOL II.) The LINK and XCTL commands may still be used for program transfer.

13. If the program(s) will reside in the Link Pack AREA(LPA), specify RENT during link-edit processing. (See JCL Requirements.)

14. Run-time options that a particular application needs that don't match your shop's defaults must be developed and INCLUDEd via the Linkage Editor. See topics later in the book on IGZEOPT (for COBOL II) and CEEUOPT (for COBOL/370).

15. With OS/VS COBOL, any uninitialized areas in WORKING STORAGE were set to binary zeros. If your current applications are dependent on those areas being binary zeros, then you need to ensure appropriate run-time options are set. (These are some of the options that are set via appropriate IGZEOPT or CEEUOPT modules.) For COBOL II, the run-time option that initializes WORKING STORAGE to binary zeros is WSCLEAR. For CO-BOL/370 (i.e., LE/370), it is STORAGE(00). Performance is best if you do *not* use these run-time options but initialize the application from within the program or at compile-time (with VALUE clauses).

    Run-time options are set at the time a task is initiated. Therefore, if your program executes a different run unit via the EXEC CICS LINK or EXEC CICS XCTL, the new run unit inherits the options from the parent run unit.

16. If you are using COBOL/370, you may specify the TEST compile option to use the CODE/370 Debug Tool. Interactive testing was not available prior to COBOL/370.

17. For COBOL/370 and COBOL II Release 3.2 and above, you may specify the compile-time option, WORD(CICS), if desired. This provides additional compiler checking to ensure nonsupported COBOL elements are not in the program (e.g., FDs, READ or WRITE statements, and other I/O statements not supported by CICS.)

18. For COBOL/370 applications (or COBOL II applications that want to take advantage of LE/370 processing) the link-edit step must use the LE/370 libraries. I suspect your technical support staff has set up a special PROC for CICS links for LE/370. This is because the CICS stub for LE/370 is named DFHELII, not DFHECI as it is for COBOL II and OS/VS COBOL.

Programming techniques for CICS. These are techniques that apply to how you write CICS code that might be different from how an application would have been coded prior to COBOL II. If you are converting an old application, these may be critical items.

1. If you use EXEC CICS HANDLE statements, the HANDLE is suspended when CALLing a separately compiled COBOL II program (reinstated upon return), but remains active when CALLing a nested program. If the CALLed program will issue any EXEC statements, it must first issue an appropriate HANDLE statement to protect against possible ABENDs.

    With COBOL/370, however, you can change this default. The run-time option is CBLPSHPOP, and the setting is ON to provide the process described in the previous paragraph. If your applications use NOHANDLE exclusively, your application will be more efficient if you specify CBLPSHPOP(OFF). This saves the cpu time of trapping existing HANDLE conditions and suspending them. Obviously (?) if your application does use HANDLE, a problem trapped in a subordinate program will cause unpredictable results (translates to ABEND) with CBLPSHPOP(OFF).

2. Do not use BLL cells. Instead, where SET or ADDRESS parameters reference BLL cells, specify the ADDRESS OF special register for the actual data area. (This was often needed with OS/VS COBOL.)
3. Do not write code to provide addressability for areas greater than 4K (usually done in OS/VS COBOL by adding 4096 to the value of a BLL cell). This function is provided for you by COBOL II.
4. The SERVICE RELOAD statement is treated as a comment, so *there is no need to code it.* (This was often needed with OS/VS COBOL.)
5. The LENGTH parameter is not needed, although it may be coded if desired. (CICS uses the LENGTH OF special register from COBOL II to access the length of the data area.)
6. STOP RUN is now a supported statement, but I encourage you to continue using EXEC CICS RETURN or GOBACK for compatibility.
7. You will improve transaction response time and use less virtual memory by converting EXEC CICS LINK commands to COBOL CALL statements.

   Converting a LINKed module to a dynamically CALLed module is simpler than you might think. (*NOTE:* This technique applies *only* when LINKING from a COBOL II or COBOL/370 program to another COBOL II or COBOL/370 program. Any interaction with OS/VS COBOL applications must still use LINK.) Here is an example of converting a LINK to a CALL:

In the main COBOL program, we convert this:

```
EXEC CICS LINK ('PROGXYZ')
          COMMAREA (MY-COMM-AREA)
          LENGTH (COMM-LENGTH)
END-EXEC
```

to this (where CALL-NAME is defined as PIC X(8)):

```
MOVE 'PROGXYZ' TO CALL-NAME
CALL CALL-NAME USING DFHEIBLK MY-COMM-AREA
```

If the subordinate program is fussy about the length of the COMM area, just precede the above MOVE with

```
MOVE COMM-LENGTH TO EIBCALEN
```

This additional MOVE fakes the subordinate program in case it tests EIBCALEN for a valid length. This MOVE would be required because, since your CALL bypasses CICS, the COMM area is not modified or checked.

Now, in the subordinate (LINKed) program, we do this:

Just replace EXEC CICS RETURN with GOBACK. That's all there is to it. Use of WORKING STORAGE or LINKAGE is irrelevant. The subprogram already has the proper PROCEDURE DIVISION USING information that directly maps to the two fields being passed to it in the CALL statement. Since the CALL was a direct route via MVS (not CICS), the GOBACK takes the same reverse path.

8. If any EXEC CICS commands include reference modification, be sure to include the LENGTH parameter. Otherwise, the CICS translator may generate incorrect code. (Reference modification was explained in Chapter 2.)
9. If your application uses the CICS GETMAIN command, change the LENGTH keyword to FLENGTH. This also requires that the length field itself be changed from S9(4) COMP to S9(8) COMP. The use of FLENGTH causes the memory to be allocated above the 16 megabyte line and also allows your program to allocate a larger chunk of memory. (*NOTE:* You may want to rethink the purpose of the GETMAIN now that you are using COBOL II or COBOL/370. If the GETMAIN was to relieve the OS/VS COBOL WORKING STORAGE constraint of 64K, you may just need to move the data area definition to the WORKING STORAGE SECTION from the LINKAGE SECTION and remove the GETMAIN (and any related FREEMAINs). Performance will improve—and your program will be easier to maintain.) The GETMAIN (with LENGTH, not FLENGTH) may still be useful if your application must issue LINKs to OS/VS COBOL applications and must allocate shared data areas in 24-bit mode.
10. Restrictions on the use of UNSTRING, STRING, and INSPECT have been removed with COBOL II and COBOL/370. These sometimes worked for OS/VS COBOL but were not supported. If you were using the EXAMINE statement in earlier programs, those must be changed to a form of the INSPECT command, since EXAMINE is no longer supported. (See examples of INSPECT elsewhere in this book.)

Accessing LINKAGE SECTION. Techniques for managing the LINKAGE SECTION were mentioned previously. Prior to COBOL II, this was often important because CICS only allowed a 64K WORKING-STORAGE for OS/VS COBOL. Now, with the availability of COBOL II and COBOL/370, that restriction no longer exists. So, while there are several examples shown here, remember that you will get maximum performance gains by simply defining the data areas in WORKING STORAGE and not using any special techniques.

If your shop has a CICS-to-COBOL II conversion software package, the conversion of BLL cells can be done automatically for OS/VS COBOL programs. Check with your technical staff. Here are some elementary (and incomplete) comparisons of how COBOL II replaces BLL processing. All differences are highlighted. All techniques are explained earlier in this section.

Accessing an area in LINKAGE SECTION.

OS/VS COBOL:

```
LINKAGE SECTION.
      .
01   BLL-CELLS.
     05   FILLER                PIC S9(8) COMP.
     05   DATA-REC-POINTER      PIC S9(8) COMP.
01 DATA-REC.
     .
     .

     EXEC CICS ADDRESS CWA(DATA-REC-POINTER)
     .
```

COBOL II:

```
LINKAGE SECTION.
     .
01 DATA-REC.
     .

     EXEC CICS ADDRESS CWA(ADDRESS OF DATA-REC)
     .
```

Reading a file in LINKAGE SECTION.

OS/VS COBOL:

```
LINKAGE SECTION.

01   BLL-CELLS.
     05   FILLER        PIC S9(8) COMP.
     05   LS1-REC-PTR   PIC S9(8) COMP.
01   LS1-DATA-REC       PIC X(1000).
        .
        .
```

```
        EXEC CICS READ FILE ('fileid')
                  SET (LS1-REC-PTR)
                  RIDFLD (keyfield)
                  LENGTH (lengthfield)
                  .
                  .
        END-EXEC
        SERVICE RELOAD LS1-DATA-REC
```

COBOL II:

```
    LINKAGE SECTION.

    01  LS1-DATA-REC        PIC X(1000).
          .
          .
        EXEC CICS READ FILE ('fileid')
                  SET (ADDRESS OF LS1-DATA-REC)
                  RIDFLD (keyfield)
                  LENGTH (lengthfield)
                  .
                  .
        END-EXEC
```

Processing a large storage area in LINKAGE SECTION.

OS/VS COBOL:

```
    WORKING-STORAGE SECTION.
          .
    01 WS1-FILE-WORK.
       05  WS1-REC-LEN      PIC S9(4) COMP VALUE 5000.
          .
          .
    LINKAGE SECTION.
          .
    01 BLL-CELLS.
          .
       05   ADDR-1          PIC S9(8)     COMP.
       05   ADDR-2          PIC S9(8)     COMP.
          .
          .
    01  DATA-REC-A          PIC X(5000).
          .
          .
```

```
    EXEC CICS READ FILE('fileid')
        RIDFLD(keyfield)
        SET(ADDR-1)
        LENGTH(WS1-REC-LEN)
    END-EXEC
    COMPUTE ADDR-2 = ADDR-1 + 4096
    SERVICE RELOAD DATA-REC-A
```

COBOL II:

```
    LINKAGE SECTION.
        .
    01  DATA-REC-A              PIC X(5000).
        .
        .

        EXEC CICS READ DATASET('fileid')
            RIDFLD(keyfield)
            SET(ADDRESS OF DATA-REC-A)
        END-EXEC
```

If you have a CICS application that accesses an IMS database (sometimes referred to as DL/I), see the next topic for additional information.

Earlier versions of CICS (e.g., version 1.6) shipped the DFHECI (CICS CO-BOL stub) module with AMODE and RMODE of 24, preventing your application from running above the 16-megabyte address. If your program link-edit listing shows an AMODE and RMODE of 24 despite specifying RENT and RES at compile-time, see your systems programmer to reinstall DFHECI with AMODE and RMODE of 31.

3.9.2. IMS Considerations

There are few special changes for IMS applications that affect the applications programmer. Some of the compile options have been streamlined to improve compatibility (e.g., COBOL II has no equivalent for the OS/VS COBOL compile option ENDJOB). Also, COBOL II offers your technical staff the ability to preload CO-BOL II applications more efficiently.

Restrictions on use of UNSTRING and INSPECT have been removed for both COBOL II and COBOL/370. However, use of previously restricted DIS-PLAY, ACCEPT, and STOP RUN varies between COBOL II and COBOL/370. With COBOL II, DISPLAY, ACCEPT, and STOP RUN can only be used in IMS/DB applications. With COBOL/370, there are no restrictions. (I still recommend that STOP RUN not be used, as documented earlier in the text.)

A new feature with COBOL/370 is that you may compile with the TEST option to use the CODE/370 Debug Tool. Prior to COBOL/370, the only IBM debug facility was BTS (Batch Terminal Simulator).

The major programming change available (optional, not required) is that you may replace CALLs to CBLTDLI with CALLs to CEETDLI. CEETDLI is available only with LE/370 and may be CALLed by both COBOL II and COBOL/370 modules. All parameters are the same so the change is easy. Primary benefit is that CEETDLI provides extended condition handling.

If you use CEETDLI, the CALL can be either static or dynamic. Since IMS is usually administered by a technical staff within your MIS shop, they may have guidelines on this for you. CEETDLI requires that a CSECT named DFSLI000 be in your load module. The module is provided by IBM and it needs to be in the SYSLIB DD of your link edit JCL. CEETDLI will work only with IMS Version 3.2 or later, so check your release level before attempting this, since CEETDLI is provided with LE/370, and your shop's version of IMS may not be at this level.

CEETDLI can also be used with the LE/370 run-time option, TRAP(ON), whereas CBLTDLI cannot. (IMS does not receive the percolated ABEND in LE/370 with TRAP(ON) when the CBLTDLI CALL interface is used, preventing IMS from doing proper database rollbacks. This can be corrected by having your technical staff write an LE/370 termination exit, if desired.)

Although not specific to COBOL II, the main programming concerns for IMS are

1. You do not need to code ENTRY DLITCBL. Use PROCEDURE DIVISION USING instead. It is easier to code and provides better readability.
2. For program termination, code GOBACK. Do not use STOP RUN.
3. Where all modules in a run unit are COBOL II and compiled with RENT, specify the RENT option at link-edit time if modules will be in the Link Pack Area (LPA).

I won't specify compile or run-time options for IMS/DC applications, as your technical staff has already made some decisions here. The selected options are dependent on the mix of COBOL II and OS/VS COBOL programs and on whether the modules are preloaded. Typical IBM recommendations include RES, RENT, TRUNC(BIN), and DATA(31), as these allow applications to run in nonpreload mode or preloaded.

Some versions of IMS still run below the 16-megabyte address line, requiring that data areas from your program be located there. That is done by the compile option DATA(24). Check with your technical staff for more particulars for your installation. If your shop is running IMS/VS Version 3, Release 1, you may specify DATA(31).

For CICS applications, you may use EXEC DLI instead of the CALL statement if your shop is running IMS Version 1, Release 3, or later. As noted above, however, BLLs are not allowed. Once the scheduling CALL is completed, there are no other differences for CICS applications. Here is an example of the differences when using the scheduling CALL statement (differences are highlighted). See the previous topic on CICS for explanations of the differences.

Differences for a scheduling CALL for CICS/DLI programs.

OS/VS COBOL:

```
LINKAGE SECTION.
    .
01   BLL-CELLS.
     05   FILLER          PIC S9(8)     COMP.
     05   DLIUIB-BLL      PIC S9(8)     COMP.
     05   PCB-ADDR-BLL    PIC S9(8)     COMP.
     05   PCB-1-BLL       PIC S9(8)     COMP.
     05   PCB-2-BLL       PIC S9(8)     COMP.

01   DLIUIB.
     05   UIBPCBAL        PIC S9(8)     COMP.
     .
01   PCB-ADDRESSES.
     05   PCB-ADDR-1      PIC S9(8)     COMP.
     05   PCB-ADDR-2      PIC S9(8)     COMP.
     .
01 PCB-1.
     .
01 PCB-2.
     .
     CALL 'CBLTDLI' USING PCB-SCHEDULE
                          psb-name
                          DLIUIB-BLL
     SERVICE RELOAD DLIUIB
     MOVE UIBPCBAL      TO PCB-ADDR-BLL
     SERVICE RELOAD PCB-ADDRESSES
     MOVE PCB-ADDR-1    TO PCB-1-BLL
     MOVE PCB-ADDR-2    TO PCB-2-BLL
     SERVICE RELOAD PCB-1
     SERVICE RELOAD PCB-2
```

COBOL II:

This example uses the POINTER technique described earlier in this chapter and in Chapter 2. It is created by modifying the DLIUIB COPYbook or by using a REDEFINES statement to place the POINTER.

```
LINKAGE SECTION.
        .
01  DLIUIB.
    05  UIBPCBAL        POINTER.
        .
01  PCB-ADDRESSES.
    05  PCB-ADDR-1      POINTER.
    05  PCB-ADDR-2      POINTER.
        .
01  PCB-1.
        .
01  PCB-2.
        .


        CALL 'CBLTDLI' USING PCB-SCHEDULE
                       psb-name
                       ADDRESS OF DLIUIB
        SET ADDRESS OF PCB-ADDRESSES TO UIBPCBAL
        SET ADDRESS OF PCB-1 TO PCB-ADDR-1
        SET ADDRESS OF PCB-2 TO PCB-ADDR-2
```

An alternative way to code the last three statements in the above example follows. Because this technique uses **EXEC CICS** commands, the DLIUIB COPYbook does not need to be changed. I don't recommend this approach, however, because it is less efficient.

```
EXEC CICS ADDRESS SET(ADDRESS OF PCB-ADDRESSES)
          USING(UIBPCBAL)     END-EXEC
EXEC CICS ADDRESS SET(ADDRESS OF PCB-1)
          USING(PCB-ADDR-1) END-EXEC
EXEC CICS ADDRESS SET(ADDRESS OF PCB-2)
          USING(PCB-ADDR-2) END-EXEC
```

A sample IMS program is included in Chapter 8. The sample was written to be compatible with OS/VS COBOL, COBOL II, and COBOL/370.

3.9.3. DB2 Considerations

While there are several issues to address with CICS and IMS, DB2 is hardly a concern. I include this topic to reassure DB2 programmers that I didn't overlook DB2. If your DB2 application operates within the CICS or IMS environment, those considerations will apply. Other than that, here are the few considerations:

1. If you are using a DB2 precompiler prior to Version 1, Release 3, the generated IF statements from the SQL WHENEVER statement that

contains a GO TO clause omits the END-IF. The END-IF must be added manually. (Later versions include it in the generated COBOL source.)

2. Whereas all types of dynamic SQL statements were not allowed with OS/VS COBOL, you may use them with COBOL II.

3. If you used an SQLDA (Structured Query Language Data Area) with OS/VS COBOL, you needed to write an assembler program to manage the address pointers. That still works, but is not needed with COBOL II. Instead, you may use POINTER variables with the SET statement. You will also need to define your SQLDA because the SQL INCLUDE for COBOL does not provide the code for it. Examples of an SQLDA, along with all other information about dynamic SQL statements, are included in the *IBM Database 2 Advanced Application Programming Guide* (see Chapter 9).

4. The COBOL II options that affect the DB2 environment are TRUNC and NOCMPR2. IBM recommends TRUNC(BIN) for DB2, as it does for CICS and IMS. If your application does not use binary arithmetic extensively, follow IBM's recommendation. If you do use binary arithmetic (COMP), you may want to test other options of TRUNC if performance is an issue. NOCMPR2 is required because of changes in COBOL II. (See Specifying COBOL II Options for more information.)

   To clarify my point, I am referring to INTEGER (4-byte) and SMALLINT (2-byte) fields. If your DB2 data is always in compliance with the COBOL PIC clauses (S9(9) COMP for INTEGER, S9(4) COMP for SMALLINT), then you probably don't need to use TRUNC(BIN) but will benefit from using TRUNC(MIG) or TRUNC(OPT).

5. If you are using COBOL/370, you can specify TEST at compile-time and use the CODE/370 Debug Tool.

6. DB2 statements used by COBOL II are OPEN, CLOSE, PREPARE, DESCRIBE, and FETCH.

7. Non-SELECT statements, as well as fixed-list and varying-list SELECT statements, may also be used with COBOL II.

3.10. CREATING A LOAD MODULE

Creating executable code (called a load module in MVS) requires that the output from the compile(s) be processed by the Linkage Editor. This is because IBM language compilers generate a standard format dataset of machine code that includes nonexecutable tables of reference (e.g., list of CALLed modules that must be resolved). Certain compile options affect this process and there are other items you can specify for your program at the time of the link.

The Linkage Editor is an intelligent software product and can do many things with the object code it processes. However, because the Linkage Editor does not know the logic structure of the application, or which program should get control at run-time, there are specific concerns you must address for a successful link-edit. This section addresses all Linkage Editor considerations except JCL. JCL for the Linkage Editor is in a later section, JCL Requirements: Compile, Link, and Execute.

3.10.1. Static Versus Dynamic CALLS

The concept of static CALLs and dynamic CALLs was explained in the section Module Structures. If you have static CALLs to resolve, you must have the needed modules in object or load format accessible to the Linkage Editor via JCL DD statements. If you use dynamic CALLs, there are no concerns to the Linkage Editor in resolving these CALLs.

3.10.2. RESIDENT and REENTRANT Options

Reentrant At run-time, MVS checks to see what attributes a load module has so it can manage the load module correctly. Those attributes might be placed in the object module by the language compiler or in the load module by the Linkage Editor. This may seem redundant, but the processing done by each is different. For example, by specifying RENT at compile-time, the COBOL II compiler generates different object code so the program will be reentrant, as well as have 31-bit addressability. The module attributes are marked for 31-bit addressability, but are not marked as reentrant. That is done by the Linkage Editor.

When the option RENT is specified to the Linkage Editor, it sets an attribute bit so MVS will assume the module is reentrant. (Linkage Editor options are in the section, JCL Requirements.) When MVS loads a run unit that is marked reentrant, it schedules the run unit to take advantage of this feature, whether the run unit is or isn't reentrant. Don't make the mistake, then, of assuming that you can specify RENT at link-edit time and not at compile-time. Each serves a different purpose. Here is a definition of reentrant code to help you determine when RENT needs to be specified to the Linkage Editor.

Reentrant code First, reentrant code has no relationship to 31-bit addressability. The COBOL II compiler packages reentrancy and 31-bit addressability with RENT, but the two features could have been done separately. Although all applications can benefit from 31-bit addressability, only specialized applications benefit from being reentrant. By being reentrant, a load module is capable of being loaded once into memory and then multiple transactions can execute concurrently, using the one copy. This feature can be useful for high-performance on-line transactions, but it is of no benefit for batch transactions. Usually, your technical staff that supports on-line transactions can assist you with this, as the decision has some dependency on how the on-line environment is initialized and where the load module is stored.

That last sentence may have confused you. Where the load module is stored is important when an application's design is dependent on sharing one copy across multiple CICS or IMS environments. MVS has special areas, called the Link Pack Area (LPA) and the Extended Link Pack Area (ELPA), that serve all MVS regions. If your application is in LPA or ELPA, one copy can be shared by different regions. Otherwise, it isn't.

Resident   The RES option (COBOL II only) affects the size of your load module, the size of your Linkage Editor listing, and how your load module accesses the COBOL II run-time modules. Since RES means that COBOL run-time modules will be resident in the system and not in your load module, there are no CALLs in your object module to COBOL routines for the Linkage Editor to resolve. (Exception: There is always a CALL to IGZEBST that must be resolved by the Linkage Editor.)

As a reminder, the RESIDENT option applies only to COBOL II, because COBOL II has a subroutine library, while COBOL/370 does not. The NORES option allowed you to create a load module that had no need for external environmental assistance, positive in one aspect but negative in the other. Execution time might be more efficient, but the load module was not protected from environmental changes. COBOL/370 has no RES option because there is no component of COBOL/370 that is subject to execution time performance. All run-time aspects of COBOL/370 are administered by LE/370, freeing the programmer from this concern.

3.10.3. Using the Linkage Editor

Despite its simple design, the Linkage Editor is one of the least understood of IBM's software. This is not an extensive treatment on the subject, but it should suffice for most applications. The JCL, options, and tips for use are in JCL Requirements. The control statements, however, are here.

Linkage Editor concepts.

First, let's review terms to be sure we're in sync. See Figure 3.2 for a simple compile and link-edit for a two-module application.

First, let's clarify the term CSECT. You will see this term whenever dealing with the Linkage Editor (or with ABENDS, for that matter). This is because a common term was needed that could be relevant, regardless of source language used. CSECT (for Control Section) represents the object code set for a single source program (even if a nested program). This means that a CSECT is generated by a single invocation of the COBOL compiler. A CSECT retains its properties (and its identity) whether in object module format or in load module format.

A *load module* is one or more CSECTs, bound together in executable format.

By this, I mean the internal offsets have been resolved by the Linkage Editor, and the module is formatted so that it can be loaded into memory for execution.

In Figure 3.2 (the datasets are double-lined), program MODA, with a CALL to MODB, is compiled. The output object module is written to the SYSLIN DD statement. The object module has a table in it (referred to as a dictionary), listing all external references that the Linkage Editor must resolve.

When the Linkage Editor reads this as input (SYSLIN), it strips nonexecutable tables from the code and searches for any external references, in this case, MODB. If the Linkage Editor cannot locate MODB elsewhere (this is explained later), it searches a DD statement named SYSLIB and locates it. The module is read from SYSLIB and combined with MODA into an executable load module.

The Linkage Editor has no idea which module should receive control at run-

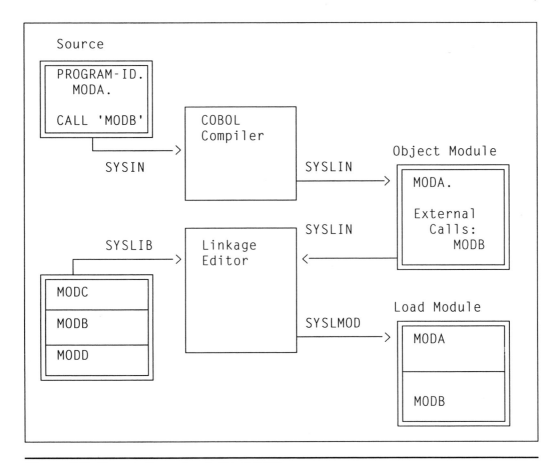

Figure 3.2. Sample flow of compile and link.

time. Unless specified elsewhere, it assumes the first module read from SYSLIN should get control (in this case, MODA).

Now, let's back up and review the process in detail. Here are the basic logic steps as executed by the Linkage Editor, presented to help you determine what, if any, special considerations need to be made.

1. First, it OPENs and READs the SYSLIN dataset. That dataset may contain object module(s), control statements, or both. If it contained only object modules, any decisions to be made would use Linkage Editor defaults (e.g., which module gets control at run-time). If it contained only control statements (covered later), they would need to specify which modules to process and where to find them. Since object modules contain tables that identify the name of all modules CALLed by them, this becomes additional input to the Linkage Editor.

   The Linkage Editor continues to read (and process in the order of appearance) control statements and object modules until either end-of-file is reached on SYSLIN or a NAME control statement (covered later) is read.

2. If *all* the object code needed to create a load module is in SYSLIN, the Linkage Editor searches no other libraries, follows any control statement instructions, writes out the load module to the SYSLMOD DD and is finished with that load module. (See step 4.)

3. If, after reading all input from SYSLIN, there were missing modules (as in our example of MODB), the Linkage Editor has a priority of search to locate the missing module(s). That priority is

   a. Was it concatenated in SYSLIN? If so, it uses it. This could occur when there are several COBOL compiles preceding the link-edit step or when JCL has concatenated several object datasets. The Linkage Editor will use all such modules up to end-of-file on SYSLIN or the appearance of a NAME control statement (explained later). Note: Concatenated modules found in SYSLIN are placed in the load module even if there are *no* CALLs to them.

   b. Was there an INCLUDE control statement specifying additional modules? An INCLUDE statement can identify object modules or load modules (not both) that are to be included in the new load module. Note: Modules specified on INCLUDE statements are included in the load module, whether needed or not. The Linkage Editor is just following your instructions.

   c. Was there a LIBRARY statement specifying where to search for the module(s) if still not located? This is useful if there might be a CALL to a unique module and you want the Linkage Editor to know where to search.

   d. Is there a SYSLIB DD statement? If this data set is present, the Linkage Editor will search there last. This is a PDS of load modules. This final search is often referred to as the automatic call library because it will be automatically searched unless one of the prior events occurs. The member name must match the name from the CALL statement AND the module name from the PROGRAM-ID. (Reminder: The Linkage Editor term for a module is CSECT (for Control Section). The Linkage Editor does not refer to a PROGRAM-ID name, but to a CSECT name (although, for COBOL, they are the same).

4. The last process done for a load module is to determine the logical entry point (the entry address that should be given control when the module is executed). That is done from the following priority list:

   a. If an ENTRY statement (maximum of one per load module) was specified, that module will be the logical entry point.

   b. If there was one or more CSECTs read directly from SYSLIN (not from an INCLUDE or other control statement), the first (or only) CSECT read from SYSLIN will be marked as the logical entry point. This is the normal situation.

   c. If all processed modules were located via INCLUDE or other control statements, the Linkage Editor marks the first one it found as the logical entry point. This is not desirable and should always be avoided.

5. After processing all the modules, the Linkage Editor writes the load module to the SYSLMOD DD dataset and names the load module. The name is done on a priority basis. The priority is

   a. Was there a NAME control statement? If so, the module gets its name from it.

   b. Was there a member name coded on the SYSLMOD DD dataset? If so, it gets its name from there. If a module already exists in the library with that name, it is overwritten.

   c. In the absence of the first two options, the module is named TEMPNAME. If a module already exists in the library with that name, it is overwritten.

   If end-of-file on SYSLIN has been reached, the Linkage Editor terminates. If the processing in step 5 was caused by the appearance of a NAME statement, the Linkage Editor starts over again at step 1. In this way, the Linkage Editor can create multiple load modules in one execution. COBOL II allows you to take advantage of this with the NAME compile option.

This wraps up Linkage Editor processing. The Linkage Editor's only function is to locate and bind all modules that you (or the object module) identify as being needed in a load module. Whether the modules are needed or not, whether control is given to the right module, whether the modules are reentrant or not, are decisions the Linkage Editor cannot make. It only follows instructions and makes assumptions in the absence of those instructions.

Linkage Editor control statements.

These are the basic control statements, presented with the options most commonly used. If you are responsible for a link-edit procedure that has additional control statements, see the appropriate Linkage Editor reference manual (Chapter 9). Overlay structures are excluded from this discussion. For the options that are specified via PARM to the Linkage Editor, see JCL Requirements.

Control statements follow traditional IBM syntax, i.e., they must begin at or after column 2, must not exceed column 71, must have a nonblank character in column 72 if continued to a following statement, and must begin in column 16 on any continued statements. In most cases, the examples shown can be combined into one statement if desired. Where a single member name is shown, there can be several, separated by commas. The examples shown are the most common format.

```
INCLUDE ddname                    <- For sequential object
                                     datasets
```

or

```
INCLUDE ddname(membername)        <- For partitioned datasets
                                     with either object or load
                                     modules
```

This statement is a demand that modules identified on the DD statement be included in the new load module. The ddname may be one of your own or you may reference SYSLIB or SYSLMOD if desired. The Linkage Editor includes them even if there are no CALLs to them and even if they are duplicates of modules already located. For example,

```
//SYSLIN   DD   *
       INCLUDE MYDD(MODB)
//MYDD    DD   DSN=MYLIB,DISP=SHR
//SYSLMOD  DD   DSN=LOAD.LIB,DISP=OLD
```

In this case, the Linkage Editor would search the dataset specified in the MYDD ddname and look for a member named MODB. Note that the name of the new load module will be TEMPNAME because no name is specified. (See above if you don't know how names are defined.)

Finally, one of the most powerful uses of the INCLUDE statement is that it causes replacement of modules (CSECTs) that have the same name. Whenever the Linkage Editor determines that it has read a CSECT from SYSLIN and an identically named one from an INCLUDE statement, it "throws away" the version found with the INCLUDE statement, using the one from SYSLIN for link-edit processing. This is especially helpful for load modules that are formed from multiple static CALLs, that is, the load module was formed from the object code of more than one COBOL source program. For example, assume we have a load module named MODA that consists of three CSECTS (programs) named PROGA, PROGB, and PROGC. We make a source change to PROGB and recompile it. Now, we want to link-edit the new PROGB with the existing versions of PROGA and PROGC, replacing the old version of PROGB in the load module. That's easier than it sounds:

```
//SYSLIN   DD   DSN=&&OBJECT,DISP=(OLD,DELETE)   <== contains PROGB
//         DD   *
   INCLUDE   SYSLMOD(MODA)
//SYSLMOD DD   DSN=LOAD.LIB(MODA),DISP=OLD
```

In the above example, a load module will be created consisting of PROGB (it was processed first), followed by PROGA and PROGC. The prior version of PROGB that was found within the INCLUDEd module is discarded. The double use of SYSLMOD is common. The member name on the INCLUDE statement specifies what member is to be processed. The member name on the SYSLMOD DD statement specifies the name of the module to be created. In this case, they happen to be the same. There is an error in this link-edit, however. (Remember, I specified earlier that the Linkage Editor only follows instructions. It doesn't know if what it creates is logically sound.) In this case, PROGB becomes the logical ENTRY point for execution. Since it is a CALLed module, the resulting load module will not execute correctly (an ABEND will occur). To correct this, see the ENTRY statement further along in this section.

```
LIBRARY   ddname(membername)          <- Specifies a PDS where a
                                         CALLed module is located.
```

or

```
LIBRARY   (CSECTname)                 <- Identifies a CALL that is
                                         not to be resolved in this
                                         link-edit.
```

or

```
LIBRARY  *(CSECTname)                 <- Identifies a CALL that is
                                         never to be resolved.
```

The LIBRARY statement has two personalities. One format is used to identify where CALLed modules can be located when you want the CALL resolved via "automatic call library," but the member is not in SYSLIB. The ddname may be one of your own or you may reference SYSLMOD if desired. As with SYSLIB searches, the member name and CSECT name must match. The second format is used when a particular module should not be included, even if the Linkage Editor could locate it. The third option is used when a module reference should be ignored from now on. Here is an example, combining all three:

```
//SYSLIN   DD DSN=&&OBJECT,DISP=(OLD,DELETE)
//         DD *
     LIBRARY LIB(MODA),(MODB),*(MODC)
//LIB    DD  DSN=DAVES.LOADLIB,DISP=SHR
//SYSLMOD  DD DSN=LOAD.LIB(NEWPROG),DISP=OLD
```

In this example, the Linkage Editor would look for MODA in DAVES.LOADLIB, would ignore the CALL to MODB, and would remove permanently the reference to MODC. Note: This, of course, does not change the program logic. If the program logic still executes CALLs to MODB or MODC at runtime, an ABEND will occur. The load module name will be NEWPROG. The entry point for the load module will be the object module in &&OBJECT.

```
MODE AMODE(a),RMODE(r)        <- Specifies memory residency and
                                 addressing capability


      where  a = 24, 31, or ANY
             r = 24, or ANY
```

This is usually not needed, as it overrides the mode specified by the compiler. Don't use it unless you are well-versed in 31-bit and 24-bit concepts. AMODE refers to the addressability of the program, while RMODE refers to where the program may reside. The COBOL compiler sets these automatically, depending on your choice of compile options RENT and RES.

This statement might be useful if you want a COBOL II module to be RES, NORENT and you want an OS/VS COBOL module to be able to CALL it or be CALLed by it. Specifying MODE AMODE(24),RMODE(24) would tell the Linkage Editor to set the load module attribute so your module would not be loaded above the 16-megabyte address, allowing programs with 24-bit addressability to interact.

As with other statements, you can fool the Linkage Editor because it only obeys your commands, but if programs aren't what you specify, anticipate some weird ABENDs. For example, you could specify AMODE(31) for an OS/VS COBOL program, but since it can't handle a 31-bit address, an ABEND is inevitable.

```
NAME        membername [(R)]   <- Names a load module
```

If used, this must be the LAST control statement for a load module. At this point, the Linkage Editor stops reading from SYSLIN and processes everything pending, creating a load module. After finishing a load module, it then picks up again reading from SYSLIN. If there are more modules or control statements, it continues to create load modules until end-of-file on SYSLIN. The (R) means REPLACE the module if one already exists with the same name. If (R), including the parentheses, is omitted, the Linkage Editor will not create the new load module if a member already exists by that name. (Note: COBOL II has the ability, based on the compile option NAME, to create this Linkage Editor control statement for you. In the section on JCL, we'll explore where this might be useful.) Here is an example, using several of the statements discussed so far, in which an object module has been created in a prior step:

```
//SYSLIN    DD  DSN=&&OBJECT,DISP=(OLD,DELETE)
//          DD  *
   INCLUDE  XTRAFILE(PROGC)
   LIBRARY  ALTFILE(PROGD)
   NAME   PROGA(R)
//XTRAFILE DD  DSN=LIBA,DISP=SHR     <- PDS containing PROGC
//ALTFILE  DD  DSN=LIBB,DISP=SHR     <- PDS containing PROGD
//SYSLMOD  DD  DSN=LIBC(MYPROG),DISP=OLD
```

In this example, the load module will be named PROGA, as that is a priority over MYPROG in the JCL. The load module will contain whatever object module(s) was in &&OBJECT, plus PROGC (even if not referenced). PROGD will be in the load module only if CALLed by one of the other object modules. The module that gets control at run-time will be the first module, as that is a default and no control statement said otherwise.

```
ENTRY        externalname     <- Specifies logical beginning of
                                 load module
```

where externalname can be PROGRAM-ID name or ENTRY name from the source program.

When the logical beginning of the program might be other than the first module's PROGRAM-ID name (CSECT name), use the ENTRY statement. This is useful when you are combining modules in different sequences and can't predict their order of appearance to the Linkage Editor. This statement is never needed on single-module load modules that have no ENTRY statement in the PROCEDURE DIVISION.

Consider an example where PROGA CALLs PROGB. Both have been previously compiled and linked. Now PROGB has been recompiled due to a change needed. Since the Linkage Editor assumes the first object module read in through SYSLIN is the entry point, an ENTRY statement is needed, such as the following:

```
//SYSLIN  DD  DSN=&&OBJECT      <- Contains PROGB object code
//       DD  *
  INCLUDE  SYSLMOD(MODA)
  ENTRY PROGA
  NAME MODA(R)
//SYSLMOD  DD  DSN=LIBC,DISP=OLD
```

PROGB will precede PROGA in the load module, although because of the ENTRY statement, PROGA will be the logical beginning point. Note: This could cause debugging complications if you assume that the entry point identified in a dump is the beginning of the load module.

```
REPLACE  module-name [(new-mod-name)]      <- Changes existing
                                              references

      where  module-name = a module or reference in a
                           FOLLOWING module
             new-mod-name = a replacement reference name
```

This is a seldom-understood control statement. It must *immediately precede* the module to which it refers. It is useful on three occasions.

1. When a new version of the CSECT has been created and relinked and you want to relink a load module to use the new version.
2. You created a new version of a module but with a different name. Without changing and recompiling all CALLs to the old name, this will change all references within the load module.
3. You accidentally INCLUDEd some modules into a load module that aren't referenced by the module. This statement can remove them.

Let's look at some examples:

```
//SYSLIN  DD  *
  REPLACE  PROGB
  INCLUDE SYSLMOD(MODA)
  ENTRY   PROGA
  NAME    MODA(R)
//SYSLMOD  DD  DSN=LIBC,DISP=OLD
```

The above example tells the Linkage Editor to remove PROGB from the member in the following INCLUDE statement. Since there is no other input, the Linkage Editor searches SYSLIB for the new version of PROGB. This process is often referred to as a replace link. If PROGB were not referenced by any module in PROGA, it would be removed and all traces deleted.

```
//SYSLIN   DD  DSN=&&OBJECT     <- Points to SUBC module
//         DD  *
   REPLACE SUBA(SUBC)
   INCLUDE OLDLOAD(MODA)
   ENTRY   PROGA
   NAME    NEWPROGA
//OLDLOAD  DD  DSN=LIBC,DISP=SHR
//SYSLMOD  DD  DSN=LIBD,DISP=OLD
```

The above does several things. First, we have the object module for SUBC in the input stream (DSN=&&OBJECT). It is a replacement for a module called SUBA. The Linkage Editor will replace all references to SUBA with SUBC. The new load module is also being written to a different library. By omitting the (R) from the NAME statement, we ensure that if a module already exists by that name we don't replace it.

```
ALIAS   external-name     <- Provides alternate name for load
                             module
```

I include this statement although I am opposed to using it. The ALIAS statement, by providing another name to a program, can create confusion in program documentation. Another little trick it does is with ENTRY statements. If the external-name shown matches an ENTRY statement within the program, that ENTRY statement becomes the logical entry point. This violates the "one entry, one exit" concept of structured programming.

```
ORDER  CSECTname [(P)] [,CSECTname,...]   <- Arranges order of
                                             CSECTs in load module
```

The ORDER statement is rarely needed. The purpose of the ORDER statement is to force the physical arrangement of modules within the load module, normally not of special concern. The ORDER statement is useful for programs where certain CSECTs are to be grouped together to minimize virtual storage paging. Since a virtual storage page is only 4K and COBOL programs tend to be much larger, this is seldom a concern with COBOL applications. (Incidentally, the "P" in the syntax specifies that the named CSECT is to begin the next virtual page.)

The only place where you will normally find that the physical arrangement of CSECTS is important is in CICS application load modules prior to LE/370. Prior to LE/370 the CICS stub (DFHECI) needed to appear first within the load module. Here is an example.

```
//SYSLIN   DD  DSN=&&OBJECT
//         DD  *
   ORDER   DFHECI
```

```
     INCLUDE   CICSLIB(DFHECI)
     NAME      CICSTRAN(R)
   //CICSLIB   DD   DSN=cics.library,DISP=SHR
   //SYSLMOD   DD   DSN=LIBD,DISP=OLD
```

CICS link-edit considerations.

Actually, even for COBOL II (only) CICS link-edits, you will not see the above example, which I created only for illustrative purposes. That's much too clumsy to require for routine link-edits. Instead, you will usually see something like the following for CICS links:

```
   //SYSLIN   DD   DSN=cicslib(DFHECI),DISP=SHR
   //         DD   DSN=&&OBJECT,DISP=(OLD,DELETE)
   //SYSLIB   DD   DSN=cics.loadlib(membername),DISP=SHR
```

The above works because the member named DFHECI in this example is not a load module but an INCLUDE statement, something like this:

```
   INCLUDE SYSLIB(DFHECI)
```

This doesn't violate the priority rule of determining the ENTRY address of the module (first module from SYSLIN is default), since this module, although specified first, is not itself in SYSLIN. Therefore the module in &&OBJECT remains the first module processed from SYSLIN, causing it to be the default ENTRY point, even with no ENTRY statement.

To close this discussion of CICS link-edit JCL (which are normally precoded by your technical support staff, anyway), the previous example was explicitly for COBOL II *only*. If your shop has LE/370 and your program is COBOL II or COBOL/370, the link JCL will probably be already structured to provide the LE/370 replacement for DFHECI. That module is DFHELII and provides more LE/370 support (although DFHECI continues to be supported). Another feature of DFHELII is that it may appear anywhere within the load module, so the rigorous requirement of placing it first is no longer necessary.

Relinking COBOL II load modules for LE/370.

By now, you know that COBOL II is so upwardly compatible with COBOL/370 that to convert source programs to COBOL/370 just requires recompiling with the COBOL/370 compiler (assuming you were using the NOCMPR2 compile option with the COBOL II compiler). That gives you full access to all COBOL/370 features, such as its new intrinsic functions. However, you might have COBOL II load modules that you want to benefit from LE/370 or want to link with COBOL/370 modules. Doing that is accomplished by what is known as a "replace link."

The term *replace link* comes from its reliance on the Linkage Editor RE-

PLACE statement, covered previously. If you wish to relink an existing COBOL II load module to benefit from LE/370, here is how to do it:

1. First, be sure that you use the proper PROC at your shop for COBOL/ 370, since that is probably the normal PROC for linking to LE/370. Using a COBOL II link PROC will accomplish nothing.
2. The name of the PROC will probably be unique to your shop. For my example, I will assume a name of CEEWL since that is the name of the IBM-supplied PROC. The following statements will probably be sufficient. If not, see the previous explanations of each statement and adjust as appropriate:

```
//      EXEC CEEWL
//SYSLIN   DD   *
   REPLACE   IGZEBST
   REPLACE   DFHECI                  <== only for CICS applications
   INCLUDE   YOURLIB(loadmodname)
   INCLUDE   CICSLIB(DFHELII)  <== only for CICS applications
   ENTRY     entryname
   NAME      loadmodname (R)
//SYSLMOD  DD   DSN=target.load.library,DISP=OLD
//YOURLIB  DD   DSN=your.load.library,DISP=SHR
//CICSLIB  DD   DSN=cics.system.library,DISP=SHR
```

Naturally, the order of appearance of DD statements is important when overriding PROC entries. In most PROCs that I've seen, SYSLIN precedes SYSLMOD, so that is why I placed these DD statements in this order. Whatever RMODE and AMODE attributes your load module had will be retained.

In the previous example, there is a REPLACE statement for only one IGZxxx module. If your load module contains other ones, such as IGZEOPT, include REPLACE statements for them as well. Presence of any ILBOxxx modules indicates a possibility that a VS/COBOL module is part of the load module. If so, REPLACE statements must also be coded for each such ILBOxxx name.

Now that we've reviewed *how* to relink your COBOL II module, remember—it isn't required. COBOL II modules will still function as before whether they are recompiled or relinked. You need do so only where you want to benefit from either new COBOL/370 features (a recompile) or new LE/370 features (a relink).

This section on the Linkage Editor was not intended to give you all possible information for using it. Instead, it was intended to help you understand the flow and to help you determine when you need various JCL and control statements. JCL for the Linkage Editor is defined in JCL Requirements.

3.11. SPECIFYING COBOL II AND COBOL/370 OPTIONS

The COBOL compile options are referenced throughout this book, often with partial explanations or examples of use. This section is somewhat more academic, explaining what each option does and its typical uses, rather than describing tips and techniques.

3.11.1. Options Available

The options available fall into three categories: (1) those you may specify at compile-time, (2) those you may specify at run-time, and (3) those you cannot specify at compile or run-time. I make you aware of that third category because, if your attempts to override an option aren't working, it may be because your company has prevented them from working. This ability to enforce compile options was new with COBOL II and is extended to COBOL/370.

COBOL compile-time options.
Since those options specified at compile-time are the most common, let's look at them first. Figure 3.3 lists them by general category. Several options appear in more than one column. The categories are

Performance: These are options that affect resource usage, either at compile-time or at run-time. "R" means the option affects run-time, "C" means the option affects compile-time, and "O" means the option affects input/output of the compiler, other than to SYSPRINT.

Documentation: These are options that affect the input or SYSPRINT output (normally, printed listings) from the compile.

Structure: These are options that affect the module-to-module structure, and the residency and addressing facilities of the run-time module.

Standards: These options provide opportunities your company may wish to use to monitor or enforce standards.

Test-debug: These options provide debugging capabilities but at the expense of extra resource usage. "C" is for compiler debugging, and is for use by systems programmers.

Run-time effect: These are options that have an effect on the run-time environment, either in required JCL, data formats, application logic, or options that may be changed from that specified at compile-time.

Option	Performance	Documentation	Structure	Standards	Test-debug	Runtime Effect?
ADV	R					X
APOST		X				
AWO	R					
BUFSIZE	C					
CMPR2*				X		
COMPILE	C			X		
CURRENCY²				X		
DATA	R		X			X
DBCS						X
DECK	O					
DUMP					C	
DYNAM*	R		X			X
EVENTS²					X	
EXIT	C	X		X		
FASTSRT	R					
FDUMP¹	R				X	
FLAG		X				
FLAGMIG				X		
FLAGSAA				X		
FLAGSTD				X		
LANGUAGE		X				
LIB	O	X				
LINECOUNT		X				
LIST		X				
MAP		X				
NAME	O		X	X		
NUMBER		X				
NUMPROC	R					X
OBJECT	O					
OFFSET		X				
OPTIMIZE	R					
OUTDD						X
RENT*	R		X	X		X

1 = COBOL II only
2 = COBOL/370 only

cont'd

Figure 3.3. COBOL II and COBOL/370 Compile options. (* = CICS-sensitive)

Option	Performance	Documentation	Structure	Standards	Test-debug	Runtime Effect?
RESIDENT*1		R		X	X	X
SEQUENCE			X			
SIZE		C				
SOURCE		X				
SPACE		X				
SSRANGE	R				X	X
TERM	O					
TEST	R				X	
TRUNC	R					X
VBREF		X				
WORD		X		X		
XREF		X				
ZWB						X

1 = COBOL II only
2 = COBOL/370 only

Figure 3.3. *(Continued)*

In reviewing the list, you may want to receive a list of the defaults at your company. You can get one by submitting any program for a compile in which you have included the SOURCE compile option. If you want a list of all COBOL error messages, use this two-statement program:

```
ID DIVISION.
PROGRAM-ID. ERRMSG.
```

ADV   Options: ADV, NOADV
                   Abbreviations: None

This option is used with the WRITE AFTER ADVANCING statement. It adds 1 byte to length of 01-level entry. For example, to write a 133-byte physical record with the first byte for carriage control requires a 132-byte record definition with ADV and requires a 133-byte record definition (with the first byte not referenced) with NOADV. ADV gives better performance and retains device independence.

```
APOST        Options: APOST, QUOTE
                  Abbreviations: APOST, Q
```

This option determines whether you will enclose literals with the apostrophe (') or with quotation marks (").

```
AWO          Options: AWO, NOAWO
                  Abbreviations: None
```

This option specifies **APPLY WRITE ONLY** for any physical sequential datasets with blocked, V-mode records. AWO gives better performance.

```
BUFSIZE      Options: BUFSIZE (integer)
                  Abbreviations: BUF (integer)
```

This option specifies how many bytes may be allocated by the compiler for the work datasets. Specifying BUF(32760) gives best performance.

```
CMPR2        Options: CMPR2, NOCMPR2
                  Abbreviations: None
```

This option provides compatibility with COBOL II, Release 2. (Note: This version of COBOL II is not covered in this book.) The Release 2 implementation of COBOL II was a subset of ANSI 85 and there are some incompatibilities. NOCMPR2 should be the option you use to take full advantage of the features of COBOL II described in this book. If you have earlier COBOL II programs, use CMPR2 and the FLAGMIG compile option to identify potential incompatibilities. CICS and DB2 applications must specify NOCMPR2. Refer to the appropriate programming guide (Chapter 9) for more guidance.

An additional restriction on using CMPR2 is that LE/370's intrinsic functions are not available to you when CMPR2 is specified. If your shop is using CMPR2 as a compile default, you're digging a deep hole. I encourage you to migrate to NOCMPR2 as soon as possible.

```
COMPILE      Options: COMPILE, NOCOMPILE, NOCOMPILE(n)
                  Abbreviations: C, NOC, NOC(n)

                  where n = W for level 4 errors (Warning)
                            E for level 8 errors (Error)
                            S for level 12 errors (Severe)
```

This option specifies whether a compile is to generate object code after detecting an error. COMPILE means to generate object code anyway. NOCOMPILE means to generate no object code, regardless. NOCOMPILE(n) means to stop generating object code if an error of that severity occurs. For example, NOCOMPILE(E) would mean to stop generating object code after appearance of the first level 8 error message. Syntax checking of the program is not affected.

CURRENCY   Options: CURRENCY(literal), NOCURRENCY
                     Abbreviations: CURR, NOCURR

(COBOL/370 only) This option allows an application to specify a symbol other than the dollar sign ($). The default is NOCURR. Since the combinations are complex and rarely used, I will omit a full description of the options. If your shop uses this feature, I'm confident that a standard set of values is available for your use.

DATA   Options: DATA(24), DATA(31)
                     Abbreviations: None

This option specifies whether DATA DIVISION entries are to be allocated below or above the 16-megabyte address. Where possible, specify DATA(31). The primary use of DATA(24) is when you are maintaining compatibility with older, non-COBOL II programs. This option is for use when RENT is specified and is ignored if NORENT is specified. See Module Structure for more information.

DBCS   Options: DBCS, NODBCS
                     Abbreviations: None

This option provides support for the Double Byte Character Set (DBCS), allowing use of non-English characters if the 256 EBCDIC character set is insufficient. There is no further reference to this option in this book. Most applications will specify NODBCS.

DECK   Options: DECK, NODECK
                     Abbreviations: D, NOD

This option specifies that object code is to be written to the SYSPUNCH data set in 80-byte records. It is normally set to NODECK. See also the OBJECT option.

DUMP   Options: DUMP, NODUMP
                     Abbreviations: DU, NODU

This option is not for application debugging. It is for use by your systems programmers when a compiler error is occurring and they are diagnosing it. This should normally be NODUMP.

DYNAM   Options: DYNAM, NODYNAM
                  Abbreviations: DYN, NODYN

This option specifies whether CALL "literal" statements are to generate static CALLS (resolved by the Linkage Editor) or dynamic CALLs (resolved at run-time). For more information, see Static versus Dynamic Calls. For CICS, this must be NODYNAM. DYNAM may not be used with NORES.

EVENTS   Options: EVENTS, NOEVENTS
                  Abbreviations: None

(COBOL/370 only) This option specifies whether the compiler should update the events file. This file is used by CODE/370 to display compile errors. If you are working from a mainframe terminal, you may find no need for this option; however, a programmer working at a PWS and using CODE/370 will find it useful.

If you specify EVENTS, your compile JCL must include a DD statement with a DDNAME of SYSEVENT. This must be a sequential file with these attributes: RECFM=V, LRECL=4095, BLKSIZE=4099.

Other compile options may cause some confusion on what is stored in the events file, since the events file stores statements based on their input sequence number, not their relative number as listed on the source listing. These options are: NOCOMPILE(W | S | E), INEXIT, FLAGSTD, LIB, and NUM.

The EVENTS option may not be specified in a PROCESS or CBL statement. Instead, you are restricted to specifying it (if not your shop's default) only via a JCL PARM at compile-time. (The PROCESS and CBL statements are covered later in this chapter.)

EXIT   Options: NOEXIT, EXIT (options)

The various options are not shown here because your installation must specify what they are. EXIT is specified where an installation has one or more of the following:

   1. A user-written routine that intercepts all requests for SYSIN statements (COBOL source), providing them via the user routine.

   2. A user-written routine that intercepts all COPY statements, providing the source statements via the routine instead of from the SYSLIB DD statement.

   3. A user-written routine that intercepts all output to SYSPRINT and reformats or otherwise processes it.

These are powerful features, allowing a company to (1) read all source statements or COPY statements prior to being processed by the compiler, (2) provide direct access to a source program management system internally instead of via JCL, or (3) provide reformatted or duplicate compiler output listings. For most installations, this is NOEXIT.

```
FASTSRT     Options: FASTSRT, NOFASTSRT
              Abbreviations: FSRT, NOFSRT
```

This option specifies whether you want DFSORT to optimize processing for a COBOL SORT application. FASTSRT can improve processing for any SORT statement that has either a USING or GIVING statement or both (i.e, a SORT... INPUT PROCEDURE...OUTPUT PROCEDURE would not be optimized). When FASTSRT is specified, COBOL II ignores it if the feature cannot improve your program performance. IF NOFASTSRT is specified, COBOL II will still produce information messages where optimization could have been realized.

```
FDUMP       Options: FDUMP, NOFDUMP
              Abbreviations: FDU, NOFDU
```

(COBOL II only) This option specifies that a formatted dump is to be produced at run-time in case of an ABEND. A SYSDBOUT data set is required (e.g., //SYSDBOUT DD SYSOUT=A). For CICS, the dump is written to the CEBRxxxx temporary storage queue (can be suppressed by EXEC CICS HANDLE ABEND command). The formatted dump is not produced if TEST was also specified as a compile option. For more information, see Chapter 4 (Debugging Techniques).

If you are using COBOL/370, the equivalent function is achieved by specifying TEST(NONE,SYM). However, if FDUMP is specified to the COBOL/370 compiler, the compiler transposes it to TEST(NONE,SYM) for you. COBOL/370 does not require the SYSDBOUT DD statement.

```
FLAG        Options: FLAG (x,y), NOFLAG
              Abbreviations: F(x,y), NOF

            where x and y =  I for Informational messages
                             W for level 4 errors (Warning)
                             E for level 8 errors (Error)
                             S for level 12 errors (Severe)
                             U for level 16 errors
                                              (Unrecoverable)
```

This option specifies whether error messages are to appear imbedded in the source listing (new with COBOL II). The x value specifies what error level messages appear at the end of the listing. The y value specifies what error level messages appear within the listing. The y value must not be lower than the x value. For example, FLAG(I,E) means all messages appear at the end, but only level 8 errors and above appear within the listing. NOFLAG specifies no error messages.

FLAGMIG   Options: FLAGMIG, NOFLAGMIG
             Abbreviations: None

This option flags migration errors for incompatibility between COBOL II Release 3.0 and prior levels. See CMPR2 for more information. Normally, this is NOFLAGMIG.

FLAGSAA   Options: FLAGSAA, NOFLAGSAA
             Abbreviations: None

This option flags statements that are incompatible with IBM's Systems Application Architecture (SAA). If your company has standardized on SAA, this should be FLAGSAA. Otherwise, it should be NOFLAGSAA. For more information on SAA, see Chapter 9 (Related Publications).

FLAGSTD   Options: FLAGSTD (options), NOFLAGSTD

This option flags statements that do not conform to the ANSI standard and specified subsets. The options are not listed here as they would be specific to your installation. If your shop enforces a level of ANSI 85 or a Federal Information Processing Standard, then your shop will be using FLAGSTD with some options specified. Otherwise, use NOFLAGSTD.

LANGUAGE Options: LANGUAGE (n)
             Abbreviations: LANG(n)

                 where n = EN for mixed-case English
                           UE for upper-case English only
                           JA or JP for the Japanese language

This option specifies the language to use to print out the compile listing. This includes diagnostic messages, page headers, and compilation summary information. A special Japanese Language Feature must be installed to use options JA or JP. To print output in mixed-case English, specify LANG(EN).

LIB   Options: LIB, NOLIB
             Abbreviations: None

This option specifies whether COPY, BASIS, or REPLACE statements can be used. Since most shops use COPY statements, this should be set to LIB. There is no further reference to BASIS or REPLACE statements in this book. (The

REPLACE statement that is used in this book is for the Linkage Editor, not the compiler.)

```
LINECOUNT    Options: LINECOUNT (n)
             Abbreviations: LC

             where n = number of lines to print per page
```

This option specifies number of lines to print per page on SYSPRINT data set during compilation. Specifying zero causes no page ejects. Since the compiler uses three lines for titles, there will be three fewer COBOL statements per page than the specified line count.

```
LIST         Options: LIST, NOLIST
             Abbreviations: None
```

This option specifies whether a listing of generated assembler code for the compiled program should be produced to SYSPRINT. This is mutually exclusive with the OFFSET option. If both are used, OFFSET receives preference. For information on using this listing, see Chapter 4 (Debugging Techniques).

```
MAP          Options: MAP, NOMAP
             Abbreviations: None
```

This option specifies whether a DATA DIVISION map for the compiled program is to be produced to SYSPRINT.

```
NAME         Options: NAME, NONAME, NAME(ALIAS)
             Abbreviations: None
```

This option specifies whether a Linkage Editor NAME control statement is to be inserted immediately following the last object statement for a program. The NAME statement will use the PROGRAM-ID. If NAME(ALIAS) is specified, ALIAS statements are also generated for all ENTRY statements. For examples of where this is useful, see JCL Requirements in this chapter. Usually the default for this is NONAME.

```
NUMBER       Options: NUMBER, NONUMBER
             Abbreviations: NUM, NONUM
```

This option specifies whether the compiler should use sequence numbers from your program in columns 1–6. If so, they are sequence-checked. To me, this was important when programs were on punched cards. Now, with most people using DASD to store source programs, I suggest using NONUMBER. With

NONUMBER, the compiler generates numbers for the compilation and all diagnostics refer to those generated numbers.

```
NUMPROC    Options: NUMPROC (n)
             Abbreviations: None

           where n = MIG    for migration support
                     PFD    for preferred sign support
                     NOPFD  for no preferred sign support
```

This option specifies how signs in data fields are to be handled by generated code. This topic is explored in Defining, Initializing, and Using Data Areas. Your shop probably has a companywide standard on this option. If, after reading the mentioned topic, you feel your application should use a different option, I suggest you test the application and discuss it with others at your shop. I say this because a book can rarely address the many possibilities that exist. If in doubt, NUMPROC(NOPFD) works, but at the cost of efficiency. The most efficient option is NUMPROC(PFD).

```
OBJECT     Options: OBJECT, NOOBJECT
             Abbreviations: OBJ, NOOBJ
```

This option specifies whether the object module is to be written to the SYSLIN data set in 80-byte records. OBJECT is required if the TEST option is also specified. See also DECK. Both options do the same thing. To generate object code, one of them should be on. I suggest setting this to OBJECT.

```
OFFSET     Options: OFFSET, NOOFFSET
             Abbreviations: OFF, NOOFF
```

This option specifies whether a condensed listing of generated code will be produced to the SYSPRINT dataset. This listing shows the beginning offset location of each procedural statement. See also LIST. If used in conjunction with LIST, LIST will be ignored. For information on using this listing, see Chapter 4 (Debugging Techniques).

```
OPTIMIZE   Options: OPTIMIZE, NOOPTIMIZE
             Abbreviations: OPT, NOOPT
```

This option specifies whether optimized code is to be generated for the compiled program. This is enhanced from the optimizing facility in OS/VS COBOL. When OPTIMIZE is specified, it not only seeks to optimize individual statements, but also to combine statements when possible. In addition, it will attempt to create inline PERFORMs when possible and to bypass any code that will not be executed. Because the generated code is often quite different on a statement-by-statement basis, you may want to specify NOOPTIMIZE during initial testing. NOOPTIMIZE also reduces costs if you do many compiles before putting a program in productional use.

```
OUTDD      Options: OUTDD (ddname)
                Abbreviations: OUT(ddname)
```

This option specifies what ddname will be used for DISPLAY messages at run-time. The option normally specified is OUTDD(SYSOUT).

```
RENT       Options: RENT, NORENT
                Abbreviations: None
```

This option specifies that the compiled program is to be generated with reentrant code. It also allows the program to be executed in memory above the 16-megabyte address. RENT programs may *not* be mixed with NORENT programs. RENT is required for CICS programs. RENT also allows use of DATA(24) or DATA(31). NORENT cannot be used with DATA(31). Unless you have special considerations, I suggest specifying RENT to take advantage of the extended memory accessibility. NORENT supports static CALLs to and from 24-bit programs. See RESIDENT for related information. Also, see the RENT Linkage Editor option in JCL Requirements and Options in the previous section, Creating a Load Module.

```
RESIDENT   Options: RESIDENT, NORESIDENT
                Abbreviations: RES, NORES
```

(COBOL II only) This option specifies that CALLs to COBOL II run-time modules will be resolved at run-time, not during the link-edit phase. This produces smaller load modules that access the most current version of the COBOL II modules. RES is required for CICS programs. See RENT for more information. The setting of RENT and RES cause the following RMODE and AMODE settings to also be made for the module. (COBOL/370 is RES by default.)

These options Allowable combinations		cause these settings RMODE	AMODE
COBOL II:			
RENT	RES	ANY	ANY
NORENT	RES	24	ANY
NORENT	NORES	24	24
RENT	NORES	not allowed	

These options Allowable combinations	cause these settings	
	RMODE	**AMODE**
COBOL/370:		
RENT	ANY	ANY
NORENT	24	ANY

RMODE refers to where a module may be loaded. AMODE refers to the addressability it has within memory, either to data areas or to other programs.

SEQUENCE   Options: SEQUENCE, NOSEQUENCE
               Abbreviations: SEQ, NOSEQ

This option specifies whether the source statement sequence numbers are to be validated. Unless your program is on punched cards, which can be dropped, NOSEQ is more efficient and prevents irrelevant error messages.

SIZE   Options: SIZE (nnnn) or SIZE(MAX) or SIZE(nnnK)
             Abbreviations: SZ(...)

             where n = memory requirements

This option specifies how much memory is to be used by the compiler. To a degree, the compiler is more efficient if more memory is specified. My suggestion is to set it to a number that exceeds REGION size, such as 4000K, with the REGION at 2000K. Setting SIZE(MAX) could cause the compiler to use all memory in the system, compromising performance of other applications.

SOURCE   Options: SOURCE, NOSOURCE
             Abbreviations: S, NOS

This option specifies whether the source listing is to be produced. See the following section on JCL for tips on using this.

SPACE   Options: SPACE (1), SPACE(2) or SPACE(3)
            Abbreviations: None

This option specifies single, double, or triple spacing of the SOURCE listing from the compile.

SSRANGE Options: SSRANGE, NOSSRANGE
             Abbreviations: SSR, NOSSR

This option specifies whether debug code for subscript and index range checking is to be included in the object module. Debug code is also included to check reference modification. This can increase cpu use during running. Output from this option is written to the MVS message log (in batch, this appears as the JES log) or to the CICS CEBRxxxx queue (COBOL II only). The program will be terminated upon occurrence of any detected error.

The SSRANGE compile-time option requires a run-time option as well. For COBOL II, the run-time option has the same name, SSRANGE. For COBOL/370 (i.e., LE/370), the option is CHECK(ON) for the equivalent of SSRANGE, and CHECK(OFF) for the equivalent of NOSSRANGE. SSRANGE at compile-time causes debug code to be inserted into your object module. Specifying the appropriate run-time option causes the debugging to take effect (or not to take effect). A common technique when developing new applications is to specify SSRANGE at compile-time and then to use the run-time options as needed. SSRANGE does reduce performance.

```
TERMINAL    Options: TERMINAL, NOTERMINAL
               Abbreviations: TERM, NOTERM
```

This option requests that messages and diagnostics be sent to the SYSTERM dataset. This was useful prior to full-screen programming environments (e.g., ISPF) when on-line programmers used typewriter terminals.

```
TEST        COBOL II:   Options: TEST, NOTEST
               Abbreviations: TES, NOTES

            COBOL/370:  Options: TEST, NOTEST, TEST(hook,symbol)
               Abbreviations: None
```

As you can see, the TEST option has different options for COBOL II and COBOL/370. In both cases, though, the purpose is the same: to generate debug code for using the compiler's debug tool (COBTEST for COBOL II and CODE/370 Debug Tool for COBOL/370). *NOTE:* With COBOL/370, the option also serves the functions performed by the COBOL II FDUMP option, which is not related to use of a debug facility.

For COBOL II the choices are simple: Use TEST when using COBTEST and use NOTEST for everything else. With COBOL II, TEST also forces NOOPTIMIZE, so performance is seriously affected by TEST.

For COBOL/370, there are a number of choices, none of them easy. COBOL/370 uses two parameters, hook and symbol. Those define to what degree you want debug code generated. Since the options affect the amount of generated output for debugging, generating too much output can be detrimental to a successful debug effort. The hook and symbol options are

hook The hooks determine what logic points are to be trapped during debugging.

NONE NO hooks generated

BLOCK Logic points will be trapped where logic flow is not sequential or can change. This includes IF . . . ELSE statements, the CALL statement, PERFORM loops, and GOTOs.

PATH Same as BLOCK, except program entry and exit points are included.

STMT Every statement and label is trapped. (This may sound like the best choice, but visualize the amount of output you will receive and you may change your mind.)

ALL Same as STMT, except all program entry and exit points are also trapped.

symbol The symbol-table option determines whether dictionary tables are to be generated. These are especially useful as data names are then available for use with the debug language or within dump output. This does increase object code noticeably.

SYM Dictionary will be generated.

NOSYM Dictionary will not be generated.

Specifying NOTEST is the equivalent of specifying TEST(NONE,NOSYM) and causes maximum performance and minimal debug assistance. Specifying TEST is equivalent to TEST(ALL,SYM). TEST(NONE,SYM) will cause output similar to the COBOL II FDUMP option. Specifying any hook value other than NONE causes NOOPTIMIZE option to take effect.

With COBOL/370, there is a run-time LE/370 option that must be specified for the debug code to take effect. The option is TEST. This is normally set to NOTEST, so you will probably need to override it with a JCL PARM, with a modification to a CEEUOPT module, or via a CALL to an LE/370 service called CEETEST. (Yes, all the techniques are reviewed in this book.) Reminder: Specifying TEST at run-time is not necessary if your compile-time option was TEST(NONE,SYM), since all that does is provide an enhanced format of the LE/370 dump in case the program ABENDs.

```
TRUNC        Options: TRUNC (n)
                Abbreviations: None


             where n = BIN    allow full binary value
                       OPT    optimize object code
                       STD    conforms to American National
                              Standard
```

This option determines how binary (COMP) data will be truncated in your application. This is because binary data is stored as 2-byte or 4-byte values, regardless of the PIC clause. Your choice of TRUNC specifies whether the maximum binary value should be allowed, TRUNC(BIN) the American National Standard should be used, TRUNC(STD) or optimized code based on an assessment of the PIC clause and the field size, TRUNC(OPT). This option is discussed at length in a prior section on data efficiency. IBM recommends that you use BIN if your program uses CICS, IMS, or DB2. Because of the performance implications, you may want to test other settings for your application.

BIN allows the maximum value, regardless of the PIC clause. STD uses a generic approach, using only the PIC clause. OPT assesses the field size (2 or 4 bytes) and the PIC clause to generate the most efficient code.

There is no one-to-one correspondence with TRUNC options of prior COBOL compilers.

```
VBREF        Options: VBREF, NOVBREF
             Abbreviations: None
```

This option generates a listing at compile-time of the different verbs used and how many times each verb is used. It can be useful to assess whether a program uses verbs that are unfamiliar to you or that do not follow your shop standards. NOVBREF causes a more efficient compilation.

```
WORD         Options: WORD (xxxx) or NOWORD
             Abbreviations: WD, NOWD

             where xxxx = 4-character name of a word table
             developed by your installation
```

This option allows a company to develop a table of verbs that are to be checked during compilation. For example, if ALTER or GO TO are not allowed, they could be placed in this table, and at compile-time generate a warning message developed by your shop.

If you're using COBOL/370 (or COBOL II, Release 3.2 or later), IBM has included a CICS-specific table to assist in monitoring CICS programs to ensure they contain no unsupported verbs. That is invoked by specifying WORD(CICS) at compile-time. If your shop is using a version of COBOL II prior to Release 3.2, but you like the idea of having a CICS-specific word table, it would be an easy task for your technical support personnel to create one since the process is well documented in IBM manuals.

```
XREF         Options: XREF, XREF(SHORT), XREF(FULL) or NOXREF
             Abbreviations: X, NOX
```

This option specifies whether a cross-reference listing is to be produced by the compiler. The cross-reference listing is at the end of the source listing and if SOURCE is specified is appended at the right of related source statements.

XREF and XREF(FULL) generate a listing of all names. XREF(SHORT) generates a listing of referenced names. XREF(SHORT) and XREF(FULL) may not be used with versions of COBOL II prior to version 3.1.

ZWB
          Options: ZWB, NOZWB
              Abbreviations: None

ZWB causes a compare of a signed numeric item with an alphanumeric item to have the sign stripped prior to the compare, e.g., a +5 (hex C5) would be equal to 5 (hex F5). Although I don't recommend it, NOZWB can be used if you compare numeric items to SPACES.

COBOL run-time options.

Run-time options are especially important to understand, as the performance of your application is dependent on them. Your technical staff may have installed the shop-wide default software options without knowing your requirements. If only a few are in conflict, you can override them for batch jobs by using a JCL PARM. If your application is CICS or IMS, you will need more drastic action to change them. Both options are covered in the text.

Since the COBOL II run-time library only needed to support requirements for COBOL II programs, there are only a handful of COBOL II run-time options. LE/370, though, because it must provide an operational environment for a growing list of languages, is much more comprehensive in its offerings. This text will not cover the more technical performance options, such as HEAP, STACK, or STORAGE, as those are normally established by systems programmers. Instead, this text will cover the LE/370 run-time options that are most commonly used by COBOL programmers and application designers.

Also, while this text implies that all run-time options may be overridden for LE/370, IBM provided the ability for systems programmers to set any combination of them as "non-modifiable." This can be productive if certain options are desired for corporate standards. Such enforcement can be costly, though, if the standard settings are for downward-compatibility (e.g., ALL31(OFF)) and prevent newer applications from taking advantage of new features. If you need to override some options that can't be overridden, discuss it with your technical support staff.

These options may be different for different environments, e.g., CICS and non-CICS. These options are usually set for an entire shop. They are presented here so you may modify (some of) them at run-time. You may need to contact your technical staff for assistance in their selection and use. Figure 3.4 lists them by some general categories. Several run-time options appear in more than one column. The categories are

Performance: These are options that affect resource usage.

Documentation: These are options that affect the input or SYSPRINT output (normally printed listings) from the compile.

Structure: These are options that affect the module-to-module structure, and the residency and addressing facilities of the run-time module.

Standards: These options provide opportunities your company may use to monitor or enforce standards.

Test-debug: These options provide debugging capabilities, but at the expense of extra resource usage.

How to specify: These two columns specify whether your company defaults may be overridden and how. For information on how to do this, see Specifying Options at Run-Time and Specifying Options via Preassembled Modules.

| OPTIONS | | | | | | | How to override | | |
| | | | | | | | COBOL II | | LE/ 370 |
COBOL II	LE/370	PERFORMANCE	DOCUMENTATION	STRUCTURE	STANDARDS	TEST-DEBUG	USE IGZEOPT	USE JCL	JCL OR CEEUOPT
AIXBLD*	AIXBLD*	X			X		X	X	X
	ALL31	X							X
	CBLOPTS		X		X				X
	CBLPSHPOP	X		X	X				X
DEBUG	DEBUG	X				X	X	X	X
LANGUAGE	NATLANG		X					X	
LIBKEEP*		X		X	X				
MIXRES*		X	X				X		X
RTEREUS*	RTEREUS*	X	X				X	X	X
SIMVRD*	SIMVRD*	X					X	X	X
SPOUT	RPTOPTS		X			X	X	X	X
	RPTSTG		X			X			X
SSRANGE	CHECK	X				X	X	X	X
STAE	TRAP	X		X	X	X	X	X	X
	TEST	X				X			X
UPSI	UPSI			X			X	X	X
WSCLEAR	STORAGE	X			X				X

Figure 3.4. COBOL II and COBOL/370 (LE/370) run-time options.

Before reviewing these, you may want to get a listing of your company defaults. This may be accomplished by submitting a program for a compile, link, and execute. If you have no program, this one works fine:

```
ID DIVISION.
PROGRAM-ID. EXAMPLE.
PROCEDURE DIVISION.
1.  STOP RUN.
```

The run-time EXEC statement for the linked program needs this format:

```
// EXEC PGM=programname,PARM='/SPOUT '        <== for COBOL II
```

or

```
// EXEC PGM=programname,PARM='/RPTOPTS(ON)' <== for LE/370
```

The options will be listed on the JES log. These options will be those for the batch environment. For a CICS or IMS/DC environment, ask your systems programmer. Normally, you won't need to override, or even know about most of these options, other than some for debugging purposes. Here is an example of the output:

```
+IGZ025I Run-time options in effect: 'SYSTYPE(OS), LANGUAGE(UE),
+       NOAIXBLD, NODEBUG, LIBKEEP, NOMIXRES, RTEREUS, NOSIMVRD, SPOUT,
+       NOSSRANGE, STAE, NOWSCLEAR, UPSI(00000000)'
+        Default options overridden: 'NOSPOUT'
+        Maximum physical space allocated by the space manager was
+       '16384' bytes above 16 megabytes and '8192' bytes below 16
+       megabytes.
```

If this doesn't work properly, that means you are using LE/370 and the run-time option CBLOPTS is set to OFF. To see a list of the run-time options, change your EXEC statement as follows:

```
// EXEC PGM=programname,PARM='RPTOPTS(ON)/'
```

This is normally an undesirable situation, and I encourage you to ask that the default for CBLOPTS at your shop be changed to CBLOPTS(ON) if this feature was commonly used with COBOL II applications. Otherwise, you face an unproductive conversion process.

So, what's happening here? When IBM introduced LE/370, the format for setting run-time options was reversed. That's right—the COBOL II run-time library expects a PARM to consist of application data, a slash (optional), and run-time options. LE/370 has it reversed. To provide coexistence with existing

COBOL applications, LE/370 provides a run-time option, CBLOPTS, to signal that the options should be switched back to the same as COBOL II.

What follows are run-time options that apply to COBOL applications. For COBOL II, all are shown. For COBOL/370, only the most typical ones for COBOL use are shown. (If you need information on all of the LE/370 options, see IBM's *LE/370 Programming Guide* (Chapter 9, Related Publications).

AIXBLD   Options: AIXBLD, NOAIXBLD

If this option is specified, the system checks for empty VSAM indexes at OPEN and invokes Access Method Services to build alternate indexes. This affects performance and also requires that a DD statement be included for Access Method Services messages. NOAIXBLD means that VSAM indexes are already defined. The DD for COBOL II is SYSPRINT; for LE/370, it is SYSOUT.

ALL31   Options: ALL31(ON|OFF)

(LE/370 only) This option has a major impact on performance. ALL31(ON) should be set to ON if all modules in the run unit are AMODE(31). This causes all memory allocated for the COBOL application (other than WORKING STORAGE, which is controlled by the DATA (31|24) option) to be allocated wherever MVS acquires it, normally above the 16 megabyte line.

Setting ALL31 to ON also stops any AMODE switching to be performed during dynamic CALLs to other run-units. This is because run-time options are set at the time the first run unit in a task or jobstep is initiated. For example, if you have a COBOL/370 application (or COBOL II application running under LE/370) that CALLs an OS/VS COBOL module dynamically, you would need to set ALL31 to OFF to allow for the run-time library to switch the AMODE to provide addressability to the other module. With CICS, the default is ALL31(ON).

For maximum compatibility, set this to ALL31(OFF). This is an excellent migration tool, but you should be working toward the day when all applications are 31-bit addressable and ALL31(ON) can be the default.

Although not covered specifically in this text due to its complexity, you need to be aware of the STACK run-time option if ALL31(OFF) is specified. The STACK option specifies where memory is allocated for temporary work areas for COBOL library routines. When ALL31(OFF) is specified, the STACK option must also be set to STACK(,,BELOW). This protects the application environment, since one or more modules are in 24-bit mode. Normally, STACK is one of the options that is tuned, based on data from the RPTSTG option. In most situations, your technical support staff will advise on this value.

CBLOPTS   Options: CBLOPTS(ON|OFF)

(LE/370 only) This option is to provide compatibility for COBOL applications that use the PARM to pass information to the application. The default with LE/370 is

```
PARM='[run-time options/][application data]'
```

With **CBLOPTS(ON)**, the PARM (only for COBOL run-units) becomes

```
PARM='[application data][/run-time options]'
```

CBLPSHPOP   Options: CBLPSHPOP(ON|OFF)

(LE/370 only) This option is only for CICS. Set to ON, all HANDLE conditions are suspended whenever a CALL is made to a COBOL II or COBOL/370 subprogram and then reinstated upon return. For maximum performance, CICS applications should use the NOHANDLE option on CICS commands and specify CBLPSHPOP(OFF).

DEBUG   Options: DEBUG, NODEBUG

This option is effective when WITH DEBUGGING MODE is specified in the source program. This is the only reference to WITH DEBUGGING MODE in this book.

LANGUAGE   Options:

(COBOL II only) See this option above, under COBOL compile-time options. (The LE/370 equivalent is NATLANG.) This specifies the language for run-time messages.

LIBKEEP   Options: LIBKEEP, NOLIBKEEP

(COBOL II only) This option causes all COBOL II run-time modules to be retained in memory during a run unit. This can increase performance, especially if COBOL modules are CALLed by non-COBOL main programs. In most cases, LIBKEEP should be specified.

Okay, you're probably wondering, "Where's the LE/370 equivalent for something this important?" Actually, LE/370 minimizes the need for such an option. If you believe your application needs this service, discuss your requirements with your technical staff. LE/370 provides many pre-initialization services and they can help you decide the best approach.

MIXRES   Options: MIXRES, NOMIXRES

(COBOL II only) This option is specified when RES and NORES programs are combined within a single run unit. It is primarily used for migration assistance to COBOL II, when NORES was the previous default. It should be used only if needed and not used as an ongoing standard. Considerations on using MIXRES are in the section Using OS/VS COBOL Programs in Module Structures.

NATLANG   Options: NATLANG(ENU|UEN|JPN)

(LE/370 only) This option does for the run-time environment what the LANGUAGE option does for the compile environment: it specifies in what language run-time error messages are produced. ENU is for upper- and lower-case English; UEN is for upper-case English, and JPN. (*NOTE:* Other national languages are available via the LE/370 CALLable service CEE3LNG, but that is beyond the scope of this book.)

RTEREUS   Options: RTEREUS, NORTEREUS

This option was discussed earlier in the section Module Structures. RTEREUS initializes the run-time environment for reusability. This option does not apply to CICS. It affects program structure and may or may not be set at your installation. Specifying RTEREUS for IMS/DC applications is dependent on several factors, including preload considerations and the use of GOBACK or STOP RUN. Check with your technical staff if you have concerns for IMS/DC applications.

SIMVRD   Options: SIMVRD, NOSIMVRD

When processing a variable length relative dataset, this option uses a VSAM KSDS to simulate that data organization.

SPOUT   Options: SPOUT, NOSPOUT

(COBOL II only) This option issues a message indicating the amount of storage allocated and the selected run-time options in effect. It uses the WTP (write-to-programmer) facility (in batch, this is the MVS JES log). In CICS, the message goes to the CEBRxxxx queue. (RPTOPTS is the LE/370 equivalent.)

RPTOPTS   Options: RPTOPTS(ON|OFF)

(LE/370 only) The RPTOPTS option causes a listing of all run-time settings to be printed on the SYSOUT dataset. This option is usually set to OFF, being overridden via a JCL PARM when a person wants to see what settings are set for an application. Output for CICS goes to a transient data queue named CESE.

RPTSTG   Options: RPTSTG(ON|OFF)

(LE/370 only) This is similar in process to RPTOPTS in that it generates a report to SYSOUT containing information on how storage was used during execution of the application. This is normally done during the test phase for performance-oriented applications. An explanation about the report produced can be found in the IBM manual *LE/370 Debugging and Run-time Messages Guide* (Chapter 9, Related Publications). The information should be reviewed with your technical staff. Output for CICS goes to a transient data queue named CESE.

SSRANGE   Options: SSRANGE, NOSSRANGE

(COBOL II only) This option activates the SSRANGE object code generated during compile-time. This feature allows you to compile with SSRANGE, yet control its use at run-time. Using NOSSRANGE at run-time can reduce cpu usage somewhat, and it eliminates the need to recompile to activate SSRANGE. Many shops set the default to NOSSRANGE to prevent inadvertent use of SSRANGE in productional applications. (The CHECK option is the LE/370 equivalent.)

CHECK   Options: CHECK(ON|OFF)

(LE/370 only) This option is used in conjunction with the SSRANGE compile option. It functions identically to the COBOL II SSRANGE run-time option. Maximum performance occurs when CHECK is set to OFF.

STAE   Options: STAE, NOSTAE

(COBOL II only) STAE causes COBOL II to intercept ABENDs, clean up the run-time environment, and produce a formatted dump (if FDUMP was specified). STAE is the normal setting and is recommended for CICS and IMS applications. (TRAP is the LE/370 equivalent.)

TRAP   Options: TRAP(ON|OFF)

(LE/370 only) TRAP specifies how LE/370 is to respond to application error conditions. Setting TRAP(ON) is the norm and is recommended for most situations. TRAP(OFF) is primarily for system level problem investigation.

TEST   Options:

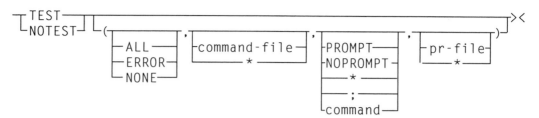

(LE/370 only) This option has a complex structure (obviously). This is the run-time component for the COBOL/370 compile-time TEST option and defines whether the CODE/370 Debug Tool will be invoked and, if so, with what options.

ALL, ERROR, and NONE These specify that the Debug Tool receives control only at a prespecified hook, on an error condition, on the attention function, or termination. ALL gives control for all conditions, good or otherwise. ERROR gives control only for error conditions. NONE specifies that the Debug Tool receives control only for prespecified hooks.

command-file or * These specify whether the Debug Tool is to receive primary commands from a dataset (command-file) or from the terminal (*). The command-file entry may be a DDNAME or a dataset name.

PROMPT or ; Specifies that the Debug Tool is to be invoked when LE/370 is initialized.

NOPROMPT or * Specifies that the Debug Tool is not to be automatically invoked when LE/370 is initialized.

command This can be a command list (normally in single quotes) of a valid Debug Tool command.

pr-file or * This specifies whether a preference file is to be allocated. The "*" indicates that it is not. The indicator for pr-file can be a DDNAME or a dataset name. This allows the programmer to specify settings for the debug environment.

The options may also be specified with NOTEST. This allows a default setting to be NOTEST, yet contain a shop's most common settings. Then, all that is needed is to specify TEST with no options. LE/370 merges the TEST and NOTEST settings at run-time.

As you probably guessed, using the TEST run-time option with LE/370 requires that you also know the CODE/370 Debug Tool. As I mentioned earlier in the book, in-depth information will not be provided since this book's focus is on development and prevention, not on correction. High-level information is in Chapter 4, Debugging Techniques with COBOL II and COBOL/370.

UPSI   Options: UPSI (nnnnnnnn)
          where *n* = digit from 0 to 7

There are 8 UPSI switches. They are provided for backward compatibility if a shop is dependent on their use. These switches cannot be referenced if the option NOCMPR2 is set. Since NOCMPR2 is the preferred option to take advantage of the newest COBOL features, the UPSI feature is meaningless at most shops.

WSCLEAR   Options: WSCLEAR, NOWSCLEAR

(COBOL II only) This option causes all external data records and working storage areas acquired by a RENT program to be set to binary zeros (other than fields with VALUE clauses). This can reduce performance. Another approach is to write initialization code in your program or use more VALUE statements. (STORAGE (00) is the LE/370 equivalent.)

STORAGE   Options: See text

(LE/370 only) This option has more complexities than this book will address. The option supports various values for Heap storage and stack frames, topics not addressed here. So, why is it in the book? It is here because you should know the normal, default setting and also the setting that may be needed by applications that are dependent on WORKING STORAGE and external data areas acquired for RENT programs being initialized to binary zeros. If your application is dependent on binary zeros being in uninitialized data areas, use STORAGE(00). This specifies that all dynamically acquired areas are to be filled with hex "00". Doing this degrades performance and I don't recommend it. The default setting is usually STORAGE(NONE,NONE,NONE).

Additional COBOL options.

There are other options that you cannot use, but that affect COBOL II and COBOL/370. They are listed here in case some of the information I've given you in other sections appears to conflict with what is happening to your code. These options are set at the time COBOL is installed or modified by your systems programmers. If you believe the options are incorrect at your installation, you will need to see your systems programmers to determine the settings.

ALOWCBL(YES) This option specifies whether PROCESS or CONTROL statements may be imbedded in source program. The default is YES. It is required for CICS. (You will want to use these statements, since they allow programmers to control SOURCE output.)

DBCSXREF(NO) The default is NO. This option specifies some cross-reference options for DBCS (the double-byte facility for languages with extensive alphabets). If you specify YES, you must order more software. If your installation needs DBCS, this option must be set to YES.

INEXIT, LIBEXIT, PRTEXIT These are the three components that make up the EXIT facility. If your company uses one or more of these, they can be set to be the default by your systems programmer.

LVLINFO This is a Systems Engineering option to specify what level is used at your company. If specified, up to four characters may follow the IBM Release number. It is a means of keeping track of different releases in your shop's terms. Default is to just print the IBM level number.

NUMCLS(PRIM) This is the technical side of NUMPROC. This setting determines what signs NUMPROC will accept. NUMPROC(PRIM) is the assumption used in this book, since it supports signs that are either C, D, or F.

3.11.2. Specifying COBOL Options via JCL at Compile-Time

The options you need to specify are those other than the installation defaults. They may be coded as follows:

```
//   EXEC cobolprocname,PARM='option-1,option-2,...'

     Example: // EXEC COBC,PARM='SOURCE,OFFSET,OPTIMIZE'
```

3.11.3. Specifying COBOL Options Within the Source Program

There will be times when you aren't familiar with the JCL or when you want to keep a program's compile options with the source code. That can be done with PROCESS statements. A PROCESS statement may be anywhere between columns 1 and 66. There may be no spaces between options. You may use more than one PROCESS statement. The format is

```
PROCESS   option-a,option-b,...

Example: PROCESS   SOURCE,OFFSET,VBREF
         PROCESS   XREF,OPTIMIZE
               ID DIVISION.
                 .
                 .
```

Other than for installation options that have been defined as not eligible for override, the PROCESS options take precedence over any in the JCL and over the installation defaults. You may use CBL in place of PROCESS if desired. (Don't confuse this with *CBL statements, covered in JCL Requirements.)

3.11.4. Specifying COBOL Options at Run-Time via JCL

As noted, the run-time options may be specified via JCL at run-time or via a module called IGZEOPT or CEEUOPT. This topic addresses the JCL approach. The JCL option may be used if your program is capable of accepting a PARM at run-time (e.g., CICS and IMS programs cannot). The syntax is to code the PARM statement with the selected run-time option(s) preceded by a slash. Any PARM the application program is to receive must be to the left of the slash mark.

The first example executes a program called MYPROG, and sets SSRANGE on (assuming program was compiled with SSRANGE). The second example has two logical PARMs, one for the application and one for the run-time options. The first PARM is WEEKLY and is made available to the program via the PROCE-DURE DIVISION USING statement. The second PARM is SSRANGE and is processed by the run-time environment.

```
//   EXEC PGM=MYPROG,PARM='/SSRANGE'
```

or

```
//   EXEC PGM=MYPROG,PARM='WEEKLY/SSRANGE'
```

By now, I hope you are able to recognize that the above examples are explic-itly for COBOL II, since SSRANGE is not a run-time option for LE/370 (and, by default, COBOL/370). Here is a similar example for a program being executed under control of LE/370 where AMODE switching is required and SSRANGE is to be activated:

```
//   EXEC PGM=MYPROG,PARM='CHECK(ON),ALL31(OFF),STACK(,,BELOW)'
```

3.11.5. Specifying COBOL Run-Time Options in Preassembled Modules

There will be times when you need to specify run-time options and can't use JCL (e.g., CICS and IMS) or you want to specify options that cannot be specified via JCL. (See Figure 3.4.) In those cases, your installation must establish a module for each combination of desired options. (IBM provides a facility that your tech-nical staff can use to create this module.) You can include the module into your program during link-edit processing. You use normal INCLUDE processing (see the previous section, Creating a Load Module) to accomplish this.

This module is never required but, if present, causes specific run-time op-tions to be in effect for this load module. This feature is possible because there is always an IBM-supplied module in every COBOL II or COBOL/370 load module. Its name is IGZEBST, and it contains a weak external reference (WXTRN) to the module. For COBOL II, the module is named IGZEOPT. For COBOL/370, the module is CEEUOPT. While coded differently by your systems programmers, they yield equivalent results to the application. (*NOTE:* If LE/370 detects the presence of an IGZEOPT module in a run unit, a message is produced, acknowledging that the IGZEOPT module exists, but it will be ignored.)

NOTE: If COBOL II or COBOL/370 is new at your shop, the needed combinations of IGZEOPT or CEEUOPT modules may not have been created. Your systems programmers need to be told all possibilities that may be needed so they can create them. For example, if the default for a COBOL II shop is NOSSRANGE, a version of IGZEOPT needs to be made available with SSRANGE. Otherwise, modules that are invoked without JCL, such as CICS, will not have access to the capability. With COBOL/370 this becomes even more critical because COBOL/370 can have many more combinations of debug run-time options that are needed. This is because COBOL/370 also uses the run-time option for invoking the CODE/370 Debug tool (covered in Chapter 4) and for optimizing use of allocated memory with the ALL31 and STACK options (covered elsewhere in this chapter).

3.12. JCL REQUIREMENTS: COMPILE, LINK AND EXECUTE

Your installation will probably use JCL differently from what is shown here. This information may be useful, however, to assist you in improving performance or in understanding some of the processing steps. While you may have other facilities at your shop, such as on-line compile and test facilities, this section deals with the batch facility. It is a common format across most installations and is usually the least expensive.

3.12.1. JCL for Compilation

In most installations, JCL procedures (PROCs) will be used for the compile, since there is so much JCL to specify. See Figure 3.5 for an example.

Typical PROCs from IBM may have names such as in this chart. Check with your technical support staff for the ones that are set up for your use.

	JCL PROC names	
Compiler	Compile	Comp&Link
COBOL II	COB2UC	COB2UCL
COBOL/370	IGYWC	IGYWCL

Examples here assume the name of the PROC is COBC, but that is probably not the case. Your shop may have developed custom PROCs and you need to know of them. As you read the next few pages, you will see that I have specific suggestions to improve the compile JCL and to make departmental standards more accessible (e.g., standardizing options for test separately from options for production).

While the JCL at your shop may be different, let's review the sample MVS compile JCL in Figure 3.5. You may find it is more efficient than what your shop is using. (Note: DD statements may be in any order.)

1. Statement 1 specifies any symbolic JCL parameters.
2. The REGION on line 2 ensures that a SIZE compile option exceeding 2048K won't access more memory than 2048K. (Having the SIZE option set to a higher value than 2048K allows the REGION to be increased if appropriate without also needing to change the SIZE parameter concurrently.)
3. The PARM on line 3 is an example of a compiler option that was not specified as a company default, but will be treated as such if no other PARMs are specified.
4. Statement number 4 should have the name of your installation's library where COBOL is stored.
5. Statement number 6 points to a partitioned dataset for COPY statements. (COBOL II and COBOL/370 allow the block size of this data set to be double that allowed with OS/VS COBOL.)

```
 1.  //COBC    PROC  OUT='*'
 2.  //COB      EXEC  PGM=IGYCRCTL,REGION=2048K,
 3.  //               PARM=NOSOURCE
 4.  //STEPLIB  DD   DSN=your.cobol.compiler.library,DISP=SHR
 5.  //SYSLIB   DD   DSN=your.cobol.COPY.library,DISP=SHR
 6.  //SYSPRINT DD   SYSOUT=&OUT,DCB=BLKSIZE=133
 7.  //SYSLIN   DD   DSN=&&OBJECT,UNIT=SYSDA,
 8.  //               DISP=(MOD,PASS),SPACE=(TRK,(40,10)),
 9.  //               DCB=(BLKSIZE=3200,RECFM=FB)
10.  //SYSUT1   DD   UNIT=SYSDA,SPACE=(CYL,(1,1))
11.  //SYSUT2   DD   UNIT=SYSDA,SPACE=(CYL,(1,1))
12.  //SYSUT3   DD   UNIT=SYSDA,SPACE=(CYL,(1,1))
13.  //SYSUT4   DD   UNIT=SYSDA,SPACE=(CYL,(1,1))
14.  //SYSUT5   DD   UNIT=SYSDA,SPACE=(CYL,(1,1))
15.  //SYSUT6   DD   UNIT=SYSDA,SPACE=(CYL,(1,1))
16.  //SYSUT7   DD   UNIT=SYSDA,SPACE=(CYL,(1,1))
```

Figure 3.5. Sample COBOL II or COBOL/370 Compile JCL for MVS.

6. The SOURCE, OFFSET, LIST, MAP, VBREF, and XREF information is written to the DD statement on line 6 (SYSPRINT). This defaults to RECFM=FBA, LRECL=133.

7. The DISP of MOD on line 8 allows multiple compiles to be in a job prior to a link-edit. This allows concatenated object modules for a multiple-module structure.

8. The DCB parameter on line 9 is the largest block size that can be processed by the Linkage Editor. If this is not specified on the JCL, COBOL defaults to a block size of 80 bytes. Use this option to reduce I/O during compiles.

9. Lines 10 through 16 are work files. They are allocated to cylinders to minimize I/O. Their block sizes are determined by the setting of the BUF compile option.

10. The source statement input dataset, SYSIN, is not in this example, since it is provided by the programmer in the job stream. It must have a record size (LRECL) of 80 bytes and may or may not be blocked. Efficiency is increased if the dataset has a large block size, especially for big programs (by large block size, I mean 12,000 or more).

11. If you are using COBOL/370 and have specified the EVENTS option, you will also need to specify a DD with DDNAME of SYSEVENT. This is a sequential file and explained with the EVENTS compile option. The dataset is used to capture compile information for display via CODE/370 at a PWS.

Tips to control the compile process.

Multiple standard options At most shops, there are usually several standard sets of compile options that people use. For example, it may be common at your installation to specify "SOURCE,OFFSET,NOOPTIMIZE" during testing and "SOURCE,LIST,OPTIMIZE,MAP" when compiling for productional use. Instead of requiring programmers to code all that and be subject to a coding error, you could set up standard combinations in a PDS using PROCESS statements (these were covered in a previous section, Specifying COBOL Options). Using my example, you might code three PDS members (LRECL=80, RECFM=FB).

Member: USEDEF
This member would have one blank record.

Member: TEST:
This member would have this statement:

```
PROCESS SOURCE,OFFSET,NOOPTIMIZE
```

Member: PROD:
 This member would have this statement:

```
PROCESS SOURCE,LIST,OPTIMIZE,MAP
```

Now, if we insert a SYSIN DD statement in the compile PROC and change the PROC statement itself (using the example in figure 3.5) to include these two statements:

```
//COBC   PROC  OUT='*',OPTION=USEDEF
      .
      .
      .

//SYSIN   DD  DSN=your.library(&OPTION),DISP=SHR
//        DD  DDNAME=SOURCE
```

we could specify the desired combinations by coding

```
// EXEC COBC                  for defaults
//SOURCE DD....
```

or

```
// EXEC COBC,OPTION=TEST      for "testing" options
//SOURCE  DD  ....
```

or

```
// EXEC COBC,OPTION=PROD      for "production" compiles
//SOURCE  DD  ....
```

Too often, systems programmers, in their desire to construct a compile PROC that meets everyone's needs, create a PROC that pleases no one. The previous suggestion eliminates all those problems. Frequently, one department is coping with batch-oriented, poorly coded modules, while another department is moving forward with on-line programs developed with structured techniques. The options that get the work done for one group will penalize the other.

A company where I provided some assistance in their move toward COBOL II found that my table-oriented technique opened several opportunities for them. They established PDS members with compile options for batch, CICS, unit test, system test, acceptance test, and production. By doing this, they were able to create tight control on what options were normally used, depending on what phase a program was in. The improved documentation of having all compile options in a single dataset instead of in each programmer's JCL dataset was an additional benefit.

Multiple compiles There are two ways to do multiple compiles with a single execution of the compile. One is to compile a main program and one or more CALLed subprograms to link them into one run unit. The other is to compile multiple programs that are each to be linked as separate run units. Let's take them separately.

Compiling a main module and subprogram(s) Insert "END PROGRAM program-id." as the last statement in each program. This lets the compiler tell the various programs apart. The second step is to arrange the sequence of source programs in the order you want the object modules to be created. Then, one execution of the compiler creates all the object modules in the specified sequence, such as:

```
//    EXEC COBC,PARM='SOURCE,OFFSET'
//SYSIN   DD    your.source.lib(MAINPROG),DISP=SHR
//        DD    your.source.lib(SUBPROGA),DISP=SHR
//        DD    your.source.lib(SUBPROGB),DISP=SHR
```

This generates the object code first for MAINPROG, then SUBPROGA, followed by SUBPROGB. From the information in the previous section, Creating a Load Module, you know that this minimizes or eliminates the need to code Linkage Editor control statements.

Compiling several independent modules Insert "END PROGRAM program-id.," as in the previous example, as the last statement in each program. This lets the compiler tell the various programs apart. The second step is to specify the NAME option (along with any other options) on the compile JCL. Then, one execution of the compiler creates all the object modules with Linkage Editor NAME control statements following each one.

This example generates the object code for PROGA, PROGC, and PROGB and places a NAME control statement after each one. From the section Creating a Load Module, you know that this causes the Linkage Editor, in one execution, to create three separate load modules with no need for Linkage Editor control statements.

```
//    EXEC COBC,PARM='SOURCE,OFFSET,NAME'
//SYSIN   DD    your.source.lib(PROGA),DISP=SHR
//        DD    your.source.lib(PROGC),DISP=SHR
//        DD    your.source.lib(PROGB),DISP=SHR
```

Limiting printed output with *CBL. You can control the printing of SOURCE statements, assembler statements (LIST option), and data maps (the

MAP option). This could be useful (and save some trees) when you have a large program, have changed a few statements, and need to see the output from one or more of those three options (SOURCE, LIST, MAP). Here is how it is done.

1. Specify appropriate compile options via JCL or PROCESS statements. These must include those which you want to control. In our example of controlling source and assembler statements, we would specify SOURCE and LIST via a JCL PARM or PROCESS statements (if not already the installation default). This causes the compile to begin with the *options set on.* That is mandatory. If the options are set to NOSOURCE, NOLIST, or NOMAP, the next steps cannot take effect.

2. Next, immediately (or wherever desired) include a statement in your source program that is similar to the PROCESS statement. This is a *CBL statement also known as a CONTROL statement. The *CBL statement is similar to PROCESS, but it can only specify SOURCE or NOSOURCE, MAP or NOMAP, LIST or NOLIST, or some combination of the three. When encountered by the compiler, the compiler adjusts the compile options according to the *CBL options specified. The *CBL statement may begin in any column, starting with column 7. As with PROCESS, no spaces may appear between options. The reason to code the *CBL immediately is to negate any listings until we reach the part of our program we want to list. For our example, we would specify

```
*CBL   NOSOURCE,NOLIST
```

3. Then, immediately preceding the code you want a listing of, insert another *CBL statement, such as

```
*CBL   SOURCE,LIST
```

4. Finally, at the end of the code you want listed, insert another *CBL statement, identical to that in step 2.

Let's put all this together in an example using PROCESS and *CBL statements. Assume that SOURCE and LIST are set to NOSOURCE and NOLIST as installation defaults. Here is the example:

```
PROCESS SOURCE,LIST
                *CBL NOSOURCE,NOLIST
Not          ┌─→  ID DIVISION.
printed      │      ·
             └─→    ·
                *CBL SOURCE,LIST
```

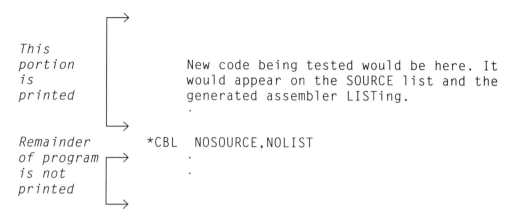

This
portion
is
printed

New code being tested would be here. It would appear on the SOURCE list and the generated assembler LISTing.

Remainder   *CBL   NOSOURCE,NOLIST
of program
is not
printed

Using *CBL statements takes practice and adds work to the compile process, but this feature puts the ability to reduce paper usage in the programmer's hands. Prior to COBOL II, it was an all-or-nothing situation. (NOTE: *CONTROL may be used in place of *CBL.)

3.12.2. JCL for Link-Edit Processing

The processing of the Linkage Editor was covered in the section Creating a Load Module. This topic deals with the JCL requirements. Here is an example of an MVS procedure to use with the previous MVS example for compiling:

```
 1.  //LKED      PROC OUT='*'
 2.  //LINK       EXEC PGM=IEWL,REGION=1700K,COND=(4,LT),
 3.  //           PARM='SIZE=(1600K,800K),LIST,LET,MAP,XREF,RENT'
 4.  //SYSPRINT  DD   SYSOUT=*
 5.  //SYSLIB    DD   DSN=your.runtime.library,DISP=SHR
 6.  //SYSLIN    DD   DSN=&&OBJECT,DISP=(OLD,DELETE)
 7.  //          DD   DDNAME=SYSIN
 8.  //SYSUT1    DD   UNIT=SYSDA,SPACE=(CYL,(5,2))
 9.  //SYSLMOD   DD   DSN=&&TEST(GO),DISP=(NEW,PASS),UNIT=SYSDA,
10.  //               SPACE=(TRK,(10,20,5)),DCB=BLKSIZE=32000
```

Figure 3.6. Sample link-edit procedure for MVS.

To review the MVS link-edit JCL (Note: DD statements may be in any order):

1. Statement 1 specifies any symbolic JCL parameters.
2. Statement 2 specifies that, if a prior step had a severity 2 error (return

code greater than 4), no link should be done. It also specifies the link-edit options you will normally require (RENT depends on the application). The SIZE option shown is intended to reduce your link-edit costs. Unlike the COBOL II compiler, which can take advantage of available memory automatically, the Linkage Editor must be told how much is available. In this example, I am specifying that it may use 1600K and should leave 800K of the 1600K for I/O buffers. This reduces I/O to SYSUT1 during link-edit processing and can reduce overhead to load the module at run-time.

3. Statement 5 must point to your COBOL II or LE/370 run-time library, since there is always an imbedded CALL to at least one of the modules.
4. Statement 6 assumes object code input is from the sample COBOL compile procedure. This could be any sequential dataset with LRECL=80 and a block size not greater than 3200.
5. Statement 7 is a JCL technique that allows logical concatenation to SYSLIN via a DD name of SYSIN. That allows you to code

```
//      EXEC LKED
//SYSIN DD *
  control statements
```

instead of

```
//      EXEC LKED
//SYSLIN  DD
//        DD *
  control statements
```

6. Statements 9 and 10 specify the output dataset, in this case a temporary library with a module name of GO.

Selecting link-edit options.

The COBOL compiler places several link-edit attributes into the object module, primarily the AMODE and RMODE attributes. The options that will normally affect you are as follows:

RENT This option marks the load module as reentrant. (Note: All modules must have been compiled with the RENT attribute.) Use this for modules where reentrant processing is desired (normally CICS and IMS/DC applications). See Creating a Load Module for more information on RENT.

This has been discussed elsewhere in this text, but I remind you here that RENT, in and of itself, does not make a load module reentrant. Also, where the load module is stored affects whether MVS will treat the module as fully reentrant across all regions. Modules must be in LPA for that to take effect.

REUS This option marks a load module as serially reusable. (This is not needed if RENT was specified—was used for OS/VS COBOL modules.)

LIST This option produces a listing of control statements used on the print dataset.

XREF Produces a cross-reference listing on the print dataset.

MAP This option produces a list of all modules in new load module on the print dataset.

LET This option lets the module be marked executable, even if errors occurred. (This is useful if some modules are known to be absent during a test.)

NCAL This option does not resolve any CALLs via the "automatic call library."

AMODE and *RMODE* These two attributes are documented elsewhere. The syntax for each is AMODE=24 | ANY RMODE=24 | ANY. For information on allowable values, see the RENT (and, for COBOL II, the RES) options. As with the MODE Linkage Editor statement, I do not recommend overriding the AMODE and RMODE that was set by the compiler. The Linkage Editor's priority in determining RMODE and AMODE is to

- Use the MODE control statement options if present.
- Use PARM values if present (and no MODE statement).
- Use what the compiler specified only if there were no MODE or PARM overrides. (This is my preference because it is more reliable than any attempt to force AMODE or RMODE.)

Be careful with options such as AMODE or RMODE. For additional information on the Linkage Editor (or AMODE and RMODE), see Creating a Load Module.

Naming the load module.

This is also explained in Creating a Load Module. The load module name is determined by this priority:

1. If there is a NAME statement, it is used.
2. If there is no NAME statement, but a member name is on the SYSLMOD JCL, it is used.
3. If neither of the above, TEMPNAME is used.

Linkage Editor listing.

The Linkage Editor listing may include weak external references (WXTRN), depicted as

```
IGZETUN $UNRESOLVED(W)
```

If the prefix of the module is IGZ or CEE, this is normal and does not require that you attempt to correct it.

3.12.3. JCL for Batch Execution

In executing a program, you need to consider these JCL requirements that are imposed on you by COBOL. They are in addition to other DD statements your application may require.

Additional DD statements.

To execute your program, there are some JCL DD statements that are required in addition to whatever other JCL you use. They are

SYSABOUT (COBOL II only) To list any COBOL II ABEND intercept information. If this DD statement is missing, summary information is written to the MVS message log (WTP route code 11). For batch, this is the JES log. The data set format is LRECL=125, RECFM=VBA. For example,

```
//SYSABOUT DD SYSOUT=*
```

SYSDBOUT (COBOL II only) To list any output from FDUMP, if specified. This is also required for some options of COBTEST (Chapter 4). Dataset format is LRECL=121, RECFM=FBA. For example,

```
//SYSDBOUT DD SYSOUT=*
```

SYSOUT To list any DISPLAY information. Dataset format is LRECL=121, RECFM=FBA. (Note: This ddname is determined by the COBOL compile option OUTDD. I assume you use SYSOUT). For example,

```
//SYSOUT    DD SYSOUT=*
```

SYSIN To process any input from an ACCEPT statement. Dataset format is LRECL=80, RECFM=FB.

NOTE to COBOL/370 programmers: Yes, special DD statements are required when running a COBOL/370 application. However, LE/370 will allocate them dynamically if they are not specified. Those DD statements are SYSOUT (for any run-time error messages for the application) and CEEDUMP (for any output from specifying TEST(xxxx,SYM) or other LE/370 ABEND information). LE/370 does not use SYSABOUT or SYSDBOUT.

WRITE AFTER ADVANCING and ADV option.

When writing reports, you probably use the WRITE AFTER ADVANCING statement. Remember the ADV option, which allows you to not include a byte in the 01-level record for the ASA control character. For example, if you are writing a report that is 115 characters wide (they don't have to be 120 or 132 as some people believe), you would code it differently, depending on the setting of ADV.

With ADV:

```
        FD  FD-REPORT-FILE
            RECORD CONTAINS 115 CHARACTERS
            RECORDING MODE IS F.
        01  FD-REPORT-RECORD PIC X(115).
                           ↑
                           └────────────────┐
         .                                   │
         .                                   │
            MOVE field-name TO FD-REPORT-RECORD
            WRITE FD-REPORT-RECORD AFTER ADVANCING 1
         .
    //ddname DD SYSOUT=A,DCB=BLKSIZE=116
```

With NOADV:

```
        FD  FD-REPORT-FILE
            RECORD CONTAINS 116 CHARACTERS
            RECORDING MODE IS F.
        01  FD-REPORT-RECORD.
            05                 PIC X.        <- Not referenced
            05 FD-DATA-AREA  PIC X(115).
                           ↑
                           └────────────┐
         .                              │
         .                              │
            MOVE field-name TO FD-DATA-AREA
            WRITE FD-REPORT-RECORD AFTER ADVANCING 1
         .
    //ddname DD SYSOUT=A,DCB=BLKSIZE=116
```

In the first example, notice that the FD and 01-level specify the actual size of the report, freeing the programmer from being concerned with machine dependencies. This still requires the JCL to acknowledge the real record and block size of 116 (record size plus ASA control character).

The second example, using NOADV, is the same size on FD, 01-level, and JCL. It requires different coding, however. The first byte of the 01-level must not be referenced and no MOVEs may be made to the 01-level name. I recommend ADV, since I don't want to be concerned with accidentally modifying an ASA control character.

3.12.4. DFSORT Control Statements

This topic appears in several places. See also the appropriate sections in this chapter. This topic contains the control statements you would most likely use in a SORT application.

GENERAL Syntax All the following statements are coded as part of the IGZSRTCD (or SORTCNTL) dataset, which must be LRECL=80. All statements must leave column 1 blank and must not exceed column 71. Statements may be continued to a following line by ending a parameter with a comma and then coding the next parameter on the next line, again leaving column 1 blank.

INCLUDE and OMIT Syntax (Use one or the other, not both.)

```
INCLUDE COND=(st,len,ty,cond, st,len,ty  [,AND or OR]...)
OMIT                          C'xxxx'
                              X'xxxx'
                              +number
                              -number
```

```
Where
    st        = first position of field
    len       = length of the field in bytes
    ty        = type of data, i.e., CH, FI, ZD, PD
    cond      = EQ,GT,LT,GE,LE,NE
```

For example, including records where positions 25–28 equal "LIFE":

```
INCLUDE  COND=(25,4,CH,EQ,C'LIFE')
```

Omitting records where positions 25–28 equal "LIFE" or positions 25–30 equal "HEALTH":

```
OMIT  COND=(25,4,CH,EQ,C'LIFE',OR,25,6,CH,EQ,C'HEALTH')
```

INREC Syntax (Only the specified fields will be in the sort record.)

```
INREC  FIELDS=(start,length,start,length,...)

              └1st field┘ └2nd field┘  etc.
```

For example, extract fields in positions 35–40 and 61–90, creating a sort input record of 36 bytes. (SORT is faster with shorter records.) Reminder: SD 01-level must show that these two fields are now in positions 1–6 and 7–36. While the new record length is now 36, the SD 01-level should continue to reflect the original length.

```
INREC FIELDS=(35,6,61,30)
```

SUM Syntax (has two different formats)

```
SUM   FIELDS=(start,length,type,...)
```

Fields must be FI, PD, or ZD. This summarizes data based on sort keys used. Fields being summarized must not be sort key fields.

```
SUM FIELDS=NONE
```

This option creates one output record where multiple records had the same sort key. For example, if you wanted to get a sorted listing by salesperson and the input file contained a record for each sale by salesperson, this option would eliminate the duplicates.

OUTREC Syntax (same as INREC, except it can insert binary zeros, blanks, or constants)

For example, reformat output from above to include 30 blanks, making the output record 66 bytes long:

```
OUTREC FIELDS=(1,36,30X)     <- inserts 30 blank bytes

OUTREC FIELDS=(1,36,30Z)     <- inserts 30 bytes of binary
                                zeros
```

For example, reformat output from above to begin with 10 blanks, followed by first 30 bytes of data, followed by a 13-byte literal, followed by the last 5 bytes from input record, creating a 58-byte record:

```
OUTREC FIELDS=(10X,1,30,C'literal value',31,5)
```

Example of SORT JCL.

Here is an example where a COBOL SORT program has a USING statement and an OUTPUT PROCEDURE statement. The OMIT and INREC provide all the logic needed to omit certain records from processing and to reformat the record to contain only the needed data fields for the OUTPUT processing. There are no COBOL changes required to use the OMIT process, but the INREC requires the SD 01-level to reflect the new data positions.

```
//        EXEC PGM=cobol-sort-program
//SORTCNTL  DD *
     OMIT     COND=(26,2,CH,EQ,C'25')
     INREC    FIELDS=(1,5,6,20,26,2,28,2,47,2)
//    .
//    .                  <- other DD's as needed
//    .
```

3.13. USING COBOL/370 INTRINSIC FUNCTIONS AND LE/370 CALLABLE SERVICES

Topics covered here are exclusive to COBOL/370 and/or LE/370. If your shop is using COBOL II, these capabilities aren't available to your application. For those of you with access to COBOL/370 and LE/370, you need to spend time experimenting with these features because you are probably currently writing code to do what these features already provide.

3.13.1. Using COBOL/370 Intrinsic Functions

As I mentioned in Chapter 2, complete examples of all the intrinsic functions will not be provided. In fact, I only show a few here to demonstrate the concept. If you haven't yet, you should read the overview of intrinsic functions in Chapter 2 prior to reviewing this material. Also, since the intrinsic functions in the examples are not explained in detail, you will need to review Section 7.12, Summary of COBOL/370 Intrinsic Functions.

To debug the use of an intrinsic function that includes any subscripts, you need to specify SSRANGE at compile-time and CHECK(ON) at run-time. This also applies to use of the ALL subscript.

Working with numeric arrays.

The following example is built around an array developed to track performance of students on an exam. The array is intentionally simple to demonstrate the technique of storing related data (in this case, student number and test grade) and then gathering information on the results by using intrinsic functions (and no SORTs).

Here are our theoretical specifications: You are to produce a report showing the highest grade and who got it, lowest grade and who got it, the range of grades attained, and the mean of the grades. Sounds complex, doesn't it? Here is how we do it:

```
05   STUDENT-INFO OCCURS 1000.
        10   STUDENT-ID      PIC XXXX.
        10   STUDENT-GRADE   PIC  999.

     COMPUTE HI-GRADE    = FUNCTION MAX (STUDENT-GRADE (ALL))
     COMPUTE HI-STU-NO   = FUNCTION ORD-MAX (STUDENT-GRADE (ALL))
     MOVE STUDENT-ID (HI-STU-NO) TO HI-STUDENT-ID
     COMPUTE LOW-GRADE   = FUNCTION MIN (STUDENT-GRADE (ALL))
     COMPUTE LOW-STU-NO  = FUNCTION ORD-MIN (STUDENT-GRADE (ALL))
     MOVE STUDENT-ID (LOW-STU-NO) TO LOW-STUDENT-ID
     COMPUTE RANGE-VAL   = FUNCTION RANGE (STUDENT-GRADE (ALL))
     COMPUTE MEAN-VAL    = FUNCTION MEAN (STUDENT-GRADE (ALL))
```

Working with dates.

There are also intrinsic functions available for working with dates. This has always been frustrating with COBOL because you often needed to write calendar subprograms that could calculate dates since there was no easy way within a COBOL program. For example, if you need to calculate the number of days between two dates, you know that, unless your shop already has a prewritten CALLable subroutine for this, you have a lot of work ahead of you. No more. Here is an example of calculating days between dates using an intrinsic function:

```
COMPUTE NUM-DAYS = FUNCTION INTEGER-OF-DATE (DATE-A) -
                   FUNCTION INTEGER-OF-DATE (DATE-B)
```

Another common requirement with dates is the need to convert dates between Gregorian format (YYYYMMDD) and Julian format (YYYYDDD). Here is also an example of nesting FUNCTIONS. This example converts a Gregorian date to Julian format. The process is accomplished by first converting the Gregorian date to a portable numeric format, followed by converting the portable numeric format to the receiving Julian format. Here is the code:

```
COMPUTE JULIAN-DATE-FLD = FUNCTION DAY-OF-INTEGER (FUNCTION
                 INTEGER-OF-DATE (GREGORIAN-DATE-FLD))
```

As a final example of working with dates, here is an example of taking a given Gregorian date and calculating what the Gregorian date will be 60 days later.

```
COMPUTE NEW-DATE = FUNCTION DATE-OF-INTEGER (60 + FUNCTION
                 INTEGER-OF-DATE (GREGORIAN-DATE-FLD))
```

Working with nonstandard data.

As a COBOL programmer, there may be times when numeric data is not in the desired format. After all, once a data field gets cluttered up with dollar signs, commas, and all, you just can't do much with it. Now there are a couple of new intrinsic functions that let you manipulate free-form numeric data.

An ideal place to use these features might be for an on-line transaction. If you've ever designed an on-line transaction that required receiving numeric input, you know the clumsiness of the process. Terminal users are required to enter numeric data that corresponds to your COBOL PIC specifications. For example, if you had a CICS MAP with a PIC specification of 999V99, the terminal user must enter digits that correspond to that—for example, 1 would need to be entered as 100 to ensure decimal alignment. (This is because CICS ignores the PIC clause for data mapping.) Here is how that might be with COBOL/370.

A numeric data field could be defined in a MAP as XXXXXXXX (e.g., PIC X(8)) and named SALARYI. A WORKING-STORAGE item might be SALARY-FIELD, defined as PIC S999V99. Here is the statement to do the work:

```
COMPUTE SALARY-FIELD = FUNCTION NUMVAL (SALARYI)
```

The FUNCTION named NUMVAL strips a free-form field and formats it into a numeric value, even with preceding or following spaces. Examples of what the data might be for the value 300.20 are

```
bb300.2b   300.20bb   300.2bbb   bbb300.2
```

If the terminal user might be also entering dollar signs ($), credit symbols (CR), or commas, then we would replace NUMVAL with NUMVAL-C. Then the options could include such additional variations as $300.20, $300.20CR, $b3,000, among others. These two FUNCTIONs can make average transaction screens become user friendly, letting the terminal user decide how to enter the numeric amount instead of needing to conform to program requirements.

Working with financial calculations.

Figuring out monthly installment amounts for a given principal amount and interest rate is not usually an assignment to give to programmers who don't have a good math background. COBOL/370 eases the difficulty. Here is the statement in COBOL/370 to calculate the monthly payment amount on a 5 year loan at 8.5%:

```
COMPUTE MONTH-PMT = LOAN-AMT * FUNCTION ANNUITY ((.085 / 12) 60)
```

A common requirement at financial institutions is computing the present value of a future amount. While a full discussion of present value is beyond the scope of this book, here is an example where we need to determine the present value of an investment that will pay $1,000 a year for 5 years at an interest rate of 8.5%. In this example, as in several others in this book, I show literals to show the structure more easily. Normally, these would be datanames. The second example demonstrates how it might be coded if all future payments were in a table defined by an OCCURS clause.

```
COMPUTE PRES-VAL = FUNCTION PRESENT-VALUE (.085 1000 1000
                                           1000 1000 1000)

COMPUTE PRES-VAL = FUNCTION PRESENT-VALUE (INT-RATE,
                                           PAYMENT-ENTRIES (ALL))
```

These examples are only to get you interested. You should review the description for each intrinsic function in Chapter 7 for specifics. Also, as I mentioned previously, I have made no attempt there to explain every FUNCTION's purpose or when to use it—for example, SIN, STANDARD-DEVIATION, LOG. If you understand the terms, though, you will have no problem. Good luck.

3.13.2. Using LE/370 CALLable Services

Although the LE/370 CALLable services provide extensive power, most of those services aren't in this text. This is because many of those services are for controlling and reacting to the LE/370 environment, not to other applications. There are a few, however, that are of general interest and may be useful to you. Those are reviewed here. You may invoke any LE/370 CALLable service either dynamically or statically.

Common to all LE/370 CALLable services is the format of the feedback data field (referred to in some LE/370 manuals as a *token* or *condition token*). It is always optional and is always the last parameter in the CALL list. The feedback area is a single parameter in this format:

```
01  FEEDBACK-AREA.
    05  SEVERITY-CODE    PIC S9(4) COMP.
    05  MESSAGE-NO       PIC S9(4) COMP.
    05  FLAG-FLD         PIC X.
    05  FACILITY-ID      PIC XXX.
    05  ISI-INFO         PIC S9(9) COMP.
```

These fields aren't used by all CALLs, but this is the general format. The intent in including this field on your CALLs is to allow your program to interrogate the success of the CALL, although this parameter is never required. The fields are defined below:

SEVERITY-CODE Similar to a return-code, where 0 indicates success, 1 a minor error, 2 a possible problem, 3 a severe error, and 4 a critical error.

MESSAGE-NO This is the message number associated with the problem. Not present when SEVERITY-CODE is 0. The contents vary with the CALL.

FLAG-FLD Not normally needed by COBOL applications.

FACILITY-ID This contains the message prefix. This is rarely useful to COBOL applications, since LE/370 always puts "IGZ" here if the run unit is COBOL.

ISI-INFO Not normally needed by COBOL applications. This is the Instance Specific Information (ISI) code associated with a given instance of a condition.

Terminating with a dump with CEE3ABD.

This service is useful if your application determines that it is preferable to ABEND rather than continue. This module, CEE3ABD, has few options. When CALLed, it produces a system dump and immediately terminates the enclave (run unit). Since this module never returns control to the CALLing application, the feedback area does not apply.

There are only two parameters to be passed:

An ABEND code This is a full-word binary value between 1 and 4095. This is the user ABEND code. With CICS, the code is first converted to EBCDIC.

A timing code This is to specify whether the ABEND should be issued immediately. At this time, the only acceptable value is zero.

Here is an example where the ABEND code is to be 125:

```
01   ABEND-INFO.
     05   USER-ABEND-CODE    PIC S9(9) COMP VALUE +125.
     05   ABEND-TIME-CODE    PIC S9(9) COMP VALUE +0.

     CALL 'CEE3ABD' USING USER-ABEND-CODE ABEND-TIME-CODE
```

Generating a dump with CEE3DMP.

There may be times when you want to force a dump to assist in debugging. One major feature of this LE/370 module is that it can be a productive tool, even in production. Usually, we find that dump tools are useful only during testing, but this one cuts through some of the haze of an ABEND. Since you can control what is or is not in the dump, you don't need to generate printouts that you don't need. Unlike CEE3ABD (above), this does *not* terminate the application.

The LE/370 module name is CEE3DMP. Output is written to a DDNAME of CEEDUMP, although this may be overridden with the FNAME option in the parameter list. (EXCEPTION: For CICS applications the dump is written to a transient data queue named CESE.)

There are three parameters that are to be passed:

A title field This is a field that is 80 bytes long. It contains the title you want to appear on each page of the dump.

An options field This is a 255-byte field that contains the options being passed to CEE3DMP. All options must be separated by a space or a comma. Options may be in any order, but if there are any conflicts, LE/370 uses the rightmost such option.

A feedback field Described above. Possible severity code values are 0 = success; 2 = incompatible options specified and ignored; 3 = error occurred while writing dump file.

The options have defaults. Those are underlined. In most cases, I think you will find the defaults are well suited for debugging COBOL applications. Here are your options:

THREAD(ALL | CURRENT) Specifies how many threads within the run-time environment (called *enclave* in LE/370). Normally, the default is all you will want. Also, LE/370 Version 1 only supports one thread.

TRACEBACK/NOTRACEBACK Specifies that a trace of prior CALLs is to be included in the dump. This is useful for applications that use several modules.

FILES/NOFILES Specifies that contents of buffers and attributes of all open files are to be included in the dump.

VARIABLES/NOVARIABLES This option is dependent on whether TEST was specified at compile-time and what options were included. If you specified an option that caused the symbol table to be generated (e.g., TEST(NONE,SYM)), the dump will include names of data areas plus their contents. This can significantly reduce your efforts in resolving a problem.

BLOCKS/NOBLOCKS Specifies that system control blocks are to be included in the dump. Unless you have serious problems (or are a true guru in the art of reading dumps), I recommend you not use this option.

STORAGE/NOSTORAGE Specifies that storage for the application is to be printed in hexadecimal and character format (i.e., the "traditional" dump). If FILES was also specified, all storage for file buffers will also be printed.

STACKFRAME(n | ALL) Specifies the number of stack frames to be included in the dump. Since this relates to more detailed LE/370 information, I recommend you leave this alone. This ensures that all options are dumped for the application, not just for the module that CALLed CEE3DMP (i.e., specifying STACKFRAME(1) would limit output to just the CALLing module).

PAGESIZE(n) Specifies number of lines to be printed per page in the dump. If zero, no page breaks are produced. Otherwise, value must be greater than 9. Default is PAGESIZE(60).

FNAME(ddname) Specifies the DDNAME for the dump. If this is not coded, the dump goes to CEEDUMP. (*NOTE:* CICS ignores this option and always uses the transient data queue named CESE.)

CONDITION/NOCONDITION Specifies that information from the Condition Information Block (CIB) is to be included in the dump for all conditions in the CALL chain. This is useful if an error or ABEND has occurred that has been trapped. (The mechanics of doing that are not part of this book.) My recommendation is to go with the default.

ENTRY/NOENTRY Specifies that register contents upon entry to CEE3DMP are to be printed. This can be helpful if CEE3DMP is CALLed from many locations and the title information isn't specified for each CALL.

Here is a sample of what a CALL might be coded:

```
01   TITLE-FLD    PIC X(80)
        VALUE 'Title for dump invoked from CEE3DMP '.

01   OPTION-FLD   PIC X(255)
        VALUE 'NOSTORAGE NOENTRY STACKFRAME(1) '.

01   FEEDBACK-AREA.
     05   SEVERITY-CODE   PIC S9(4) COMP.
     05   MESSAGE-NO      PIC S9(4) COMP.
     05   FLAG-FLD        PIC X.
     05   FACILITY-ID     PIC XXX.
     05   ISI-INFO        PIC S9(9) COMP.

     CALL 'CEE3DMP' USING TITLE-FLD OPTION-FLD FEEDBACK-AREA
```

Invoking the Debug Tool with CEETEST.

This module is to programmatically invoke the CODE/370 Debug Tool. The choices in doing that are identified in Chapter 4, Debugging Techniques with COBOL II and COBOL/370. To use this, you also need to know the available commands available with CODE/370. Being specific to the tool itself, they are not included here. (*NOTE:* In this text, I assume the debug tool of choice is IBM's CODE/370. In truth, the CEETEST module can invoke any test tool that follows the CODE/370 protocol.)

There are two parameters to code and both are optional:

A command field This is a variable-length field containing debug commands to be passed to CODE/370. The first two bytes must be a binary field containing the number of bytes, not counting the first two bytes, in the command string.

A feedback area Described above. Possible severity code values are 0 = success; anything else = error; Debug Tool not invoked.

Here is an example of using CEETEST:

```
01   DEBUG-COMMANDS.
     05               PIC S9(4)  COMP VALUE +40.
     05               PIC X(40)
        VALUE 'AT STATEMENT 40 LIST (FIELD-Z); GO;'.

     CALL 'CEETEST' USING DEBUG-COMMANDS FEEDBACK-AREA
```

In this example, the Debug Tool is invoked, sets a breakpoint at statement 40, lists a variable, then executes the GO command, which causes control to return to the application.

In Chapter 7 there is a listing of all of the LE/370 CALLable services. If you need information on using those other services, see IBM's *LE/370 Programming Guide* (Chapter 9, Related Publications).

SUMMARY

This chapter covers a lot of material, all of which is designed to help you be a better, more knowledgeable, more efficient programmer. Some techniques may appear not to work correctly in your shop. If that happens, first review the material to ensure you followed the guidelines carefully. Many of these techniques are not routinely used and you may encounter people who swear the techniques will never work. This is because for many years many of us have viewed COBOL as just a black box and had no understanding of it. You won't master all these techniques by reading. Keep the book nearby and try something new on your next program.

4

Debugging Techniques with COBOL II and COBOL/370

Unlike other chapters, where the use of the term COBOL II represented both COBOL II and COBOL/370 (because COBOL/370 can do anything that COBOL II can do), this chapter will be more explicit on whether a given approach works with one or both compilers. This is because COBOL II and COBOL/370 use different debug tools. The first sections of this chapter (Sections 4.1, 4.2, and 4.3) remain generic from the first edition, since basic debug skills from the source listing and Linkage Editor listing remain the same. Sections 4.4 and 4.5 combine COBOL II and COBOL/370 approaches since both are done in a similar fashion. Section 4.6 (Using the COBTEST facility for COBOL II) is unique to COBOL II and has no information for COBOL/370 programmers. Likewise, Section 4.7 (Using the CODE/370 Debug Tool) is explicitly for COBOL/370 programmers. I hope that, by placing generic information first, followed by common debug approaches, followed by explicit information on language-specific tools, this chapter can assist you.

I chose to combine information on the debug techniques for COBOL II and COBOL/370 in a single chapter because they have a lot in common, the only major difference being in their respective debug tools. What happened is that, while COBOL II has a specific mainframe-only test tool called COBTEST (that is largely a major enhancement over the much older TESTCOB for OS/VS COBOL), COBOL/370's debug approach is to use a programmable workstation (PWS) for part of the debugging and a component product on the mainframe to tie the two together.

This COBOL/370 product, called SAA AD/Cycle Cooperative Development Environment (CODE/370, for short), is further broken down into two primary components, each with their own considerations. There is the PWS Debug Tool (which obviously runs on the PWS) and the MFI (for Mainframe Interface) Debug Tool, which is for mainframe-only debugging, either in batch mode or from a nonprogrammable terminal. Here is a basic summary of approaches available. You may find it helpful to refer to this table as you review various techniques in this chapter.

Function desired	With COBOL II	With COBOL/370
Get system dump	CALL 'ILBOABN0'	CALL 'CEE3ABD'
Get formatted dump	FDUMP option	TEST (NONE,SYM) option or CALL 'CEE3DMP'
Trap subscript error	SSRANGE option	SSRANGE option
Interact with program	COBTEST tool & TEST option	CODE/370 Debug Tool & TEST(xxxx,xxx) option or CALL 'CEETEST'
Use batch test script	COBTEST tool & TEST option	CODE/370 Debug Tool & TEST(xxxx,xxx) option or CALL 'CEETEST'

The CALL modules are covered elsewhere, but I mention them here because they do qualify as debug facilities. The CALL modules are easy to code and, in many cases, provide adequate information for the majority of problems. They are especially helpful for production use, since they (other than CEETEST) use no system resources until needed.

As the table shows, COBOL II uses a specific compile-time option (FDUMP) to specify that a formatted dump should be produced upon ABEND and uses a different option (TEST) to specify that extra code should be generated to interact with the debug facility (COBTEST). COBOL/370 made the issue a bit clumsier by using one option (TEST) to serve both functions.

As with the first edition of this book, focus of this chapter remains on awareness of debug facilities and not on mastery. There is only so much time in our lives to devote to improving our professional skills. That being true, time spent mastering other skills (such as those in Chapter 3 and Chapter 5) will always yield a higher payoff than what you will receive by mastering debug tools. I should also acknowledge that attempting to cover all of COBTEST and CODE/370 within the framework of a single book would not be feasible.

This chapter will not teach you how to debug specific problems. Instead, the goal of this chapter is to ensure you know what information is available and how it may be used. As a professional programmer, your interest is in developing a foundation of knowledge on which to build, not to learn tricks for specific situations. Despite this statement, the first section of this chapter is a tutorial, presenting some concepts about dumps to readers with limited background. If you need special information about COBOL dumps beyond what is covered in this section, see Chapter 9 (Related Publications).

Unfortunately, many programmers think debugging means reading dumps. Not true. Reading a dump is a last resort and should be postponed as long as possible. Additionally, with several proprietary dump interpretation software products on the market, the pain from reading system dumps is a memory. (Note: If your shop still reads raw dumps from the system, I suggest you encourage your management to investigate the dump interpretation software products available. They save a mountain of paper, reduce costly training time, and usually isolate most problems, often including a statement of the problem in plain language and how to solve it.)

COBOL II and COBOL/370 provide several aids to assist you in solving problems, including options for compile output, object code generation, and error interception. In fact, some problems that caused an ABEND in prior versions of COBOL cause only an error message and termination today. You will also notice that COBOL II and COBOL/370 provide facilities to let you be proactive in anticipating and resolving ABENDs.

Because the focus of this book is on helping you develop efficient applications with COBOL and not on teaching various work practices to solve problems, the debugging environment (called COBTEST for COBOL II and CODE/370 Debug Tool for COBOL/370) is not covered in depth. Another reason is that COBTEST and the Debug Tool are separate products that may not be at your installation. For specifics on the compile options that support debugging, see Specifying COBOL Options in Chapter 3.

4.1. REMOVING THE MYSTERY FROM DUMPS

This section is a tutorial, taking some license with the actual specifics that occur. If you are comfortable with dumps and using compiler output to resolve them, you will find little here. You may even disagree with some of the details as I present them. The goal of this section is to ensure there is no mystery surrounding dumps for people with little experience. So long as a topic is mysterious, you cannot learn techniques to deal with it.

With many debug courses oriented around specific problems (e.g., "How to solve an 0C7," "How to solve multimodule problems"), junior programmers often view dumps as a mystery. Let's tackle that first. With a grasp of how the elements fit together, it is easier to develop a strategy for a variety of application problems.

4.1.1. 1. Why Is the Dump in Hex, Anyway?

Contrary to a popular belief, the computer does NOT do hexadecimal arithmetic (yes, you can buy one of many hand-held calculators that do hex arithmetic, but the mainframe cannot). Instead, the mainframe does binary arithmetic for memory management and uses hexadecimal as a shorthand format. (If a dump were nothing but 1s and 0s, life would be tough indeed.) Also, the operating system has no idea whether the data components of your program were EBCDIC, binary, packed-decimal, or floating point. The common format for all formats is the bit configuration they use, so this is what you get. The operating system correctly assumes that the compiler with which you compiled your program will provide documentation to assist in locating your program and data elements. The operating system further assumes, also correctly, that the Linkage Editor listing will provide assistance in determining which program was involved in the ABEND. I'll cover that information shortly.

Do you need to be good at hex arithmetic? Although I may incur the wrath of many senior programmers, my answer is no. For most of us, we have a sufficient knowledge of hex if we can

- Write our name in hex
- Count from 1 to 20 in hex
- Write our age in binary, in hex, and in packed-decimal
- Using our fingers, subtract numbers such as 4A minus 3C

The above items aren't difficult and emphasize that what we need is the ability to recognize patterns. For example

- C4C1E5C5 is a pattern of EBCDIC characters ("DAVE")
- F2F5, 19, and 025C are patterns of the decimal value 25 in EBCDIC, hex, and packed-decimal. (No, I'm not 25, but it was a nice age when I was.)
- In the subtraction example, I know that 4A is greater than 3C. That also means I know that 3D through 49 are numbers that occur between these two. With my fingers, I can do whatever is needed there.

In most cases, the information you have from the compiler and Linkage Editor are hex numbers. Usually, all you need to do is search high/low and match values. You'll see that later. If, for your application, it is necessary to consistently do arithmetic such as

```
 3A2CD4        4C9A0F
-2FC19A       +19CDF0
```

you should consider buying one of the many calculators on the market that do this for you. Why? They aren't expensive and their use removes a lot of drudgery. For a person to be a superior programmer, there are many skills to master that are more important than hex arithmetic, so why waste the time? I stopped teaching the details of hex arithmetic years ago and have no regrets.

Other questions you may have are, "Do I need to be able to convert decimal numbers to hex and hex numbers to decimal?" and "Do I need to be able to read negative hex numbers, i.e., master the technique of two's-complement notation?" Unfortunately, these two techniques can be frightening but are in many textbooks. Instead of answering those questions, let's turn them around. A better question is, "How do I eliminate the need to convert hex to decimal and cope with two's-complement notation?" Now the answer is simple. Just don't use the COMP format. That's all there is to it. Yes, you may still have to add or subtract hex numbers to locate programs or statements or data elements, but you never need to convert those answers to decimal and you won't be dealing with negative numbers.

From the above, you may wonder why some programmers use COMP. For one thing, they were probably taught it was more efficient (see Chapter 3 for more information). One of the reasons many programmers use packed-decimal (COMP-3) is that it requires no hex conversion in a dump. That in itself improves your productivity. If you would like to learn more about hexadecimal values, see Chapter 7.

4.1.2. Identifying Where Information Is Located

Earlier, I mentioned that the operating system assumed information was available to assist you in reading a dump. Using Figure 4.1, let's look at how that information is constructed. For our example, assume a batch program, PROGA, has an ADD statement on line 23 of the program and that it will ABEND because of a bad data field. (In our example, it also CALLs PROGB, but that is incidental to the problem.) Here are the steps:

1. The first step, the compile, produces two important pieces of information. One, the SOURCE option shows that the ADD statement is on line 23. Two, the OFFSET option shows that it is in the range 2FC through 305. (Remember my comment about knowing ranges. ABENDS never occur where a failing instruction begins.) Those two items will be important in the event of an ABEND. The purpose of the compiler-produced information is to locate which statement or data element within a specific program caused the ABEND.

2. Next, the Linkage Editor prints a listing of how the load module is constructed. It shows that PROGA is at the beginning, with an offset into the load module of 0. You may also note that PROGA occupies addresses 0 through 4CEF and that PROGB occupies addresses 4CF0 through 52BF. The purpose of the Linkage Editor listing when debugging is to locate which program within a load module caused the ABEND (although this information is rarely needed when using compiler-produced debugging aids, such as FDUMP).

3. Third, when the program ABENDs, MVS has two outputs. One is a series of messages, normally available via the JCL sysout queue (JES) for

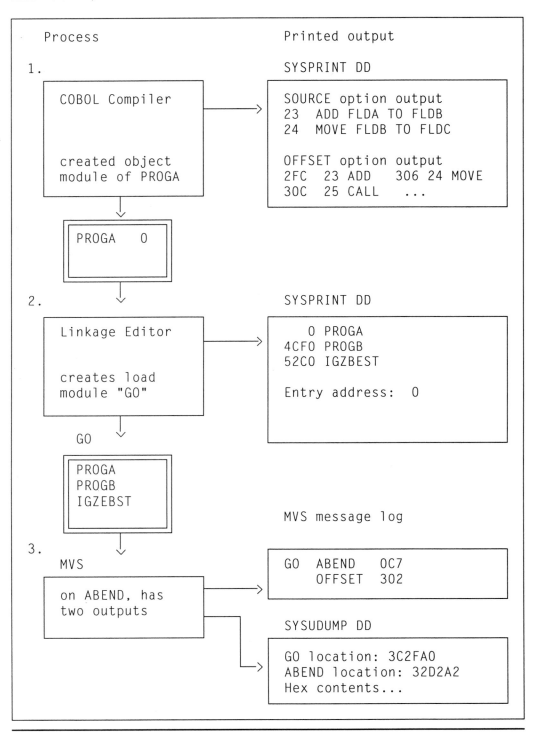

Figure 4.1. Sample of information to analyze a dump.

batch applications. (The COBOL II or LE/370 run-time error intercept routines also put messages here.) The second output is the dump itself. The dump is produced only if there is an appropriate DD statement, such as SYSUDUMP or SYSABEND. (Check with your installation standards for which one you should use.) Information from MVS confirms in which load module the ABEND occurred.

Now, let's follow that flow in reverse, going from MVS to the Linkage Editor to the COBOL listing. By following these steps as a standard routine, you will solve most of the ABENDs you will encounter. Sample listings of actual output will be in following topics. We're still on basics in this section.

From MVS. On ABEND, MVS prints that the load module was named GO, the ABEND was 0C7, and that the offset in the load module was 302. The dump shows the actual memory location, 32D2A2. Locating location 32D2A2 in the dump will be a waste of time because it will be all in hex. So don't do it. Notice also the MVS message saying offset 302. Where did 302 come from? MVS has *already* subtracted 32CFA0 from 32D2A2, giving a result of 302. This is the offset of the instruction beyond the logical beginning point of the load module. To confirm which program that is in, you look at the Linkage Editor listing. Reminder: MVS always shows the next sequential instruction's address, not the address of the offending instruction. When you locate the correct offset in the correct program, you will be looking at the instruction just beyond the one that caused the ABEND.

From the Linkage Editor. From this listing, you want to confirm the location of the ABEND from the physical beginning, not the logical beginning, of the load module. Since the physical beginning (always 0) matches the logical beginning (entry address) in the example, you know the offset of 302 needs no further adjustment. (Note: If the entry address (logical beginning) was other than 0, you would need to add it to the number from MVS to get an address relative to the Linkage Editor listing.)

Since the Linkage Editor listing shows us that instructions between relative location 0 and 4CEF are in the program PROGA, you now know in which program to search for the problem. Notice that you haven't done any hex arithmetic yet. When you are using debug facilities from COBOL II or COBOL/370, you usually do not need to reference the Linkage Editor listing, as the error message will include the name of the offending program.

From the compiler listing. Here is where planning helps. If you compiled the program and specified none of the possible options to help in debugging, you should stop pursuing the problem until you recompile the program with some debugging options (see Chapter 3). Assuming you specified SOURCE (to list all source code and sequence numbers) and OFFSET (to show at what offset the instructions begin), you can continue with this problem. In our example, the OFFSET listing in figure 4.1 shows that location 302 occurs somewhere between the beginning of an ADD statement on line 23 and a MOVE statement on line 24. Again, notice that no hex arithmetic has been needed. This confirms that the ABEND was caused by the ADD statement on line 23.

A reminder about an OFFSET listing: Earlier, I mentioned that MVS always points, not to the instruction causing the error but to the next sequential instruction. For example, if the offset address had been 306 (the address of the MOVE instruction), it would still confirm the ADD instruction as the one causing the ABEND. Likewise, had the offset address been 2FC, it would confirm whatever instruction preceded this ADD statement. With the specific instruction confirmed, it is usually a small matter to determine whether it was FLDA or FLDB in the example that caused the 0C7.

Review. To review that flow again, all programs must go through three steps in their life. One, to be compiled into machine code. Two, to be transformed into executable code as a load module. Three, to be loaded into memory and executed. On an ABEND

- MVS indicates which load module.
- The Linkage Editor listing shows which program.
- The compiler listing shows which statement.

Bypassing any of those three steps can cause confusion in solving the problem. These steps are needed whenever MVS or the run-time modules cannot identify the problem.

My suggested steps in solving a dump follow:

1. At the risk of offending programmers everywhere, I suggest not using the system dump information (e.g., SYSUDUMP DD) when testing a program, unless other approaches fail. A large number of ABENDs can be solved without wasting so many trees. If you get an unsolvable ABEND, you can always add the DD statement and reexecute the program. In most cases, it isn't needed. From my experience, programmers tend to read (or keep) everything the computer prints for a testing error. If that is true at your shop, you will get a productivity gain by not even seeing the unnecessary dump. For example, I once got an ABEND for misspelling a DDNAME. One of the system messages was "Missing DD statement" (or words to that effect). With that message, I corrected the situation in minutes. Despite this, MVS still produced a dump of 100+ pages for me to throw away. When I discussed this with several other

programmers, many felt I should have read (or kept) the dump anyway. Why? Because it was there. Let's get out of that trap.

2. Read the system messages first. This may solve the problem. For example, if you meant to execute a program called GLOP, but coded EXEC PGM=FLOP on the JCL statement, MVS produces an 806 ABEND message, stating that the load module called FLOP could not be located. The problem is solved. No dump is needed.

3. Even if the system messages do not produce any clear solution, check them anyway for ABEND messages that have an OFFSET address or ABEND code. The OFFSET can be checked against your Linkage Editor listing to confirm which program was involved and the ABEND code may be sufficient in itself. For example, once I got an ABEND of 0C9 (divide by zero). Since I had just added a group of statements to the program, one of which was a COMPUTE statement with the divide operator, I knew where to look for the problem.

4. Unless your program has a complex link-edit structure, you can now go to the source listing and locate the offending statement with the OFFSET value.

Most of the time, these steps will do it for you. If they solve 90 percent of your problems, you will be viewed as a technical genius and you can then afford to seek additional assistance beyond that. Our goal in this topic is to remove the magic, not make you an expert. In the following topics, you will see additional information to assist you. If you desire to master every facet of dump reading, you may want to get the appropriate IBM manuals. (See Chapter 9, Related Publications.)

4.2. READING THE SYSTEM MESSAGES

Earlier, I suggested that you check the system messages first. Let's get a feel for that here. One of the most difficult challenges is being patient as you read the many messages logged during your job. Some are useful; some are not. Here is a simple example where a program received an 0CB (decimal divide exception) and, although there is a lot of information here, most of it is useless for this problem. I highlighted the useful data but, even with this aid, it can be difficult to bypass the other information. Since MVS never knows the true cause of a problem, it gives you every shred of information it has, leaving it to you to discard most of it.

In this example, the load module ABEND offset is 6C2. If I know the module to contain only one COBOL program, beginning at location 0, then I can proceed directly to the COBOL listing to locate the error. The dump, if present, can be tossed.

```
IEA995I SYMPTOM DUMP OUTPUT
SYSTEM COMPLETION CODE=0CB REASON CODE=0000000B
 TIME=12.41.54 SEQ=32563 CPU=0000 ASID=0052
 PSW AT TIME OF ERROR 478D2000 00006E22 ILC 6 INTC 0B
  ACTIVE LOAD MODULE=DKA10100 ADDRESS=00006760 OFFSET=000006C2
  DATA AT PSW 00006E1C - FD41D17B 9006F822 9008D17B
  GPR  0-3   00000000 00006FD0 0000A930 30006FDC
  GPR  4-7   000140B0 007EEE88 000067B4 0000A930
  GPR  8-11  0000EAB4 00007000 000067F4 00006B5C
  GPR 12-15 000067E0 00006E58 50006E06 00000000
END OF SYMPTOM DUMP
+IGZ057I An ABEND was intercepted by the COBOL execution time ABEND
+        handler. It is described by a corresponding IEA995I message.
```

This next message is indicative of the type of assistance COBOL gives the programmer. What would once have been a difficult ABEND to solve is now a simple error message. The ABEND occurred when the program attempted to READ the file. Again, an example of an error where no SYSUDUMP DD is needed. This gives the program name, so the Linkage Editor listing also isn't needed. With the offset of 0516 from the message, the OPEN causing the error can be found from an OFFSET or LIST option.

```
+IGZ035I There was an unsuccessful OPEN or CLOSE of file 'PAY102' in
+        program 'DKA10200' at relative location X'0516'. Neither FILE
+        STATUS nor an ERROR declarative were specified. The I-O status
+        code was '39'.
```

These next messages don't give much information, except to tell you that the COBOL II run-time intercept module is active and the SYSABOUT DD is missing. The SYSABOUT DD statement is used at ABEND to record information for you. For an example of SYSABOUT information, see Using FDUMP and SYSABOUT (COBOL II only).

```
+IGZ043I A SYSABOUT error occurred. The ABEND information may be
+        incomplete.
+IGZ057I An ABEND was intercepted by the COBOL execution time ABEND
+        handler. It is described by a corresponding IEA995I message.
```

These examples are by no means complete or thorough. I hope you now have a better anticipation of the type of messages that COBOL II and COBOL/370 (via LE/370) generate so you may adjust your debugging technique accordingly. Our goal here is to "work smarter, not harder." For information and detailed explanations of the run-time messages, see the *VS COBOL II Application Program Debugging* manual or the *LE/370 Debugging and Run-time Messages Guide*. The prefix for COBOL II messages is IGZ, and the prefix for messages from LE/370 will be either IGZ (if COBOL-specific) or CEE for other LE/370 error messages. (*NOTE:* If the message has a prefix of IKF, it will indicate that an OS/VS COBOL module was involved.)

4.3. READING THE OFFSET AND LIST OUTPUT FROM A COMPILE

These two options, OFFSET and LIST, are mutually exclusive. If both are selected, OFFSET gets priority. I recommend that OFFSET, as a minimum, be specified for every compile where you anticipate executing the module. Without one of the two, you will be unable to identify a specific COBOL statement in case of an ABEND, and OFFSET uses less paper.

Here is an example, showing both the OFFSET list for part of a program, plus the LIST for that part of the program. In this example, the LIST option is needed due to the complexity of the ABENDing statement. The statement causing the error is the ADD statement on line 76. With so many data-names represented, the OFFSET listing is, by itself, insufficient to locate the problem. The LIST, because it shows every instruction, helps us identify the data field at the added expense of producing more paper at compile-time.

The messages from MVS. The messages from MVS show the ABEND occurred at offset 464 in the program. Using the number 464 as a search argument, you can locate the ADD statement in the OFFSET or the LIST output.

```
IEA995I SYMPTOM DUMP OUTPUT
 SYSTEM COMPLETION CODE=0C7 REASON CODE=00000007
  TIME=12.35.47 SEQ=09141 CPU=0000 ASID=0057
  PSW AT TIME OF ERROR 078D1000 843005CC ILC 6 INTC 07
    ACTIVE LOAD MODULE=GO        ADDRESS=04300168 OFFSET=00000464
    DATA AT PSW 043005C6 - FA32D1B4 D1BDF224 D1BD801E
    GPR  0-3   00000001 0004C300 043005A2 00045090
    GPR  4-7   00045090 84300674 007C5FF8 00007FD8
    GPR  8-11  0004C300 00045210 0430020C 0430041C
    GPR 12-15  043001E8 04303028 500323EC 800323FC
 END OF SYMPTOM DUMP
+IGZ057I An ABEND was intercepted by the COBOL execution time ABEND
+        handler. It is described by a corresponding IEA995I message.
```

The SOURCE listing. The numbers to the right of the listing are produced by the XREF option and show the line numbers where the data elements are defined. The number 1, to the left of the COBOL statements in lines 75 through 78, shows the depth of nested statements.

```
000071
000072     2000-PROCESS.
000073         PERFORM 2100-READ-DATA                                    80
000074         IF NOT END-OF-FILE                                        49
000075 1           MOVE FD2-EMP-NAME TO WS2-EMP-NAME                     34 53
000076 1           ADD FD2-DED1 FD2-DED2 FD2-DED3 FD2-DED4 TO WS1-ACCUM  35 36 37 38 45
000077 1           MOVE WS1-ACCUM TO WS2-TOTAL-DED                       45 55
000078 1           WRITE FD1-OUT-REC FROM WS2-OUT-REC.                   27 51
```

The OFFSET listing. Notice how many statements can be identified in so little space. The OFFSET listing has the line number, the hex offset, and the verb. The OFFSET listing should be read from left to right, not from top to bottom. In our example, the offset of 464 occurs between lines 76 and 77, confirming the ADD statement. Because this ADD statement contains so many data-names, more information will be needed. See the LIST output for a comparison.

```
LINE # HEXLOC VERB          LINE # HEXLOC VERB           LINE # HEXLOC VERB
000062 00035A PERFORM       000063 000376 PERFORM        000064 00039A PERFORM
000065 0003B2 STOP          000068 0003C6 INITIALIZE     000069 0003E6 OPEN
000073 000428 PERFORM       000074 000440 IF            000075 00044C MOVE
000076 000452 ADD           000077 000488 MOVE           000078 0004AA WRITE
000081 0004E8 READ          000083 000532 MOVE           000085 00053A ADD
000089 00054C MOVE          000090 000558 WRITE          000091 000590 CLOSE
```

The LIST output. The LIST option is mutually exclusive with OFFSET. If you specify both, OFFSET takes effect. You do not need to know assembler language to use the LIST option. This lists every machine instruction generated for COBOL statements. To the right of each instruction are some abbreviated words and codes to assist you in deciphering what data elements are involved. It takes practice and an occasional leap of faith to interpret them, but it isn't difficult to survive here.

Since you know the address of the next sequential instruction is 464, you can determine that the offending instruction was at location 45E, the preceding instruction. That instruction, AP (for ADD Packed-decimal data) is adding the contents of temporary storage area # 2 (TS2-n) to the contents of temporary storage area # 1 (TS1-n). You know this from reading the comments at the right. (Note: Temporary storage areas are just intermediate work areas the compiler added to our program to accomplish various functions. The numbers of the storage areas used have no special meaning.)

```
       00043A                  GN=12 EQU *
       00043A D203 D17C D18C    MVC 380(4,13),396(13)     VN=5          PSV=4
000074 IF
       000440 95E8 900A         CLI 10(9),X'E8'           WS1-EOF-SW
       000444 58B0 C020         L                         11,32(0,12)   PBL=1
       000448 4780 B22E         BC 8,558(0,11)            GN=3(0004E2)
```

```
000075 MOVE
       00044C D213 9012 8000      MVC 18(20,9),0(8)        WS2-EMP-NAME    FD2-EMP-NAME
000076 ADD
       000452 F274 D1B0 8019      PACK 432(8,13),25(5,8)   TS1=0           FD2-DED2
       000458 F224 D1BD 8014      PACK 445(3,13),20(5,8)   TS2=5           FD2-DED1
       00045E FA32 D1B4 D1BD      AP 436(4,13),445(3,13)   TS1=4           TS2=5
       000464 F224 D1BD 801E      PACK 445(3,13),30(5,8)   TS2=5           FD2-DED3
       00046A FA32 D1B4 D1BD      AP 436(4,13),445(3,13)   TS1=4           TS2=5
       000470 F224 D1BD 8023      PACK 445(3,13),35(5,8)   TS2=5           FD2-DED4
       000476 FA42 D1B3 D1BD      AP 435(5,13),445(3,13)   TS1=3           TS2=5
       00047C FA34 9002 D1B3      AP 2(4,9),435(5,13)      WS1-ACCUM       TS1=3
       000482 F833 9002 9002      ZAP 2(4,9),2(4,9)        WS1-ACCUM       WS1-ACCUM
000077 MOVE
       000488 D209 D1BE A063      MVC 446(10,13),99(10)    TS2=6           PGMLIT AT +79
       00048E D203 D1CC 9002      MVC 460(4,13),2(9)       TS2=20          WS1-ACCUM
```

If you look at the preceding instructions that are affiliated with the ADD statement, you find two statements, one at location 452 and one at location 458. Both are PACK instructions (a PACK instruction converts EBCDIC DISPLAY data to COMP-3 format data and moves the result to a receiving field). The first PACK instruction moves a data field called FD2-DED2 to TS1, and the second PACK instruction moves the data field FD2-DED1 to TS2.

Now things are beginning to take shape. The two PACK instructions moved FD2-DED1 and FD2-DED2 to the two temporary fields TS1 and TS2. The AP instruction that ABENDed was adding those two fields. Therefore, of all the data fields specified in the ADD instruction, the error was either FD2-DED1 or FD2-DED2. The other fields on the ADD statement on line 76 may also cause errors, but the program never got that far. At this point, you can look at those two areas in the dump. One of them probably has a blank in it.

That wasn't so hard, was it? Usually, the LIST option isn't needed, but it's nice to know it is available. If you sometimes find it difficult to locate the source statement with LIST, it may be because the program was compiled with OPTIMIZE. While OPTIMIZE is recommended for production use, its ability to restructure the program at the machine code level can make it difficult to match instructions to source statements. In such a situation, recompile with NOOPTIMIZE and rerun the test.

4.4. USING FORMATTED DUMPS, SYSABOUT, AND SSRANGE

4.4.1. SYSABOUT (COBOL II only)

The SYSABOUT DD statement, although not required, is used to record elementary information in case of an ABEND (for CICS, this information goes to the CEBRxxxx queue). The STAE option must be set for this to take effect. (STAE causes the COBOL II run-time error intercept code to take control in the event of an ABEND.) See JCL Requirements for specifics on the SYSABOUT DD. The purpose of using SYSABOUT is to determine the program name that caused the ABEND, including the date compiled. For me, that is all I get from it. Here is an example:

```
- VS COBOL II ABEND Information -
Program = 'PRTFILE' compiled on '04/17/91' at '12:35:37'    <- Useful
    TGT = '04303028'
Contents of base locators for files are:
    0-00007FD8                    1-0004C300
Contents of base locators for working storage are:
    0-00045210
Contents of base locators for the linkage section are:
    0-00000000
No variably located areas were used in this program.
No EXTERNAL data was used in this program.
No indexes were used in this program.                  <- Possibly useful
- End of VS COBOL II ABEND Information -
```

As you see, this shows you the PROGRAM-ID, the date compiled, plus some other bits and pieces. For most of us, the SYSABOUT information is only to confirm the name of the offending program. Since STAE is the default at most installations (see compile run-time options for more information), you may want to have this information. Getting the SYSABOUT information does not override other information sources, such as FDUMP.

Note to COBOL/370 programmers: The benefit from using the SYSABOUT DD with COBOL II has never been significant. With COBOL/370 and LE/370, this DD is no longer used. LE/370 includes this information in a standard format.

4.4.2. Formatted Dumps

One big benefit of both COBOL II and COBOL/370 is that they each provide a simple way to get easy-to-read dumps. This is called a formatted dump because, while it is produced at ABEND, it contains datanames from the source program, and the data values from the dump are adjusted for readability within the PIC for the dataname. One of the main reasons I like them is that there's virtually no tradeoff to requesting them throughout the development and testing process.

For both compilers, the formatted dump is triggered by a compile-time option. However, the process of producing a formatted dump upon ABEND is different for each because, as you recall, the run-time environments are different. COBOL II uses its own run-time library, while COBOL/370 relies on LE/370. Also, both require that equivalent run-time options (STAE for COBOL II, TRAP(ON) and TERMTHDACT(DUMP) for LE/370) be set. Since those settings are the norm (and are usually set by systems programmers), I won't get embroiled in the issues for NOSTAE or TRAP or TERMTHDACT.

To get the formatted dump with COBOL II, you must specify FDUMP as a compile-time option. COBOL II also requires a SYSDBOUT DD at run-time for non-CICS applications and a CEBRxxxx temporary storage queue for CICS applications. If you specify SYSDBOUT and SYSUDUMP, you will get both dumps. In most cases, you will find you don't need two dumps, as the FDUMP will usually be more than sufficient (and saves trees). See JCL requirements for specifics of the SYSDBOUT DD.

To get the formatted dump with COBOL/370, you must specify SYM as the second parameter with the TEST option at compile-time—TEST(NONE,SYM). COBOL/370 also supports the FDUMP option (indirectly) in that it replaces FDUMP, if encountered, with TEST(NONE,SYM). The run-time requirement is a CEEDUMP DD for non-CICS applications and a CESE transient data queue for CICS. If the CEEDUMP DD is not present, LE/370 allocates one for you. If all you want is a formatted dump (i.e., you do not want additional code generated to interact with the Debug Tool), always specify TEST(NONE,SYM). The use of any first parameter other than NONE causes extra code to be generated (and also forces NOOPTIMIZE). (*NOTE:* You can still use the CODE/370 Debug Tool with TEST(NONE,SYM), but with limited functions available.)

Specifying that a formatted dump is desired upon ABEND increases the size of your load module and the amount of virtual memory used, so the option should be set off (NOFDUMP for COBOL II, NOTEST or TEST(NONE,NOSYM) for COBOL/370) after testing applications that need high performance. This added size is due primarily to the inclusion of a dictionary of your program's datanames and their attributes, not the inclusion of active code. Therefore, if the application is volatile, new, or not performance-sensitive, you may decide to leave the formatted dump option set even when used in production. (See the next section, A Proactive Approach to Problem Resolution, for more information.)

A formatted dump presents you with a format of the DATA DIVISION, using names from the source code, with the data converted for readability if needed. Additionally, it presents you with the line number and statement number of the verb that caused the ABEND if NOOPTIMIZE was specified, and the hex offset of the verb (remember the OFFSET and LIST features?) if OPTIMIZE was specified. This eliminates virtually all hex arithmetic when reading dumps, the need to review the Linkage Editor listing to determine what program caused the ABEND, and the need to review the dump to determine the value of various data fields.

Here is an FDUMP example, produced for a COBOL II application (information would be similar for COBOL/370).

```
VS COBOL II Formatted Dump at ABEND —
Program = 'PRTFILE'
```

```
Completion code = 'S0C7'
PSW at ABEND = '078D1000843005CC'
Line number or verb number being executed: '0000076'/'1'   <- line number in
The GP registers at entry to ABEND were                        source program
    Regs  0 - 3  - '00000001 0004C300 043005A2 00045090'
    Regs  4 - 7  - '00045090 84300674 007C5FF8 00007FD8'
    Regs  8 - 11 - '0004C300 00045210 0430020C 0430041C'
    Regs 12 - 15 - '043001E8 04303028 500323EC 800323FC'
Data Division dump of 'PRTFILE'
000023 FD PRTFILE.FD1-REPORT FD
FILE SPECIFIED AS:
   ORGANIZATION=SEQUENTIAL   ACCESS MODE=SEQUENTIAL
   RECFM=FIXED BLOCKED
CURRENT STATUS OF FILE IS:
   OPEN STATUS=EXTEND
   QSAM STATUS CODE=00                        <-File status information
000027 01 PRTFILE.FD1-OUT-REC X(37)
       DISP   ===> JOHN E. DOE            213.35
000029 FD PRTFILE.FD2-INPUT FD
FILE SPECIFIED AS:
  ORGANIZATION=SEQUENTIAL ACCESS MODE=SEQUENTIAL
  RECFM=FIXED BLOCKED
CURRENT STATUS OF FILE IS:
  OPEN STATUS=INPUT
  QSAM STATUS CODE=00
000033 01 PRTFILE.FD2-INP-REC AN-GR
000034 02 PRTFILE.FD2-EMP-NAME X(20)
     DISP    ===>JANE S. DOE
000035 02 PRTFILE.FD2-DED1 S999V99
                                            INVALID SIGN
   DISP   ===>+000.00
           HEX> FFF FF
                000 00
000036 02 PRTFILE.FD2-DED2 S999V99
                                            INVALID DATA FOR THIS DATA TYPE
   DISP    HEX> 44444
                00000
000037 02 PRTFILE.FD2-DED3 S999V99
                                            INVALID SIGN
   DISP   ===>+020.00
           HEX> FFF FF
                020 00
000038 02 PRTFILE.FD2-DED4 S999V99
                                            INVALID SIGN
   DISP      ===>+030.00
           HEX> FFF FF
                030 00
```

```
000039 02 PRTFILE.FILLER X(40)
   DISP      ===>04000
```

— End of VS COBOL II Formatted Dump at ABEND —

In reviewing the sample FDUMP output, you noticed that it states the error was caused on line 76, the 1st (and only) verb on that line. If the program had been compiled with OPTIMIZE, the statement would have shown the hex offset, instead. Here is that verb and the 01-level entry it was referencing:

```
000033        01 FD2-INP-REC.
000034           05 FD2-EMP-NAME    PIC X(20).
000035           05 FD2-DED1        PIC S999V99.
000036           05 FD2-DED2        PIC S999V99.
000037           05 FD2-DED3        PIC S999V99.
000038           05 FD2-DED4        PIC S999V99.
000039           05                 PIC X(40).


000076           ADD FD2-DED1 FD2-DED2 . . .
```

Since the ABEND was an 0C7, you know that FD2-DED1 or FD2-DED2 probably contained blanks. By looking at the FDUMP, you can confirm this. Also notice how FDUMP points out incorrect signs—acceptable, but incorrect for this choice of the NUMPROC option. This could be useful information if the program logic had IF NUMERIC statements.

4.4.3. SSRANGE

SSRANGE is an excellent aid when testing a program that has subscripts, indexes, or uses reference modification and is not dependent on DD statements. (Chapter 2 explains reference modification, and subscripting and indexing are described in Chapter 3). SSRANGE may be used with FDUMP (COBOL II only) or TEST and appears as a compile-time option and as a run-time option. This provides you with the opportunity to control its impact on performance. Here are your choices:

	Run-time option		
Compile option	**COBOL II**	**COBOL/370**	
SSRANGE	SSRANGE	CHECK(ON)	Debugging is activated, with some impact on performance.

| Compile option | Run-time option | | |
	COBOL II	COBOL/370	
SSRANGE	NOSSRANGE	CHECK(OFF)	No SSRANGE monitoring, but run unit may be activated by changing run-time option.
NOSSRANGE	SSRANGE	CHECK(ON)	No SSRANGE monitoring. Program must be recompiled with SSRANGE before monitoring takes effect.
NOSSRANGE	NOSSRANGE	CHECK(OFF)	No SSRANGE monitoring.

Many companies have the run-time option default set to NOSSRANGE or CHECK(OFF) to prevent inadvertent productional running of programs with SSRANGE specified at compile-time. If you are unsure about your shop's default setting, see Specifying COBOL Options in Chapter 3 for instruction on how to determine them. That topic also specifies how to turn run-time options on or off. (There is an example of doing this in the next topic, but the example assumes you are familiar with the mechanics from Chapter 3.)

SSRANGE should normally be part of your proactive debug technique, covered in the next topic. Testing programs with untested subscripts, indexes, or reference modification without specifying SSRANGE is not professional.

4.5. A PROACTIVE APPROACH TO PROBLEM RESOLUTION

Usually, problem solving is done when a program is being tested, when you have time to use a variety of techniques to solve a problem. Sometimes, however, you are trying to debug productional applications and can't afford the luxury of extensive use of DISPLAY statements or other code modifications. Here are a couple of tips to use when the program won't cooperate. These tips work for all environments.

4.5.1. In Test Mode

First, compile the suspected (or untested) module with FDUMP (or TEST (NONE,SYM) if using COBOL/370) and NOOPTIMIZE. Yes, this will affect performance, but if the program is having problems, you are not getting the desired performance anyway. I recommend NOOPTIMIZE because the formatted dump accompanied with OFFSET or LIST output from the compilation is easier to use than when OPTIMIZE is specified.

A formatted dump, as explained previously, does increase load module size (due to the tables, not due to extra code) and also increases use of virtual memory. While you normally do not have debug code in productional applications, doing so will position you to get maximum usable information at the time of an ABEND. The use of NOOPTIMIZE is to let you see the specific code generated (via LIST option) if you're having major problems. NOOPTIMIZE is also recommended in IBM manuals for debugging because optimized code is less predictable when interacting with debug tools.

Second, if subscripts, indexes, or reference modification code are suspect, include SSRANGE in the compile-time options specified. If performance is an issue even when testing, specify NOSSRANGE (if COBOL II) or CHECK(OFF) (if COBOL/370) at run-time to minimize performance degradation. (See Chapter 3 under Specifying COBOL II and COBOL/370 Options for information on setting options.) Now run the program. If it ABENDs, you will have the formatted dump. If the problem appears to be one of the types that SSRANGE handles (and you specified NOSSRANGE or CHECK(OFF) at run-time), all you need to do is the following:

1. If the module is executed by the JCL EXEC statement with PGM=modulename, change the PARM to '/SSRANGE' or '/CHECK(ON)', as appropriate, and reexecute.
2. If you were not running from the JCL EXEC (e.g., CICS or IMS), relink the module with a copy of IGZEOPT (COBOL II) or CEEUOPT (COBOL/ 370) that includes the SSRANGE or CHECK(ON) option, as appropriate, and reexecute.

Since the load module contains extra code that will reduce performance (and may even contain a copy of IGZEOPT or CEEUOPT with debugging options), you must recompile with normal production options (e.g., NOFDUMP, NOTEST, OPTIMIZE). While continuing to run with a PARM of '/NOSSRANGE' or '/CHECK(OFF)' or relinking with a REPLACE statement to remove any unwanted IGZEOPT or CEEUOPT modules will improve performance of the module as tested, the improvement is only a reduction of overhead. Only a recompile will rid you of the full overhead.

NOTE: This example assumed that the installation default for the run-time option was NOSSRANGE or CHECK(OFF). That is the situation I normally encounter. If the installation run-time default had been SSRANGE or CHECK(ON), you could have left the load module as is, running with degraded performance until the problem surfaced.

The downside of an installation having SSRANGE or CHECK(ON) as the default is that moving a module into production that was compiled with SSRANGE can significantly affect performance of the greater environment. By setting run-time defaults so debug options are OFF, a shop has better control and less likelihood that an application will accidentally be moved to production with test options set. Incidentally, your shop might have different options set for different environments (e.g., CICS) than it does for batch, so don't assume what is set for one environment applies to the other.

4.5.2. In Production Mode

This approach is more long term than the previous one. If you have an application that isn't sensitive to performance concerns, you might want to use formatted dumps all of the time. This can be useful if an application is volatile or is being maintained by a less experienced programmer.

With a formatted dump, less experienced programmers build confidence more rapidly than if they continually face a hex dump, and problems are generally resolved more quickly. This can also be beneficial for those applications that usually run during the night shift. Often, performance isn't as critical, and a formatted dump sure eliminates (some of) the pain of attempting to read a dump at 2 A.M.

Unless the run unit is complex, I suggest omitting the SYSUDUMP DD also, relying solely on the formatted dump. While some of you will dismiss the thought out of hand (because "we've always used hex dumps"), I encourage you to consider the option. There are just so many trees.

If your shop is using one of the available dump interception and formatting software products on the market, this approach may not be relevant. If your shop doesn't use such software, though, then this deserves some consideration. If you're afraid of the " performance issue," set up back-to-back tests, running with the module compiled with a formatted dump option and again without. In most situations (primarily batch) I doubt you will see much difference.

Reminder: With COBOL/370, any combination of TEST options will produce the formatted dump. This includes combinations such a s TEST(ALL,SYM), which includes a significant amount of extra code over and above the amount needed to get a formatted dump. If using formatted dumps in production, TEST(NONE,SYM) is my recommendation.

4.6. USING THE COBTEST FACILITY FOR COBOL II

COBTEST is a separate product from IBM and may not be installed at your shop. There was a similar (but not identical) product with OS/VS COBOL called TESTCOB. The COBTEST facility is embedded within your object module by using the compile option TEST. COBTEST runs with these options even

if they are not specified: TRUNC(STD), NOZWB, NUMPROC(NOPFD). I want
you to be aware of COBTEST, but it is not a focus of this book. I find it useful for
the professional who uses test scripts and I have included some examples. The
on-line environments are described but without details. For more information
on work practices with COBTEST, or for a complete list of all commands and
syntax, see *VS COBOL II Application Program Debugging* (Chapter 9).

4.6.1. COBTEST Debug Environments

One of the reasons some companies don't use COBTEST, or don't use it extensively, is because COBTEST does not support all MVS platforms nor does it
provide equal services on those that are supported. This is unfortunate because
COBTEST is a much-improved testing tool with COBOL II and has much to
recommend it.

COBTEST supports three modes: batch, full-screen (TSO), and line mode
(TSO). Full functionality is available only from full-screen mode. Full-screen
mode and line mode are not available for CICS. Batch mode is available for CICS
in a restricted fashion (using "CICS" and "batch" in the same sentence clearly
speaks to restricted use). Line and batch modes are available for IMS, but require the IMS/VS BTS product. (See Chapter 9.)

Programs that run easily in TSO (e.g., DB2) and those that do not use CICS
or IMS are the prime beneficiaries of COBTEST. Here are brief descriptions of
the three modes.

Batch mode.

Batch mode is straightforward for batch programs using JCL. Instead of specifying the name of your program on the PGM= parameter, specify COBDBG, instead. For example, assume a program was compiled with the TEST option and
linked into a load library called TESTRUN.LOAD, with a member name of
DAVEMOD1. The PROGRAM-ID of the COBOL II program is DAVEPROG. To
test in batch mode, my JCL might look something like Figure 4.2.

While the JCL in Figure 4.2 is relatively simple, the function of each, plus a
brief description of the control statements will help you get a feeling for the
power of COBTEST in batch mode. The commands are read from the SYSDBIN
dataset. The numbers were added for clarity.

Statement 2 executes COBTEST.
Statement 3 contains the name of the load library where the module to be
tested was linked.
Statements 4 through 6 have been discussed elsewhere and are for any
debugging output from this test.
Statement 7 is required for batch mode operation. COBTEST opens this
input file to receive instructions. While I haven't explained these statements (and will not, extensively, in this book), let's review them here.

```
 1. //jobname    JOB  ....
 2. //GO         EXEC PGM=COBDBG
 3. //STEPLIB    DD   DSN=TESTRUN.LOAD,DISP=SHR
 4. //SYSABOUT   DD   SYSOUT=*
 5. //SYSDBOUT   DD   SYSOUT=*
 6. //SYSOUT     DD   SYSOUT=*
 7. //SYSDBIN    DD   *
 8. COBTEST DAVEMOD1
 9. RECORD
10. QUALIFY DAVEPROG
11. SET WS3-TASK-CODE = '01'
12. TRACE PARA PRINT
13. FLOW ON
14. AT DAVEPROG.36 (IF (WS3-TASK-CODE NE '01'),
    (LIST WS3-TASK-CODE))
15. ONABEND (FLOW (25))
    //
```

Figure 4.2. Sample COBTEST in batch.

COBTEST DAVEMOD1 tells COBTEST the name of the load module to
   load for this execution.
RECORD tells COBTEST to create a log on SYSDBOUT of all commands.
QUALIFY DAVEPROG tells COBTEST the name of the PROGRAM-ID to
   which the following statements apply.
SET WS3-TASK-CODE = '01' forces an initial value into a WORKING-
   STORAGE field.
TRACE PARA PRINT specifies that a trace (similar to TRACE ON in OS/
   VS COBOL) of paragraph names is to be printed (default is to
   SYSDBOUT).
FLOW ON specifies that a log of paragraphs executed is to be kept by
   COBTEST (later referenced by line 13).
AT DAVEPROG.36 ... specifies that an IF statement is to be executed when
   the statement on line 36 is executed, in this case printing out the value
   of WS3-TASK-CODE whenever it is not equal to '01'. (The commands
   inside the parentheses, IF and LIST, are also COBTEST commands.)
ONABEND (FLOW(25)) specifies that, if an ABEND occurs, print out the
   most recent 25 paragraphs executed (similar to the FLOW option from
   OS/VS COBOL).

In the example, you would normally not want both a TRACE and a FLOW, since these two options overlap. A restriction of batch mode is that all commands are processed immediately, preventing any interaction. This restricts you to a limited set of commands, but batch mode has much to offer, as you'll see.

For me, I like to keep things simple, because there are so many skills that a professional programmer needs to have. I use standard batch facilities whenever I suspect a potential problem and that relieves me from mastering all the various commands. By setting up a test script of basic debug commands, I have a tool that can be reused with minor changes for many programs. I'll cover the use of test scripts in the next topic, after describing the other modes of COBTEST.

Line mode.

Line mode allows interaction from a TSO terminal and the syntax of commands matches those of batch mode. An added feature is that, by selecting commands, you can stop execution, modify values, and continue. Since it is the same product as the batch product, you would expect the TSO CLIST to appear similar to the batch JCL. It does. Since this is not a text on CLISTs, I won't explain their syntax here. Here is a sample CLIST:

```
PROC 0
FREE DDNAME(SYSDBOUT)
FREE DDNAME(SYSABOUT)FREE DDNAME(LOADLIB)
ALLOCATE DDNAME(SYSDBOUT)    DSN(SYSDBOUT.JCL)  OLD
ALLOCATE DDNAME(SYSABOUT)    DSN(SYSABOUT.JCL)  OLD
ALLOCATE DDNAME(LOADLIB)     DSN(TESTRUN.LOAD)  OLD
COBTEST LOAD(DAVEMOD1:LOADLIB)
QUALIFY DAVEPROG
```

In the example, I created datasets of logonid.SYSDBOUT.JCL and logonid.SYSABOUT.JCL for the SYSDBOUT and SYSABOUT datasets. (For information on their data set attributes, see the section JCL Requirements in Chapter 3.)

Notice that the COBTEST command is different from that used in batch mode. Not only does it execute the COBTEST program, it specifies in what DDNAME the named load module is in (in batch mode, it was in the STEPLIB DD). If I place the CLIST above in a dataset named DAVE.TSO.UTIL, with a member name of DEBUG, Figure 4.3 shows what the screen might look like after typing in the TSO command.

As Figure 4.3 shows, you will see a COBTEST message appear each time the software is ready for instructions from you. At this point, you could type in commands such as shown for batch mode and press the terminal Enter key.

A down side of line mode is that you can't see anything unless you request it. Much of this is (to me) a throwback to the early days of on-line terminals before CRTs. A programmer using TSO 20 years ago didn't have a CRT, only an on-line typewriter. In that era, line mode made sense. It still has use when used with prewritten scripts, as I mentioned earlier for batch mode. The Debug language is a rich language, allowing sophisticated test scripts to be developed and reused. This can eliminate the common problem in which a programmer, after typing in commands at a terminal for an hour or more, doesn't remember what was tested.

You can place prewritten scripts in a dataset (LRECL=80) and allocate to TSO with a DDNAME of SYSDBIN. For example,

```
ALLOC DDNAME(SYSDBIN) DSN(SYSDBIN.TXT) SHR
```

As with batch mode, use of SYSDBIN is limited. COBTEST will open and read commands from SYSDBIN if the DDNAME is allocated. All commands are executed immediately, so such use is usually limited to commands that are repeated, such as QUALIFY, RECORD.

```
-------------------- TSO COMMAND PROCESSOR --------------
ENTER TSO COMMAND OR CLIST BELOW:

===> EX 'DAVE.TSO.UTIL(DEBUG)'




IKJ56247I FILE SYSDBOUT NOT FREED, IS NOT ALLOCATED
IKJ56247I FILE SYSABOUT NOT FREED, IS NOT ALLOCATED
IKJ56247I FILE LOADLIB NOT FREED, IS NOT ALLOCATED
IGZ100I PP - 5668-958 VS COBOL II DEBUG FACILITY - REL 3.2
IGZ100I (C) COPYRIGHT IBM CORPORATION
IGZ101I COBTEST
```

Figure 4.3. Sample of COBTEST screen in line mode.

Full-screen mode.

Full-screen mode has all the commands available under batch and line modes, and several more. Whereas line mode can be invoked from a CLIST, the full-screen mode must be installed by a systems programmer to run as an ISPF menu. Check with your technical staff to see if this is available. Full-screen mode allows you to see source code during execution and to have several windows open on screen. Since this operates under ISPF, many of ISPF's features are available also. Since ISPF invokes full-screen mode for you, the COBTEST command is not appropriate in this environment, nor will it work.

This book's focus is on program development techniques, not work practices, so I avoided doing more than make you aware of the tool and present some techniques for packaging standard commands. For a thorough reference to COBTEST, see *VS COBOL II Application Program Debugging* (Chapter 9, Related Publications). You will need that manual since it includes all the error messages for COBTEST.

4.6.2. Sample Batch Mode Scripts

Here are my suggestions for some common COBTEST statements that you can use with most applications where you need simple, canned scripts. While the examples use batch JCL, the commands could also be used for DB2, CICS, and IMS applications. (See CICS/IMS/DB2 Debug Considerations.) With these examples, you must change the name of the load module on the COBTEST statement and the name of the PROGRAM-ID on the QUALIFY statement.

Sample trace.

Unlike OS/VS COBOL, where READY TRACE printed the name of every paragraph executed, this prints only the names where logic flow changed:

```
//GO       EXEC PGM=COBDBG
//STEPLIB  DD   DSN=TESTRUN.LOAD,DISP=SHR
//SYSABOUT DD   SYSOUT=*
//SYSDBOUT DD   SYSOUT=*
//SYSOUT   DD   SYSOUT=*
//SYSDBIN  DD   *
COBTEST module-name
RECORD
QUALIFY program-id
TRACE PARA PRINT
//
```

Sample flow trace.

This is useful where you are getting an ABEND, but do not know how the logic flow is creating it. This example produces a list of the 25 most recently executed paragraphs that caused a change in the logic flow prior to the ABEND:

```
//GO          EXEC PGM=COBDBG
//STEPLIB     DD   DSN=TESTRUN.LOAD,DISP=SHR
//SYSABOUT    DD   SYSOUT=*
//SYSDBOUT    DD   SYSOUT=*
//SYSOUT      DD   SYSOUT=*
//SYSDBIN     DD   *
COBTEST module-name
RECORD
QUALIFY program-id
FLOW ON
ONABEND (FLOW (25))
//
```

Sample subroutine test.

This is useful if you are testing a CALLed subprogram and have no module to initiate the CALL or you want to test how it performs with certain variables. With this script, a subprogram with PROCEDURE DIVISION USING can be tested alone. In this example, the subprogram is a variation of one of the examples in Chapter 8, DKA101BN. Part of that program is here:

```
LINKAGE SECTION.

01   LS1-RECORD.
     05   LS1-JOB-CODE          PIC XX.
     05   LS1-SICK-DAYS         PIC 99.
     05   LS1-VACATION-DAYS     PIC 99.
     05   LS1-ERROR-SW          PIC X.
       .
       .

     PROCEDURE DIVISION USING LS1-RECORD.
```

Here are sample control statements to test it with a value of LS1-JOB-CODE equal to '05'. (I continue to use the FLOW and ONABEND statement because, being proactive, I don't want an ABEND to leave me wondering what happened.)

```
//GO          EXEC PGM=COBDBG
//STEPLIB     DD   DSN=TESTRUN.LOAD,DISP=SHR
//SYSABOUT    DD   SYSOUT=*
//SYSDBOUT    DD   SYSOUT=*
//SYSOUT      DD   SYSOUT=*
//SYSDBIN     DD   *
COBTEST DAVEPROG
RECORD
QUALIFY DKA101BN
LINK (LS1-RECORD)
```

```
SET LS1-JOB-CODE = '05'
TRACE PARA PRINT
WHEN TST1 (LS1-ERROR-SW = 'Y') (LIST ALL)
FLOW ON
ONABEND (FLOW (25))
//
```

This example introduced a new statement, LINK. You may have already figured out what it does. LINK establishes addressability for an 01-level entry in the LINKAGE SECTION. In practice, it simulates a CALL statement. LINK can be followed (not preceded) by a SET statement to initialize the field. In effect, the program is CALLed, passing a value of '05' to it. Once you have developed such canned statements, you will find this is easier than locating the parent CALLing program and setting it up to CALL the subprogram.

The WHEN statement is testing a switch in the program. Whenever the named data element has a value of 'Y', this statement will list the entire DATA DIVISION. Since this is a small program, it was easier to code than naming the fields with which I was concerned. Also, LIST ALL fits better in my philosophy of having several canned tools in my arsenal for program testing. (Note: While the command summary below may indicate that IF and WHEN are equivalent, they are not. IF takes place immediately, which is inappropriate for batch. WHEN tests constantly throughout the run.) Here is sample output from the script, as written to SYSDBOUT:

```
                        ┌───────> RECORD
Printed by              │   QUALIFY DKA101BN
RECORD                  │   LINK (LS1-RECORD)
statement               │   SET LS1-JOB-CODE = '05'
                        │   TRACE PARA PRINT
                        │   WHEN TST1 (LS1-ERROR-SW = 'Y') (LIST ALL)
                        │   FLOW ON
                        └───────> ONABEND (FLOW (25))
                            IGZ100I PP - 5668-958 VS COBOL II DEBUG FACILITY — REL 3.2
                            IGZ100I (C) COPYRIGHT IBM CORPORATION
                            IGZ102I DKA101BN.000035.1
                        ┌───────> IGZ106I TRACING DKA101BN
Program TRACE           │   IGZ109I 000040.1
                        └───────> IGZ109I 000051.1
                        ┌───────> IGZ103I WHEN TST1 DKA101BN.000037.1
Output from             │   000025 01 DKA101BN.LS1-RECORD AN-GR
WHEN statement          │   000026 02 DKA101BN.LS1-JOB-CODE XX
condition               │          DISP    ===>05
being set               │   000027 02 DKA101BN.LS1-SICK-DAYS 99
                        │          DISP    ===>00
                        │   000028 02 DKA101BN.LS1-VACATION-DAYS 99
                        └───────>    DISP    ===>00
```

```
IGZ129I PROGRAM UNDER COBTEST ENDED NORMALLY
IGZ350I ******** END OF COBTEST ********
```

In the previous example, the program was to set LS1-ERROR-SW if it passed an invalid value. If you browsed through the program listing in Chapter 8, you noticed that only values of 01, 02, or 03 were valid in LS1-JOB-CODE. By asking for a listing only if the error switch was set, I confirmed that the program worked correctly for this set of test data. The commands were also listed because I included a RECORD statement.

All of this can also be used in line mode by establishing a SYSDBIN dataset as shown in the previous section with the ALLOCATE command for TSO or by combining into the CLIST.

4.7.   USING THE CODE/370 DEBUG TOOL

Learning to use the CODE/370 Debug Tool (sometimes referenced in this text as just Debug Tool) easily requires more information than I will give you here. IBM has developed several useful manuals on CODE/370 (listed in Chapter 9), and you will need those if you will be actively using CODE/370, either from a PWS or from the mainframe. As with the topic on COBTEST, this section is primarily to make you familiar with the product. You should also be aware that CODE/370 is not COBOL-specific and that IBM's documentation on CODE/ 370 includes information on other languages as well. First, let's review the fundamental differences.

4.7.1.   Differences from COBTEST in Initiation

With COBTEST, the debug environment was initiated by explicitly invoking the COBTEST program, specifying in various ways the name of the module that was to be debugged. CODE/370 has more options than that, none of which are so simple but easily more elegant.

With CODE/370, the TEST run-time option is the primary vehicle that specifies that a program is to be debugged with the Debug Tool. This means that, to invoke the Debug Tool, you will normally just execute your program, whether batch, CICS, or whatever, in the same way you normally do. For this reason, you will probably find that your shop needs many different flavors of the CEEUOPT run-time module to provide the different combinations of the TEST run-time option that you will need.

This transparency is because the Debug Tool is invoked *after* your program begins, not before as with COBTEST. In fact, determining when the Debug Tool becomes involved is highly dependent on your TEST run-time option specifications. The TEST option not only specifies whether the Debug Tool should be initialized prior to the beginning of your program, but also specifies the name of the script file (if any). With COBOL II, you need one set of JCL to execute a program without COBTEST and one to execute the program with COBTEST. With the Debug Tool, just use the same JCL for both environments. Here is a conceptual presentation of the structure.

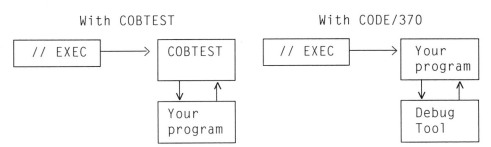

This approach gives you considerable flexibility. With this structure, you might always compile with TEST(ALL,SYM) during program development, using the formatted dump (always available when SYM is specified), yet having full access to the Debug Tool without needing to recompile.

Another option you have in invoking the Debug Tool, in addition to the runtime TEST option, is to use the CALL statement. The Debug Tool can be invoked from within your program by a CALL to CEETEST, documented in Chapter 3. This provides the same basic approach to invoking the Debug Tool with the additional feature of having it invoked only for specific situations. Although the syntax is complete in this book, there are no examples of using CEETEST here.

Finally, you may use the Debug Tool even if you specified NOTEST (or TEST(NONE,NYSYM) or TEST(NONE,SYM) at compile-time). That was impossible with COBOL II. Admittedly, the Debug Tool can't do much for you with these options, but the tool is still there. I don't recommend doing it, by the way, since these options allow the generated code to be OPTIMIZEd (all other TEST options generate code with NOOPTIMIZE automatically), and you may get incorrect results when attempting to debug optimized code.

4.7.2. CODE/370 Environments

For an overview of debug environments, see Section 4.6.1, COBTEST Debug Environments, as the concept is the same. CODE/370 supports all environments that COBTEST supports (line mode, batch, full-screen) and provides more options for environments, such as CICS.

As mentioned earlier in this book, CODE/370 is more than one product (and runs on more platforms than mentioned in this book). One component is the Mainframe Interface component (MFI Debug Tool) and one component is the Programmable Workstation component (PWS Debug Tool). Incidentally, the Debug Tool on the PWS is only one part of CODE/370. It also has edit and compile capabilities that are extensive that are not part of this topic. In this book, I have limited discussion to the MFI Debug Tool, since that is accessible whether or not you are using a PWS.

What makes CODE/370 so different from COBTEST is found in the subtlety of its execution, being from within the application instead of from without. The benefit to the programmer is that there are no changes to whatever JCL or other preparatory planning is done to execute the program, whether DB2, IMS, CICS, or batch. Since COBOL II required that a separate program (COBDBG) be executed instead of the actual application, the requirements for setting up a COBOL II application for use with COBTEST will always be more demanding than with COBOL/370.

Using CODE/370 successfully, either from a PWS or with MFI on the mainframe, will require material beyond the scope of this book. My goal in reviewing it was to make you aware of the interfaces and how it contrasted with COBTEST for COBOL II. If you work as I do, you will find the formatted dump services and the LE/370 services adequate for most situations.

4.8. CICS/IMS/DB2 DEBUG CONSIDERATIONS

This section assumes you are familiar with prior topics in this chapter, as this section presents only those details that are unique for these environments. For instructions on the mechanics of using COBTEST or the CODE/370 Debug Tool, see the IBM manuals *VS COBOL II Application Debugging* or *SAA AD/Cycle CODE/370 Using the Debug Tool* (Chapter 9). With LE/370, you will also need access to *LE/370 Debugging and Run-time Messages Guide* (Chapter 9).

4.8.1. CICS Debug Considerations

Most of these specifics for CICS were covered previously. Other CICS services supplied by IBM, such as the CEDF transaction, can be used in conjunction with any COBOL II or COBOL/370 debug facilities. Those services are covered in depth in the QED book *CICS: A How-to for COBOL Programmers* (Chapter 9). Changes to run-time options must be made by link-editing with custom IGZEOPT (COBOL II) or CEEUOPT (COBOL/370) modules.

Using formatted dumps and SSRANGE.

COBOL II. Output from SYSABOUT or FDUMP or SSRANGE goes to the CEBRxxxx temporary storage queue instead of to a DD dataset (where " xxxx" is the terminal-id of the transaction). You can browse this queue with the CICS CEBR transaction.

COBOL/370. Output from TEST(NONE,SYM) or SSRANGE goes to the CESE transient data queue instead of to a DD dataset.

Using software debug facilities.

COBOL II. COBTEST can be used only in batch mode—that is, all commands must be prepared prior to running the CICS transaction. The commands must be stored in the CSCOxxxx temporary storage queue, where xxxx is your terminal-id. Commands follow the same syntax as that shown previously and follow the same order. For example,

```
COBTEST loadmodulename
RECORD
QUALIFY program-id-name
  .
  .
```

COBOL/370. CODE/370 can be used in batch (but not for pseudoconversational transactions) and in full-screen interactive mode. If debugging in batch mode, all commands must be specified in the primary commands and log files in the TEST command itself. In such cases, the filename specified in the TEST command must *not* be the DD name, but must be the actual dataset name.

If debugging an application that does screen I/O, your best bet is to use two terminals, as follows:

- Invoke CEDF from terminal 1 with the command CEDF nnnn,ON,I where nnnn is the terminal-id where the actual application will be invoked.
- Invoke the application transaction from terminal 2. This causes the transaction to run on terminal 2, while the debug session is active on terminal 1.

This approach is somewhat clumsy, but it allows you to respond to screen I/O from one terminal without impacting on the screen I/O from the debug session to the other terminal.

4.8.2. IMS Debug Considerations

IMS programs can use most test aids, but you must remember that your application program is not the only program in the run unit, even in batch mode. Here is a summary of IMS considerations:

- COBTEST may not be used in full-screen mode.
- COBTEST requires access via the IMS/VS BTS (Batch Terminal Simulator) software product from IBM (this needs to be installed by your systems programmer). See the IBM manual *IMS/VS Batch Terminal Simulator Program Reference* for more information (Chapter 9).
- SSRANGE and FDUMP should be used with the BTS product when testing on-line transactions due to DD restrictions in an on-line environment and the possible conflict between COBOL II's use of STAE and IMS/VS's use of STAE.
- Changes to run-time options must be made via custom IGZEOPT (COBOL II) or CEEUOPT (COBOL/370) modules.
- The RENT option must be specified when using BTS.

4.8.3. DB2 Debug Considerations

There are fewer restrictions for DB2, primarily because it works within the TSO environment, whereas CICS and IMS do not. Also, these considerations apply only for COBOL II. Since COBOL/370 indirectly invokes the Debug Tool after the application has been invoked, there are no special changes for DB2 applications with COBOL/370 other than specifying debug commands in the appropriate command file. Here are considerations for DB2 with COBOL II:

- DB2 can use FDUMP, SYSABOUT, and SSRANGE, as described in earlier topics, with no restrictions.
- DB2 can use COBTEST in batch, line, and full-screen modes, but the mechanics for each are different. For batch, in the bind, the RUN statement should specify COBDBG (COBTEST's batch name) as in this example:

```
RUN PROGRAM(COBDBG) PLAN(xxxxxxx) LIB('cobolII.library')
```

where 'cobolii.library' identifies the name of the load library at your shop where the COBOL II run-time modules are stored. Your program library should be concatenated with this one, such as in Figure 4.4.
- Running DB2 in line or full-screen mode follows the same concept as batch in that

STEPLIB must concatenate the COBOL II run-time library.

The RUN statement should identify COBTEST, for example,

```
DSN SYSTEM( . . . )

RUN CP PLAN(planname)
```

For line mode, enter COBTEST as a TSO command.

For full-screen mode, use the appropriate ISPF menu.

4.9. THE DEBUG LANGUAGE—SUMMARY

This includes rudimentary definitions of some of the commands discussed in this chapter. For full syntax you will need either the *VS COBOL II Application Programming Debugging* manual or the *SAA AD/Cycle CODE/370 Debug Tool Reference* (Chapter 9).

While the command names are the same or similar in many instances, the syntax differs. If you have developed scripts for COBTEST and are now using CODE/370, there is a command translator supplied with CODE/370 that will convert your COBTEST scripts to CODE /370 scripts.

```
//DB2RUN  EXEC PGM=IKJEFT01
//STEPLIB  DD  DSN=cobolii.library,DISP=SHR
//         DD  DSN=db2load.library,DISP=SHR
//         DD  DSN=yourload.library,DISP=SHR      <-Your
//SYSABOUT DD  SYSOUT=*                             load
//SYSDBOUT DD  SYSOUT=*                             library
//SYSTSPRT DD  SYSOUT=*
            .
            .
            .
//SYSTSIN  DD  *
DSN SYSTEM( . . . )
BIND PLAN(planname) . . . .
RUN PROGRAM(COBDBG) PLAN(planname) LIB('cobolii.library')
END
//SYSDBIN  DD  *
COBTEST planname
     .
     .          <- COBTEST commands go here
     .
//
```

Figure 4.4. Sample DB2 batch COBTEST (COBOL II only).

COBOL II	CODE/370	
AT	**AT**	Establish breakpoints in program. This is helpful when you want to pause at a statement or execute other commands at a given statement. This is a major command for scripts.
AUTO	**MONITOR**	Activates an automatic monitoring portion of the screen (full-screen mode only).
COBTEST	**n/a**	Invokes COBTEST in line mode and specifies name of load module in both line and batch modes.

```
 -COBTEST-┬─LOAD (loadmodname:ddname)─┬┬──────────────────────>-<
          └──loadmodname──────────────┘└PARM('your_parm')─┘
```

COLOR	PANEL	
COLOR	**PANEL**	Used only in full-screen mode, this command allows you to modify color attributes for your session.

COBOL II	CODE/370	
DROP	CLEAR	Deletes symbols established with EQUATE or SET EQUATE.
DUMP	CALL %DUMP	Terminates a debug session and prints a SNAP dump of storage areas.
EQUATE	SET EQUATE	This allows you to use a shorthand technique to assign names for various parts of the debug session. Where you will be developing complex scripts, this is a must.
FLOW	LIST LAST	This specifies to turn on (or off) an internal trace of program flow. The flow is printed by a second execution of the statement with different options.
FREQ	SET FREQUENCY	This tallies how many times verbs were executed.
GO	GO	Starts, or resumes execution of, a program.
HELP	HELP	Not available in batch mode, this command provides information about any debug command.
IF	IF	A powerful debug command, this provides logic capability to your debug script.
LINK	LOAD or CALL	Useful when debugging CALLed subprograms when you are testing them without the CALLing program, it sets up the LINKAGE SECTION addressability. This must be followed by the SET command to initialize the values of the variables.
LIST	LIST	Displays or prints data areas from program.
LISTBRKS	LIST AT	This is a useful command when you've set many breakpoints with AT, NEXT, or WHEN commands and need a refresher on what is still set. This is helpful when you are in a debug session and wanting to determine the next step to take.
LISTEQ	QUERY EQUATES	Similar to LISTBRKS, this lists all active EQUATEs in your program. Useful if you didn't write them down.
LISTFREQ	LIST FREQUENCY	This lists the number of times verbs were executed for all programs for which FREQ was specified. This may be useful if seeing the count of verbs gives you information on what was/was not properly executed.

COBOL II	CODE/370	
LISTINGS	**PANEL**	Available only in full-screen mode, this gives access to the various source listings to be available during test.
MOVECURS	**CURSOR**	Available only in full-screen mode, this command moves the cursor between the command line and the source or auto monitoring area.
NEXT	**STEP**	Sets a temporary breakpoint at the next verb. Useful when you want a breakpoint set from the current position in the program for one iteration.
OFF	**CLEAR AT**	This resets breakpoints that were set with AT.
OFFWN	**CLEAR AT**	This resets breakpoints that were set with WHEN.
ONABEND	**AT OCCURRENCE**	This specifies a list of commands to execute if the program ABENDs. Very useful if you want information listed or other processes to occur only at ABEND.
PEEK	**QUERY**	Useful only in full-screen mode, this allows you to see the line number that is obscured by the AT breakpoint information on the screen.
POSITION	**SCROLL TO**	Available only in full-screen mode, this causes the current line to move to the top of its area on the screen.
PREVDISP	**n/a**	Full-screen mode only, this redisplays the previous screen.
PRINTDD	**n/a**	Not meaningful with CICS, this specifies a DDNAME for RECORD output. Default is SYSDBOUT. Useful if you want to send RECORD information to different data sets during the debug session. Each occurrence of PRINTDD closes the previously open file.
PROC	**AT CALL**	A powerful command, this allows you to intercept CALLs to an existing (or nonexisting) subprogram. From this, you can specify SET commands that dictate what values to return to the CALLing program.

COBOL II	CODE/370	
PROFILE	**PANEL**	For full-screen mode only, this command brings up a screen where you can change your default debug parameters.
QUALIFY	**SET QUALIFY**	This command does double duty. It identifies the name of the PROGRAM-ID to which following commands apply. It also can qualify datanames (e.g., where the same name exists in two or more programs being tested together).
QUIT	**QUIT**	Terminates the session.
RECORD	**SET LOG ON**	Starts (or stops) recording of the debug session. Useful for reviewing what happened during a debug session. Records to the PRINTDD for COBOL II (default is SYSDBOUT).
RESTART	**RESTART**	Deletes and reloads a program, making it available in its initial state. Does not apply to CICS.
RESTORE	**SET**	Full-screen mode only, this restores the source listing area of the screen to the last point of execution.
RUN	**CLEAR AT** then **GO**	Causes the program to ignore all breakpoints and begin/continue execution. If the program does not ABEND, this will cause it to proceed to STOP RUN or GOBACK.
SEARCH	**FIND**	Full-screen mode only, this searches for a given character string. Similar to the ISPF FIND command.
SELECT	**SHOW**	Full-screen mode only; useful to see frequency counts for other than the first verb on a line. Not usually needed, as most (?) programmers no longer attempt to put more than one COBOL statement on a line.
SET	**SET** or **MOVE**	Sets a variable to a value. Useful when initializing areas or, at a breakpoint, changing them to monitor program logic.
SOURCE	**WINDOW OPEN**	Available only for full-screen mode, this command opens, closes, or resizes the source area of the screen.

COBOL II	CODE/370	
STEP	**STEP**	Causes a specified number of statements to be executed before stopping execution and returning control to the terminal.
SUFFIX	**SET SUFFIX**	Similar to SOURCE, this opens or closes the suffix area for full-screen mode.
TRACE	**AT GLOBAL**	Displays a flow of program or paragraph execution.
VTRACE	**STEP**	Full-screen only, this allows you to view dynamic program execution.
WHEN	**AT * IF**	An excellent command for scripts, this command continuously tests a condition while the program is executing. It also establishes a name for the condition for reference.
WHERE	**QUERY LOCATION**	Useful in line or full-screen mode, this displays what statement the program is at during program suspension.

In addition to these commands, CODE/370 also supports elementary use of several COBOL statements. Those include CALL, COMPUTE, EVALUATE, IF, MOVE, PERFORM, and SET. These can simplify coding commands, as they use COBOL syntax. The commands are restricted, so see the CODE/370 manuals mentioned elsewhere in this chapter for specifics.

SUMMARY

In writing this book, I was torn about whether to include this chapter. Debugging is not a skill for building better productional systems. By following the guidelines in Chapter 5 (Program Design), problems will diminish. I finally decided to include this chapter because FDUMP & SSRANGE can help. I use COBTEST only for packaging scripts, not for interacting with a terminal.

While I attempted to be as thorough as possible in other chapters, I avoided it here. IBM's COBOL II debugging manual covers it thoroughly (over 300 pages) and you will need that manual anyway, as that is where error messages are located. Still, I hope you picked up a few tricks here that will help you be proactive in your approach to resolving problems.

The best programmers often do poorly at debugging or reading dumps. The better the code, the less opportunity to engage in debugging practices. Writing error-free code is possible. Believe it and you will write it—but first you *must* believe.

5

COBOL Program
Design Guidelines

Unlike the previous chapters that focused on exploiting COBOL II and COBOL/ 370, this chapter focuses on program design. This chapter is presented because 1) some shops have no design guidelines at all, 2) others have design guidelines so outdated that no one uses them, and 3) still others have design standards that use terminology that prevents direct translation to the programming process. Effort has been placed on simplicity and clarity instead of more rigorous definitions of the design process. Emphasis has been placed on structure and style components, using COBOL II facilities where they enhance those issues. Some awareness of structured design and structured programming concepts is necessary to use these guidelines. This chapter relates to the next chapter, COBOL Coding Guidelines. Both are presented to assist you in evaluating and establishing your own program design and coding guidelines.

In reading this chapter, you may find areas in which this book is in conflict with your shop's standards. Since your shop has its own circumstances, this is anticipated. What I hope occurs is active dialogue on some of the differences and why your company's standards disagree with these. At too many companies, the standards manuals were developed with an unconscious awareness of the restrictions of earlier versions of COBOL. This is an effort to remove those restrictions. Too often, the programmer is criticized for poor program structure, when the real culprit was a design so convoluted that the programmer had to patch it together.

5.1. STRUCTURE VERSUS STYLE—DEFINITIONS

Quality finds its way into a program by two routes: structure and style. Good structure ensures the application does exactly what is required and also minimizes debug efforts. Style is a contribution by the programmer to ensure clarity in the structure. Here are my definitions.

5.1.1. Structure

Structure is an end product, not a process or a technique. Good structure is evidenced by balance and consistent decomposition of a program's components. Common examples of structure within the code are verbs such as CALL, PER-FORM, EVALUATE, INITIALIZE. Their appearance alone is not, however, proof of good structure. A program gets its structure during the Program Design phase of application development.

5.1.2. Style

Style is the approach taken by the programmer to achieve clarity, consistency, maintainability, and portability. Good style is simple, using as few syntax elements as possible to represent the solution. This is apparent in the coding by a uniform format with predictable and recurrent placement of both data and procedural items. A programmer will be able to absorb the structure and processes of a program designed with good style using a minimum number of eye movements. A program gets its style during the coding phase of application development. Most style aspects are addressed in the section, Program Layout Guidelines.

5.2. ACHIEVING GOOD STRUCTURE

These are practical tips to assist the programmer in developing good structure. Reasonable effort has been made to ensure these steps do not conflict with the majority of design processes being used.

5.2.1. Use Top-Down Development

This initial step is where you should do the JCL for batch processes and ensure all screen-to-screen interactions for on-line applications are complete. By doing this now, before getting into the details of each program, you ensure the structure is complete from the top down. For example, in doing the JCL you will complete all external names (e.g., DDNAME, PROGRAM-IDs) required and may discover that some processes, such as the use of various utilities (e.g., IDCAMS, DFSORT) were overlooked. This step should also confirm what processes should be daily, weekly, on-line, batch, and so on.

A side benefit of this step is that it allows a programming team to start dividing the work effort, with senior programmers beginning program design while junior programmers begin coding JCL or statements for utility programs.

If documentation specialists are on the team, they can begin structuring the documentation for the system.

Note: If the application will use VSAM, IMS, CICS, or DB2, ensure the data design has been properly done. See the topic Data Structures and System Environments in Chapter 3 for more information.

5.2.2. Design Each Program from the Top Down

This is a major factor for success. Here are some techniques to assist you.

Decompose each box on the structure chart into subordinate boxes. Decomposition allows you to focus on the solution and not on the mechanics. Decomposition begins with a high-level statement of what is to be done. If you can state it in one sentence, you can depict it as a box on a chart. For example, decomposing a box called "Do final processes" might create these subordinate processes: "Print totals," "Update audit file," "Close files." Each description begins with a verb. Together, they represent the processing described by the parent box. Descriptions such as "Error routine" or "Handle I/O" are invalid; they can't be decomposed and reflect an incomplete decomposition. Where possible, the subordinate boxes should be shown from left to right in their anticipated processing sequence.

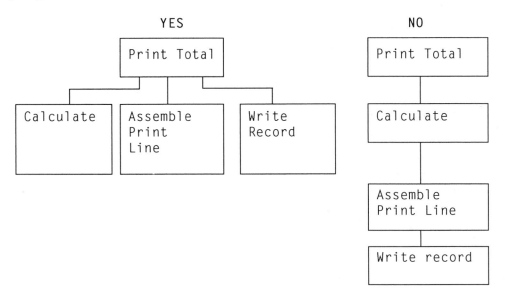

Represent one COBOL paragraph or CALLed subprogram per box. This ensures decomposition occurs and that too many functions aren't attempted within a single module. This can be easily tested. You should be able to fully code any module above the lowest level (e.g., after editing the third level of a structure chart, you should be able to code the first and second levels of the program). GO TO statements that are required during the coding phase are evidence that the decomposition was incomplete or incorrect. (NOTE: I use the term *module* to refer to a box on a structure chart, normally a COBOL paragraph.)

Place control higher and action lower. By placing control (e.g., IF) in upper-level modules and action (e.g., COMPUTE) in lower-level modules, you contain the scope of each module. Moving action to a lower level is the management equivalent of delegation, whereas moving control to a lower-level is the management equivalent of abdication. Not following this guideline is a major reason that lower level modules must abort or GO TO another module to correct an error in the structure or resolve an issue caused by a higher module's abdication. Note: The authority to terminate the program (STOP RUN or GOBACK) should never be delegated to a lower-level module. This verb should appear only in the highest module.

Be sensitive to cohesion and coupling aspects. Here are basic definitions.

> **COUPLING:**   The degree that two modules are dependent on each other. This should be low.
>
> **COHESION.**   The degree that all the code within a paragraph or program relates to the purpose of the paragraph or program. This should be high.

For example, a module titled "Initialize work areas" might consist of many MOVE or INITIALIZE statements and even the loading of a data table. All of these processes are setting data areas to initial values before processing and therefore this module would have high cohesion (desirable). Here are some tips to increase cohesion and reduce coupling:

1. Isolate functions. For example, the READ of a file should be alone in one module (paragraph). Other examples might be "Compute withholding tax" or "Assemble print line."
2. Separate one-time processes from repetitive processes. This is often the first decomposition within a program, separating those processes that occur at program initiation, those that occur at program termination, and those that are repetitive.
3. Avoid setting switches to trigger action in peer-level or lower-level modules. This is known as pathological coupling, the tying of one module's actions to another's without higher-level modules being involved or aware. This defeats the isolation desired within modules and creates complexity in maintenance when higher-level modules are not in control of processes.

4. Avoid defining general-purpose modules. Modules such as "Do database I/O" are not functional and are difficult to debug. Instead, identify what must occur (e.g., "Read policy segment" or "Add beneficiary segment").

5.2.3. Use Structured Programming Techniques

Structured programming is a process and a technique, not an end product. It is a process of building programs by a rigid discipline, following a technique of combining logically related components. Each of the five possible structures has one entry and one exit. (See Figure 5.1.) With structured programming, all modules whether paragraphs or programs should also have one entry and one exit. Definitions for terms are given.

SEQUENCE: Verbs that manipulate data or cause an event to occur. This includes MOVE, ADD, and WRITE among others.

SELECTION: These are conditional statements that are often dependent on the particular implementation of COBOL to be easily used. These include IF, ON SIZE ERROR and AT END among others.

DO-WHILE: In COBOL, this is implemented as PERFORM and PERFORM UNTIL. By determining what condition should terminate processing, you prevent abdicating the decision to a lower-level module that must control the process with a GO TO. Repetitive processes should be controlled by the PERFORM UNTIL statement.

DO-UNTIL: Not available prior to COBOL II, this requires the WITH TEST AFTER clause in the PERFORM statement. Where the DO-WHILE tested a value prior to each repetition, the DO-UNTIL tests the control value after each repetition. The choice is often moot with COBOL, but does affect the resulting value of any data elements being incremented in the iterations.

CASE: Available only in COBOL II and COBOL/370, this is executed with the EVALUATE statement. Because this verb has several different formats, you should be familiar with it; its capabilities may enhance your program design.

Structuring an application cannot be done by simple prose. Check your program design specifications to see if they 1) have an implied GO TO to return to the beginning to repeat the process for the next record, or 2) have imbedded alternate selection logic in the body of the processing specifications. These are two common errors that occur in developing specifications. They are usually avoided only by a conscious view of the entire application as a large DO WHILE or DO UNTIL.

SEQUENCE

SELECTION

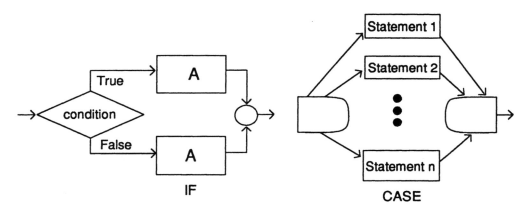

ITERATION

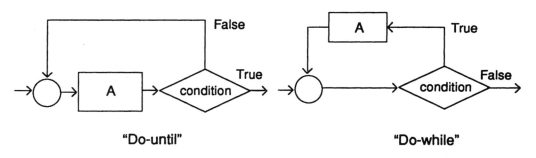

Figure 5.1. Structured programming components.

5.2.4. Use CALL and PERFORM to Transfer Control and Delegate Processes

This often begs the question "How big should a program be?" Do not subdivide a program into smaller programs based on some arbitrary limit, such as the number of modules (boxes) or the anticipated number of source statements. A program may stay a single program so long as its primary function is well defined. That consideration, itself, will ensure that the program stays relatively small.

5.2.5. Use Structure Charts with Consistent Style and Numbering

Consistency and the ability to readily convert a structure chart into code are key factors determining whether structure charts improve productivity. Also, since the programmer will develop paragraph names from this chart, the naming technique should be predictable. A sample structure should follow these guidelines:

1. Define one uppermost module.
2. Decompose each module in a left-to-right fashion.
3. Define names for each module consisting of one verb followed by at least one word, preferably two.
4. Assign module numbers to each box as follows:
   - (1) Level 1 (top) Set to 0.
   - (2) Level 2   Increment by 1000.
   - (3) Level 3   Increment by 100.
   - (4) Level 4   Increment by 10.
   - (5) Level 5   Increment by 1.
   - (6) Level 6   Increment by Alphabet (A, B, etc.)
5. Include a horizontal line across the box to depict CALLed subprograms.
6. Draw an angled mark across the upper-right corner to depict modules that are accessed from more than one module.

The benefit of the above numbering scheme is that each module's name contains its origin. For example, a box titled 1100 will be a subset of the box titled 1000. When this numbering scheme is carried into the program's paragraph names, there is a good one-to-one relationship that is easy to read and understand.

Simple Structure Chart

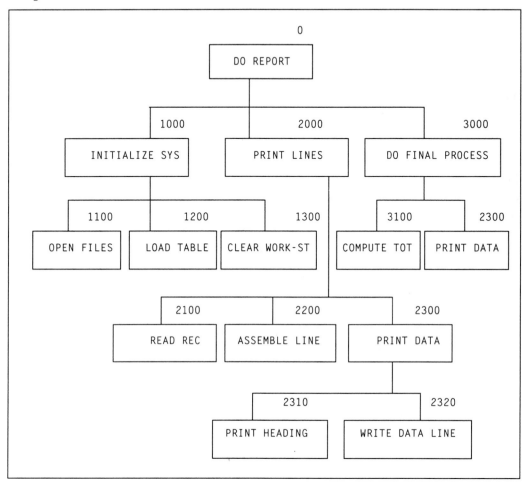

This example represents only one approach to the application. If coded directly from the structure chart, there would be 12 paragraphs (one is a prewritten subprogram and one is PERFORMed from two locations). It also demonstrates the style of the designer, since it depicts where files are OPENed, but leaves it to the programmer to determine where to CLOSE them. (Ideally, there would be a module numbered 3200 named "Close files.") Notice that all paragraphs other than the top one are to be PERFORMed (i.e., no fall throughs, no GO TOs).

The style of the programmer may also affect the final structure. For example, the programmer may determine that modules 1100, 1200, and 1300 consist only of one OPEN, one CALL, and a couple of INITIALIZE and MOVE statements. Being only four or five statements, the programmer might decide to put all of them in module 1000. As this is a style issue, there are no firm rules. If this occurs too frequently in the coding of an application, the structure can be defeated by ending up with a few very large paragraphs that are difficult to decipher and maintain. There should be periodic reviews during the coding process to ensure the structure is intact.

5.3. SORT DESIGN TECHNIQUES

Sorting has unique aspects because it is a separate program being activated under control of COBOL within the run unit. Here are some considerations to take whenever specifications indicate a sort is needed.

5.3.1. DFSORT versus a COBOL SORT

Consider using DFSORT instead of a COBOL SORT with INPUT/OUTPUT procedures.

DFSORT is advantageous when (1) the output will be used by more than one application, (2) the volume of records to be sorted is such that restart or recovery processing is not feasible, or (3) the speed of development is primary (DFSORT statements may be coded more quickly than COBOL SORT statements).

Consider a COBOL SORT when (1) the selection criteria is complex, (2) many of the data fields will not be needed after sorting, (3) the number of records to be sorted will be significantly reduced by using COBOL record selection, or (4) the sorted data is needed by a single application and run-time performance is primary.

5.3.2. DFSORT Control Statements versus INPUT or OUTPUT PROCEDURE

Specify that the DFSORT control DD * dataset (IGZSRTCD or SORTCNTL) be used with SORTs whenever selection criteria are simple or the OUTPUT PROCEDURE does not need access to all data fields. This can reduce development and run-time costs. This technique combines the positive features of using DFSORT alone with the positive features of a COBOL SORT.

5.3.3. SORT Performance Issues

Consider performance issues of sort applications even though such information is not part of the user's requirements. The volume of records involved in a sort will be the major influence on run time and cost. This can be reduced by sorting only the records needed *and* by sorting only the fields necessary for subsequent processing. This can be accomplished by the IGZSRTCD control dataset or by an INPUT procedure.

5.4. SUMMARY OF PROGRAM DESIGN GUIDELINES

While not complete, the following represent highlights to remember in designing programs. Refer to the previous pages for specifics.

1. Do JCL and external processes first.
2. Decompose each program and module.
3. Do control processes first and action ones later.
4. Design each module to be a single paragraph or program.
5. Maintain one entry and one exit for each module.
6. Identify all modules with a verb.
7. Consider management terms such as *span of control*, *delegation*, and *abdication*.

SUMMARY

These design guidelines omit any COBOL examples and assume the reader is familiar with the terms and techniques defined in Chapters 2 and 3. I would appreciate hearing from you whether they help you organize the up-front part of your programming.

COBOL Coding Guidelines

This chapter complements the previous chapter, providing a framework for program coding. As with Chapter 5, this section is provided because many shops either have no guidelines or their guidelines were developed in the 1970s. These guidelines may be used to help you develop your own coding guidelines, or you can use them as they stand. While Chapter 3 showed various ways of using COBOL for specific applications, this chapter focuses only on the mechanics of the coding process. I'm sure these guidelines differ from any your shop may have. How do I know this? Because most guidelines I have seen emphasize that the programmer should code every entry in a program. You will find the guidelines in this chapter are different:

- Code the fewest statements necessary for the application (optional entries keep getting dropped by ANSI, only creating future conversion headaches).
- Some verbs should never be coded. This includes some popular verbs.
- The period (.) is a curse and should be coded only to end paragraphs.

Surprisingly, most of these guidelines (other than new verbs) work fine with older versions of COBOL. In fact, the main reason people find it difficult to convert to COBOL II or COBOL/370 is because they are still coding syntax from ANSI 68, not because they were using the OS/VS COBOL compiler.

Examples of programs developed using these guidelines are in Chapter 8. You will notice that the examples do not follow these guidelines completely. I believe the programmer must have some latitude in interpreting any guidelines on the programming process.

Notice to OS/VS COBOL readers: I do not encourage you to change existing programs so they incorporate new techniques. Programs that do not follow these guidelines should not be changed except when it will be beneficial. "If it ain't broke, don't fix it" is my motto for program maintenance.

6.1. GENERAL LAYOUT GUIDELINES

This section deals with general guidelines that apply to all divisions. Emphasis is on neatness and on preventing the program from becoming dense (i.e., having too many statements per page).

6.1.1. Format—White Space and Indentation Guidelines

Spacing

1. DIVISION statements should be preceded and followed by at least two blank lines.
2. SECTION statements should be preceded and followed by at least one blank line.
3. Paragraphs, FDs, SDs, and 01-levels should be preceded by at least one blank line.
4. Place each statement (this includes ELSE) on a separate line. This does not include clauses that are subordinate to a statement.
5. Place paragraph names on a separate line.

Indentation

1. Margin A entries (FD, SD, DIVISION, SECTION, Paragraph names, 01-level entries) must begin in column 8 and margin B entries (procedural statements, subordinate data definitions) must begin in column 12.
2. Entries that are subordinate (e.g., 05-level data definitions and related clauses) or are components of the same definition (e.g., FD) should be indented 4 columns and aligned in columnar fashion.

6.1.2. Use of Comments

Use comments liberally to make code more meaningful or to explain complicated logic.

1. Use the * in column 7 for comments.
2. At the end of the program, document every project that causes a change to the program. Here is an example:

```
*- - - - - - - - - - - - - - - - - - - - - - - - - - - - - - - - - - - - - - - - - - - - - - -
- - - - - - -*
*    MAINTENANCE LOG                                                    *
* DATE    * WHO         *    DESCRIPTION                                *
*- - - - - - - - - - - - - - - - - - - - - - - - - - - - - - - - - - - - - - - - - - - -*
* 05/26/92* ANNA LIST   *  CC12345 - NEW BILL OPTION                    *
* 07/20/93* JOEL FIXIT  *  NP23456 - NEW TERM RIDER                     *
*- - - - - - - - - - - - - - - - - - - - - - - - - - - - - - - - - - - - - - - - - - - -*
```

3. At the end of the program, place the COBOL II statement "END PRO-
   GRAM program-id." The END PROGRAM statement begins in column
   8 and does not include a hyphen. The program-id must match that coded
   in PROGRAM-ID of the IDENTIFICATION DIVISION.
4. Place the TITLE statement at the beginning of the program and at the
   beginning of all parts of the program that would benefit, e.g. a SORT
   INPUT PROCEDURE.
5. Place comments as paragraphs, not as single lines interspersed between
   other statements. See examples in Chapter 8.

6.1.3. COPY Statement Use

Use the COPY statement for record formats and complex procedural processes
that are used in several programs. COPY members should carry a comment line
showing the last date changed and why, in addition to a comment line identifying
the COPY member's function (e.g., STATE-NAME TABLE).

The COPY statement should *not* be used for data values that control logic of
the application. This includes 88-levels and tables of business-dependent variables. For example, a table of months of the year never changes, so it would not
be "business-dependent," while a table of customer account numbers is subject to
periodic change. Having such information in COPYbooks mandates that many
programs be recompiled for every change. Record formats and complex procedural processes are less likely to be affected with frequent changes and are,
therefore, more suitable.

6.1.4. Resolving Compiler Error Messages

Resolve warning messages before maintaining the program. If the compiler generates a return code other than zero, you are receiving warning messages that
could cause complications later. The compiler routinely is upgraded to change
some warning messages to major error messages. Keep your program listings
clean.

6.2. IDENTIFICATION DIVISION GUIDELINES

6.2.1. Specific Layout Guidelines

None, other than general guidelines specified previously.

6.2.2. Minimum Entries and PROGRAM-ID Guidelines

1. PROGRAM-ID must be eight characters long, matching the productional name of the program.
2. Enter one or more comment paragraphs to describe the purpose and functions of the program. These should be in comment format (* in column 7). Avoid generic descriptions such as "SORT FILE AND PRODUCE REPORT."
3. Use comments to provide information on AUTHOR and on DATE WRITTEN.
4. Do NOT use the COBOL elements, AUTHOR, DATE-WRITTEN, INSTALLATION, or DATE-COMPILED. They are obsolete elements.

6.3. ENVIRONMENT DIVISION GUIDELINES

6.3.1. Specific Layout Guidelines

None, other than general guidelines specified previously.

6.3.2. Minimum Requirements

1. The ENVIRONMENT DIVISION is not needed if there are no external MVS files to be processed (those processed with OPEN and CLOSE verbs).
2. The CONFIGURATION SECTION is not usually needed and should not be coded.
3. No I-O-CONTROL entries are usually needed.
4. INPUT-OUTPUT SECTION, followed by FILE-CONTROL, followed by SELECT statements are all that are usually necessary in this division (assuming external files are processed).

6.3.3. SELECT Statement Use and DDNAME Guidelines

1. The ASSIGN clause must specify "AS-ddname" for VSAM sequential files, but just "ddname" for QSAM sequential files and VSAM indexed or relative files. Example, where DDNAME will be MASTERIN:

```
SELECT FD-PAYROLL-FILE
    ASSIGN TO MASTERIN.          <— For QSAM & VSAM indexed or
                                    relative files


SELECT FD-PAYROLL-FILE
    ASSIGN TO AS-MASTERIN.       <— For VSAM sequential files
```

2. For SORT files, use ASSIGN TO SORTWORK.
3. ORGANIZATION should be specified *only* for nonsequential files.
4. RESERVE clause should not be specified (use JCL if more data buffers are needed).
5. The selection of DDNAMEs for the application should not be left to the individual programmer. It needs to follow a predefined company standard. This becomes critical when multiple programs are combined into a run unit.

6.4. DATA DIVISION GUIDELINES

6.4.1. Specific Layout Guidelines

1. **Datanames.** Datanames must be sufficient for a knowledgeable reader to understand (e.g., FLDA is unacceptable). Datanames must be hyphenated and use a prefix convention that is consistent throughout the division.
   - FDs and SDs should have a prefix of FDn- or SDn- and end with the word FILE. (The phrases, LABEL RECORDS ARE and DATA RECORD IS are obsolete and should NOT be used.) The suffix "n" should reflect the file's relative number within the program. Examples:

```
FD1-identifier-FILE
    RECORD CONTAINS nn CHARACTERS
    BLOCK CONTAINS O RECORDS
    RECORDING MODE IS F.

(Note: nn refers to the number of characters in the record. For
variable-length records, use RECORDING MODE IS V.)

SD2-identifier-FILE
    RECORD CONTAINS nn CHARACTERS.
```

   - 01-level entries for FD and SD should retain the prefix of the file description and end with the term RECORD.

- 01-level entries for WORKING STORAGE should have the prefix WSn- and end with the term RECORD.
- 01-level entries for LINKAGE SECTION should use the prefix LSn- and end with the term RECORD. Examples:

```
FILE SECTION              01 FD1-identifier-RECORD

WORKING-STORAGE SECTION:  01 WS1-identifier-RECORD

LINKAGE SECTION:          01 LS1-identifier-RECORD
```

2. **Format for subordinate levels.** Subordinate entries are indented four columns to the right of their parent entry. If the entry is an elementary item, the PIC and VALUE clauses may appear on the same line. Subordinate entries should begin at level 05 and increment by 5. Their dataname should bear the same prefix as the 01Dlevel entry.

3. **Categories for 01-level entries in WORKING STORAGE.** Group like items together, such as in the following example:
   - 01-level entries that contain various switches and counters
   - 01-level entries that are used to store data records during processing
   - 01-level entries that are used to format print records
   - 01-level entries that are used in CALL statements.

4. **Definition of data types.** Specify data fields as either alphanumeric or numeric. Follow these techniques to minimize inefficiencies:
   - Use PIC X for all items that are not used in arithmetic or are not intrinsically numeric (e.g., a person's age is intrinsically numeric, whereas a part number is a coding mechanism that could become nonnumeric).
   - Define COMP-3 (packed) items as an odd number of digits, plus a sign, to ensure optimum code is generated.
   - Define COMP items that will contain a number of 9,999 or less as PIC S9(4) for optimum memory use.
   - Define COMP items that will contain a value between 10,000 and 999,999,999 as PIC S9(9) for the same reason.

5. **Definition of switches.** Define switches as PIC X and show a value of 'Y' if true and 'N' if not true. The name of the switch must specify a readily understood condition, with 88-level entries also provided, e.g.,

```
05 WS3-FD1-PAYROLL-FILE-EOF    PIC  X   VALUE 'N'.
   88  WS3-FD1-PAYROLL-AT-END           VALUE 'Y'.
   88  WS3-FD1-PAYROLL-NOT-AT-END       VALUE 'N'.
```

6. **Use of 88-level entries.** The 88-level removes literals from the PROCEDURE DIVISION, improving readability of the procedural

code, and simplifying conditional statements. Use them wherever they accomplish this. Use a meaningful name that will be appropriate in the procedural code.

6.4.2. Minimum Requirements and Restrictions

1. Use SECTION names only when there are entries within them (e.g., the FILE SECTION is not required if there are no FDs or SDs to be processed).
2. Do not use the 77 level or 66 level entries. Instead, combine what would be 77 entries into a common 01-level. Common data types (e.g., counters, switches) are easier for maintenance than 77 level entries. Likewise, a REDEFINES entry is clearer and more readily understood than 66 level entries.
3. Do not use the word USAGE and abbreviate PICTURE and COMPUTA-TIONAL. For example,

```
05 WS2-PAGE-COUNTER    PIC S9(5)    COMP-3.
```

6.4.3. Performance Considerations

To improve performance of programs, use the following guidelines:

1. **Define tables with indexes** and, where possible, in ascending order. This supports binary search techniques (SEARCH ALL) and is more efficient than using subscripts. Note: As a general rule, subscripts are no less efficient than indexes when the subscript data element is changed for each use. In all other cases, indexes are more efficient. For example,

```
IF WS-PREM-AMT (WS-APP-AGE) = WS-APP-PAID
    PERFORM 2300-PROCESS-FULL-PREM
ELSE
    IF WS-PREM-AMT (WS-APP-AGE) > WS-APP-PAID
        PERFORM 2400-PROCESS-OVERPMT
```

could cause the location within the table of WS-PREM-AMT to be calculated twice. With indexes, this additional calculation would not happen.
2. **Use S in PIC for numeric items** (e.g., PIC S999) if a sign is present. This reduces generation of object code that resets the sign after each operation.
3. **Use COMP-3 or COMP** for data elements that are involved in arithmetic operations.
   • Use COMP-3 for application data elements and accumulators used to assist the programmer. COMP-3 is more efficient than DISPLAY and more readable in a dump than COMP. For example, the number

123456789 would require this storage and would appear this way in a dump:

```
Data      Bytes
Type      required      As seen in a dump
DISPLAY   9             F1F2F3F4F5F6F7F8F9
COMP-3    5             123456789C
COMP      4             075BCD15
```

- Use COMP only where specific subprograms or system functions require them. For example, PARM processing requires COMP. Also, use COMP for subscript control elements (i.e., where indexing is not being used).

4. If possible, define arithmetic items that are used in the same computation with the same number of decimal places.

6.5. PROCEDURE DIVISION GUIDELINES

6.5.1. Specific Layout Guidelines

1. Indent conditionally executed statements at least 4 columns beyond invoking statement. For example,

```
IF WS-FD-EOF-SWITCH = 'N'
    PERFORM 3200-PRINT-DETAIL
```

2. Place Scope terminators and ELSE statements in same column as previous statement to which it relates. For example,

```
IF WS-SALARY-CODE = 'H'
    PERFORM 2300-COMPUTE-HOURLY-PAY
ELSE
    PERFORM 2400-VALIDATE-SALARY-EMP
END-IF
```

3. Code statements that exceed one line to next line with a minimum 2-column indentation. For example,

```
MOVE ZEROS TO WS-HOURLY-RATE
              WS-GROSS-PAY
```

4. Develop paragraph names with a structure, such that the name of PERFORMed paragraphs is an extension of the parent paragraph. This should match the structure chart numbering scheme. For example,

```
2000-PRODUCE-FINAL-TOTAL.
    PERFORM 2100-CALCULATE-DATA
    PERFORM 2200-ASSEMBLE-TOTAL-LINE
    PERFORM 2300-WRITE-TOTALS.
```

5. Focus on function. Paragraphs with several functions tend to be large and can become difficult to debug.
6. Be conscious of the overuse of literals. They can lead to maintenance headaches. If a literal is used often, consider defining a WORKING-STORAGE data element for it instead.
7. Be conscious of the overuse of switches. With good design, fewer switches are needed. Switches are usually misused when a paragraph does not have the authority to take a specific action, but must set a switch to show a condition.
8. Code all paragraphs using structured programming elements such that only one period is used at the end of the paragraph, causing the paragraph itself to be one COBOL sentence.

6.5.2. Minimum Structural Requirements and Constraints

1. There must be only one STOP RUN (main program) or GOBACK (subprogram). Do not use STOP RUN in IMS or CICS programs. For CICS, use the EXEC CICS RETURN only when returning to CICS or to a program that invoked the program with EXEC CICS LINK. The STOP RUN, GOBACK, or EXEC CICS RETURN statement must be in the first paragraph of the program (i.e., highest level of the structure).
2. SECTION entries should not be used.
3. One paragraph, one period.

6.5.3. Program Structure Guidelines

Here is a summary of general considerations to assist you in coding the program.

1. Keep paragraphs small.
2. Code top-to-bottom, left-to-right.
3. Keep balance. Don't string out PERFORMs through a series of serially executed paragraphs.

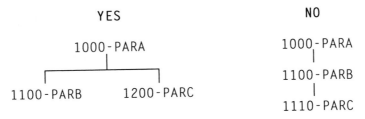

4. Ensure all paragraphs return control to the PERFORMing paragraph.
5. Place control statements higher and action statements lower.
6. Place I/O processes in separate paragraphs and include a record counter for potential debug assistance.
7. Don't mix several functions in one paragraph. Decompose the paragraph so imbedded functions become new paragraphs that are PERFORMed from the original paragraph.

6.5.4. Use of Control and Action Paragraphs/Subprograms

Ensure PERFORMed action paragraphs return status when the outcome is conditional. For example:

PERFORMing a paragraph that can have multiple outcomes and then checking results:

```
PERFORM 2300-READ-RECORD
IF WS-EOF-SWITCH = 'N'
    . . . .
```

Making a decision first and then PERFORMing the action paragraph:

```
IF VALID-DETAIL-RECORD
    PERFORM 2400-PRINT-DETAIL
    . . . .
```

6.5.5. Preferred COBOL Statements

Appearance of any of the following statements within a program generally indicates that the program is using COBOL II facilities and good structure.

1. **COMPUTE.** Usually more efficient than other arithmetic statements, especially when more than one arithmetic operation takes place.
2. **EVALUATE.** See examples in Chapter 2.
3. **CONTINUE.** See examples in Chapter 2.
4. **INITIALIZE.** If you group common items together, such as accumulators, the INITIALIZE can reset all entries under a group name, numeric fields to zero, and alphanumeric fields to spaces.
5. **SET.** The SET statement has two formats, SET TO TRUE and SET to adjust indexes or POINTERs. (Reminder: When setting indexes, always test that the range of an index is within the table being accessed to prevent causing major program problems.) For example, if a table has 99 entries, you could program this:

```
IF WS-AGE > 0 AND < 100
    SET WS-PREM-INDEX TO WS-AGE
ELSE
    ...   <- process for invalid age goes here
```

6. **PERFORM and PERFORM UNTIL.** The presence of a PERFORM UNTIL denotes a DO WHILE or a DO UNTIL, both of which show the repetitive portions of a process. See examples in Chapter 2.

7. **SEARCH and SEARCH ALL.** Although not new, many programmers are unaware of their features. You are encouraged to consider their use. See Chapter 3 for more information. Here is an example of a binary search:

Assumed table definition

```
01  WS-STATE-CODE.
    05 WS-STATE OCCURS 50 TIMES ASCENDING KEY STATE-ID
            INDEXED BY ST-INDEX.
      10 STATE-ID        PIC XX.
```

Binary search, indexed

```
SEARCH ALL WS-STATE
  AT END
      PERFORM 2300-RECORD-STATE-ERROR
WHEN STATE-ID (ST-INDEX) = WS-APP-STATE
      PERFORM 2400-RECORD-STATE-VALID
END-SEARCH
```

8. **Nested programs.** Nested programs offer many benefits and their use is encouraged. For more information on nested programs, see the section Module Structures in Chapter 3.

9. **CALL extensions.** Extensions to the CALL statement, including clauses such as BY CONTENT, LENGTH OF, and ADDRESS OF provide opportunities to develop a cleaner module-to-module structure. Their use is not required, and there are many situations in which they serve no purpose, so don't use them unnecessarily.

6.5.6. COBOL Statements That Should Be Used with Caution

While the following statements are useful, consider them carefully before using them. They are listed here to acknowledge that situations may exist when they will contribute to structure and clarity.

1. **PERFORM WITH TEST AFTER.** This format works exactly like PERFORM UNTIL except that the test of the associated variable occurs after the PERFORM instead of before it. The difficulty is that programmers used to one format may have difficulty rethinking the logic flow.
2. **Inline PERFORM.** While it is no longer necessary to PERFORM outside a paragraph, this statement increases the size of a paragraph, increases the complexity of any paragraph, and increases the possibility of introducing an error into program logic. See the example in Chapter 2.
3. **Nested COPY.** The ability to include a COPY statement within another COPY member introduces administrative complexity to maintain the entries.
4. **Hexadecimal literals.** These are machine-dependent and require a knowledge of bit configurations. They are coded as X'literal', e.g.,

```
MOVE X'OF' TO WS-PROCESS-ERROR-SWITCH
```

5. **Reference modification.** This feature allows reference to specific bytes within a data element, e.g., MOVE WS-EMP-NAME (3:10) TO WS-EMP-NAME would move ten bytes, beginning with the third byte.

6.5.7. COBOL Statements That Should Not Be Used

Most of these elements violate structured programming techniques or could introduce external problems (e.g., COPY OF). (Note: The PERFORM THRU, EXIT, and GO TO were once required to construct a meaningful structure with CICS applications. That is no longer true.)

1. **ALTER.** Do not use.
2. **COPY OF.** This feature allows a programmer to specify from what library a COPY member will be extracted. This creates a dependency on the location of COPYbooks, which should be an administrative issue, not a programming one.
3. **PERFORM THRU.** PERFORM THRU requires a minimum of two paragraphs, encourages the use of GO TO, and violates the concept of decomposition. The format is never required and should be avoided.
4. **EXIT.** The EXIT verb only serves to place a paragraph name. Since it is linked with PERFORM THRU, avoiding use of PERFORM THRU should eliminate this verb also.
5. **GO TO.** Using GO TO indicates an incomplete or inadequate structure. In OS/VS COBOL, it was required to function within some restrictions of that compiler (e.g., SORTs), but no longer has validity.
6. **ENTRY.** The ENTRY statement gives a program more than one entry. Since this is a violation of structured programming, avoid its use. If a subprogram requires multiple entry points, write multiple subprograms instead. Also, it is not required for IMS programs.

7. **NEXT SENTENCE** clause.   NEXT SENTENCE is an implied GO TO. Use other approaches, such as the CONTINUE statement, or rewrite the statement so NEXT SENTENCE is not required.

6.5.8. Compound Conditions

Conditions are used in IF, EVALUATE, SEARCH, and PERFORM statements. A compound condition is one that combines two or more conditions with AND, OR, or NOT. While these are useful, here are some guidelines to prevent problems.

1. Use arithmetic expressions with caution. They have two potential problems. The first is that if used more than once, you lose efficiency and should use a COMPUTE statement to store the result prior to the conditional statement. The second is that the computed value is not truncated into a PICTURE clause, preventing an exact value from being used (e.g., 10 divided by 3 is a never-ending quotient).

2. Use parenthesis around conditions to clarify and document what each condition is. For example,

```
IF A > B AND = C OR D is equivalent to

IF (A > B AND = C) OR
   (A = D)
```

3. Use NOT carefully. When possible use a positive test, not a negative one. Also, remember that NOT combined with OR is always true. Consider,

IF A NOT EQUAL 1 OR 2. The field, A, will always be unequal to one of those values, therefore the condition will always be true.

6.6.   COBOL SORT TECHNIQUES

Sorting has unique aspects, since it is actually a separate program being activated under control of COBOL. Here are some considerations to take whenever specifications indicate a sort is needed. For performance considerations or to determine whether to use DFSORT alone or a COBOL SORT, see Chapter 5 ("Program Design Guidelines"). For usage techniques, see Chapter 3.

1. Address SORT performance issues.
   - Sort only the records needed, not the entire file.
   - Sort only the fields necessary for subsequent processing, not the entire record.
2. Use paragraphs, not SECTIONs. The INPUT PROCEDURE and OUTPUT PROCEDURE must specify paragraphs, not SECTIONs. Use a

single paragraph for the INPUT and OUTPUT PROCEDURES, i.e., do not specify "paragraph-a THRU paragraph-n."

3. Validate correct SORT execution. The SORT-RETURN special register will be nonzero if the SORT process terminated prematurely. This field should be tested immediately following the SORT statement.

4. Terminate a SORT correctly. If a processing discrepancy occurs during an INPUT or OUTPUT PROCEDURE, move 16 to SORT-RETURN, and then issue one more RETURN or RELEASE statement, (i.e, do not immediately issue a STOP RUN, GOBACK, or ABEND). This will terminate the sort and will return control to the statement following the SORT statement, at which time you can test SORT-RETURN and then act accordingly.

5. Consider using the IGZSRTCD Interface. Using DFSORT's INCLUDE or OMIT statements with the IGZSRTCD DD statement (SORTCNTL is also allowed) may eliminate the need for an INPUT or OUTPUT PROCEDURE.

In developing a COBOL SORT, here are the basics for the COBOL statements that are used, assuming that both an INPUT and an OUTPUT PROCEDURE are needed. Some portions of the program are omitted. The action taken in this example for a sorting error is an example only.

```
SELECT SD1-sortfile-FILE ASSIGN TO SORTWORK.
   .
   .

SD  SD1-sortfile-FILE
    RECORD CONTAINS nn CHARACTERS.
01  SD1-sortfile-RECORD.
    05  SD1-sortkey-a  PIC ...
       .
    05  SD1-sortkey-z  PIC ...
       .


  SORT SD1-sortfile-FILE
    ASCENDING KEY  SD1-sortkey-a  SD1-sortkey-z
    INPUT PROCEDURE 1000-SELECT-DATA
    OUTPUT PROCEDURE 2000-PRODUCE-REPORT
  IF SORT-RETURN > 0
      DISPLAY ' SORT ERROR OCCURRED' UPON CONSOLE
      CALL 'ILBOABNO' USING WS3-ABEND-CODE
  ELSE
      MOVE 0 TO RETURN-CODE
      STOP RUN
  END-IF.
```

```
1000-SELECT-DATA.
   PERFORM 1010-READ-INPUT
   IF NOT WS-MASTER-EOF
      .
      .          <- Processing to validate or modify data
      .                prior to the sort goes here.
      .

      RELEASE SD-sortfile-RECORD
   END-IF.
2000-PRODUCE-REPORT.
   RETURN SD-sortfile-FILE
      NOT AT END
      .
      .          <- Processing of data after the sort
      .                goes here.
   END-RETURN.
```

SUMMARY

Admittedly, the format of this chapter was different, rather terse, and procedural. The focus was on mechanics, not on logic or design. My goal was to give you a format for assessment. Many times, we don't know what we want to do until we hear someone else suggest what we clearly do not want to do. If this document helped you determine how you want to change your programming standards, I'll consider it a success. Your comments will be appreciated.

Summaries, Tables, and References

7.1. SUGGESTED COBOL COMPILE AND EXECUTION JCL OPTIONS

These options are presented here in summary fashion and, in many cases, options for different situations may be combined. For each situation, only the options that normally affect the category are listed (e.g., options such as SOURCE, SEQUENCE, and OBJECT do not appear). You should refer to Chapter 3 for specific options and to Chapter 4 for debugging specifics. You should also know your shop's defaults before using these suggestions.

7.1.1. Options for Syntax Compile

If you're compiling a program to determine whether it is coded correctly, but you do not intend to execute it, you incur minimum costs and resource use by coding:

```
NOCOMPILE,XREF,VBREF
```

7.1.2. Options for Routine Tests

Routine testing is for programs that have executed several times and are beyond the unstable phase. These options are proactive. (See Chapter 4.)

```
OFFSET,FDUMP
```

7.1.3. Options for Minimum Compile Resource Use

This option is for use when you want minimum resource use during the compile (see also, Options for Maximum Compiler Performance, following):

```
NOOPTIMIZE
```

7.1.4. Options for Debugging Assistance

These options may be useful for unstable programs or those that have not been tested. SSRANGE increases run-time resource use. Debugging options also require JCL at run-time.

Compile options.

These options will provide adequate information in most cases and do not require use of debug tools such as COBTEST or CODE/370 Debug Tool. (Reminder: FDUMP, although technically a COBOL II option, is transposed to TEST (NONE,SYM) with COBOL/370, yielding an equivalent result.) For debugging with COBTEST or the Debug Tool, see Chapter 4.

```
MAP,XREF(SHORT),OFFSET,SSRANGE,FDUMP
```

Run-time requirements.

For batch programs, the JCL requirements for COBOL II are different from those required for COBOL/370. COBOL II programs that have been linked with LE/370 will use the same JCL as COBOL/370 programs.

For COBOL II:

```
//SYSABOUT  DD  SYSOUT=*    For ABEND messages (optional)
//SYSDBOUT  DD  SYSOUT=*    For FDUMP output
//SYSOUT    DD  SYSOUT=*    For DISPLAY statements
//SYSPRINT  DD  SYSOUT=*    If AIXBLD run-time option specified
//SYSDBIN   DD  . . .       If COBTEST is being used in batch
//SYSIN     DD  . . .       If ACCEPT FROM SYSIN statements used
```

For COBOL/370:

```
//CEEDUMP  DD  SYSOUT=*     For formatted dumps (specified with
                           FDUMP or TEST(xxxx,SYM)). (NOTE:
                           This is optional. If not defined,
                           LE/370 will allocate the DD for
                           you.)
```

```
//SYSOUT   DD  SYSOUT=*        For DISPLAY statements and any run-
                               time error messages. (NOTE: This is
                               optional. If not defined, LE/370
                               will allocate the DD for you.)
//SYSIN    DD  . . .           If ACCEPT FROM SYSIN statements
                               used
```

Note: If you specify SSRANGE, you must also specify appropriate information at run-time to activate the debugging code for this feature. That can be done in either of two ways:

1. On the EXEC JCL statement if your program can receive a PARM (IMS and CICS programs cannot). The format is

```
//stepname  EXEC PGM=pgmname,PARM='/SSRANGE'
```

(If your program also expects a PARM value, it must be coded to the left of the / mark.)

2. If your program cannot accept a PARM (CICS and IMS) or if you prefer not to use this technique, you can include the appropriate code at link-edit time. That is done by adding the following link-edit control statement during the link-edit step. The desired options must have been previously set in the module named IGZEOPT or CEEUOPT.

```
INCLUDE ddname(IGZEOPT) or INCLUDE ddname (CEEUOPT)
```

See the section Specifying COBOL Options in Chapter 3 for more information.

7.1.5. Options for Minimum Run-Time Costs

These options are for programs that are stable and you want minimum cpu use. You should check Chapter 3 for specifics of each option, since some might affect run-time logic. *NOTE:* The RES option applies only to COBOL II.

```
OPTIMIZE,TRUNC(OPT),NUMPROC(PFD),NOSSRANGE,
NODYNAM,RENT,RES,ADV,AWO,NOTEST
```

7.1.6. Options for Maximum Compiler Performance

These options are my personal suggestion for your shop to use as defaults for maximum performance by the compiler. These options should be used with the sample JCL PROC that is in Chapter 3. This supports a REGION size up to 4000K.

```
SIZE(4000K),BUF(32760)
```

Note: An additional step that should be considered is re-blocking your shop's COPY library if COPY statements are used a lot. COBOL II allows the block size to be up to 32,767, double the size that OS/VS COBOL allowed.

7.1.7. Options for CICS

CICS programs need the following options set. You should read the section CICS/IMS/DB2 Issues in Chapter 3 for specifics and additional considerations.

```
RES,RENT,NODYNAM,NOCMPR2,TRUNC(BIN),NODBCS
```

7.1.8. Options for IMS/DC

IMS programs normally use the following options. You should read the section CICS/IMS/DB2 Issues in Chapter 3 for specifics and additional considerations.

```
RES,RENT,DATA(31),TRUNC(BIN)
```

7.1.9. Options for DB2

DB2 programs are not as sensitive as those for CICS and IMS, although they benefit from the same options that improve performance (e.g., RENT, RES). You should read the section CICS/IMS/DB2 Issues in Chapter 3, for specifics.

```
TRUNC(BIN),NOCMPR2
```

7.2. SUMMARY OF MAJOR COBOL STATEMENTS

This section includes a subset definition of syntax for a subset of the available CO-BOL statements with emphasis on the major new facilities (e.g., you won't find the syntax for the ALTER or GO TO statements here, nor the more esoteric options of some of the other statements). Where any clause is omitted, it is noted. Statements that are not new and have no variables (e.g., GOBACK, STOP RUN) are omitted.

Where a loop is evident in the syntax, it represents an optional clause or repetition. Charts should be read from top to bottom, left to right. Each complete statement ends with "—><". Where, due to complexity, I redirected the flow of the syntax from right to left, I inserted arrows (e.g., <———<———) to assist you. Clauses that are new are highlighted.

My goal was to provide a ready reference for the majority of statements that you will encounter, not provide a reference to every option. For explanations and examples of new statements, see Chapter 2. For complete syntax, see the appropriate IBM language reference (Chapter 9).

IDENTIFICATION DIVISION (obsolete clauses omitted).

```
──┬──IDENTIFICATION DIVISION.──┬──────────────────────────>
  └────ID DIVISION.────────────┘

──── PROGRAM-ID.   program-name──┬──────────┬─┬──────────┬─.─><
                                 └─COMMON───┘ └─INITIAL──┘
```

Partial ENVIRONMENT DIVISION (VSAM options and CONFIGURATION SECTION omitted).

```
──┬──────────────────────────────────────────────────────┬─><
  └── ENVIRONMENT DIVISION.──────────────────────────>   │
                                                         │
──── INPUT-OUTPUT SECTION.───────────────────────────>   ^
                    ┌─────────────────────────────────┐  │
                    v                                 │  │
──── FILE-CONTROL. SELECT─┬────────────┬─ file-name ──>  │  ^
                          └─OPTIONAL───┘              │  │
                                                      │  │
──── ASSIGN─┬────┬─ddname─┬──────────────────────────┬─> │
            └─TO─┘        └─┬──────────────────┬─SEQUENTIAL┘
                            └─ORGANIZATION─┬────┬─┘   │  │
                                           └─IS─┘     │  │
──┬───────────────────────────────────────────────────┘──┘
  └── FILE STATUS ─┬────┬─ data name 1 ─┬───────────────┬
                   └─IS─┘               └─data-name-2───┘
```

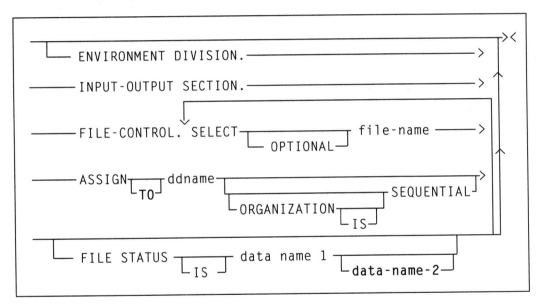

DATA DIVISION.

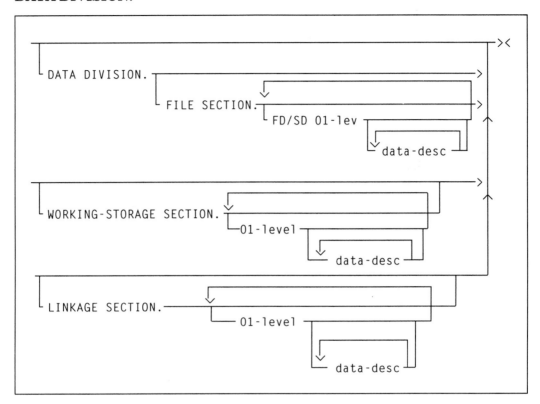

New USAGE and VALUE options.

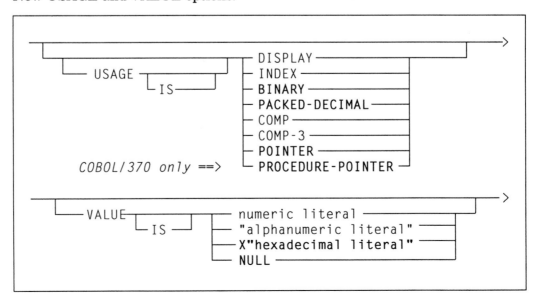

Partial PROCEDURE DIVISION (declaratives and SECTIONs omitted).

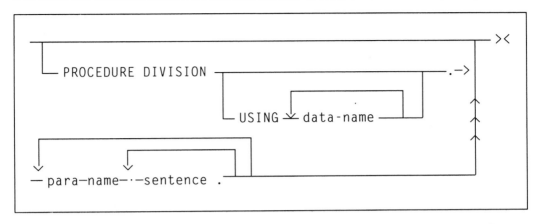

Relational operators.

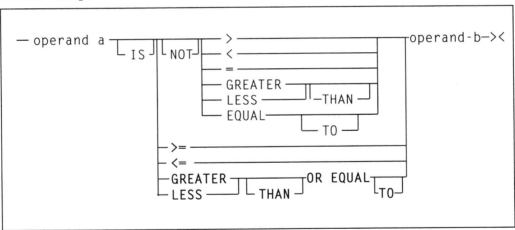

Precedence rules for conditions and arithmetic expressions. Elements are listed in the priority in which they are evaluated.

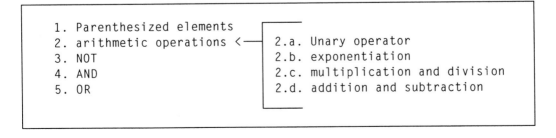

Class condition.

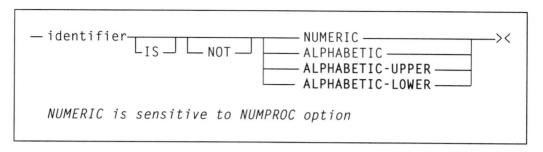

Sign condition.

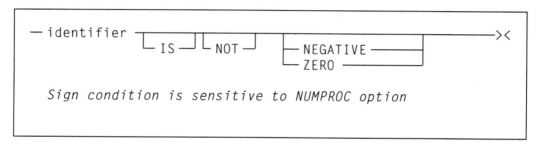

Reference modification.

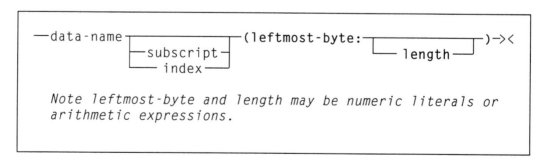

ACCEPT statement for system transfer.

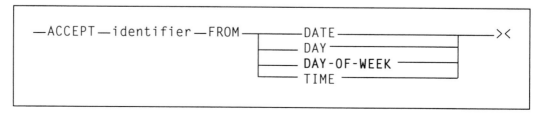

ADD statement.

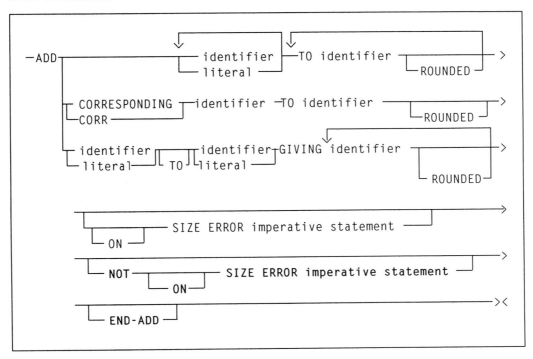

CALL statement.

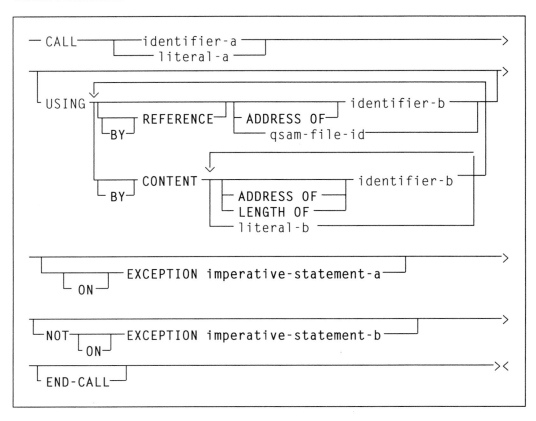

CANCEL statement.

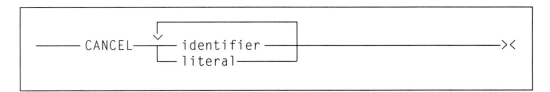

CLOSE statement (tape reel options omitted).

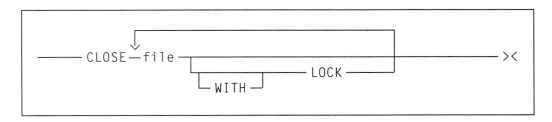

COMPUTE statement.

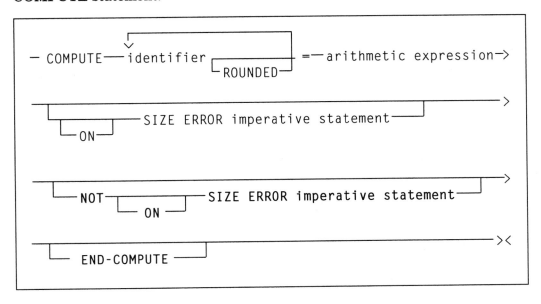

CONTINUE statement.

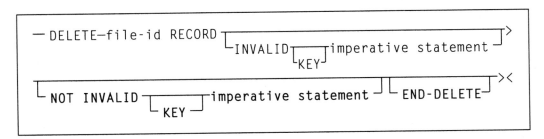

DELETE statement.

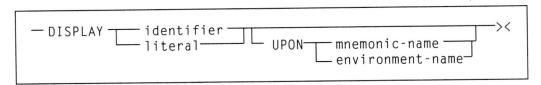

DISPLAY statement, abbreviated.

DIVIDE statement.

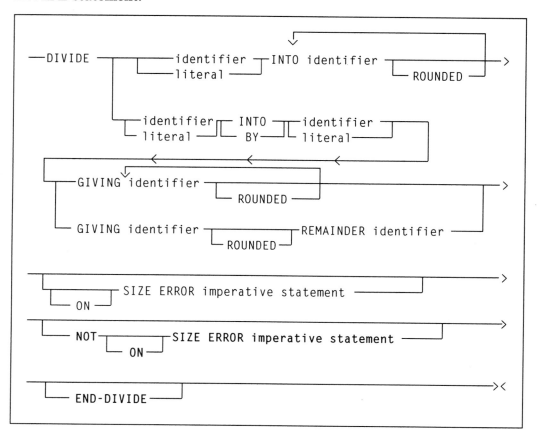

ENTRY statement.

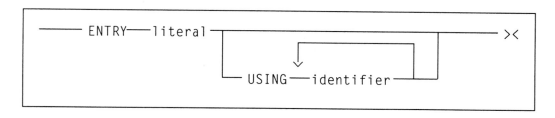

EVALUATE statement.

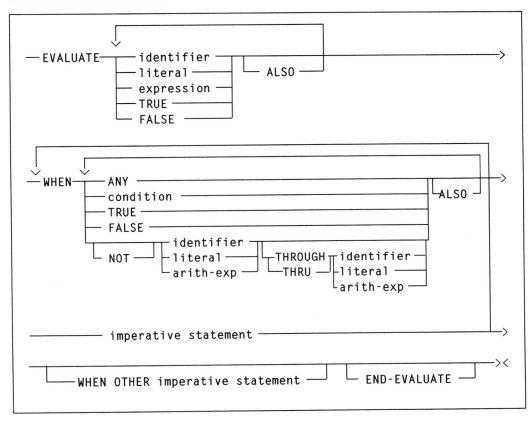

IF statement (NEXT SENTENCE clause omitted).

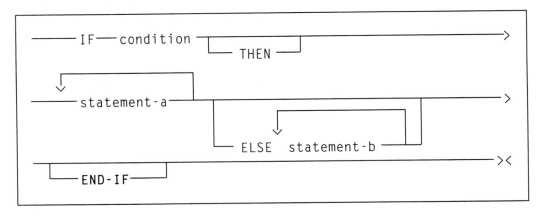

INITIALIZE statement.

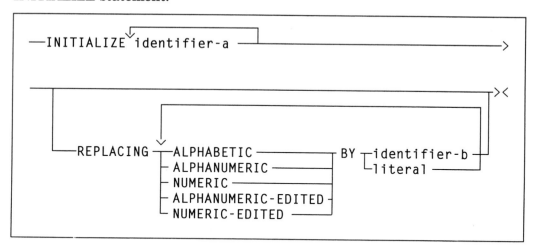

INSPECT statement.

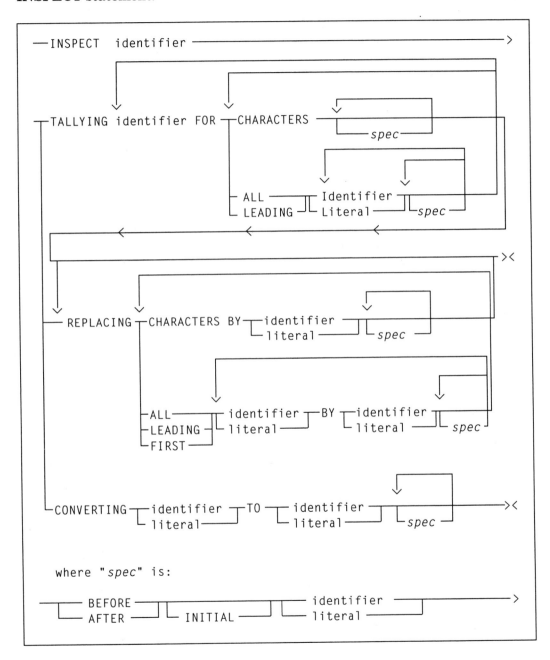

MERGE statement.

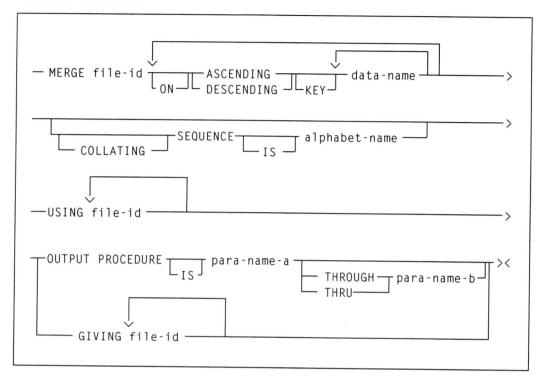

MOVE statement.

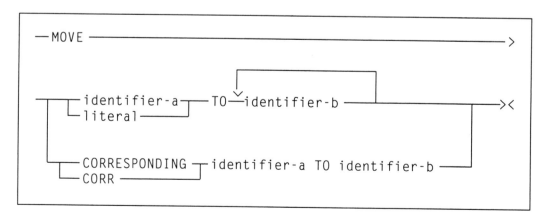

MULTIPLY statement.

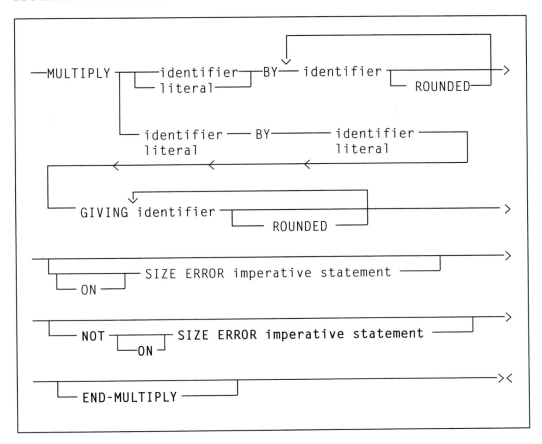

OPEN statement (tape reel options omitted).

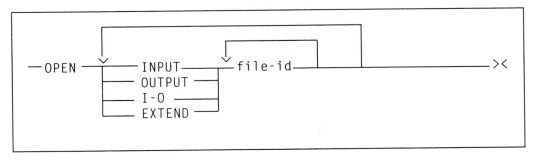

PERFORM statement, except Inline PERFORM.

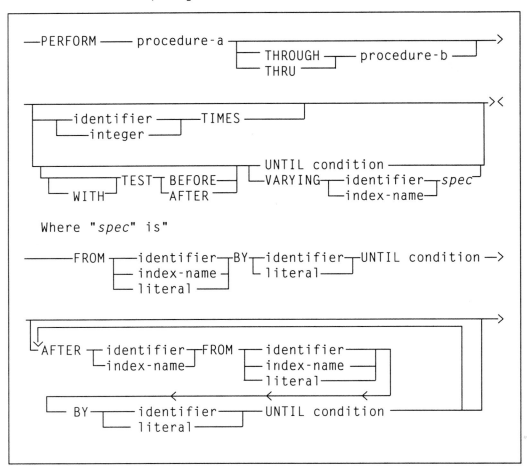

Where "*spec*" is"

Inline PERFORM.

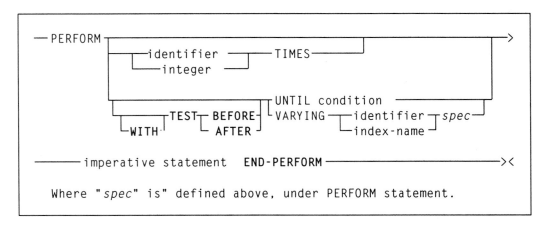

READ statement. AT END/NOT AT END cannot be intermixed with INVALID KEY/NOT INVALID KEY. NEXT has meaning only for VSAM.

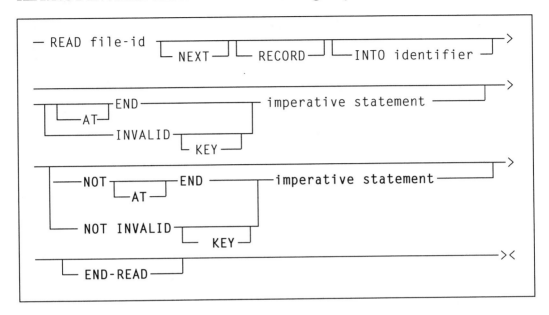

RELEASE statement.

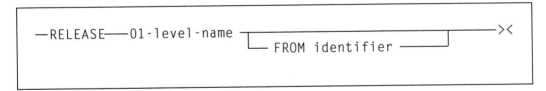

RETURN statement.

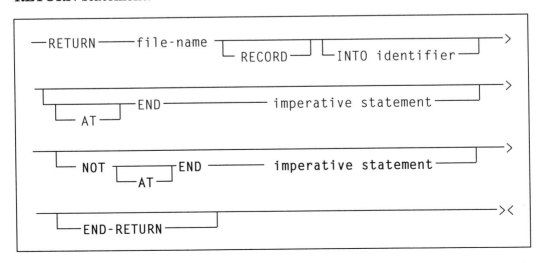

REWRITE statement.

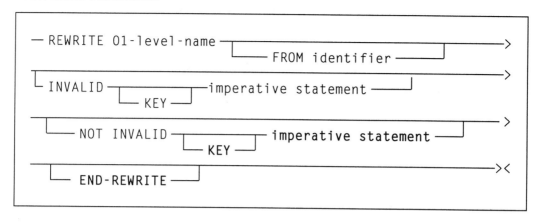

Serial SEARCH statement (NEXT SENTENCE clause omitted).

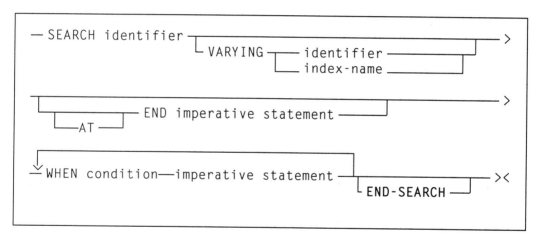

Binary SEARCH ALL statement (IS EQUAL TO omitted).

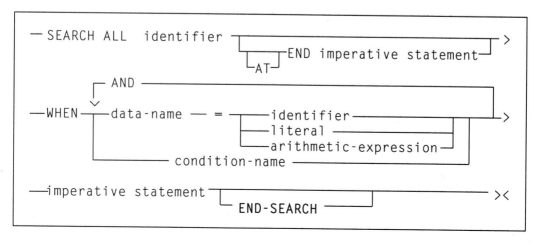

SET statement.

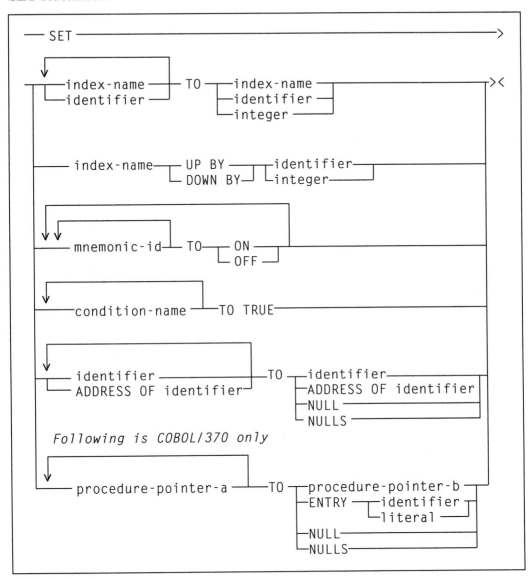

SORT statement.

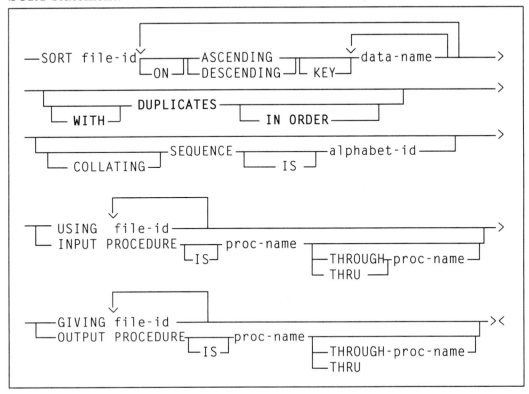

START statement (fully spelled operators, e.g., EQUAL TO, omitted).

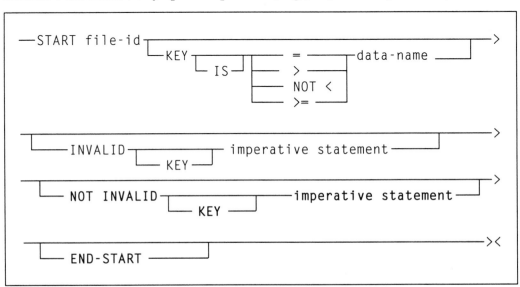

STRING statement.

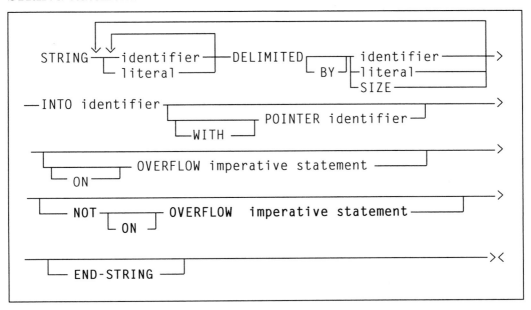

SUBTRACT statement.

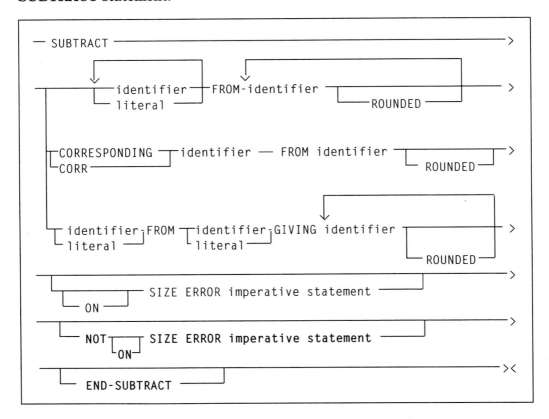

UNSTRING statement.

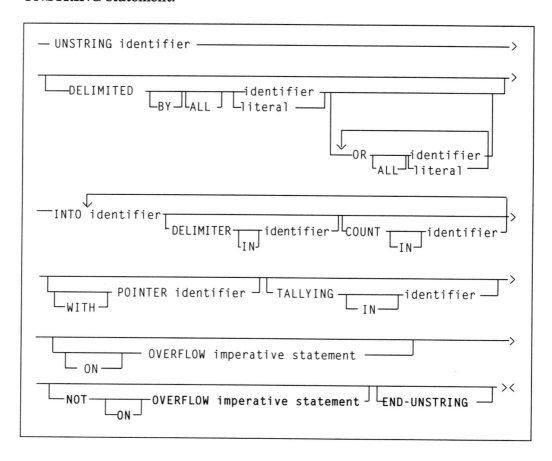

USE statement.

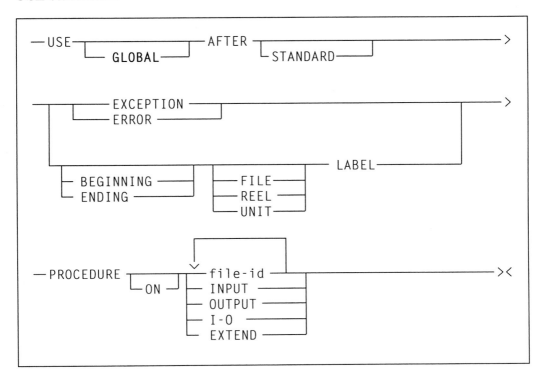

WRITE statement (sequential).

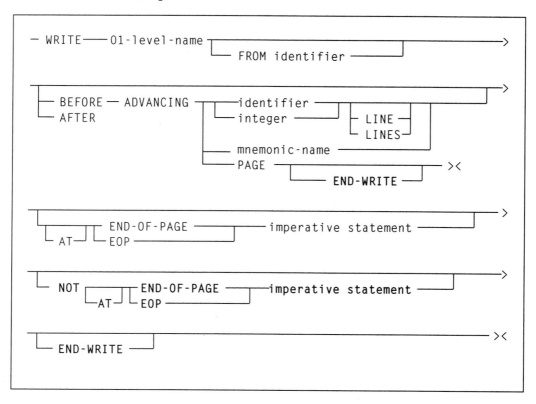

WRITE statement (non-sequential).

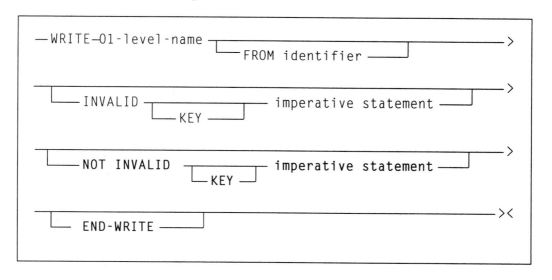

7.3. FILE STATUS CODES

This table of status codes is primarily for quick reference. The keys shown for COBOL II and COBOL/370 are for use with the NOCMPR2 compile option.

QSAM		VSAM		
COBOL/370 & COBOL II	OS/VS COBOL	COBOL/370 & COBOL II	OS/VS COBOL	
00	00	00	00	Successful completion
N/A	N/A	02	02	Duplicate key
04	N\A	04	00	Wrong length record
05	N/A	05	00	Optional file not present
07	N/A	N/A	N/A	Not a reel-type device, yet was specified
10	10	10	10	End-of-file detected
N/A	N/A	14	N/A	Relative rec # too large— sequential READ
N/A	N/A	20	20	Invalid key
N/A	N/A	21	21	Invalid key, sequence error
N/A	N/A	22	22	Invalid key, duplicate key or not allowed
N/A	N/A	23	23	Invalid key, no record found
N/A	N/A	24	24	Invalid key, attempt to write beyond file limit
30	30	30	30	Permanent error
34	34	N/A	N/A	Permanent error, violation of file boundary
35	93 96	35	93 96	File missing that was not OPTIONAL
37	93	37	90	Device conflict
38	92	N/A	N/A	OPEN error, closed WITH LOCK
39	95	39	95	OPEN fail, conflict of attributes
41	92	41	92	OPEN attempted for open file
42	92	42	92	CLOSE attempted, file not open
43	92	43	92	REWRITE attempted when prior I/O not proper
44	92	N/A	N/A	Attempted REWRITE with different record size

continued on next page

QSAM		**VSAM**		
COBOL/370 & COBOL II	OS/VS COBOL	COBOL/370 & COBOL II	OS/VS COBOL	
46	92	46	92	READ attempted (sequential), no next record
47	92	47	92	READ attempted when file not OPENed for input
48	92	48	92	WRITE attempted when file not OPENed for output
49	92	49	92	DELETE or REWRITE attempted - OPEN incorrect
90	90	90	90	Undocumented errors
91	91	91	91	VSAM password failed
92	92	N/A	N/A	Logic error
93	93	93	93	VSAM resource not available
94	94	N/A*	94	VSAM file position indicator missing (COBOL II with CMPR2 option)
95	95	95	95	VSAM file information wrong or incomplete
96	96	96	96	NO DD for VSAM file
N/A	N/A	97	97	OPEN successful - integrity verified

A more thorough review of file status codes is available in the appropriate language reference manual. Sample scenarios are in the programming guides (Chapter 9).

Note: When using FILE STATUS for QSAM files, there may be situations in which recovery may be inhibited if the ERROPT=ACC parameter is not coded on the file's DCB parameter.

7.4. TABLES AND WORKSHEETS

7.4.1. Installation Options

COBOL II and COBOL/370 compile-time options.

Use this section to fill in your shop's default options. For information on each option, see the section Specifying COBOL II and COBOL/370 Options in Chapter 3.

Option	Sample Settings	Your Installation Defaults
ADV	ADV	_____
APOST	APOST	_____
AWO	NOAWO	_____
BUFSIZE	32760	_____
CMPR2	NOCMPR2	_____
COMPILE	NOCOMPILE(E)	_____
CURRENCY[2]	NOCURRENCY	_____
DATA	31	_____
DBCS	NODBCS	_____
DECK	NODECK	_____
DUMP	NODUMP	_____
DYNAM*	NODYNAM	_____
EVENTS[2]	EVENTS	_____
EXIT	NOEXIT	_____
FASTSRT	FASTSRT	_____
FDUMP[1]	NOFDUMP	_____
FLAG	FLAG(I,W)	_____
FLAGMIG	NOFLAGMIG	_____
FLAGSAA	NOFLAGSAA	_____
FLAGSTD	NOFLAGSTD	_____
LANGUAGE	UE	_____
LIB	LIB	_____
LINECOUNT	60	_____
LIST	NOLIST	_____

Option	Sample Settings	Your Installation Defaults
MAP	NOMAP	_____
NAME	NONAME	_____
NUMBER	NONUMBER	_____
NUMPROC	PFD	_____
OBJECT	OBJECT	_____
OFFSET	NOOFFSET	_____
OPTIMIZE	NOOPTIMIZE	_____
OUTDD	SYSOUT	_____
RENT*	RENT	_____
RESIDENT*1	RESIDENT	_____
SEQUENCE	NOSEQUENCE	_____
SIZE	4194304	_____
SOURCE	NOSOURCE	_____
SPACE	1	_____
SSRANGE	NOSSRANGE	_____
TERM	NOTERM	_____
TEST	NOTEST	_____
TRUNC	BIN	_____
VBREF	NOVBREF	_____
WORD	NOWORD	_____
XREF	NOXREF	_____
ZWB	ZWB	_____

* = CICS-sensitive
1 = COBOL II only
2 = COBOL/370 only

COBOL II and COBOL/370 run-time options.

This may be separate for different environments. For information on how to determine these settings, see the section Specifying COBOL Options in Chapter 3. Also, some of these settings cannot be overridden for individual applications.

COBOL II Options	LE/370 Options	Your Installation Defaults	
		Other	CICS
AIXBLD*	AIXBLD*	_____	_____
	ALL31	_____	_____
	CBLOPTS	_____	_____
	CBLPSHPOP	_____	_____
DEBUG	DEBUG	_____	_____
LANGUAGE	NATLANG	_____	_____
LIBKEEP*		_____	_____
MIXRES*		_____	_____
RTEREUS*	RTEREUS*	_____	_____
SIMVRD*	SIMVRD*	_____	_____
SPOUT	RPTOPTS	_____	_____
SSRANGE	CHECK	_____	_____
STAE	TRAP	_____	_____
	TEST	_____	_____
UPSI	UPSI	_____	_____
WSCLEAR	STORAGE(00)	_____	_____

* Option ignored for CICS

Run-time options may be forced via IGZEOPT or CEEUOPT assembler modules. Global defaults are in IGZEOPD or CEEUOPD.

7.4.2. Compile Options: COBOL II and COBOL/370 versus OS/VS COBOL

This list is to assist programmers familiar with OS/VS COBOL compile options who want to locate the similar option for COBOL II or COBOL/370. For information on each option, see the section Specifying COBOL Options in Chapter 3.

COBOL/370 & COBOL II Options	OS/VS COBOL Option Settings	Comments
ADV	ADV	
APOST/QUOTE	APOST/QUOTE	
AWO	n/a	
n/a	BATCH	Batch compiles are available by specifying END PROGRAM statement.
BUFSIZE	BUF	For OS/VS COBOL, this specified the total amount of memory for buffers. For COBOL II and COBOL/370, it specifies the maximum per buffer.
CMPR2	n/a	
COMPILE	SYNTAX CSYNTAX SUPMAP	There is no 1-to-1 relation, although the function is similar.
n/a	COUNT	This function was moved to COBTEST.
CURRENCY[2]	n/a	
DATA	n/a	
DBCS	n/a	
DECK	DECK	
DUMP	DUMP	
DYNAM	DYNAM	
n/a	ENDJOB	The ENDJOB function is always in effect in COBOL II.
EVENTS[2]	n/a	
EXIT	n/a	
FASTSRT	n/a	
FDUMP[1]	SYMDMP STATE	COBOL/370 uses TEST(NONE, SYM)
FLAG	FLAGW FLAGE	

COBOL/370 & COBOL II Options	OS/VS COBOL Option Settings	Comments
FLAGMIG	MIGR	All three compilers use it to monitor migration toward the current release of COBOL. OS/VS COBOL only checks for ANSI 74 compatibility.
FLAGSAA	n/a	
FLAGSTD	FIPS	These two have similar goals, but are different.
n/a	FLOW	This function was moved to COBTEST. (LE/370 supports FLOW for OS/VS COBOL only.)
n/a	LANGLVL	COBOL II and COBOL/370 do not support ANSI 68.
LANGUAGE	n/a	
LIB	LIB	
LINECOUNT	60	
LIST	PMAP	
n/a	LSTnnn	The LISTER feature is not available with COBOL II or COBOL/370.
	LCOLn	
	L120/L132	
	FDECK	
	CDECK	
MAP	DMAP	
NAME	NAME	COBOL II and COBOL/370 provide extended features here.
NUMBER	n/a	
NUMPROC	n/a	
OBJECT	LOAD	
OFFSET	CLIST	
OPTIMIZE	OPTIMIZE	COBOL II and COBOL/370 do significantly more optimization.

COBOL/370 & COBOL II Options	OS/VS COBOL Option Settings	Comments
OUTDD	SYS	
RENT	n/a	
RESIDENT[1]	RESIDENT	COBOL/370 is always RESIDENT.
SEQUENCE	SEQ	
SIZE	SIZE	
SOURCE	SOURCE	
SPACE	SPACE	
SSRANGE	n/a	
TERM	TERM	
TEST	TEST	
TRUNC	TRUNC	In OS/VS COBOL, this was a yes/no option. In COBOL II and COBOL/370, it is a more complex issue. See Chapter 3.
VBREF	VBREF	
	VBSUM	
WORD	n/a	
XREF	SXREF	
ZWB	ZWB	

1 = COBOL II only
2 = COBOL/370 only

7.5. HEXADECIMAL CONVERSION CHART

The following table represents some hexadecimal and decimal values. Notice that two hex values occupy a byte. The values shown are built from right to left, showing the hex and decimal values that each bit occupies within a binary value.

The techniques shown following the table are simple ways to convert from different numbering systems to others by using the table. I apologize to the mathematicians and others among you who prefer more elegant approaches. I use this approach because, unless hex arithmetic comes easy to you, it is a skill that is rarely needed. As I mentioned in Chapter 4 ("Debugging"), if you need to do hex arithmetic a lot, get a hand-held hex calculator.

Finding binary numbers.

The row titled "Binary value of bit within hex number" lets you see what bits will be on or off for any hex representation. The value will be true for any column,

Binary value of bit within hex number

Bit position within byte

Hex	Dec	Hex	Dec	Hex	Dec	Hex	Dec	Hex	Dec	Hex	Dec
0	0	0	0	0	0	0	0	0	0	0	0
1	1,048,576	1	65,536	1	4,096	1	256	1	16	1	1
2	2,097,152	2	131,072	2	8,192	2	512	2	32	2	2
3	3,145,728	3	196,608	3	12,288	3	768	3	48	3	3
4	4,194,304	4	262,144	4	16,384	4	1,024	4	64	4	4
5	5,242,880	5	327,680	5	20,480	5	1,280	5	80	5	5
6	6,291,456	6	393,216	6	24,576	6	1,536	6	96	6	6
7	7,340,032	7	458,752	7	28,672	7	1,792	7	112	7	7
8	8,388,608	8	524,288	8	32,768	8	2,048	8	128	8	8
9	9,437,184	9	589,824	9	36,864	9	2,304	9	144	9	9
A	10,485,760	A	655,360	A	40,960	A	2,560	A	160	A	10
B	11,534,336	B	720,896	B	45,056	B	2,816	B	176	B	11
C	12,582,912	C	786,432	C	49,152	C	3,072	C	192	C	12
D	13,631,488	D	851,968	D	53,248	D	3,328	D	208	D	13
E	14,680,064	E	917,504	E	57,344	E	3,584	E	224	E	14
F	15,728,640	F	983,040	F	61,440	F	3,840	F	240	F	15
→	0 1 2 3		4 5 6 7		0 1 2 3		4 5 6 7		0 1 2 3		4 5 6 7
→	8 4 2 1		8 4 2 1		8 4 2 1		8 4 2 1		8 4 2 1		8 4 2 1
	one byte				one byte				one byte		

since this represents the bit configuration, not the numeric value. For example, the hex number A will have the binary value 1010 because A (decimal 10) is formed with the 8 and 2 bits on and the 4 and 1 bits off. This lets us determine the binary number directly from a hex number or construct a hex number from a binary one. If you can remember the hex numbers from 0 to 15, you don't even need the table. For example,

To convert E7C to binary, you examine each hex number and break it down into the appropriate bit value combination of 8, 4, 2, and 1, using "1" for on and "0" for off.

E becomes 1110 because it requires the 8, 4, and 2 bits.
7 becomes 0111 because it requires the 4, 2, and 1 bits.
C becomes 1100 because it requires the 8 and 4 bits.
Putting the result end to end you get 1110 0111 1100.

To convert 10110110 from binary to hex, you first mark the number off in units of 4 bits from right to left.

The rightmost 4 bits, 0110, represent 6 (4 and 2 bits).
The next 4 bits, 1011, represent B (8, 2 and 1 bits).
Our hex number, then, is B6.

Converting from hexadecimal to decimal.

To convert a number from hexadecimal to decimal, take the decimal value from each column that corresponds to your hex value and add the decimal values together. For example, to convert 05FA to a decimal value:

A in the rightmost column has the decimal value of	10
F in the next column has the decimal value of	240
5 in the next column has the decimal value of	1,280
TOTAL:	1,530

Converting from decimal to hexadecimal.

Similarly, to convert a decimal number to hexadecimal, locate the largest decimal number on the chart that is not greater than your decimal number. Subtract it from your decimal number and mark its hex value. Repeat the above until done, finding the largest number on the chart that is less than the remainder, marking its hex value. For example, to convert the decimal number 1,100 to a hex value:

1,024 in the third column from right is nearest to 1,100. The hex value from that column is 4. The 4 will then be the hex number that occupies the third position from the right, since it came from that column. Our hex value so far is 4xx.

With a remainder of 76 (1,100 − 1,024), our next decimal number found is 64 in the second column. Using its hex value (4 again) our hex value so far is 44x.

Our final remainder is 12. Taking the hex value C from the rightmost column our final hex number is 44C.

7.6. EBCDIC COLLATING SEQUENCE

This is not a complete EBCDIC chart. The focus is on alpha and numeric.

dec	hex	char	dec	hex	char	dec	hex	char
0	00		125	7D	'	196	C4	D
			126	7E	=	197	C5	E
			127	7F	"	198	C6	F
63	3F		128	80	**	199	C7	G
64	40	SPACE	129	81	A	200	C8	H
65	41		130	82	b	201	C9	I
			131	83	c	202	CA	
			132	84	d			
			133	85	e			
73	49		134	86	f	208	D0	
74	4A	¢	135	87	g	209	D1	J
75	4B	.	136	88	h	210	D2	K
76	4C	<	137	89	i	211	D3	L
77	4D	(	138	8A		212	D4	M
78	4E	+				213	D5	N
79	4F	|				214	D6	O
80	50	&	144	90		215	D7	P
81	51		145	91	j	216	D8	Q
			146	92	k	217	D9	R
			147	93	l	218	DA	
89	59		148	94	m			
90	5A	!	149	95	n			
91	5B	$	150	96	o	225	E1	
92	5C	*	151	97	p	226	E2	S
93	5D	)	152	98	q	227	E3	T
94	5E	;	153	99	r	228	E4	U
95	5F	¬	154	9A		229	E5	V
96	60	-				230	E6	W
97	61	/				231	E7	X
98	62		161	A1		232	E8	Y
			162	A2	s	233	E9	Z
			163	A3	t	234	EA	
106	6A		164	A4	u			
107	6B	,	165	A5	v			
108	6C	%	166	A6	w	239	EF	
109	6D	_	167	A7	x	240	F0	0
110	6E	>	168	A8	y	241	F1	1
111	6F	?	169	A9	z	242	F2	2
112	70		170	AA		243	F3	3
						244	F4	4
						245	F5	5
121	79		192	C0		246	F6	6
122	7A	:	193	C1	A	247	F7	7
123	7B	#	194	C2	B	248	F8	8
124	7C	@	195	C3	C	249	F9	9
						250	FA	
						255	FF	

7.7. COMMON ABEND CODES AND MESSAGES

COBOL run-time module ABENDs.

When an ABEND occurs from the COBOL II or LE/370 run-time modules, there will be a message associated with it. See the appropriate IBM manual (Chapter 9) for an explanation of the error. If the run unit includes any OS/VS COBOL modules, the associated run-time error message will have the prefix IKF. ABEND codes will range from 1000 to 1999.

Common application ABENDs.

0C1 Often due to error in OPEN or attempted READ before OPEN. CALLs to nonexisting subprograms may also cause this.

0C4 Usually caused by subscript errors in COBOL. The SSRANGE option will identify this error. Other possibilities include incorrect specification of passed parameters in a CALLing/CALLed structure (e.g., one module passes one parameter and the CALLed module attempts to access two parameters. Other possibilities associated with the LINKAGE SECTION include mishandling of PARMs and failure to SET addresses with POINTER items, where appropriate.

0C7 Bad data in arithmetic operation. The OFFSET or LIST compile option can assist in identifying the offending COBOL statement. Usually caused when spaces are allowed to be in a numeric field.

0C9 or 0CB Usually caused by a divide by zero.

x37 Normally caused by data storage specifications. It may be too little DASD for an output file or incorrect JCL for a tape file.

1037 CICS transaction "fell through" the last statement in the program, causing an implicit EXIT PROGRAM statement to be executed.

Messages from other system components.

When an error occurs within MVS, an MVS component will usually issue a message. The prefix can be helpful in locating where the issued message is documented. Common prefixes are

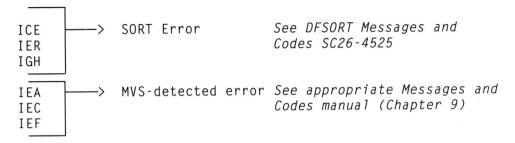

7.8. JCL SUMMARY

The information in this section is summary information. The intent was to combine various pieces of JCL information that are sometimes forgotten. For specific JCL statements and their options, see the appropriate JCL manual (Chapter 9).

7.8.1. Summary of Syntax and Major Statements

This depicts the basic statements of JCL and their description.

```
 1 3       12      16      <—— thru ——>        71
//NAME     OPCODE  OPERANDS
```

JOB statement Identifies the set of run units as one complete unit of work and identifies appropriate accounting information.

```
//jobname JOB      operands.....      comments...
```

EXEC statement Identifies the run unit that is to have control of the cpu. EXEC statements run in the order of appearance.

```
//stepname EXEC      operands....      comments...
```

DD statement Identifies a dataset that may be accessed by the run unit identified in the preceding EXEC statement.

```
//ddname DD      operands...      comments...
```

Comment statement Provides comments within the JCL.

```
//*          comments.........
```

Null statement Identifies the end of the JOB.

```
//
```

Delimiter statement Identifies the end of an in-stream dataset (optional).

```
/*
```

7.8.2. Summary of JCL Coding Syntax

All JCL statements must have slash marks in columns 1 and 2. All entries must be between columns 1 and 71. Each separate component of a JCL statement must be separated by at least one blank. Components are name, opcode, and operands, as shown above. No space must appear between operands, except where a continuation is done to a following line. Comments may appear after the rightmost operand by placing at least one space before coding the comment. Operands may be continued to the next line by coding a comma at any legitimate point within the operand and continuing on the next line between columns 4 and 16. For example,

```
//PAY103   JOB        123456,'MONTHLY PAYROLL' monthly payroll
//PAYPRINT EXEC    PGM=PAYROLL,REGION=256K,
//    PARM='HOURLY'
//PAYMAST  DD  DSN=PAYROLL.MASTER.WEEKLY,DISP=(,KEEP),
//          UNIT=TAPE,DCB=BLKSIZE=13000
//
```

7.8.3. Coding Guidelines for JCL Positional and Keyword Parameters

In this summary, *operand* and *parameter* have the same meaning, since both are frequently used. Multiple rules are normally in effect concurrently.

COMMON RULES

- Positional operands precede keyword operands.
- Single quotes are needed if nonstandard characters are used.
- An operand is not required if the default is acceptable.
- Operands are separated by commas.

- Subparameters are also separated by commas.
- Parentheses are needed if any commas are used to separate subparameters.

POSITIONAL

- It is denoted by position, not by content.
- The absence of a subparameter requires a comma if more subparameters to the right are to be coded.

KEYWORD

- It begins with "keyword=".
- It may contain positional and keyword subparameters.
- Keyword parameters and keyword subparameters may be coded in any sequence.

Examples:

`//JOBA     JOB     123456`	one positional parameter
`//JOBA     JOB     (123456,4321),SMITH`	two positional parameters, the first having further subparameters
`//JOBA     JOB     (123456,'RM-A',,,9999),'SALLY SMITH'`	two positional parameters, the 1st having several internal subparameters and the 2nd using quotes because of an imbedded space
`LABEL=1`	one positional subparameter
`LABEL=(,SL)`	second positional subparameter
`LABEL=EXPDT=91365`	no positional parameters
`LABEL=(EXPDT=91365)`	as above (parentheses cause no harm when they contain a complete parameter list)
`LABEL=(2,SUL,RETPD=35)`	two positional subparameters and a single keyword subparameter

```
SPACE=(TRK,10)
```
two subparameters

```
SPACE=(TRK,(8,2))
```
two subparameters, one of which has further subparameters

```
SPACE=(TRK,(8,,20))
```
two subparameters, one of which uses first and third positional subparameters

```
SPACE=(TRK,(8,2),,CONTIG)
```
three positional parameters within a keyword parameter; the second has further subparameters, the third is not coded, and the fourth is CONTIG.

7.8.4. JCL DD Parameters for Sequential Datasets

NOTE: Depending on the degree to which your shop utilizes IBM's SMS (System Managed Storage), some of this information may not apply. SMS allows a shop to eliminate the need for some JCL options and to standardize how DASD is allocated. Check with your technical staff.

Many programmers try to remember the many parameters that need to be on DD statements and, as a result, often code them when they aren't necessary. The table below is an attempt to put some order to this.

JCL	NEED	SL	Non-JCL means to provide CATALOG	JES	COBOL FD
UNIT	REQUIRED		X	X	
DISP	REQUIRED*			X	
VOL	REQUIRED***		X	X	
SPACE	DASD ONLY	X		X	
DSN	OPTIONAL**			X	
DCB	REQUIRED	X			optional

*Default is NEW,DELETE.

**Required for preexisting datasets.

***Your shop probably has some unit types defined (e.g., SYSDA) that do not require the VOL parameter.

In the table, the left column depicts the JCL parameter to provide a DD variable. The four columns on the right depict other means by which this information is provided. Where an "X" appears, the associated parameter may be omitted. If your shop uses system managed storage, the table may be incorrect. A definition or clarification for each of the terms in the table follows.

> SL means Standard Label (the dataset exists prior to the run unit).
> CATALOG means Catalogued dataset (The dataset exists prior to the run unit and is catalogued in either the system catalog or the temporary job catalog, i.e., DISP was PASS.)
> JES means Job Entry Subsystem (for SYSOUT and DD * datasets).
> COBOL FD means COBOL program, limited to RECFM, LRECL and BLKSIZE subparameters.

UNIT. Required, but is not needed if the dataset is catalogued or the dataset is processed via JES (either SYSOUT or DD *).

DISP. Unless a JES dataset, you must code it anytime you do not want the default.

VOL. Not needed for catalogued or JES datasets or those where your installation has predefined special UNIT types.

SPACE. For DASD datasets only, this need not be coded if the dataset existed prior to the current step or is a JES dataset.

DSN. This is required for access to any dataset created before this step.

DCB. Unless the dataset existed before this step or the COBOL program has information in the FD, this must be coded.

Catalogued Dataset:

```
DSN=SYS1.PROCLIB,DISP=SHR
```

Sysout (JES) Dataset:

```
SYSOUT=A,DCB=BLKSIZE=137
```

Uncatalogued Dataset:

```
DSN=XXX,DISP=OLD,UNIT=TAPE,
VOL=SER=123456
```

Temporary New Dataset: (with DCB in program)

```
UNIT=SYSDA,SPACE=(TRK,10)
```

7.8.5. JCL JOB and STEP Conflicts

Several JCL parameters appear on both the JOB and the EXEC statements. While the function of the variables is the same, the range varies. For example, the table shows that a REGION on a JOB statement sets the limit for all steps in the job, whereas REGION on an EXEC statement affects only that step, up to the limit of the JOB statement (i.e, if a JOB statement has REGION=150K and an EXEC statement has REGION=2000K, the step will be allocated only 150K of memory).

Parameter	JOB	STEP
REGION	Limit	Step
TIME	Entire job	Step
COND	flushes rest of job	controls one step
(JOB/STEP)LIB	If no STEPLIB	If STEPLIB

Note that JOBLIB and STEPLIB are mutually exclusive. MVS will check one but not both.

7.8.6. JCL for Tape Files

Many of us code JCL for tape files so seldom that we forget that additional parameters are sometimes needed. For the full syntax, see the appropriate JCL manual in Chapter 9.

LABEL= Is sometimes required because you might not have standard labels or you are processing other than the first file on the tape. Retention dates or expiration dates are coded here as well.

UNIT=AFF= This parameter allows tape files to share the physical drive of another file and can be beneficial when one file is processed prior to another file or several tape files are concatenated together.

VOL= Since tape files may have many volume serial numbers, this is sometimes needed to identify them. Also, if the file will have more than five reels, this must be coded.

DCB=DEN= Different tape drives create tapes with different densities. While this information is recorded on SL files, it would be needed to override defaults for a drive when file is opened for OUTPUT.

17 RIGHTMOST CHARS IN DSN I include this as a reminder that tape labels only record the rightmost 17 characters of a dataset label. Be sure not to focus unique naming standards on the leftmost characters, leaving some datasets with the same rightmost characters.

7.8.7. JCL: Using PROCs

Some programmers have trouble with PROCs, even though they do fine when coding JCL from scratch. There are a few differences in how the JCL is constructed.

PROC keywords.

To assign a value to a keyword on a PROC statement, code

```
KEYWORD=value
```

To nullify a default value on a keyword on a PROC statement, code

```
KEYWORD=
```

For example, for a compile PROC set up this way with a default of LIST:

```
//COB2UC  PROC  OPTION=LIST
//COB2    EXEC  PGM=IGYCRCTL,PARM=&OPTION
          .
          .
```

you could code

```
//  EXEC COB2UC,OPTION=OFFSET
```

to replace the default value with a new value or you could code

```
//  EXEC COB2UC,OPTION=
```

to remove the PROC default (in this example, you would then get the installation default for that option).

Coding EXEC parameters.

When coding standard EXEC statement parameters (e.g., PARM, RE-GION), the overrides must be done in the sequence of the steps within the PROC. For a PROC with two steps, named COB2 and LKED, the following example would be appropriate, coding all parameters for COB2 before coding them for LKED:

```
//    EXEC COB2UC,PARM.COB2=SOURCE,REGION.COB2=2000K,
//       PARM.LKED=RENT
```

If stepname is not coded with the parameter, here is how each of the following EXEC parameters affects the steps in the PROC:

PARM   First step only, PARMs (if any) on remaining steps
                in PROC are nullified
TIME   All steps in PROC (not each step)
REGION   Each step
COND   Each Step

DD overrides.

Overrides to DD statements within a PROC are done in their order of physical appearance within each step. You need only code the parameter to be replaced, not the entire DD statement. Exception: For the DCB parameter, you need only code the desired subparameter, preceded by DCB=.

If overrides are not in the proper sequence, you do not get a JCL error at the time the job is submitted. In fact, you will receive no error messages if the job is capable of executing with the original values of the DD statement as they appear within the PROC. (No, this is not magic. Since DD statements are merged in the order of physical appearance, you end up with two allocations in the step. The OPEN process allocates the first one—the one from the PROC.)

7.9. ACRONYMS

This list represents many of the acronyms that a mainframe MVS programmer sees. Some are used in this book, some are not.

ABEND   ABnormal END
ALC   Assembler Language Code
AMS   Access Method Services
ANSI   American National Standards Institute
BAL   see ALC.
BLL   Base Locator for Linkage Section
CICS   Customer Information Control System

CMS	Conversational Monitor System
COBOL	COmmon Business Oriented Language
DASD	Direct Access Storage Device
DBCS	Double Byte Character Set
DB2	Database 2
DL/1	Data Language/One (See IMS/VS.)
DFSORT	Data Facility Sort
EBCDIC	Extended Binary Coded Decimal Interchange Code
HDAM	Hierarchical Direct Access Method for IMS
HIDAM	Hierarchical Indexed Direct Access Method for IMS.
IMS	See IMS/VS.
IMS/VS	Information Management System/Virtual Storage
ISPF	Interactive Structured Programming Facility
JCL	Job Control Language
JES	Job Entry Subsystem
MVS/SP	Multiple Virtual Storage/System Product
MVS/XA	Multiple Virtual Storage/Extended Architecture
MVS/ESA	Multiple Virtual Storage/Enterprise Systems Architecture
PDS	Partitioned Dataset
PL/1	Programming Language/One
QSAM	Queued Sequential Access Method
RACF	Resource Access Control Facility
SAA	Systems Application Architecture
SQL	Structured Query Language
TSO	Time Sharing Option
TGT	Task Global Table
VSAM	Virtual Storage Access Method
VTAM	Virtual Telecommunications Access Method

7.10. REPORT WRITER STRUCTURE

Report Writer is not covered in this book. This is a summary of the basic structure used. See Chapter 9 for the IBM reference manual.

Structure of DD to FD to RD.

```
//ddname    DD  SYSOUT=x,DCB=(BLKSIZE=141,LRECL=137)
        ↑
        └──────────────────────────────────────────┐
                                                    |
                SELECT fd-name ASSIGN TO ddname.
                      ↑
                      └──────────┐
                                 |
            FD  fd-name
                RECORDING MODE IS V
                RECORD CONTAINS 137 CHARACTERS
                BLOCK CONTAINS 0 RECORDS
                REPORT IS report-name.
                                    │
            REPORT SECTION.         │
            RD report-name <────────┘
                CONTROL FINAL major-field minor-field
                PAGE LIMIT IS 60 LINES
                    HEADING        1
                    FIRST DETAIL   7
                    LAST DETAIL    55
                    FOOTING        57.
```

Structure of data record clauses.

```
    01  RH        report heading
            PH        page heading
                CH        control heading
                    DE        detail line(s)
                CF        control footing
            PF        page footing
        RF        report footing
```

Structure of procedural statements.

```
    OPEN            done once
        INITIATE        done once
            GENERATE    each detail
        TERMINATE       done once
    CLOSE           done once
```

7.11. COMPILER LIMITS AND MACHINE CAPACITIES

Compiler limits.

There are many limits on the compiler, most of which do not interest us. (Do you really care that you can have 999,999 source statements in a program? I hope not and I sure wouldn't want to have maintenance responsibility for it.) Here are some of the limits that are probably of more use to you in designing applications

Block size of copy library:

COBOL/370 & COBOL II	OS/VS COBOL
32,767	16,000

If your shop uses COPY statements extensively, you should consider reblocking your COPY library to reduce I/O.

WORKING-STORAGE total bytes:

COBOL/370 & COBOL II	OS/VS COBOL
127M	1M

With 127 megabytes available, this can change the way you design applications. In some cases, you may find an entire database might fit within WORKING-STORAGE for a batch application, allowing high performance direct retrieval.

	COBOL/370 & COBOL II	OS/VS COBOL
Number of data-names	16M	1M
Number of OCCURS levels	N/A	3
OCCURS value	16M	32K

The above three expansions open opportunities to build large multidimension tables for complex applications that would have been impossible with OS/VS COBOL.

LINKAGE SECTION total bytes

COBOL/370 & COBOL II	OS/VS COBOL
127M	1M

Combined with other options above, this allows sharing of large data areas with other programs.

Machine capacities.

When doing arithmetic, the compiler is aware of the maximum value that can be manipulated in the machine. When the compiler determines that there is the possibility for an intermediate or final value to exceed machine capacity, it invokes a CALL to a run-time module to do the arithmetic operation procedurally. This keeps the logic intact and ensures correct numbers, but it could have a major impact on applications with many computations. Naturally, there are situations in which you can't prevent it, but an awareness of machine limitations may help you determine when it may be more appropriate to do several smaller calculations instead of one large one.

For packed-decimal, the largest number is 16 bytes, which translates into 31 decimal digits. In multiplication and division, the SUM of the two data fields (multiplicand and multiplier, dividend and divisor) cannot exceed 16 bytes, including the sign.

For binary numbers, the largest value for a half-word field is 32,767 and the largest number for a full-word field is 2,147,483,647. (Whether your program can contain those values is dependent on what TRUNC option you specified.)

From the above information you can see that packed-decimal is preferable anytime you are manipulating large numbers. (Yes, the computer can also do floating-point arithmetic, but you rarely encounter the need in business applications.) In fairness to binary arithmetic, its instruction set is faster than the packed-decimal instruction set, but to benefit from it you need to use TRUNC (OPT).

7.12. SUMMARY OF COBOL/370 INTRINSIC FUNCTIONS

Intrinsic functions were explained back in Chapter 2 and examples were shown in Chapter 3. This is a summary of syntax for each FUNCTION. See the other chapters for rules of use and examples.

For these intrinsic functions, I have followed IBM's lead on using a shorthand format. Since FUNCTIONs use either alphabetic, alphanumeric, numeric, or integer arguments, the arguments will be shown as follows:

Prefix	Meaning
N	Numeric (may have data to right of decimal point). Arguments would be shown as N1, N2. These are defined as PIC 9(n) fields, with or without a decimal point and may be DISPLAY, COMP, or COMP-3.
A	Alphabetic. Arguments would be shown as A1, A2. These are defined as PIC A(n) or PIC X(n).

I	Integer (contains whole numbers). Arguments would be shown as I1, I2. These are defined as PIC 9(n) with no decimal point and may be DISPLAY, COMP, or COMP-3.
X	Alphanumeric. Arguments shown as X1, X2. These are defined as PIC X(n).

If the FUNCTION allows an unrestricted number of arguments, the argument will be followed by . . . ; in those cases, you may list multiple arguments or may specify the name of a table (defined by OCCURS clause) and use ALL to cause all data items in the table to be in the argument list if desired. Arguments may be literals, arithmetic expressions (where a numeric argument is allowed), another FUNCTION (i.e., a FUNCTION within a FUNCTION), a dataname, or a special register or a combination. Arguments may *not* be figurative constants, such as ZERO or SPACE.

If a FUNCTION returns alphabetic or alphanumeric values, it may be used as a sending field wherever alphanumeric data elements may be used, such as a MOVE statement. If the FUNCTION returns numeric values, it may only be used where an arithmetic expression is allowed. That is not dependent on the arguments but on the function itself. For example, the LENGTH intrinsic function might be returning the length of an alphanumeric field.

What follows is a summary of the syntax for each intrinsic function. Each would be referenced in a COBOL program by preceding the function name with the word FUNCTION.

```
ACOS        Arguments: N1
```

Returns a numeric value in radians that approximates the arccosine of the argument.

```
ANNUITY     Arguments: N1, I2
```

Returns a numeric value that represents the ratio (to an initial value of one) of an annuity paid at the end of each period, for a given number of periods, at a given interest rate. The interest rate is N1 and the number of periods is I2. This can be used to figure periodic payments (an annuity) for a given principal and interest.

```
ASIN        Arguments: N1
```

Returns a numeric value in radians that approximates the arcsine of the argument.

```
ATAN        Arguments: N1
```

Returns a numeric value in radians that approximates the arctangent of the argument.

CHAR   Arguments: I1

Returns a one-byte alphanumeric value that represents the character within the collating sequence that corresponds to the integer argument (between 1 and 256 for EBCDIC, which is the default).

COS   Arguments: N1

Returns a numeric value that approximates the cosine of the arc or angle of the argument.

CURRENT-DATE   Arguments: none

Returns a 21-byte alphanumeric value, representing the date, time, and time differential from Coordinated Universal Time (UTC, also known as World Time, Greenwich Mean Time, or Zulu Time). Format is:

Bytes	Description
1–4	year
5–6	month
7–8	day
9–10	number of hours past midnight (00 through 23)
11–12	number of minutes past the hour (00 through 59)
13–14	Number of seconds past the minute (00 through 59)
15–16	Number of hundredths of a second past the second (00 through 99)
17	Either a "+" or a "–". This specifies whether the time returned is behind UTC (–) or ahead (+).
18–19	Number of hours that the time is ahead or behind UTC.
20–21	Number of minutes that the time is ahead or behind UTC.

TIP: If you just want the date, you can extract it with reference modification, for example,

```
MOVE FUNCTION CURRENT-DATE (1:8) TO receiving-field
```

DATE-OF-INTEGER   Arguments: I1

Returns a numeric value that represents a date in the Gregorian form, YYYYMMDD. See also INTEGER-OF-DATE. The argument is an integer date form. This is a number representing the number of days since December 31, 1600 (e.g., 1 would represent January 1, 1601). That format is referred to in this topic as *integer date form.*

Please note: With this and other FUNCTIONs that manipulate dates and days, the integer date form is primarily for portability between different date FUNCTIONs. It also can be stored in a 4-byte field, whereas YYYYMMDD requires 8 bytes. My guess is that, if you use DATE-OF-INTEGER, you will be using INTEGER-OF-DATE. See examples in Chapter 3.

`DAY-OF-INTEGER`   Arguments: I1

Returns a numeric value that represents a date in the Julian form, YYYYDDD. The argument is an integer date form. See DATE-OF-INTEGER for definition of integer date form.

`FACTORIAL`   Arguments: I1

Returns an integer that is the factorial of the argument. The argument must be between 0 and 28. If zero, the value 1 is returned.

`INTEGER`   Arguments: N1

Returns an integer that is the greatest integer that is less than or equal to the argument (e.g., would return 5 for 5.5 and -6 for -5.5).

`INTEGER-OF-DATE`   Arguments: I1

Returns an integer date form that represents a Gregorian date. Argument must be in form YYYYMMDD. Se e DATE-OF-INTEGER for definition of integer date form.

`INTEGER-OF-DAY`   Arguments: I1

Returns an integer date form that represents a Julian date. Argument must be in form YYYYDDD. See DATE-OF-INTEGER for definition of integer date form.

`INTEGER-PART`   Arguments: N1

Returns an integer that represents the integer portion of the argument.

`LENGTH`   Arguments: A1 or N1 or X1

Returns a nine-digit integer that represents the length in bytes of the argument.

TIP: This yields the same result as the LENGTH special register but may be used in different constructs because it is treated as an integer. For example, the LENGTH FUNCTION may be used in reference modification, for example,

```
MOVE FLD-A TO VARIABLE-ARRAY (LOC: FUNCTION LENGTH (FLD-A)
```

LOG   Arguments: N1

Returns a numeric value that approximates the natural log (logarithm to base e). Argument must be positive.

LOG10   Arguments: N1

This is similar to LOG, except the logarithm is to base 10 of the argument.

LOWER-CASE   Arguments: A1 or X1

Returns an alphanumeric value of the same length as the argument with all characters replaced by lower case. Argument must be alphabetic or alphanumeric. Argument may be mixed upper- and lower-case text.

MAX   Arguments: A1 . . . or I1 . . . or N1 . . . or X1 . . .

Returns the maximum value of the arguments. The value returned is consistent with the arguments—that is, alphanumeric value if arguments are alphanumeric and numeric value if arguments are numeric. This allows the MAX FUNCTION to be used both where alphanumeric variables are allowed as well as where arithmetic expressions are allowed.

MEAN   Arguments: N1

Returns a numeric value that represents the arithmetic average of the arguments.

MEDIAN   Arguments: N1

Returns a numeric value representing the value of the argument that appears in the middle of the arguments after sorting.

MIDRANGE   Arguments: N1

Returns a numeric value that represents the arithmetic average of the minimum and maximum arguments.

MIN   Arguments: A1 . . . or I1 . . . or N1 . . . or X1 . . .

The opposite of MAX.

MOD   Arguments: I1, I2

Returns an integer that is represents argument-1 modulo argument-2. In many cases this will return the same result as REM, but not always.

NUMVAL   Arguments: X1

Returns a numeric value extracted from within the alphanumeric character string of the argument. This is useful when numeric data is in a PIC X format. The number of digits must not exceed 18. See examples in Chapter 3.

NUMVAL-C   Arguments: X1

This same as NUMVAL, except the alphanumeric character string may also include edit characters, such as dollar sign ($), comma, and credit symbol (CR). See examples in Chapter 3.

ORD   Arguments: A1 or X1

Returns an integer representing the ordinal position within the collating sequence for the argument (e.g., "S" is 227, X'FF' is 256). Argument must be one byte long. Returned integer will be between 1 and 256 (not 0 to 255).

ORD-MAX   Arguments: A1 . . . or N1 . . . or X1 . . .

Returns an integer that represents the sequence within the arguments of the one with the maximum value. See Chapter 3 for an example.

ORD-MIN   Arguments: A1 . . . or N1 . . . or X1 . . .

The opposite of ORD-MAX.

PRESENT-VALUE   Arguments: N1, N2 . . .

Returns a numeric value that represents the present value of a future series of payments that occur at the end of each period (argument-2) at the discount rate specified in argument-1. This is useful if your application needs to calculate the present value of a future amount, whether it's a life insurance policy or other investment. There is an example of this in Chapter 3.

RANDOM   Arguments: I1 or none

Returns a random numeric value between zero and one. If referenced with a new argument, a new random series begins. If referenced with no argument, the returned value will be the next calculated value for the original argument. For any given argument, the sequence of returned values will always be the same.

RANGE   Arguments: I1 . . . or N1 . . .

Returns a numeric value that represents the value of the maximum argument minus the minimum argument.

REM   Arguments: N1, N2

Returns a numeric value that is the remainder of argument-1 divided by argument-2. See also MOD.

REVERSE   Arguments: A1 or X1

Returns an alphanumeric value that represents the argument, but in reverse order. The returned value has the same length as the argument. For example, if the argument was "Programmer" the returned value would be "remmargorP".

SIN   Arguments: N1

Returns a numeric value that represents the sine of the arc or angle of the argument. The argument must be specified in radians.

SQRT   Arguments: N1

Returns a numeric value that is the square root of the argument. The argument must not be negative.

STANDARD-DEVIATION   Arguments: N1 . . .

Returns a numeric value that represents the standard deviation of the arguments. If the argument contains only one value, zero is returned.

SUM   Arguments: I1 . . . or N1 . . .

Returns a numeric value representing the sum of all arguments. See example in Chapter 3.

```
TAN        Arguments: N1
```

Returns a numeric value that represents the tangent of the arc or angle as specified by the argument. The argument must be in radians.

```
UPPER-CASE  Arguments: A1 or X1
```

Opposite of LOWER-CASE.

```
VARIANCE    Arguments: N1 . . .
```

Returns a numeric value that represents the variance of the arguments.

```
WHEN-COMPILED     Arguments: none
```

Returns the date and time of compilation in a 21-byte format. See CURRENT-DATE FUNCTION for format.

7.13. SUMMARY OF LE/370 CALLABLE SERVICES

In Chapter 3 you found examples of several CALLable services. Those are the ones that I felt would be most commonly used. Since the other services require more in-depth involvement with LE/370, I list the available services here, but with no specifics. If you need to use these, see the *LE/370 Programming Guide* (Chapter 9). Primarily because most of their services are provided by intrinsic functions, the math routines are not listed.

7.13.1. Dynamic Storage Services

These services allow an application program to dynamically allocate and free storage while the application is running. The term *heap* is used with LE/370 to specify storage that is allocated by LE/370 for use by application programs.

CEECRHP	Create Additional Storage
CEECZST	Reallocate or Change Size of Storage
CEEDSHP	Discard Heap
CEEFRST	Free Heap Storage
CEEGTST	Get Heap Storage
CEE3RPH	Set Report Heading (Used with RPTSTG and RPTOPTS run-time options.)

7.13.2. Condition Handling Services

These services allow the application program to interrogate complex feedback codes and to signal conditions. These also allow an application to specify a module to receive control for conditions. These services can be useful for applications that need to stay on-line and trap potential ABENDs or other problems. The term *token* refers to the 12-byte feedback area associated with LE/370 CALLable services.

CEEDCOD	Decompose a Condition Token
CEEGPID	Retrieve the LE/370 Version and Platform ID
CEEGQDT	Retrieve Q_Data_Token
CEEHDLR	Register User Condition Handler
CEEHDLU	Unregister User Condition Handler
CEEITOK	Return Initial Condition Token
CEEMRCR	Move Resume Cursor Relative to Handle Cursor
CEENCOD	Construct a Condition Token
CEESGL	Signal a Condition
CEE3ABD	Terminate Enclave with ABEND (See Chapter 3 for example.)
CEE3CNC	Allow Nested Conditions
CEE3GRN	Get Name of Routine That Incurred Condition
CEE3SPM	Query and Modify LE/370 Hardware Condition Enablement

7.13.3. Message Handling Services

LE/370 provides the facility for messages to be generated for communication between programs in an enclave.

CEEMGET	Get a Message
CEEMOUT	Dispatch a Message
CEEMSG	Get, Format, and Dispatch a Message

7.13.4. National Language Services

With LE/370, multiple languages can be supported. These services allow the application to access these features.

CEEFMDA	Obtain Default Date Format
CEEFMDS	Obtain Default Decimal Separator
CEEFMDT	Obtain Default Date and Time Format
CEEFMTM	Obtain Default Time Format
CEE3CTY	Set Default Country
CEE3LNG	Set National Language
CEE3MCS	Obtain Default Currency Symbol
CEE3MTS	Obtain Default Thousands Separator

7.13.5. Date and Time Services

With the intrinsic functions for COBOL/370, you may not need these services, many of which provide similar services. The term *Lilian* refers to an integer date form similar, but not equal, to the integer date form used by COBOL/370 intrinsic functions. With COBOL/370, the integer date form is a number representing the number of days since December 31, 1600. With LE/370 CALLable services, the integer date form is the number of days since October 14, 1582.

One possible advantage of using these date services is that they allow the year to be two digits, whereas the COBOL/370 intrinsic functions demand that the year be four digits. Since many current data files use a two-digit year, this might offer some compatibility as the end of the century looms nearer.

CEEDAYS	Convert Date to Lilian Format
CEEDATE	Convert Lilian Date to Character Format
CEEDATM	Convert Seconds to Character Timestamp
CEEDYWK	Calculate Day of Week from Lilian Date
CEEGMT	(see CEEUTC below)
CEEGMTO	Get Offset from Greenwich Mean Time to Local Time
CEEISEC	Convert Integers to Seconds
CEELOCT	Get Current Local Time
CEEQCEN	Query the Century Window
CEESCEN	Set the Century Window
CEESECI	Convert Seconds to Integers
CEESECS	Convert Timestamp to Number of Seconds
CEEUTC	Get Coordinated Universal Time (same as CEEGMT)

7.13.6. General LE/370 Services

These are nonspecific services. Two of them appear in examples in Chapter 3.

CEE3PRM	Query Parameter String
CEE3USR	Set or Query User Parameter Fields
CEETEST	Invoke Debug Tool (See Chapter 3 for example.)
CEE3DMP	Generate dump (See Chapter 3 for example.)
CEERAN0	Calculate Uniform Random Number

EXAMPLES of COBOL Programs

This chapter is unique in this book. It is not a reference chapter and includes no new information. Instead, it contains complete source programs to demonstrate the guidelines presented in Chapters 5 and 6 ("Program Design" and "Program Coding"). Some are COBOL II and some work with COBOL II and OS/VS CO-BOL. The intent of this chapter is not to dazzle you with code, but to demonstrate some of the benefits of structure and decomposition, as well as a few of the new components of COBOL. The focus is on structure and ways to preserve compatibility, not on using some new features. For examples of specific COBOL statements, please refer to previous chapters.

Importance of style and simplicity.

If you've been writing "GO TO-less" code for years, you won't find anything new here. However, if you are accustomed to coding all 4 divisions and think GO TO is a fact of life, I encourage you to walk through each example. All the programs demonstrate a bit of programmer style. I believe it is important to allow some degree of freedom for the programmer to code less-than-perfect programs.

The style of some of these programs conflicts with several major structured techniques, primarily in the initialization process. Some books suggest that the first record(s) to be processed should be read immediately after OPEN. I don't follow that belief. After years of teaching new programmers (and reteaching old programmers), I have found that many logic problems occur because of that practice. I have found programs to be simpler to code and to debug if you

1. Code one-time housekeeping processes in an initialization routine.
2. Code all repeated processes under the umbrella of a DO-WHILE (PER-FORM UNTIL) statement
3. Code one-time termination processes in a termination routine.

I included the IMS example because over the years I have heard complaints from programmers that it is impossible to use structured code with such a complex data structure. On the contrary, my approach is to blend the data structure with the program structure. Since IMS and structured programming both follow a hierarchical format, the two components can blend well.

Comments and small paragraphs.

I asked several programmers for comments prior to including these programs in the book. Two frequent comments were "Why are there so many comments in the code?" and "Why are some paragraphs so small?" Since you may have the same questions, let me give my response.

I include comments in code whenever I believe a rookie programmer may not understand the structure or the logic. I wanted to emphasize to you, the reader, where I was and was not, so you could follow my approach to structure. Also, while I often see comments in programs that explain a process, I have never seen comments that explain the structure—and this is exactly what most programmers need. Knowing what to do is usually straightforward. Knowing where in the logic flow to do it is sometimes impossible.

I compare programming to architecture. As an industry, we fail in teaching new programmers if we encourage them to use shortcuts for small classroom programs, hoping they will do differently on large, real systems. Consider architects: they follow certain disciplines whether they are building a one-story house or a 30-story building. A small building is a big building in miniature. We should do the same for programming: use specific disciplines, regardless of program size. Decomposition is decomposition is decomposition. Novice programmers who are taught to combine many small functions in one paragraph become senior programmers who write indecipherable paragraphs that run several pages long.

Knowing that somewhere, for some reason, someone will want to eliminate small paragraphs, I redid Example 8.1 using COBOL II features, allowing the entire logic of the SORT OUTPUT PROCEDURE to be accomplished in a single paragraph. I don't recommend this type of programming, but the example does display how far COBOL has come.

Aren't the examples too simple?

These programs are indeed, simple. I've been asked on occasion to use more complex programs to demonstrate ideas in my programming classes. Unfortunately, 5,000-line programs only confuse students and drown them in the application's logic. These simple structures demonstrate techniques. Where the structure is simple, a program can be easily expanded and retain the simple structure. Also, when a program gets too big to grasp quickly, I break it into several programs. Life's too short to spend it wading through monster programs just to prove you can do it.

8.1. SORT EXAMPLE WITH COBOL II

If you're used to seeing SORT programs with lots of noise, such as SECTION headers, PERFORM THRUs, GO TOs, and EXIT statements, you'll find this to be quite different. The techniques in this program are covered in the section on SORT techniques in both Chapter 5 and Chapter 6. If the use of SORT-RETURN or the comments about IGZSRTCD leave you confused, I suggest you review those sections. This program also appears in other examples.

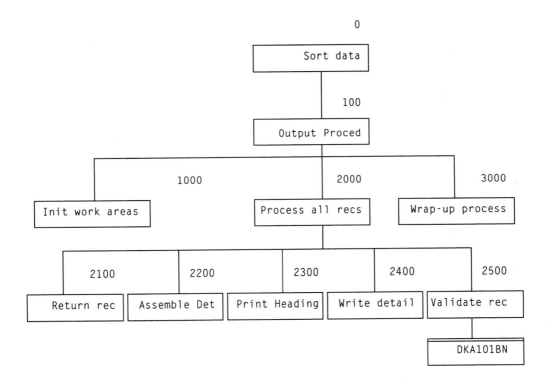

```
TITLE 'SORT Program with external CALL'
IDENTIFICATION DIVISION.

PROGRAM-ID.
    DKA10200.

*AUTHOR.
*    David S. Kirk.
```

```
**************************************************************
*       SORT Example                                        *
*                                                           *
*   The imbedded comments are tutorial and are not          *
*   meant to indicate you should explain the basics         *
*   of programs you write in this fashion, although         *
*   use of comments liberally is encouraged.                *
*                                                           *
*   There are several compromises in this example,          *
*   as the programmer's style is always a component.        *
*                                                           *
**************************************************************


    ENVIRONMENT DIVISION.

    INPUT-OUTPUT SECTION.

    FILE-CONTROL.

        SELECT FD1-PAYROLL-FILE
            ASSIGN TO PAY102.

        SELECT FD2-PRINT-FILE
            ASSIGN TO REPT102.

        SELECT SD3-SORT-FILE
            ASSIGN TO SORTWORK.

    DATA DIVISION.

    FILE SECTION.

    FD  FD1-PAYROLL-FILE
        RECORD CONTAINS 74 CHARACTERS
        BLOCK CONTAINS 0 RECORDS
        RECORDING MODE IS F.

    01  FD1-PAYROLL-REC                       PIC X(74).

    FD  FD2-PRINT-FILE
        RECORD CONTAINS 132 CHARACTERS
        BLOCK CONTAINS 0 RECORDS
        RECORDING MODE IS F.
```

```
*  ---------------------------------------------
*  Notice that the record specifies 132 positions.
*  Actually, the LRECL on JCL will be 133 if the compile
*  option ADV is used. This keeps the program "machine
*  independent," allowing COBOL to insert the ASA control
*  character external to the program logic. If compile option
*  NOADV were specified, the programmer would need to leave
*  the first byte in the record untouched by the program logic.
*  ---------------------------------------------
   01  FD2-PRINT-REC                      PIC X(132).
   SD  SD3-SORT-FILE
       RECORD CONTAINS 74 CHARACTERS.

   01  SD1-SORT-REC.
       05  SD3-EMP-NO-IN                  PIC X(5).
       05  SD3-EMP-NAME-IN                PIC X(20).
       05  SD3-TERRITORY-NO-IN            PIC X(2).
       05  SD3-OFFICE-NO-IN               PIC X(2).
       05  SD3-JOB-CODE-IN                PIC X(2).
       05                                 PIC X(43).

WORKING-STORAGE SECTION.

*  -------------------------------
*  All counters and switches are combined in the following
*  01 level.  This simplifies maintenance and saves memory use.
*  -------------------------------
   01  WS1-WORK-FIELDS.
       05  WS1-EOF-SW             PIC X.
           88 ALL-DONE               VALUE 'Y'.
           88 NOT-EOF                VALUE 'N'.
       05  WS1-DATE.
           10  WS1-YY             PIC XX.
           10  WS1-MM             PIC 99.
           10  WS1-DD             PIC XX.
       05  WS1-ERROR-MSG          PIC X(16).
           88  WS4-JOBCODE-ERROR     VALUE 'INVALID JOB CODE'.
           88  WS4-GOOD-JOBCODE      VALUE SPACES.
       05  WS1-INCOUNT            PIC S9(3)  COMP-3.
       05  WS1-LINE-SPACE         PIC S9(3)  COMP-3.
       05  WS1-LINECOUNT          PIC S9(3)  COMP-3.
       05  WS1-PAGENUM            PIC S9(3)  COMP-3.
       05  WS1-PAGESIZE           PIC S9(3)  COMP-3
                                     VALUE +50.
```

```
01   WS2-HEADING-LINE1.
     05                              PIC X(40) VALUE SPACES.
     05                              PIC X(17)
                                     VALUE 'EMPLOYEE BENEFITS'.
     05                              PIC X(3)  VALUE SPACES.
     05   WS2-DATE-OUT.
          10   WS2-MM-OUT            PIC Z9.
          10                         PIC X VALUE '/'.
          10   WS2-DD-OUT            PIC XX.
          10                         PIC X VALUE '/'.
          10   WS2-YY-OUT            PIC XX.
     05                              PIC X(5) VALUE SPACES.
     05                              PIC X(5) VALUE 'PAGE '.
     05   WS2-PAGENUM                PIC ZZ9.

01   WS2-HEADING-LINE2.
     05                              PIC X(10) VALUE SPACES.
     05                              PIC X(3)  VALUE 'JOB'.
     05                              PIC X(10) VALUE SPACES.
     05                              PIC X(8)  VALUE 'EMPLOYEE'.
     05                              PIC X(5)  VALUE SPACES.
     05                              PIC X(8)  VALUE 'EMPLOYEE'.
     05                              PIC X(19) VALUE SPACES.
     05                              PIC X(4)  VALUE 'SICK'.
     05                              PIC X(5)  VALUE SPACES.
     05                              PIC X(8)  VALUE 'VACATION'.

01   WS3-HEADING-LINE3.
     05                              PIC X(5)  VALUE SPACES.
     05                              PIC X(14)
                                     VALUE 'CLASSIFICATION'.
     05                              PIC X(7)  VALUE SPACES.
     05                              PIC X(9)  VALUE 'NO. '.
     05                              PIC X(3)  VALUE SPACES.
     05                              PIC X(4)  VALUE 'NAME'.
     05                              PIC X(21) VALUE SPACES.
     05                              PIC X(4)  VALUE 'DAYS'.
     05                              PIC X(7)  VALUE SPACES.
     05                              PIC X(4)  VALUE 'DAYS'.

01 WS4-DETAIL.
     05                              PIC X(10) VALUE SPACES.
     05   WS4-JOB-CODE-OUT           PIC X(2).
     05                              PIC X(12) VALUE SPACES.
     05   WS4-EMP-NO-OUT             PIC X(5).
     05                              PIC X(9)  VALUE SPACES.
```

```
        05   WS4-EMP-NAME-OUT              PIC X(20).
        05                                 PIC X(6)  VALUE SPACES.
        05   WS4-SICK-DAYS-OUT             PIC Z9.
        05                                 PIC X(9) VALUE SPACES.
        05   WS4-VACA-DAYS-OUT             PIC Z9.
        05                                 PIC X(5) VALUE SPACES.
        05   WS4-ERROR-MSG-OUT             PIC X(16).

   01   WS5-DATA-PASSED.
        05   WS5-JOB-CODE                  PIC XX.
        05   WS5-SICK-DAYS                 PIC 9(2).
        05   WS5-VACA-DAYS                 PIC 9(2).
        05   WS5-ERROR-SWITCH              PIC X     VALUE 'N'.

   PROCEDURE DIVISION.
*  -------------
* This paragraph is the highest level.
* While there is no INPUT PROCEDURE, this program
* can still select which records to sort and can even have
* the data records reformatted prior to the sort. This can
* be accomplished by inserting an IGZSRTCD DD (or SORTCNTL
* DD) at run time that contains valid DFSORT statements.
* Example:
*   //IGZSRTCD DD  *
*       OMIT   COND=(26,2,CH,EQ,C'25')
*       INREC  FIELDS=(1,5,6,20,26,2,28,2,47,2)
*  -------------
   000-SORT.
       SORT SD3-SORT-FILE
                  ASCENDING   SD3-TERRITORY-NO-IN
                              SD3-OFFICE-NO-IN
                              SD3-EMP-NAME-IN
                  USING FD1-PAYROLL-FILE
                  OUTPUT PROCEDURE 100-MAIN-MODULE
       IF SORT-RETURN EQUAL ZERO
           MOVE ZERO TO RETURN-CODE
           STOP RUN
       ELSE
           DISPLAY 'SORT ERROR IN DKA10200' UPON CONSOLE
           MOVE 16 TO RETURN-CODE
           STOP RUN.
```

```
*   --------------------------------------
*   The following paragraph is the SORT OUTPUT PROCEDURE.
*   --------------------------------------
    100-MAIN-MODULE.
        PERFORM 1000-INITIALIZE
        PERFORM 2000-PROCESS-ROUTINE UNTIL ALL-DONE
        PERFORM 3000-WRAPUP.


*   --------------
*   This paragraph does initialization. It is a compromise
*   since it does everything in one paragraph. In a larger
*   program, it should PERFORM a separate paragraph to OPEN
*   files and one to initialize variables.
*   The initialization part of a program should do nothing that
*   routinely repeats, such as READing files or WRITEing
*   headings.
*   --------------
    1000-INITIALIZE.
        OPEN OUTPUT FD2-PRINT-FILE
        MOVE ZEROS TO WS1-DATE
                      WS1-INCOUNT
                      WS1-PAGENUM
        MOVE 999 TO WS1-LINECOUNT
        ACCEPT WS1-DATE FROM DATE
        MOVE WS1-YY TO WS2-YY-OUT
        MOVE WS1-MM TO WS2-MM-OUT
        MOVE WS1-DD TO WS2-DD-OUT.


*   --------------
*   This paragraph controls processing of each detail record.
*   Because it follows the same path each time, it is simpler
*   to locate problems in page headings or other conditional
*   processes. The END-IF is used instead of a period because
*       it is more visible and less prone to problems and
*       it eliminates need to recode IF NOT ALL-DONE.
*   --------------
    2000-PROCESS-ROUTINE.
        PERFORM 2100-RETURN-PAYROLL
        IF NOT ALL-DONE
            IF WS1-LINECOUNT GREATER THAN WS1-PAGESIZE
                PERFORM 2300-PRINT-HEADING
            END-IF
            PERFORM 2500-VALIDATE-JOB-CODE
            PERFORM 2200-ASSEMBLE-DETAIL
            PERFORM 2400-WRITE-DETAIL.
```

```
*  - - - - - - - - - - - - - -
* This paragraph does the only RETURN of the input file.
* The END-RETURN statement isn't needed here, but minimizes
* problems if additional code is added later.
*  - - - - - - - - - - - - - -
  2100-RETURN-PAYROLL.
      RETURN SD3-SORT-FILE
          AT END
              MOVE 'Y' TO WS1-EOF-SW
          NOT AT END
              ADD 1 TO WS1-INCOUNT
      END-RETURN.


*  - - - - - - - - - - - - - -
* Because this paragraph does all of the assembly of the
* detail line, adding or changing fields is an easier
* process.
*  - - - - - - - - - - - - - -
  2200-ASSEMBLE-DETAIL.
      MOVE WS5-JOB-CODE TO WS4-JOB-CODE-OUT
      MOVE SD3-EMP-NO-IN TO WS4-EMP-NO-OUT
      MOVE SD3-EMP-NAME-IN TO WS4-EMP-NAME-OUT
      MOVE WS5-SICK-DAYS TO WS4-SICK-DAYS-OUT
      MOVE WS5-VACA-DAYS TO WS4-VACA-DAYS-OUT
      MOVE WS1-ERROR-MSG TO WS4-ERROR-MSG-OUT
      MOVE WS4-DETAIL TO FD2-PRINT-REC.


*  - - - - - - - - - - - - - -
* This paragraph prints all page headings, making it
* easy to keep track of page numbers or heading alignment.
* This is a compromise for readibility, as it does not
* PERFORM a single WRITE paragraph but repeats the WRITE
* statement for each heading line. In this case,
* the repeated statements make the ADVANCING options
* easier to see.
*  - - - - - - - - - - - - - -
  2300-PRINT-HEADING.
      ADD 1 TO WS1-PAGENUM
      MOVE WS1-PAGENUM TO WS2-PAGENUM
      WRITE FD2-PRINT-REC FROM WS2-HEADING-LINE1
        AFTER ADVANCING PAGE
      WRITE FD2-PRINT-REC FROM WS2-HEADING-LINE2
        AFTER ADVANCING 3 LINES
      WRITE FD2-PRINT-REC FROM WS3-HEADING-LINE3
      MOVE 2 TO WS1-LINE-SPACE
      MOVE ZEROS TO WS1-LINECOUNT.
```

```
*  - - - - - - - - - - - - -
*  This paragraph prints all output except page headings.
*  - - - - - - - - - - - - -
   2400-WRITE-DETAIL.
       WRITE FD2-PRINT-REC AFTER ADVANCING WS1-LINE-SPACE
       MOVE 1 TO WS1-LINE-SPACE
       ADD 1 TO WS1-LINECOUNT.


*  - - - - - - - - - - - - -
*  This paragraph calls subroutine to validate job code
*  and set benefit data. Notice that the paragraph
*  handles not only the CALL, but does the actions
*  that it dictates. If error handling were extensive
*  it would be appropriate to PERFORM that portion in
*  a separate paragraph.
*  - - - - - - - - - - - - -
   2500-VALIDATE-JOB-CODE.
       MOVE SD3-JOB-CODE-IN TO WS5-JOB-CODE
       CALL 'DKA101BN' USING WS5-DATA-PASSED
       IF WS5-ERROR-SWITCH EQUAL 'Y'
           SET WS4-JOBCODE-ERROR TO TRUE
       ELSE
           SET WS4-GOOD-JOBCODE TO TRUE
       END-IF.


*  - - - - - - - - - - - - -
*  This paragraph wraps up processing. If there were final
*  totals or similar end-of-job processing, those would be
*  PERFORMed from here as separate paragraphs.
*  - - - - - - - - - - - - -
   3000-WRAPUP.
       CLOSE FD2-PRINT-FILE.
   END PROGRAM DKA10200.
```

8.2. THE SORT EXAMPLE WITH OUTPUT PROCEDURE AS ONE PARAGRAPH

This is the previous program, redone by decomposing within a single structure instead of decomposing to subordinate paragraphs. As I mentioned elsewhere, I don't recommend this approach to programming because it is difficult to maintain. It is included to emphasize the power of COBOL II in support of structured programming. Any senior level programmer can read this, but the goal of program design is to develop code that a less skilled programmer can maintain. Managers judge code by the ease of maintenance, not by the purity of style it may exhibit.

I omitted all except the PROCEDURE DIVISION from this listing. The tight structure was accomplished by Scope Terminators (END-IF, END-RETURN, and END-PERFORM), an inline PERFORM, and extensions to the RETURN statement. Periods are used only at the end of the two paragraphs.

```
PROCEDURE DIVISION.

000-SORT.
     SORT SD3-SORT-FILE
                ASCENDING  SD3-TERRITORY-NO-IN
                           SD3-OFFICE-NO-IN
                           SD3-EMP-NAME-IN
                USING FD1-PAYROLL-FILE
                OUTPUT PROCEDURE 100-MAIN-MODULE
     IF SORT-RETURN EQUAL ZERO
          MOVE ZERO TO RETURN-CODE
          STOP RUN
     ELSE
          DISPLAY 'SORT ERROR IN DKA10200' UPON CONSOLE
          MOVE 16 TO RETURN-CODE
          STOP RUN
     END-IF.

 100-MAIN-MODULE.
* Initialization process
     OPEN OUTPUT FD2-PRINT-FILE
     MOVE ZEROS TO WS1-DATE
                   WS1-INCOUNT
                   WS1-PAGENUM
     MOVE 999 TO WS1-LINECOUNT
     ACCEPT WS1-DATE FROM DATEMOVE WS1-YY TO WS2-YY-OUT
     MOVE WS1-MM TO WS2-MM-OUT
     MOVE WS1-DD TO WS2-DD-OUT
* DO-WHILE loop
     PERFORM UNTIL ALL-DONE
          RETURN SD3-SORT-FILE
               AT END
                    MOVE 'Y' TO WS1-EOF-SW
               NOT AT END
                    ADD 1 TO WS1-INCOUNT
                    IF WS1-LINECOUNT GREATER THAN WS1-PAGESIZE
* Page heading routine
                         ADD 1 TO WS1-PAGENUM
                         MOVE WS1-PAGENUM TO WS2-PAGENUM
                         WRITE FD2-PRINT-REC FROM WS2-HEADING-LINE1
                           AFTER ADVANCING PAGE
```

```
                              WRITE FD2-PRINT-REC FROM WS2-HEADING-LINE2
                                 AFTER ADVANCING 3 LINES
                              WRITE FD2-PRINT-REC FROM WS3-HEADING-LINE3
                              MOVE 2 TO WS1-LINE-SPACE
                              MOVE ZEROS TO WS1-LINECOUNT
                      END-IF
* Validate job code routine
                      MOVE SD3-JOB-CODE-IN TO WS5-JOB-CODE
                      CALL 'DKA101BN' USING WS5-DATA-PASSED
                      IF WS5-ERROR-SWITCH EQUAL 'Y'
                          SET WS4-JOBCODE-ERROR TO TRUE
                      ELSE
                          SET WS4-GOOD-JOBCODE TO TRUE
                      END-IF
* Assemble detail line routine
                      MOVE WS5-JOB-CODE TO WS4-JOB-CODE-OUT
                      MOVE SD3-EMP-NO-IN TO WS4-EMP-NO-OUT
                      MOVE SD3-EMP-NAME-IN TO WS4-EMP-NAME-OUT
                      MOVE WS5-SICK-DAYS TO WS4-SICK-DAYS-OUT
                      MOVE WS5-VACA-DAYS TO WS4-VACA-DAYS-OUT
                      MOVE WS1-ERROR-MSG TO WS4-ERROR-MSG-OUT
                      MOVE WS4-DETAIL TO FD2-PRINT-REC
* Write detail line routine
                      WRITE FD2-PRINT-REC AFTER
                         ADVANCING WS1-LINE-SPACE
                      MOVE 1 TO WS1-LINE-SPACE
                      ADD 1 TO WS1-LINECOUNT
             END-RETURN
          END-PERFORM
* Termination routine
       CLOSE FD2-PRINT-FILE.
 END PROGRAM DKA10200.
```

8.3. CALLED SUBPROGRAM EXAMPLE WITH COBOL II

This program is CALLed by DKA10200, the previous program. Notice the missing ENVIRONMENT division and the use of EVALUATE and SET statements. In this example, the SET statement provides clearer documentation than using MOVE statements.

```
IDENTIFICATION DIVISION.

PROGRAM-ID.
    DKA101BN.
*AUTHOR.
*    David S. Kirk.


*  ---------------------------------------------
* Validates job code and returns appropriate sick and
* vacation days allowed.
*  ---------------------------------------------


DATA DIVISION.

LINKAGE SECTION.

01   LS1-RECORD.
        05   LS1-JOB-CODE           PIC XX.
        05   LS1-SICK-VAC-DAYS      PIC XXXX.
            88  BEN01                   VALUE '1421'.
            88  BEN02                   VALUE '1014'.
            88  BEN03                   VALUE '2128'.
        05   LS1-ERROR-SW           PIC X.

PROCEDURE DIVISION USING LS1-RECORD.

    100-MAIN-MODULE.
        MOVE 'N' TO LS1-ERROR-SW
        PERFORM 200-VALIDATE
        GOBACK.

    200-VALIDATE.
        EVALUATE LS1-JOB-CODE
            WHEN '01'    SET BEN01 TO TRUE
            WHEN '02'    SET BEN02 TO TRUE
            WHEN '03'    SET BEN03 TO TRUE
            WHEN OTHER   MOVE '0000' TO LS1-SICK-VAC-DAYS
                         MOVE 'Y' TO LS1-ERROR-SW
        END-EVALUATE.
    END PROGRAM DKA101BN.
```

8.4. SAMPLE SUBPROGRAM COMPATIBLE WITH BOTH COMPILERS

This program is the OS/VS COBOL compatible version of the prior program (DKA101BN). The EVALUATE and SET were replaced by IF and MOVE statements and the END PROGRAM statement was removed. Other than that, even with no ENVIRONMENT DIVISION, it compiles with no fatal errors under both COBOL II and OS/VS COBOL.

```
 IDENTIFICATION DIVISION.

 PROGRAM-ID.
     DKA101B2.

*AUTHOR.
*     David S. Kirk.


*  --------------------------------------------
* Validates job code and returns appropriate sick and
* vacation days allowed.
*  --------------------------------------------

 DATA DIVISION.
 LINKAGE SECTION.

 01  LS1-RECORD.
     05  LS1-JOB-CODE              PIC XX.
     05  LS1-SICK-VAC-DAYS         PIC XXXX.
     05  LS1-ERROR-SW              PIC X.

 PROCEDURE DIVISION USING LS1-RECORD.

 100-MAIN-MODULE.
     MOVE 'N' TO LS1-ERROR-SW
     PERFORM 200-VALIDATE
     GOBACK.

 200-VALIDATE.
     IF LS1-JOB-CODE = '01'
         MOVE '1421' TO LS1-SICK-VAC-DAYS
     ELSE
         IF LS1-JOB-CODE = '02'
             MOVE '1014' TO LS1-SICK-VAC-DAYS
         ELSE
             IF LS1-JOB-CODE = '03'
                 MOVE '2128' TO LS1-SICK-VAC-DAYS
             ELSE
                 MOVE '0000' TO LS1-SICK-VAC-DAYS
                 MOVE 'Y' TO LS1-ERROR-SW.
* This is the end of source.
```

8.5. SAMPLE SORT WITH A NESTED STRUCTURE

This program is the SORT program and its CALLed subprogram combined into a nested program structure. Many parts of the SORT program have been removed to focus on the nested structure. Notice that the CALL statement passes no data, the CALLed subprogram has no PROCEDURE DIVISION USING statement, nor does it have a DATA DIVISION. Because both programs now reference the same data-names, debugging and documentation are improved.

```
TITLE 'SORT Program with nested CALL'
IDENTIFICATION DIVISION.
PROGRAM-ID. DKA10200.
ENVIRONMENT DIVISION.
INPUT-OUTPUT SECTION.
FILE-CONTROL.
     .
     .

DATA DIVISION.
FILE SECTION.
     .
     .

WORKING-STORAGE SECTION.
     .
     .
01  WS5-DATA-PASSED          GLOBAL.
    05  WS5-JOB-CODE               PIC XX.
    05  WS5-SICK-VAC-DAYS.
        10  WS5-SICK-DAYS          PIC 9(2).
        10  WS5-VACA-DAYS          PIC 9(2).
    05  WS5-SUB-DATA REDEFINES WS5-SICK-VAC-DAYS  PIC X(4).
        88  BEN01                  VALUE '1421'.
        88  BEN02                  VALUE '1014'.
        88  BEN03                  VALUE '2128'.
    05  WS5-ERROR-SWITCH           PIC X      VALUE 'N'.

PROCEDURE DIVISION.
000-SORT.
    SORT SD3-SORT-FILE
     .
     .

100-MAIN-MODULE.
    PERFORM 1000-INITIALIZE
    PERFORM 2000-PROCESS-ROUTINE UNTIL ALL-DONE
    PERFORM 3000-WRAPUP.
```

```
1000-INITIALIZE.
    OPEN OUTPUT FD2-PRINT-FILE
    MOVE ZEROS TO WS1-DATE
    .
    .


2000-PROCESS-ROUTINE.
    PERFORM 2100-RETURN-PAYROLL
    IF NOT ALL-DONE
    .
    .


2100-RETURN-PAYROLL.
    RETURN SD3-SORT-FILE
        AT END
            MOVE 'Y' TO WS1-EOF-SW
        NOT AT END
            ADD 1 TO WS1-INCOUNT
    END-RETURN.
2200-ASSEMBLE-DETAIL.
    MOVE WS5-JOB-CODE TO WS4-JOB-CODE-OUT
    .
    .


2300-PRINT-HEADING.
    ADD 1 TO WS1-PAGENUM
    .
    .


2400-WRITE-DETAIL.
    WRITE FD2-PRINT-REC AFTER ADVANCING WS1-LINE-SPACE
    MOVE 1 TO WS1-LINE-SPACE
    ADD 1 TO WS1-LINECOUNT.

2500-VALIDATE-JOB-CODE.
    MOVE SD3-JOB-CODE-IN TO WS5-JOB-CODE
    CALL 'DKA101BN'
    IF WS5-ERROR-SWITCH EQUAL 'Y'
        SET WS4-JOBCODE-ERROR TO TRUE
    ELSE
        SET WS4-GOOD-JOBCODE TO TRUE
    END-IF.
3000-WRAPUP.
    CLOSE FD2-PRINT-FILE.
```

```
TITLE 'This is the shortened subprogram'
IDENTIFICATION DIVISION.
PROGRAM-ID. DKA101BN.
PROCEDURE DIVISION.
1.  MOVE 'N' TO WS5-ERROR-SWITCH
    PERFORM 200-VALIDATE
    GOBACK.

200-VALIDATE.
    EVALUATE WS5-JOB-CODE
        WHEN '01'    SET BEN01 TO TRUE
        WHEN '02'    SET BEN02 TO TRUE
        WHEN '03'    SET BEN03 TO TRUE
        WHEN OTHER   MOVE '0000' TO WS5-SUB-DATA
                     MOVE 'Y' TO WS5-ERROR-SWITCH
    END-EVALUATE.
END PROGRAM DKA101BN.
END PROGRAM DKA10200.
```

8.6.   IMS SAMPLE PROGRAM THAT WORKS WITH ALL COMPILERS

This program contains minor violating rules as did the previous programs. This is to be expected, rather than blindly accepting programming rules. Notice the balance of control and action, and that the status from PERFORMs is checked immediately. Keeping control at the higher level produces cleaner code. Note also that each paragraph contains only one period.

If you are familiar with IMS programs, you will notice it does not contain the usual ENTRY 'DLITCBL' statement. That requirement still appears in many IMS reference manuals, but it hasn't been needed since the PROCEDURE DIVISION USING statement became available.

The structure contains a DO WHILE within another DO WHILE. This lets the program use its own structure to access structured data.

This program compiles under:

- OS/VS COBOL with LANGLVL(1) for ANSI 68
- OS/VS COBOL with LANGLVL(2) for ANSI 74
- COBOL II
- COBOL/370

yet follows all the guidelines in the book. Compatibility was preserved by including FILLER entries and by not using the END PROGRAM statement.

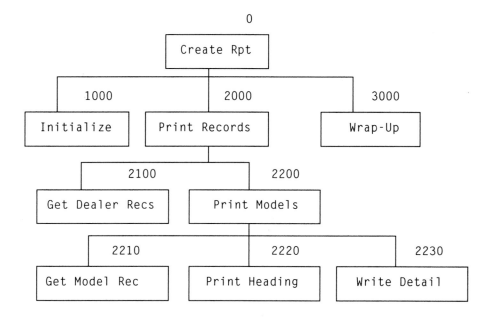

```
 IDENTIFICATION DIVISION.

 PROGRAM-ID.
     DKA10300.
*AUTHOR.
*    David S. Kirk.

***********************************************************
*                                                         *
* PROGRAM: Reads a training database and prepares         *
* a simple report. The database structure is              *
*                                                         *
*                                                         *
*              +---------------+                          *
*              |    VENDOR     |                          *
*              |   segment     |                          *
*              +---------------+                          *
*                      |                                  *
*              +---------------+                          *
*              |     PART      |                          *
*              |   segment     |                          *
*              +---------------+                          *
*                                                         *
***********************************************************
```

```
ENVIRONMENT DIVISION.

 INPUT-OUTPUT SECTION.

 FILE-CONTROL.
      SELECT FD1-PRINT-FILE
          ASSIGN TO REPT103.

 DATA DIVISION.

 FILE SECTION.

 FD  FD1-PRINT-FILE
     RECORD CONTAINS 132 CHARACTERS
     BLOCK CONTAINS 0 RECORDS
     RECORDING MODE IS F.

 01  FD1-PRINT-REC                    PIC X(132).

 WORKING-STORAGE SECTION.

 01  WS1-WORK-FIELDS-REC.
     05  WS1-EOF-SW                   PIC X.
         88 ALL-DONE                      VALUE 'Y'.
         88 NOT-EOF                        VALUE 'N'.
     05  WS1-PAGENUM              PIC S999   COMP-3.
     05  WS1-SPACE               PIC S999   COMP-3 VALUE 1.
     05  WS1-LINES               PIC S999   COMP-3 VALUE 55.

 01  WS2-HEADING-LINE1-REC.
     05  FILLER                       PIC X(40)  VALUE SPACES.
     05  FILLER                       PIC X(17)
                                  VALUE 'IMS DL/1 WORKSHOP'.
     05  FILLER                       PIC X(3)   VALUE SPACES.
     05  FILLER                       PIC X(5)   VALUE SPACES.
     05  FILLER                       PIC X(5)   VALUE 'PAGE '.
     05  WS2-PAGENUM                  PIC ZZ9.
     05  FILLER                       PIC X(51)  VALUE SPACES.

 01  WS3-DETAIL-REC.
     05  FILLER                       PIC X(2)   VALUE SPACES.
     05  WS3-VENDOR                   PIC X(30)  VALUE SPACES.
     05  FILLER                       PIC X(1)   VALUE SPACES.
     05  WS3-PART-DESC                PIC X(20)  VALUE SPACES.
     05  FILLER                       PIC X(5)   VALUE SPACES.
     05  WS3-PART-PRICE               PIC $$$$,$99.
     05  FILLER                       PIC X(20)  VALUE SPACES.
```

```
* --------IMS WORK AREAS BEGIN HERE ----------------------------

   01   WS4-UNQUAL-VENDOR-SSA.
        05  FILLER              PIC X(9)      VALUE 'VENDOR   '.

   01   WS5-QUAL-PART-SSA.
        05  FILLER              PIC X(9)      VALUE 'PART    ('.
        05  FILLER              PIC X(8)      VALUE 'PARTYPE '.
        05  FILLER              PIC X(2)      VALUE ' ='.
        05  FILLER              PIC X         VALUE 'B'.
        05  FILLER              PIC X         VALUE '&'.
        05  FILLER              PIC X(10)     VALUE 'PARTPRIC >'.
        05  FILLER              PIC S9(6)     VALUE 000100.
        05  FILLER              PIC X         VALUE ')'.

* #### VENDOR SEGMENT FOLLOWS
       COPY VENDSEG.

* #### PART SEGMENT FOLLOWS
       COPY PARTSEG.

       COPY IMSFUNC.

   LINKAGE SECTION.

       COPY VENDPCB.

   PROCEDURE DIVISION USING IMS-DB-PCB.

   000-CREATE-REPORT.
       PERFORM 1000-INITIALIZE
       PERFORM 2000-PRINT-RECORDS
               UNTIL IMS-DB-STAT-CODE = 'GB'
       PERFORM 3000-WRAP-UP
       MOVE 0 TO RETURN-CODE
       GOBACK.

   1000-INITIALIZE.
       OPEN OUTPUT FD1-PRINT-FILE
       MOVE SPACES TO IMS-DB-STAT-CODE
       MOVE ZEROS TO WS1-PAGENUM.

   2000-PRINT-RECORDS.
       PERFORM 2100-GET-VENDOR
       IF IMS-DB-STAT-CODE NOT EQUAL 'GB'
           MOVE 3 TO WS1-SPACE
           MOVE VEND-NAME TO WS3-VENDOR
```

```
         PERFORM 2200-PRINT-PARTS
                 UNTIL IMS-DB-STAT-CODE = 'GE'.

 2100-GET-VENDOR.
     CALL 'CBLTDLI' USING
         GN
         IMS-DB-PCB
         VEND-SEG
         WS4-UNQUAL-VENDOR-SSA.

 2200-PRINT-PARTS.
     PERFORM 2210-GET-PARTS
     IF IMS-DB-STAT-CODE = ' '
         MOVE PART-DESC TO WS3-PART-DESC
         MOVE PART-PRICE TO WS3-PART-PRICE
         PERFORM 2220-PRINT-HEADING
         PERFORM 2230-WRITE-DETAIL.

 2210-GET-PARTS.
     CALL 'CBLTDLI' USING
         GNP
         IMS-DB-PCB
         PART-SEG
         WS5-QUAL-PART-SSA.

 2220-PRINT-HEADING.
     IF WS1-LINES > 50
         ADD 1 TO WS1-PAGENUM
         MOVE WS1-PAGENUM TO WS2-PAGENUM
         MOVE 1 TO WS1-LINES
         MOVE 2 TO WS1-SPACE
         WRITE FD1-PRINT-REC FROM WS2-HEADING-LINE1-REC
                 AFTER ADVANCING PAGE.

 2230-WRITE-DETAIL.
     WRITE FD1-PRINT-REC FROM WS3-DETAIL-REC
                 AFTER ADVANCING WS1-SPACE LINES
     ADD WS1-SPACE TO WS1-LINES
     MOVE 1 TO WS1-SPACE.

 3000-WRAP-UP.
     CLOSE FD1-PRINT-FILE.

* THIS IS THE END OF SOURCE
```

8.7. SAMPLE STUB PROGRAM

One of the strengths of structured, top-down development is the use of stub programs. A stub program is one that does nothing, but must be CALLed from a program higher in the structure during early development stages. This allows subordinate programs to be executed, even though nothing is being done. Here is a simple stub program that works well. This example takes maximum advantage of the optional entries in COBOL II and the presence of the implicit EXIT PROGRAM code that is generated. CALLs to this subprogram will execute successfully and set a RETURN-CODE of zero. The END PROGRAM statement is optional.

```
ID DIVISION.
PROGRAM-ID.  programname.
END PROGRAM programname.
```

8.8. SAMPLE CICS PROGRAM

This program is part of a set of CICS programs used in the QED book *CICS, A How-to for COBOL Programmers*, so related modules and MAPS are not included here. As with other programs in this chapter, this program is simple— and somewhat incomplete. For example, on detection of a MAPFAIL condition, the program simply terminates. Normally, that would be an inadequate response. Such error recovery procedures, however, can detract from basic structure, and demonstrating structure and minor use of COBOL II features is the purpose of this chapter.

   This program is a simple menu application that receives a single input variable that causes it to determine which of three other programs should be invoked (via XCTL). Emphasis in the program is on structure with only a few COBOL II features shown. The EVALUATE is used to make the many decisions and related CICS instructions visible with one sweep of the eyes. A flaw (to me) of reading CICS programs is that, too often, the CICS commands themselves require many lines of code and, with the many IF . . . ELSE statements surrounding them, it can be difficult for novice programmers to detect the logic flow. This program also successfully uses the SET statement to make setting of flags more readable.

   The structure of the program is the following:

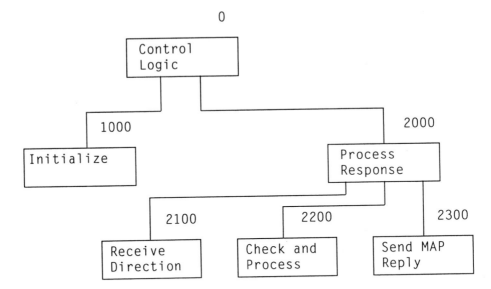

You may notice that the paragraph name for the first paragraph seems to violate normal naming standards. After all, it has no meaningful words in it, nor does it explain in any way what the first paragraph does. Since, with top-down development, it is impossible to adequately define the first paragraph (defining a paragraph, remember, is to define all subordinate processes as well), I have abandoned the attempt. Just naming the paragraph "1" does the trick.

```
IDENTIFICATION DIVISION.
PROGRAM-ID. MENUPGM.
*AUTHOR. David Shelby Kirk.
*
*   This is a sample CICS menu application, written to be
*   pseudo-conversational. The logic is simple, intended to
*   emphasize the structure. A complete explanation of the
*   program, its COPYbooks, and logic are in the QED book
*   CICS, A How-to for COBOL Programmers.
*


DATA DIVISION.
WORKING-STORAGE SECTION.
 01  LOCAL-WORK-AREAS.
*   Normally, I abhor use of flags and switches. Still, there
*   are valid places for them, especially when lower-level
*   paragraphs must return status information to higher-level
*   modules. Here I use a single flag field to indicate all
*   control information for the application. By having only
*   one flag to test, program structure is easier.
*
```

```
      05  STATUS-FLAG        PIC X       VALUE ' '.
          88  INPUT-ERROR      VALUE 'E'.
          88  TIME-TO-QUIT     VALUE 'Q'.
          88  TIME-TO-LOGOFF   VALUE 'L'.
          88  TRANSFER-NEEDED  VALUE 'A', 'U', 'D'.
          88  HELP-WANTED      VALUE 'H'.
      05  MAP-NAME           PIC X(8)    VALUE 'MENUMAP '.
      05  XCTL-NAME          PIC X(8).
      05  TERM-MSG           PIC X(24)   VALUE
          ' Transaction terminated.'.

  01  MAP-AREA               PIC X(1920) VALUE LOW-VALUES.

  01  MY-COMM-AREA.
      05  COMM-LAST-MAP    PIC X(4)  VALUE 'MENU'.
      05  COMM-PRIOR-PGM   PIC X(8)  VALUE 'MENUPGM '.
      05  COMM-ACTION-FLAG PIC X     VALUE ' '.

      COPY CICSRESP.

      COPY CICSATTR.

      COPY DFHAID.

      COPY MENUAPPC.

  LINKAGE SECTION.
  01  DFHCOMMAREA.
      05  LINK-LAST-MAP  PIC XXXX.
      05  LINK-PRIOR-PGM PIC X(8).
      05  FILLER         PIC X.

  PROCEDURE DIVISION.
  *  The first paragraph of a CICS module should be to fully
  *  determine how the program received control and to act
  *  on it. This eliminates the typical need for program
  *  switches. All application processes are PERFORMed from
  *  this top-level statement.
  *
  1.  IF EIBCALEN < 13 OR EIBAID = DFHCLEAR
         OR LINK-PRIOR-PGM NOT = 'MENUPGM '
         OR LINK-LAST-MAP = 'HELP'
             PERFORM 1000-SETUP
      ELSE
             PERFORM 2000-PROCESS-RESP
      END-IF
```

```
*
*    Still within the highest-level paragraph, the module needs
*    to determine how to exit. Too often this logic is found
*    in lower-level paragraphs. "Top-down" means the decision to
*    terminate the program cannot be delegated. This use of the
*    EVALUATE statement lets the program depict the logic and
*    subsequent choices more easily than having many IF...ELSE
*    statements.
*
     EVALUATE TRUE
         WHEN TIME-TO-QUIT
             EXEC CICS SEND TEXT
                             FROM   (TERM-MSG)
                             ERASE
                             NOHANDLE
                             RESP   (CICS-RESP-CODE)
             END-EXEC
             EXEC CICS RETURN END-EXEC
         WHEN TIME-TO-LOGOFF
             EXEC CICS START TRANSID ('CSSF')
                             TERMID (EIBTRMID)
             END-EXEC
             EXEC CICS RETURN END-EXEC
         WHEN TRANSFER-NEEDED
             EXEC CICS XCTL
                             PROGRAM  (XCTL-NAME)
                             COMMAREA (MY-COMM-AREA)
                             NOHANDLE
                             RESP     (CICS-RESP-CODE)
             END-EXEC
             IF CICS-PGMIDERR
                 EXEC CICS  ABEND
                             ABCODE('1234')
                             NODUMP
                 END-EXEC
             END-IF
     END-EVALUATE
     EXEC CICS RETURN
             TRANSID  ('M401')
             COMMAREA (MY-COMM-AREA)
     END-EXEC.

 1000-SETUP.
*    Despite being a simple program, the setup or initialization
*    logic path can seldom justify being more than a single
*    paragraph. This is because there should normally be no
*    variable information or decisions to initialize for
```

```
*   processing. Having a single paragraph also allows the
*   maintenance programmer to quickly understand the flow.
*

        MOVE LOW-VALUES TO MENUMAPI
        MOVE -1 TO PROCESSL
        EXEC CICS SEND MAP     ('MENUMAP')
                       MAPSET  ('MENUAPP')
                       FROM    (MENUMAPI)
                       ERASE
                       CURSOR
        END-EXEC.

    2000-PROCESS-RESP.
*   This is highest-level paragraph for processing a response
*   from a terminal. Notice that the logic decomposes the
*   environmental decisions (good RECEIVE, quit, logoff)
*   into one paragraph and the application data (what was typed
*   in as data) into a separate paragraph. Again, this helps
*   eliminate the need for switches and spaghetti-type logic.
*

        PERFORM 2100-RECEIVE-DIRECTION
        IF STATUS-FLAG NOT = 'Q' AND NOT = 'L'
            PERFORM 2200-CHECK-DATA
            IF HELP-WANTED OR INPUT-ERROR
                PERFORM 2300-SEND-MAP.

    2100-RECEIVE-DIRECTION.
*   Some people prefer that I/O always be the only process in
*   a paragraph. My preference is somewhat different. I use
*   a single paragraph to handle I/O and also to determine
*   if the I/O result should cause separate processing to
*   be done. In this case, that includes testing for PFkeys
*   that signal an end of processing.
*   Notice that, since the STATUS-FLAG field uses 88-levels,
*   the program can use the SET statement to provide a one-to-one
*   relation between the setting of a flag here and the testing
*   of the flag in higher-level paragraphs.
*

        EXEC CICS RECEIVE MAP    ('MENUMAP')
                          MAPSET ('MENUAPP')
                          INTO   (MENUMAPI)
                          NOHANDLE
                          RESP   (CICS-RESP-CODE)
        END-EXEC
```

```
     IF EIBAID = DFHPF3
         SET TIME-TO-QUIT TO TRUE
     ELSE
         IF EIBAID = DFHPF2
             SET TIME-TO-LOGOFF TO TRUE
         ELSE
             IF CICS-MAPFAIL
                 SET TIME-TO-QUIT TO TRUE.

 2200-CHECK-DATA.
*  Notice how this application is able to support a help
*  screen. Many programmers believe help screens are too
*  complicated but, in most cases, it takes little extra code.
*  Admittedly, if the normal data screen is needed to capture
*  and save data then a TS QUEUE might be needed to save data
*  while the help screen is sent. In this example, being only
*  a simple menu selection application, no data need be saved.
*
     IF EIBAID = DFHPF1
         MOVE 'HELP' TO COMM-LAST-MAP
         MOVE LOW-VALUES TO HELPMAPO
         MOVE HELPMAPO TO MAP-AREA
         MOVE 'HELPMAP' TO MAP-NAME
         MOVE 'H' TO STATUS-FLAG
     ELSE
         IF PROCESSI = 'A' OR 'U' OR 'D'
             MOVE PROCESSI TO STATUS-FLAG
                              COMM-ACTION-FLAG
             EVALUATE PROCESSI
                 WHEN 'A' MOVE 'ADDPGM  ' TO XCTL-NAME
                 WHEN 'D' MOVE 'DELETPGM' TO XCTL-NAME
                 WHEN 'U' MOVE 'UPDATPGM' TO XCTL-NAME
             END-EVALUATE
         ELSE
             SET INPUT-ERROR TO TRUE
             MOVE CICS-UNPROT-BRT-MDT TO PROCESSA
             MOVE CICS-PROT-BRT     TO MSG1A
             MOVE -1 TO PROCESSL
             MOVE 'Please enter a valid code  ' TO MSG1O
             MOVE MENUMAPO TO MAP-AREA.

 2300-SEND-MAP.
*  As noted in prior paragraphs, this paragraph is capable
*  of sending either the normal menu map or a help map,
*  depending on whether PF1 was pressed.
*
```

```
EXEC CICS SEND MAP    (MAP-NAME)
                MAPSET ('MENUAPP')
                FROM   (MAP-AREA)
                ERASE
                CURSOR
END-EXEC.
```

SUMMARY

Other than the second example, none of these programs made extensive use of new features. In fact, many of the examples demonstrated coexistence techniques instead. If possible, I encourage a migration from OS/VS COBOL with all deliberate speed. Continuing to code at the ANSI 74 level when you have access to ANSI 85 features is frustrating. These sample programs are not recommendations. Instead, they are examples of what you can code in a COBOL subset.

Large shops with a variety of CICS, IMS, and other environments may need to adopt a subset of COBOL, especially if many of the programs are reusable. Once you have your programs migrated to COBOL II or COBOL/370, start using the new features. The use will refuel your momentum. Otherwise, you will find yourself continuing to code using older techniques. Until you feel comfortable with the new features, the pressure of the moment will constrain your growth. Don't let that happen.

Related Publications

One of the goals of professional programmers is to have an adequate reference library, not full of "concepts" books or other books for novices, but those that contribute to building applications. It was with that view that I developed this list.

The reason I include a publications chapter in my books is because I turn to books when I want answers. Relying on some sponsor to send me to a formal training course is putting the control of my destiny in someone else's hands. Not for me. Classroom training is helpful, sure, but having the answers sitting on your bookshelf is a great feeling. Since there are many areas where my knowledge is limited or not up to a power programming level, I had the choice of omitting those topics from this book or sharing titles of other books with you that address the strengths that I lack. I chose the latter.

Selecting the book list was no easy task. In building my list, I required that the books (in my opinion, no one else's) be oriented to the application developer, not the systems programmer, and offer topics that address skills for building productional COBOL-based applications.

This caused my list with this edition to be different from the first edition, where I included peripheral texts that weren't necessarily focused on building systems. This means excellent texts on TSO, REXX, JCL, and VSAM, among others, don't appear here. You need books such as those for a complete MVS reference library, but I had to draw the line somewhere or the list would be much larger and would lose focus.

9.1   FROM QED

Each of these QED books complements the material in this book by providing in-depth information about specific IBM platforms in which COBOL applications run. These books should not be referenced for COBOL-specific information. Their value is in their specialization in the topics specified. You still need access to IBM manuals (and many are excellent), but books such as these help readers see a bigger picture.

These books may be ordered directly from QED. See the order card in this book, or call QED at 1-800-343-4848. In MA, call 617-237-5656. Or fax QED at 617-235-0826.

CICS: A How-to for COBOL Programmers This book focuses on pseudoconversational techniques, incorporates new features of CICS/ESA, provides a complete reference for building MAPs, and complements this book with more techniques for COBOL II and COBOL/370.

Embedded SQL for DB2: Application Design & Programming This is not only a complete course in using SQL with COBOL, it also addresses performance-oriented issues of building applications with COBOL and SQL for a DB2 environment.

DB2: Maximizing Performance of Online Production Systems This addresses the larger DB2 environmental aspects that must be addressed for high-performance on-line DB2 systems.

VSAM: The Complete Guide to Optimization & Design This book concentrates on the performance aspects of design and use of VSAM files.

IMS Design and Implementation Techniques, 2nd Edition If you work with IMS, this is a thorough reference on design and performance.

9.2. FROM IBM

Your shop may already have a library of IBM manuals, but all too often they are out of date. This listing may help you confirm whether appropriate IBM reference material is available to you. Most of these books contain information you may need only occasionally if at all. These books were selected by me because they either provide more in-depth information about COBOL or they provide information on the MVS operating environment. You should check with your technical staff to confirm what IBM publications are appropriate for your environment, as this list may be incomplete or list the incorrect IBM manual for your shop. Where books are shown in brackets, the books are mutually exclusive. For example, the following indicates that you need one of three possible JCL reference manuals:

```
GC28-1300, MVS/SP JCL Reference
GC28-1352, MVS/XA JCL Reference
GC28-1829, MVS/ESA JCL Reference
```

Whenever using IBM manuals, you should check that the release level of the book corresponds with the level of software you are using. For example, if

your shop is using COBOL II, Release 3.0, and your COBOL II manuals reflect
support for Release 3.1 or 3.2, there will be features in the manual that won't
function. Likewise, if your library's JCL manual specifies MVS/SP and you are
using MVS/XA, there will be features available that you will be unaware of.
When in doubt, check with your technical staff.

9.2.1. For Programming with COBOL II

GC26-4047, *VS COBOL II Language Reference*. This is a complete definition of
the COBOL II language, including all syntax.

SC26-4045, *VS COBOL II Application Programming Guide*. This provides a variety of tips and instructions for coding, compiling, and executing applications.

SC26-4049, *VS COBOL II Debugging*. This is a complete guide to debugging, including instructions on the debug language and mechanics of using COBTEST
in batch and on-line. A complete presentation on dump reading mechanics is
also included.

SX26-3721, *VS COBOL II Reference Summary*. This is a small book (not a reference card) that contains all COBOL II statements. It contains no material
not found in other texts here.

SC26-4301, *Report Writer Programmer Guide*. This book provides syntax and
other instructions for using the Report Writer Preprocessor with COBOL II
or COBOL/370. (This is a separate software product and may not be installed at your company.)

SC28-6483, *OS/VS COBOL Compiler and Library Programmer's Guide*. This
book is needed if your run unit includes OS/VS COBOL modules. You will
need this book to diagnose any run-time error messages that have the
prefix IKF.

9.2.2. For Programming with COBOL/370

SC26-4769, *SAA AD/Cycle COBOL/370 Language Reference*. This is the complete
reference of COBOL/370 coding syntax.

SC26-4767, *SAA AD/Cycle COBOL/370 Programming Guide*. This contains programming information for the system environment, various programming
techniques, and compile/debug information.

SC26-4818, *SAA AD/Cycle LE/370 Programming Guide*. This contains information on linking, CALLable services, storage management, and run-time options.

SC26-4829, *SAA AD/Cycle LE/370 Debug and Run-time Message Guide*. This
contains information on debugging applications with LE/370 facilities.

SC26-4664, *SAA AD/Cycle CODE/370 Debug Tool Reference*. This contains full
information on the Debug Tool commands and syntax.

SC26-4662, *SAA AD/Cycle CODE/370 Using the Debug Tool*. This provides information on using the Debug Tool.

9.2.3. For SAA Information

SC26-4354, *SAA Common Programming Interface, COBOL Reference.* This defines SAA considerations for COBOL. If your shop is committed to SAA across several platforms, this will help you.

GC26-4341, *SAA Overview*

GC26-4531, *SAA AD / Cycle Concepts*

9.2.4. For CICS

⌐SC33-0512, *CICS/MVS Application Programmer's Reference*
⌊SC33-0676, *CICS/ESA Application Programming Reference*
 SC33-0675, *CICS/ESA Application Programming Guide*
⌐SC33-0514, *CICS/MVS Messages and Codes*
⌊SC33-0672, *CICS/ESA Messages and Codes*
 SC26-4177, *IMS/VS Version 2 Application Programming for CICS Users*
 SC26-4080, *IBM Database 2 Application Programming Guide for CICS Users*

9.2.5. For IMS

⌐SH20-9026, *IMS/VS Version 1 Application Programming*
 SH26-4178, *IMS/VS Version 2 Application Programming*
⌊SH26-4274, *IMS/ESA Application Programming*
⌐SH20-9030, *IMS/VS Version 1 Messages & Codes*
 SC26-4174, *IMS/VS Version 2 Messages & Codes*
⌊SC26-4290, *IMS/ESA Messages & Codes*
 SH20-5523, *IMS/VS Batch Terminal Simulator Program Reference* (This book is needed if you will be using COBTEST for IMS applications.)

9.2.6. For DB2

⌐SC26-4346, *IBM Database 2 SQL Reference*
⌊SC26-4380, *IBM Database 2 Version 2 SQL Reference*
⌐SC26-4293, *IBM Database 2 Application Programming Guide*
⌊SC26-4377, *IBM Database 2 Version 2 Application Programming Guide*
 SC26-4292, *IBM Database 2 Advanced Application Programming Guide*

9.2.7. For MVS System Services

⌐GC28-1352, *MVS/XA JCL Reference*
 GC28-1829, *MVS/ESA JCL Reference (Version 3)*
⌊SC28-1654, *MVS/ESA JCL Reference (Version 4)*

GC28-1157, *MVS/XA System Codes*
GC28-1815, *MVS/ESA System Codes (Version 3)*
SC28-1664, *MVS/ESA System Codes (Version 4)*
GC28-1376 and GC28-1377, *MVS/XA System Messages*
GC28-1812 and GC28-1813, *MVS/ESA System Messages*
GC26-4011, *MVS/XA Linkage Editor & Loader User's Guide (Version 1)*
GC26-4143, *MVS/XA Linkage Editor & Loader User's Guide (Version 2)*
SC26-4510, *MVS/ESA Linkage Editor & Loader User's Guide*
SC26-4559, *MVS/DFP Version 3: Linkage Editor & Loader*
SC33-4035, *DFSORT Application Programming Guide*
GC26-4051, *MVS/370 Access Method Services Reference*
GC26-4019, *MVS/XA Access Method Services Reference (Version 1)*
GC26-4135, *MVS/XA Access Method Services Reference (Version 2)*
GC26-4074, *MVS/SP VSAM Administration: Macro Instruction Reference*
GC26-4016, *MVS/XA VSAM Administration: Macro Instruction Reference (Version 1)*
GC26-4152, *MVS/XA VSAM Administration: Macro Instruction Reference (Version 2)*
SC26-4517, *MVS/ESA VSAM Administration: Macro Instruction Reference*
GC26-4018, *MVS/XA Data Administration: Utilities (Version 1)*
GC26-4150, *MVS/XA Data Administration: Utilities (Version 2)*
SC26-4559, *MVS/DFP Version 3: Utilities*

Index

SUBSTRING
Page 66
(Ref modification)